"As the bullets are flying and the bodies are falling across the race line in America once again, precious few Christian theologians dare examine the issue at its theological roots. Andrew Draper's concise and insightful engagement with the bravest and most exciting thinkers doing so today is a real gift. His own contribution takes the conversation a big step forward by offering us a winsome vision of a church that does not aspire to go beyond race, but to learn what it means to embrace a vulnerable communion in the middle of a world characterized by racial strife."

—Brian Brock, Reader in Moral and Practical Theology, Department of Divinity, History and Philosophy, King's College, Aberdeen

"In this deeply engaging and transforming book, Andrew Draper teases out the Christological and ecclesiological implications of the theories on the origin of the racial imagination posited by noted theologians Willie James Jennings and J. Kameron Carter. His constructive task is to ground Jennings' 'ecclesiology of joining' within the lived space of his multicultural congregation. Those yearning to overcome the tortured ways that 'reconciliation' gets deployed by the racial logic and practices inscribed within Western Christian theology must read this book."

—James W. Lewis, Retired Dean, Anderson University School of Theology, Anderson, IN

A Theology of Race and Place

A Theology of Race and Place

Liberation and Reconciliation in the Works of Jennings and Carter

Andrew T. Draper

PICKWICK *Publications* • Eugene, Oregon

A THEOLOGY OF RACE AND PLACE
Liberation and Reconciliation in the Works of Jennings and Carter

Pickwick Publications
An Imprint of Wipf and Stock Publishers
199 W. 8th Ave., Suite 3
Eugene, OR 97401

www.wipfandstock.com

PAPERBACK ISBN: 978-1-4982-8082-2
HARDCOVER ISBN: 978-1-4982-8084-6
EBOOK ISBN: 978-1-4982-8083-9

Cataloguing-in-Publication data:

Names: Draper, Andrew T.

Title: A theology of race and place : liberation and reconciliation in the works of jennings and carter / Andrew T. Draper

Description: Eugene, OR : Pickwick Publications, 2016 | Includes bibliographical references and index(es).

Identifiers: ISBN 978-1-4982-8082-2 (paperback) | ISBN 978-1-4982-8084-6 (hardcover) | ISBN 978-1-4982-8083-9 (ebook)

Subjects: LSCH: Carter, J. Kameron, 1967– | Jennings, Willie James, 1961– | Race—Religious aspects—Christianity. | Racism—Religious aspects—Christianity.

Classification: BT734 .D52 2016 (print) | BT734 .D52 (ebook)

Manufactured in the U.S.A.   08/26/16

This book is dedicated to Bishop H. Royce Mitchell, whose faithful love and patient mentoring guided me through many of the relational processes that led to the writing of this text. I do not take his sacrificial investment for granted.

"Therefore remember that at one time you Gentiles in the flesh . . . remember that you were at that time separated from Christ, alienated from the commonwealth of Israel and strangers to the covenants of promise, having no hope and without God in the world."

—Ephesians 2:11–12

"But if some of the branches were broken off, and you, although a wild olive shoot, were grafted in among the others and now share in the nourishing root of the olive tree, do not be arrogant toward the branches. If you are, remember it is not you who support the root, but the root that supports you . . . So do not become proud, but fear."

—Romans 11:17–20

Contents

Acknowledgments

I would like to thank my parents, Dr. and Dr. David and Linda Draper, who have consistently encouraged me in my pastoral and scholarly work. They have modeled for me lives committed to Jesus Christ, which is the greatest of gifts. Three pastors whose counsel has been important at key points in my life are: Charles Gifford, Guy Pfanz, and David Smith. I would also like to thank my teacher Phil Harrold for teaching me to love reading theology.

The congregation of which I am senior pastor, Urban Light Community Church, has been generous in respecting the space I needed to complete this research and has been the space in which I have experienced joined lives marked by difference. I am thankful for the opportunity to participate in one another's ongoing conversion. I would especially like to thank Toddrick Gordon, Joe Carpenter, Maria Wilson, Dori Granados, Nichole and Danny Smith, Lezlie McCrory, Elisabeth Taylor, Jody Powers, Shameka Gordon, James Rediger, Carol Jackson, Brenda Miller, Emilie Carpenter, and Seth Winn—the pastors, ministers, and leaders with whom I work. I also thank the leaders of the Churches of God, General Conference and Midwest Region for their support of me and my work.

The Lilly Endowment's provision of a pastoral sabbatical grant was indispensable in allowing me and my family to journey to Aberdeen as I began the doctoral process that would lead to the writing of an early draft of this text. I thank my father-in-law, Russ Wood, for suggesting the Scottish divinity milieu as an environment appropriate to my research. I can credit only the hand of God with allowing me to find Brian Brock, whose hospitality, gentleness, and humility led me in directions I would never have been able to find on my own. I am privileged to call him both a doctoral father and a friend. Stephanie, Adam, Caleb, and Agnes joined Brian in welcoming me and my family.

I also credit the writings of John Perkins and conversations with Wayne Gordon, the founders of the Christian Community Development Association, with initially alerting me to many of the issues I later sought to address in this text. As my questions have matured, Willie James Jennings has consistently gone above and beyond my expectations in offering me guidance and hospitality as I have dialogued with him about issues in this text. Prof.

Jennings' generosity is more than I could have hoped for. I also thank J. Kameron Carter for meeting with me and pointing me in fruitful directions. I would like to thank Andre Mitchell, Kevin Hargaden, Josh Arthur, Danny Smith, Terrance Bridges, Eric Wood, Adam Stichter, and Leslie Draper for reading portions or the entirety of various versions of this text and patiently conversing with me about the material and its presentation. Thanks are due to Stanley Hauerwas and Jonathan Tran for offering invaluable constructive criticism that helped me clarify my positions. I deeply respect Prof. Hauerwas's grace and humility in disagreeing with me. I would also like to thank my colleagues at Taylor University. They have been an encouragement in my research, teaching, and ministry.

Finally, I would like to acknowledge and thank my wife, Leslie Eleanor, whose pursuit of the truth and whose commitment to justice have discipled and guided me. I respect her more than words can say and I am so thankful for her love in our shared journey. My two sons, Aidan and Alister, are supportive beyond their years as our family seeks to follow the Way together. The path is often circuitous and I am so thankful that we do not walk it alone.

Introduction

The Racial Imaginary at Work

On February 26, 2012, an unarmed African American teenager named Trayvon Martin was fatally shot by neighborhood watch volunteer George Zimmerman. Zimmerman was detained by police, questioned, and then released claiming self-defense under the state of Florida's "Stand Your Ground" laws, which justify the use of lethal force in an altercation if believing one is in danger. Zimmerman did admit, however, that he had followed Martin, and that he had initiated the contact between the two, as evidenced by a call he made to the 911 emergency operator, who had instructed him to cease following Trayvon.[1] Exiting his car after speaking to the dispatcher, Zimmerman initiated the altercation that ended in Martin's death at the hands of Zimmerman. Zimmerman was charged with murder six weeks later only in response to public outrage. On July 13, 2013, Zimmerman was acquitted of all charges, including those of second-degree murder and manslaughter.

This case received international media attention and the judgment sparked intense debates in American society surrounding the intersection of race, violence, gun laws, profiling, and the criminal justice system. It served to make visible a slew of killings of unarmed black males, many by police. Names such as Eric Garner, Michael Brown, Tamir Rice, Walter Scott, and Freddie Gray became part of the growing list of the deceased. These killings were often accompanied by a lack of indictment or prosecution of the officers responsible. Riots in Ferguson, Missouri in 2014 and in Baltimore, Maryland in 2015 hearkened back to the civil unrest after the assassination

---

1. Throughout this text, I will be referencing the transcript of the call Zimmerman placed to 911 that evening. Zimmerman, "Full Transcript."

In reference to Zimmerman being told not to follow Martin after Martin saw Zimmerman tailing him and responded by running away, the text reads as follows: Zimmerman: "Shit, he's running." Dispatcher: "He's running? Which way is he running?" Zimmerman: "Down towards the other entrance to the neighborhood." Dispatcher: "Which entrance is that that he's heading towards?" Zimmerman: "The back entrance ... f**king [unintelligible]." Dispatcher: "Are you following him?" Zimmerman: "Yeah." Dispatcher: "Ok, we don't need you to do that."

1

of Dr. Martin Luther King Jr. in 1968. In a supposedly "post-racial" twenty-first-century society, strongly-held and often unstated assumptions about race boiled just beneath the surface of American public discourse. Many citizens and activists saw in the Trayvon Martin case a clear-cut example of a white man profiling an unarmed black youth. Resistance to this view was swift, most often pointing to "black-on-black" crimes or cases in which a white person had been the victim of violence at the hands of an African American person. Four and a half years after the inauguration of the first African American president of the United States of America, the public discourse of the nation was embroiled in tense disputes about the role of race in societal relations and commutative justice. Paradoxically, the election of Barack Obama served to strengthen the resolve of those who contended that there was no longer any such thing as a "race problem" in the United States. Such voices presented the media coverage surrounding Martin's shooting as a ploy to stoke the flames of racial discord anew or to covertly advance anti-gun or other "liberal" agendas.

During the days of Zimmerman's trial, my wife Leslie, in her position as School Leader of an urban public charter school, attended a civil rights learning expedition in Little Rock, Arkansas, and was privileged to interview Ms. Thelma Mothershed-Wair in her home. Ms. Mothershed-Wair was one of the leaders of the Little Rock Nine, the group of African American students who in 1957 integrated Central High School in the face of intense persecution by community residents, students, faculty, administration, and government officials. The entrance of the Little Rock Nine to the school was aided by armed protection from the National Guard under mandate from the federal government. As Leslie entered the home of Ms. Mothershed-Wair, she was greeted by a man who subsequently excused himself in order to continue watching "the Trayvon Martin case" in the next room. While Martin's death and Zimmerman's trial were not discussed during the interview, Leslie could not but recognize the parallels for this man between his care for Ms. Mothershed-Wair, who as a teenager had been subjected to violence because of her ethnicity, and his interest in the proceedings surrounding the violence committed against Trayvon. When reflecting on this parallel in her portion of the report about the civil rights expedition, my wife was encouraged by several of the "progressive" staff who had planned the expedition to refrain from referring to the Martin case. While their primary concern was that Leslie not form connections not made explicit by Ms. Mothershed-Wair, the staff leaders did not seem to want to draw attention to the contemporary political ramifications of an interview with a member of the Little Rock Nine being conducted with the sounds of the Trayvon Martin case playing in the background. While both staff leaders preferred that she remove the reference altogether, the African American staff person "did not disagree" that the two events may be related while the Caucasian staff person did not seem to recognize the correlation. Leslie persevered in including the reference but was obligated to leave it as an observation about the interview's setting and to draw no conclusions about its significance.

My reflection upon the shooting of Trayvon Martin is intrinsically linked to the place in which I live and the community of which I am a part. I am a white pastor living and ministering in an urban community that is primarily black and white.[2] The primary focus of our church, our lives, and our education has been reconciliation across ethnic lines, particularly across the black–white divide, or what W. E. B. DuBois called "the problem of the color line."[3] We are a community struggling to experience Christ's reconciliation as it is embodied in a new sociopolitical order in which old kinship networks give way to new and unlikely claims of familial connection. Joining to one another is not something to be "had" or "accomplished"; it is a journey, fraught with difficulties, messiness, misunderstanding, and beauty. After a decade of fostering deep and intentional connections with "unlike" others, I am still often perplexed about what to say or what to do when faced with ignorance in myself or others, misunderstandings in relationships marked by a historical power disparity, and injustice within societal systems.

Being mentored by a prominent African American Bishop in our community and pastoring a church which strives to be representative of the diversity of our community at every level of leadership brings abundant opportunities for correction, redirection, and affirmation. As I write this, I am reflecting on being confronted recently by a fellow leader in regard to a set of assumptions that I had unwittingly displayed through my comments at a board meeting. While at times it would undoubtedly be more comfortable to not place oneself in a position of displaying one's own ignorance and prejudice, a continual journey of repentance and growth entails having sisters and brothers who participate in one's salvation.

I am introducing myself as narrator neither to indict nor to pardon myself. I do not intend my reflections to be an exercise in self-flagellation or in self-referential exculpation. While I am aware that positioning oneself is a common introductory move within various works dealing with identity politics, I read the majority of said statements as displaying a self-conscious hermeneutic that may tend to confine the author within his or her own

2. While family stories hold that my great-grandmother's father was Sioux, and while there are aspects of claiming that heritage that have influenced the way I perceive the world, my light skin and community of origin mean that I functionally exist in modern society as a white male.

3. DuBois, *The Souls of Black Folk*, 15.

perspectivism.[4] While a full Christian doctrine of creation necessitates that we view ourselves as bounded creatures shaped by particular contexts, the doctrine of redemption affords transcendence that can deliver us from being sealed in static identity silos. I introduce myself to make apparent how I have been led to interacting with the works of the theologians who ground my research into a theology of race and place and how my questions have led to the constructive heart of my thesis: the lived problem of racial reconciliation. Before I introduce their works, however, it remains to articulate the difficulty I faced when reflecting upon and explicating the racial vision that animated the death of an unarmed teenager and the acquittal of his murderer. I was convinced that a similar racial vision had enabled the exclusion of particular children from specific schools fifty years earlier. How could it be that what was taken for granted by Ms. Mothershed-Wair's caregiver could ostensibly be hidden from so many others?

The resistance my wife faced to drawing seemingly obvious parallels between Martin's death and the historic exclusion of black children from white schools served to remind me that history vindicates the oppressed only years after the unpopularity of standing in the place of resistance has faded. It also served to call me to the necessity of utilizing my platform as pastor, scholar, community leader, and activist to speak clearly about the reality of a society founded upon the subjugation of non-white bodies and the underlying racial calculus that determines the seeming disposability of the life of a young person of color. The immediate and strong reaction against my careful public comments, particularly from people of faith, was a bit surprising to me. While this reaction did not come from members of the faith community which I pastor or from people who have invited me into ecclesial and relational structures not my own, and while I had expected that my statements would not meet with universal approval, the strong resistance to what seemed to be straightforward conclusions about our society's racial sight and its embodiment in the justification of violence was quite perplexing.

My initial statements, which took place several days before the verdict, had been on social media and immediately received a flood of comments from many loved ones and acquaintances who claimed to not understanding how the killing of Martin or the reaction of the public could have had anything to do with race. I was told that the facts of the case did not make it clear that Martin was not killed in self-defense, that race was not involved because Zimmerman was in fact not white but of mixed white and Hispanic racial ancestry, and that it is our constitutional right to carry arms and our

---

4. See Patte, *Ethics of Biblical Interpretation*, 1–2.

legal right to "stand our ground." I was forwarded a news story about black youth shooting a white woman and her baby, with the added comment that there were no "White Panthers" protesting that occurrence. The ironic fact that said youth were not acquitted seemed to escape the recognition of that view's proponents. As "evidence" that race was not a factor in this case, I was sent one of the few speeches the press could find given by a black man in defense of Zimmerman. An historically controversial African American pastor told his New York congregation that if they would only look at this situation "through the blood of Jesus" instead of through their "black eyes" they would see that Zimmerman was justified in killing Martin, whom he named a "pot-smoking munchies, paranoid 17-year-old boy."[5] I was accused of being "taken in" by the "racist left" and was demanded to explain how I, as a Christian, could speak out for justice for Trayvon. What was most saddening about these interchanges was that most of my interlocutors were self-avowed defenders of "Christian morals."

After several days, I noticed that, of the hundreds of people who had responded, every person who had challenged me was white. People of various ethnicities had shared a sense of concern or outrage at the manner in which the trial was progressing. When I publicly noted this observation, I was chastised with the "post-racial" assumption that we now live in a "color-blind" society in which the ethnicity of a view's proponents means nothing. What matters is whether or not a person's observations are "right." Invoked to bolster this view was Martin Luther King Jr.'s dream that his children would be judged not by "the color of their skin but by the content of their character."[6] It seemed to me that this utilization of King appropriated his words out of context and insinuated that while ethnicity meant nothing, the innate character of the nonwhite other was readily discernible.

I was told that to talk about race as playing a substantial role in ethical discourse serves to stoke the flames of racial division and strife, turning back all the "progress" we have made as a society. How was I to interpret these critiques from "good" people about a society that has presumably "gotten over" ethnic division? Were it not for my experience of the racial calculus that operates reflexively within contemporary theological and ecclesial

5. Pastor James David Manning's problematic view of blackness as taint was on display as he preached: "You have not changed yet. You're black . . . So why do you blame George Zimmerman? Why? Because you're black, that's why. You're not saved, you don't know nothing about Jesus and you're full of hate . . . There ain't no truth in you, ain't no Jesus in you, condemning George Zimmerman, ain't no Jesus in you. You're black, that's all you're ever gonna be" (Blair, "Pastor Calls Trayvon Martin . . .").

6. King, "I Have a Dream . . ."

formation, I might have more seriously questioned my assumptions about the death of a black youth and the acquittal of his killer.

While I had long recognized problematic aspects of my own formation in regard to the assumed universality of what were highly culturally-constructed theological, aesthetic, and ethical frameworks, it is through the works of Willie James Jennings and J. Kameron Carter that I began to link things I had observed, but not been able to connect or explain in a coherent fashion. What had been troublesome in the way "reconciliation" was imagined within the ecclesiological frameworks I had received was explicated in their texts in a cogent manner that purposed to expose the inception of the racial vision and its subsequent masquerade as universality. Jennings' and Carter's related genealogical accounts present whiteness as a sociopolitical order that must be maintained and invested in so as to be given life.[7] As such, whiteness as a comprehensive way of life can function as a challenge to the Way of Life embodied in the One who is the Way. It will become clear throughout this study that what I am referencing as problematic is not the particularity of European experience, but the particularity-as-universality that is whiteness and which competes with the reign of Christ as it invites all flesh into its sociopolitical order.

The major portion of this book pursues an in-depth analysis of the theological race theory of Jennings and Carter. Taken together, their works form an emerging school of thought that finds the genesis of the modern racial imagination to be the racialized scale inaugurated by colonization and coming to maturation in the structure of Enlightenment. Jennings, in *The Christian Imagination*, explores the colonial underpinnings of whiteness while Carter, in *Race: A Theological Account*, reads modernity as the evolution of this way of being in the world.[8] Jennings and Carter contend that the trajectory of "whiteness" as sociopolitical order is enabled by a supersessionist tendency that undervalues the particularity of the work of YHWH through the chosen people Israel in favor of a universalizing framework characteristic of European hegemony. In other words, Occidental dominance functions within a problematic theological legacy in which the particularity of the Jewish body of Jesus Christ is of little importance. This minimizing of the particular locus of salvation can be seen as underemphasizing the particularity of all people groups. This loss of particularity is

---

7. Although I will use the term *genealogy* to describe both Jennings' and Carter's methodology, I must qualify this categorization: Carter's archeological account is a sort of "anti-genealogy" to theological retrievals of Hellenic virtue while Jennings' historical methodology is consonant with Stephen Greenblatt's "New Historicist" account. See Greenblatt, *Practicing New Historicism*.

8. Jennings, *Christian Imagination*, and Carter, *Race*.

experienced as a loss of the importance of place—tangible, local space—in the constitution of a people. Without a spatial constitution, bodies are called upon to stand in for place and are accordingly racialized along a hierarchical continuum. Racialized bodies are then understood to be drawn into the *telos* of whiteness as the salvific hope for those trapped within the taint of dark flesh, which stands as signifier of a more primitive nature. This configuration of thought and practice bars genuine joining of peoples except through assimilationist motifs in which European aesthetic, ontological, and ethical constructs are held to be the norm toward which all of creation is maturing. This book will explicate in much more detail how Carter and Jennings build this sequence of arguments.

Returning now to my experiences following Zimmerman's acquittal will allow me to illustrate my claim that whiteness is a sociopolitical order that demands continual maintenance. On the second day of the jury's deliberations, the jury found Zimmerman "not guilty" on all counts. Having lived and ministered for a decade in my inner city neighborhood located on the "color line," I had seen countless African American male youth faced with a sense of nihilism at the hopelessness of resisting the forces of categorization, exclusion from empowering education, police profiling, and a criminal "justice" system which has functioned to effectively eliminate the threat of the nonwhite body through mass incarceration. I had watched as tender young boys were streamlined down the pipeline from ghetto school to state-of-the-art prison. I had seen sensitive young men waived as adults and hardened by several years of warehousing in the prison industrial complex. I had witnessed adult men with fates largely predetermined as they faced a daunting job market with little formal education, branded with the scarlet letter of "felon" for crimes that would have been ignored or received a slap on the wrist in suburban or rural contexts. I had witnessed on my street several of the young men who spent time in our home or Bible studies as children now finding the easiest option to be one of violence in the face of seemingly pointless resistance. Defying this predetermined fate was the experience of only a few young men who had the good fortune to experience a convergence of: being afforded the possibility of non-traditional educational opportunities, connecting to a strong local faith community, receiving the approbation of multiple caring adults who intentionally and sacrificially invested in them, and possessing an uncommon mix of self-esteem, tenacity, and an extroverted personality that won favor in the eyes of those with whom they came in contact. This seemingly serendipitous confluence was the exception and not the norm and took massive amounts of effort on the part of all involved to maintain, largely because it brought one into direct conflict with the principalities and powers.[9] When Zimmerman was declared "not guilty," I realized that I was at a loss regarding what I could now tell these young men. Could I tell them that if only they made sure to do the "right" thing society would protect them? How could they have any confidence that if they, like Trayvon, were walking home with a bag of Skittles and a soda, their lives would be viewed as being worthy of protection? Could I assure them that if they attempted to avoid conflict and yet were attacked, the trial of their murderer would not turn into a judgment based on society's perception of their "character" and relative worth?

As I lay in bed that evening, I choked back tears and prayed that the grace of God would keep our local community and our country from taking ten steps backward in our ability to know and trust each other. While it was a foregone conclusion for my brothers and sisters in the black community that in some way every aspect of this tragedy had been about race, and while I took comfort in the strength I borrowed from them, I was not sure how I would be received the next morning. Zimmerman was acquitted on a Saturday night and Sunday morning I would be standing to preach before the joined black and white community that makes up the congregation which I pastor. I needed to put into words the sadness and outrage which we felt, while clinging to the hope that mutuality is possible within the body of Jesus of Nazareth. What happened was not what I expected. The building in which we worshiped was full and our members, black and white, were there and ready to worship. The African American members of the body experientially led our congregation, including those of a lighter hue, into an affirmation of God's goodness in the face of injustice. Even after having lived and ministered in my community for years and after having availed myself of many autobiographical, theological, and sociological resources related to the struggle for black liberation upon the soil of the New World, I was existentially unprepared for the familiarity of the black worshipper with exalting the name of the Lord while walking through the valley of despair. While I was able to speak to the deep sense of betrayal we as a community were experiencing, the maintenance of an affirmation of God's goodness did not rely primarily upon me. We had together formed a bond strong enough that we were able to be vulnerable with each other in the midst of our pain instead of alienating each other because of the perpetration of evil. I will never forget the heroic posture of my black brothers and sisters that morning as those of us who had not been on the receiving end of racial profiling were invited into the shared experience of lament and celebration.

9. I use this phrase to refer to what I take to be both a spiritual and political reality (Eph 6:12; Wink, *The Powers that Be.*)

There can be no "proof" that George Zimmerman targeted Trayvon Martin because he was black. To frame the issue in this manner radically misunderstands the nature of the racial imagination as inaugurated by whiteness. The point is that both Zimmerman and the contemporary church and academy often operate within similar evaluative frameworks: the former judging the intentions of a black youth and the latter posing ethical and aesthetic theories and submitting non-Western cultural forms to those judgments. While I identify Zimmerman as "racist" in ways that many Christian theologians are not, it will be my task in this book to demonstrate the ways in which a similar racial imagination enlivens both overt racism and the dominance of many "white" forms of Christian community and theological inquiry.

Within rhetoric of ethics and beauty, the racial imagination has tended to align both criminality and immorality with blackness while aligning guardianship and goodness with whiteness. Zimmerman's 911 call, in which he maintained that Martin was "a real suspicious guy" who "look[ed] like" he was "up to no good" illustrates this contention in an overt manner. "He's got his hand in his waistband and he's a black male" linked a judgment about Martin's personal intentions with a categorization of Martin as a typological character: "These assholes they always get away." This assessment was not primarily about Martin, but about what Martin represented. As a young black man in a hoodie walking through a gated community he became one of "these assholes." Run as he might, Trayvon would be overtaken by Zimmerman, who had been warned by the 911 dispatcher not to follow Martin. What happened from there, while being hotly contested, is of little consequence to the "facts" of the case or their theological significance. It is indisputable that Martin ran away at the sight of Zimmerman (Zimmerman: "Shit he's running"). The blood from Zimmerman's head and nose suggests that he was beaten after he followed and accosted Martin. Why this fact changes anything is beyond comprehension. If the tables were turned, it is unthinkable that a white youth fighting back against a darker–skinned assailant would effectively be put on trial as an aggressor.[10] It is likewise ab-

10. There was an effort on the part of some white folk to take offense at the testimony of Rachel Jeantel, a close friend of Trayvon who was on the phone with him while he was being pursued by Zimmerman. She testified that Martin was aware that he was being followed, was fleeing, had communicated to her his fear of the man following him, and had described the man as a "creepy-ass cracker." In the days following her testimony, many people found Martin's description of Zimmerman as evidence of Martin's racism. However, such a judgment drastically misunderstands (or misrepresents) the phrase used by Martin. First, Martin's description of Zimmerman came from the underside of modernity, from the bottom of the power structure. The term "cracker" was historically applied by African Americans to the white masters who "cracked" their whips at the backs of livestock and black slaves. It was a term of resistance, subverting

surd to imagine that if a darker-skinned armed man had followed and confronted an unarmed teenager forty pounds and several shades lighter than him, he would ever have been acquitted based on a claim of "self-defense."[11] The essential point is that before the final altercation, Trayvon had already been tried and found guilty. The judgment of guilt was made the moment the descriptive glance of whiteness discerned Trayvon's nefarious purposes as member of a suspicious type. That this judgment is theological in nature is evidenced by Zimmerman's later reflection to Fox News' Sean Hannity that "it was all God's plan" for him to kill Trayvon and that he could neither "regret" nor "second-guess" anything he did that night.[12]

If, as I am claiming, an observatory stance which categorizes based upon a racialized hierarchy is at work in our collective Western imagination, the debate over whether Zimmerman was white or of white and Hispanic mixed racial ancestry is of little importance. As we have seen, the pervasiveness of the racial gaze is such that an African American pastor in New York can succumb to the same reflexive disdain for blackness. Zimmerman as white male or as Hispanic male can be interpreted as functioning within this social imaginary. While the orientation of whiteness was historically inaugurated by those of lighter skin, whose re-ordering of the world produced such a descriptive stance, all flesh has been forced into this manner of categorization. It has often been the case historically that those who are "nearest" to being white are those most effective in policing the lines of racial purity, as their own identity depends on it. The popular debate about the purity or lack thereof of Zimmerman's ethnicity is indicative of

---

the impossible load of subjugation whiteness had forced others to bear. A white person referring to a person of color with a derogatory racial slur and Martin referring to Zimmerman as a "cracker" are not as similar as often assumed. While it is undoubtedly the case that neither terminology encourages the sort of mutuality toward which Jennings and Carter are pointing, it is important to remember that the former was that which classified and kept others "in their place," while the latter was defense against such categorization. Second, it should be remembered that to "creep" is to surreptitiously maneuver oneself so as to avoid detection, usually for nefarious purposes. Tracking a person in a car certainly fits this definition. It turns out that perhaps the phrase "creepy-ass cracker" is not an altogether inappropriate designation for a white man with a gun trailing a black youth running in fear. Either way, the outrage over Jeantel using this term seems to be hollow or manufactured.

11. Consider the Florida case of Marissa Alexander, who, one year before Zimmerman was acquitted in the same state, was sentenced to twenty years in prison for firing a shot into the air, from a gun she legally owned, as a warning to her husband, who had a history of abusing Alexander. Alexander stated that she was afraid that her husband was going to seriously injure or kill her. While she neither shot at nor killed her husband, the jury deliberated for only twelve minutes before finding her guilty. Alexander is black.

12. Capeheart, "George Zimmerman."

the classificatory structure of whiteness. Much in the same way that nay-sayers declared that Obama the candidate was not truly "black" because his mother was white, defenders of Zimmerman were quick to point out that race could not have been involved in this case because Zimmerman was not truly "white." This obsession with genetic makeup is reminiscent of sixteenth-century laws related to "blood purity" and drastically under-estimates the force of the racial imagination. The racial imagination sees in lighter skin a potential for "civilized" behavior and in darker skin the existence of "savage" instincts. Within the racial gaze of whiteness, people are reflexively assigned a spot somewhere along this continuum. Those who ride the fence between racial "types" are often forced to decide with which group they will identify. In much the same way that lighter-skinned persons of African descent are often looked upon more favorably by both white society and black communities, and in much the same way that "mulatto" people historically survived in the marketplace by claiming to be of some other ethnicity,[13] a black teenager named Trayvon Martin was measured on the scale of whiteness and found wanting.

Those who looked primarily for a clear sign of "racial animus" in this case were not looking deep enough. While it is certainly not the case that racism (as a matter of the will) has been eradicated, what I am describing here is the gaze that animates the ability to make racialized judgments. It is this gaze that is not primarily dependent on the conscious choice of an individual in a moment of hatred or discrimination, although it does serve to produce such animosity. It is this gaze that Jennings and Carter con-tend must be named, recognized, and resisted. Our contemporary public rhetoric, with its laudable emphasis on rooting out racism, is able to ad-dress only clearly defined acts of discrimination in an attempt to discern the prejudicial intentions of the perpetrator behind said bias. Paradoxically, the almost exclusive focus on racism as a matter of the will can distract from the underlying problem. This could be one reason why the racial judgment was purportedly so difficult for white persons to discern in the Martin/Zimmer-man case. Yet for those who have experienced both sides of the objectify-ing gaze of judgment that assumes the transparency of the nonwhite body, the racial imaginary can be seen in the assumptions made about Trayvon's intentions. Although the only language available to observers of these legal proceedings was the language of racism, many black and white Americans intuitively understood that there was more at stake in this case. I am making

13. See, for example, Williams, *Life on the Color Line*, in which Williams' father, Buster, passed himself off as Italian in order to be able to run a business. The majority of this story took place in Muncie, Indiana, the town in which I live and minister, in the 1950s and 1960s.

a hermeneutical judgment here. Yet I must stress that it is not a hermeneutical judgment that proceeds primarily from my "will"; it is a judgment that is inescapable because of the reality of being joined with those whose daily experience and historical reality directs and instructs me. Fundamentally, it is a judgment from outside me: encouraged by my position before black and white congregants as we stand together before the throne of Jesus Christ. It is the judgment of divine grace that affords us the opportunity to transcend a static ontology while remaining grounded as particular creatures.

The State of Theological Race Studies

These reflections on Martin's death and Zimmerman's acquittal have exposed common responses of many contemporary Christians, as well as the strikingly different response of my local worshipping community, shaped by intentional joining amidst diversity. This contrast suggests several different ways of theologically engaging with race. This diversity of perspectives may be demonstrated by surveying the field of contemporary literature surrounding the intersection of race and theology.

I read the theological school of race theory initiated by Jennings and Carter as both a culmination and a redirection of the field of theological race studies. Academic theological race studies have often been produced in the form of liberation theologies or reflections on identity politics. Beginning with the work of Gustavo Gutierrez in *A Theology of Liberation*, a "preferential option for the poor" began to be invoked as a framework within which to understand the liberating work of Christ.[14] Developing this impulse, James H. Cone's work almost singlehandedly inaugurated the field of black liberation theology through works such as *Black Theology and Black Power*, *A Black Theology of Liberation*, and *God of the Oppressed*.[15] Cone famously combined liberation theology and identity politics with his identification of African Americans as "God's poor people" and his assertion that "God is black." Shaped by the spirits of Stokely Carmichael and Malcolm X, Cone's sophisticated texts set the trajectory for theological race studies for a generation. Vine Deloria Jr. is often mentioned alongside Cone, his works on religion and Native spirituality emphasizing the opacity of being and presenting Native religious frameworks as offering a more satisfactory account of creation than that articulated by Christian theology. In books such as *Custer Died for Your Sins* and *God is Red: A Native View of Religion*,

14. Gutierrez, *A Theology of Liberation*.

15. Cone, *Black Theology and Black Power*; Cone, *A Black Theology of Liberation*; and Cone, *God of the Oppressed*.

Deloria Jr. offers wry and astute observations on the confluence of Christianity and colonization.[16] Deloria Jr.'s purpose is not so much to essentialize race as it is to suggest an intrinsic link between land and a people's self-understanding. This observation distinguishes Deloria Jr.'s account from the general trajectory of identity politics.

Early theologies of liberation focused on race or socioeconomic status have been followed by identity theologies dealing with gender and sexual orientation.[17] While not discounting the important anthropological insights and hermeneutical practices advanced in these works, it will become apparent throughout my treatment that I read the general trajectory of identity politics as locked within an essentialization of identity that reinforces the very strictures it seeks to overcome. While it is not within the scope of my work to address this theme as it is related to theologies of gender or sexual orientation, suffice it to say that the trajectory inaugurated by Cone tends to reinforce a hermeneutic of suspicion and has difficulty moving beyond reification of identity distinctions. The *telos* of such an intellectual arrangement does a disservice to theologies of race by allowing them no distinction from theologies of sexual orientation, for instance. While Jennings and Carter clearly enumerate the connections between the hierarchical arrangement of modern racialized bodies, modern gendered bodies, and the body politic, I read both scholars as together striking out upon a new path not locked within the hermeneutical ghetto within which theologies of identity have often been consigned.

Scholars such as Charles H. Long, Albert J. Raboteau, Dwight Hopkins Jr., J. Deotis Roberts, James Noel, William R. Jones, and Angela Sims have all made important contributions in the fields of religious studies and African American church studies. While Hopkins has focused primarily upon early Afro-Christian slave religion[18] and Sims is well known for her seminal work on Ida B. Wells, *The Ethical Complications of Lynching*,[19] Noel has published

---

16. Deloria, *God is Red*; and Deloria, *Custer Died for Your Sins*.

17. See Reuther, *Sexism and God–Talk*; Reuther, *Gaia and God*; Schussler Fiorenza, *In Memory of Her*; Schussler Fiorenza, *But She Said*; Coakley, *God, Sexuality and the Self*; Rogers, *Sexuality and the Christian Body*; and Loughlin, *Queer Theology*. This is not to say that there have not been advances in critical queer theory toward resisting gender essentialization. One example of a post-structuralist account of gender is Sullivan, *A Critical Introduction to Queer Theory*. While I am sensitive to the manner in which Sullivan builds her case, I am resistant to her overly tidy conflation of race and gender identity and am unconvinced that her conclusions hold up theologically.

18. See Hopkins, *Shoes that Fit Our Feet*; Hopkins, *Down, Up, and Over*; and Hopkins, *Cut Loose Your Stammering Tongue*.

19. Sims, *Ethical Complications of Lynching*.

more generally regarding African American religion.[20] In *Is God a White Racist?*, Jones details his "conversion from black Christian fundamentalism to black religious humanism," eschewing the God of orthodox Christianity in favor of what he calls "humanocentric theism."[21] Through classic texts like *Liberation and Reconciliation*, Roberts drafted a black theology in response to Cone, emphasizing the need for liberation and reconciliation to be experienced through active nonviolent protest.[22] Of these scholars, the two who arguably have had the greatest impact in the field of religious studies are Raboteau and Long, with whom I will interact in some detail in my treatment of Carter in chapter 1.

In the realm of public intellectualism, scholars such as Cornel West and Henry Louis Gates Jr. have influenced contemporary rhetoric and debate surrounding the role of race in society, economics, and politics.[23] While not strictly doctrinal in their theological approach, the works of West and Gates cannot be underestimated in their impact in shaping the role of race in America in the twenty-first century. While intersecting with the historical focus of scholars such as Hopkins, Sims, and Noel, and while being sensitive to the general trajectory of scholars such as West and Gates, the works of Jennings and Carter will be seen throughout this analysis to be distinct from the field of religious studies in several important ways, most clearly exhibited by their resistance to the essentialization of identity characteristic of comparative religious analysis.

At the level of popular missiology, perhaps no other organization has published so widely about racial reconciliation as the Christian Community Development Association. The CCDA is a network of several hundred urban ministries which are guided by John M. Perkins' framework of *Relocation, Reconciliation,* and *Redistribution.* Perkins, who has stressed incarnational relocation to communities not one's own, primarily post–industrial inner-city neighborhoods, founded the CCDA in 1989 after a lifetime of work focused on racial reconciliation and community development. Perkins was active in the civil rights movement in Mississippi in the late nineteen–sixties, experiencing his brother's murder and his own imprisonment and torture at the hands of white police officers. Perkins has been extremely influential

20. See Noel, *Black Religion*; Noel, "African American Art"; and Noel, "African American Religions."

21. Jones, *Is God a White Racist?*

22. Roberts, *Liberation and Reconciliation.*

23. See West, *Race Matters*; and Gates and West, *The Future of the Race*, among many other works. The public impact of neither author can be limited to his publications. Countless interviews, articles, public statements, and television appearances mark the career of each scholar.

in advancing both dialogue and praxis surrounding reconciliation and justice. As a grassroots organization of practitioners, the theological vision of the CCDA has been somewhat limited.[24] While often acknowledging the links between "community development" and colonizing sensibilities and seeking to resist the latter, the CCDA's invocation of *relocation* tends to be framed in a unilateral manner that too strongly reads the "relocator" into the place of Christ, suggesting a latent supersessionism in the CCDA's implicit Christology. The mutuality often experienced in CCDA ministries (of which my local church is an organizational member) tends to be had at the expense of the systematic integrity of its "incarnational" Christology. At this point Jennings could be a helpful conversation partner for the CCDA as his theology of place and particularity provides a more sufficient framework for considering the joining of diverse peoples. While the CCDA is invaluable as an unlikely community of diverse practitioners joined together as advocates with those on the margins, it is not first and foremost a theological school.

Somewhat more sophisticated works have been produced recently which share similar theological sensibilities to those of the CCDA. From the Duke Divinity School Center for Reconciliation, Emmanuel Katongole and Chris Rice have edited a series called *Resources for Reconciliation*, in which they pen *Reconciling All Things: A Christian Vision for Justice, Peace, and Healing*.[25] Katongole and Rice attempt to move beyond truncated visions of reconciliation often expressed in Evangelical circles by expanding those accounts into a holistic vision of the reconciliation of all things in Christ. Likewise, Jonathan Wilson-Hartgrove explores a practical theological vision of reconciliation in his semi-autobiographical account *Free to Be Bound: Church Beyond the Color Line*.[26] Wilson-Hartgrove reflects on learning to "hear the Gospel in a new key" as he was welcomed into a historically black church in Durham, and what this journey has meant for his understanding of identity and ecclesiology. While referencing Jennings and Carter as his teachers, and acknowledging their works as an important emerging "school" in "American theology,"[27] the genre of Wilson-Hartgrove's text limits the scope of his explorations of the theological genesis of the racial imagination.

In many ways, the intersection of religious thought and race in contemporary American public discourse can be shown to be inextricably linked

---

24. See Perkins, *Let Justice Roll Down*; Perkins, *Beyond Charity*; Perkins, *Restoring At-Risk Communities*; Gordon, *Real Hope in Chicago*; Gordon, *Making Neighborhoods Whole*; Lupton, *Compassion, Justice, and the Christian Life*; Lupton, *Theirs Is the Kingdom*; and Fuder, *A Heart for the Community*.

25. Katongole, *Reconciling All Things*.

26. Wilson-Hartgrove, *Free to Be Bound*.

27. Ibid., 18.

to the dual legacies of Martin Luther King Jr. and Malcolm X. As Cone demonstrates in *Martin and Malcolm and America*, the divergent emphases of Martin and Malcolm, which were heading toward greater convergence when the life of each religious leader and activist was violently snuffed out, demonstrate two distinct yet interconnected ways of viewing relationships across lines of ethnicity.[28] As demonstrated through MLK's collected papers and speeches in *The Autobiography of Martin Luther King, Jr.*[29] and the two preeminent accounts of Malcolm X's life, Alex Haley's famous interviews with X entitled *The Autobiography of Malcolm X* and the recent acclaimed biography *Malcolm X: A Life of Reinvention* by Manning Marable,[30] the trajectories of both men overlapped in ways not acknowledged in common conventional accounts of their legacies. While MLK is famous for his invocation of "the beloved community," he died somewhat of a pariah for his outspoken resistance to militarism and the systemic nature of poverty in the modern capitalist West. Likewise, while X is famous for his resistance to the evils perpetrated by the "white devil," his religious experiences through his pilgrimage to Mecca and his theological insistence upon particularity as a path toward universality marked a later more inclusive shift that would cost him his life. Neither man advocated mutuality without justice. Both paid the ultimate price for resisting the sociopolitical order of whiteness.

Two of the most recent works relating to the intersection of theology and race are Brian Bantum's academic text *Redeeming Mulatto: A Theology of Race and Christian Hybridity*[31] and John Piper's popular text *Bloodlines: Race, Cross, and the Christian*.[32] The former is sensitive to the theological sensibilities of Jennings and Carter, while the latter exemplifies the manner in which the race antinomianism of supersessionist logic is often refracted through popular Christian works. Bantum's review criticizing Piper's manner of envisioning racial reconciliation by rendering ethnicity inconsequential clearly draws from the works of Jennings and Carter.[33] While I

---

28. Cone, *Martin and Malcolm and America*.

29. Carson, *Autobiography of Martin Luther King, Jr.*

30. Haley, *The Autobiography of Malcolm X*; and Marable, *Malcolm X*.

31. Bantum, *Redeeming Mulatto*.

32. Piper, *Bloodlines*.

33. See Bantum, "Bloodlines," where he states that "Piper's Christ is a raceless God-man, focused intently on a violent sacrifice that achieves the salvation of our souls with the happy consequence of taking our bodies along for the ride." Bantum lauds Piper's desire to foster a diverse Christian community, but laments that in excluding voices from outside of his own trajectory (especially liberation and womanist thought), Piper has pre-determined that his ecclesial community will take the shape of his own theological convictions and tradition without leaving room for "*sincere* dialogue." The process envisioned by Piper arguably has very little to do with reconciliation.

will interact in some detail with each text at key points in this treatment, I introduce them here so as to indicate the ways in which they converge with or diverge from the theological school of Jennings and Carter. Bantum, as a student of Stanley Hauerwas at Duke Divinity School, had the opportunity to learn from both Jennings and Carter and aims his theological reflections in roughly the same direction as that inaugurated by the two latter thinkers. In my constructive Conclusion, I will utilize Bantum's Christological reflections on hybridity to orient my ecclesiological focus. At that point, I will enumerate what I read as Bantum's dual relationship to the theological race theory of Jennings and Carter and the classical retrieval impulse of Hauerwas. My intention is not to exaggerate Bantum's divergence from Jennings and Carter, but rather to indicate an inclination in his work not entirely at home in their theological trajectory.

I do not read Jennings and Carter as opposed to theological retrieval; their work is much more open to engaging with the "tradition" than that of many other scholars who write about identity issues. At the same time they do not uncritically incorporate the tradition; they recognize the fallibility of the luminaries of both orthodoxy and liberalism. They contend that it is within orthodoxy itself that supersessionism took root. Appeals to tradition as the preeminent theological norm can obscure this reality. Much like Kierkegaard and Barth, Carter and Jennings recognize that each generation must engage afresh and anew with the word of God. In their theological race theory, neither tradition nor liberalism alone is sufficient to this task.

I read Piper's *Bloodlines*, which is a non-academic theological work, as evincing a manner of imagining racial identity which is utterly divergent from Jennings' and Carter's vision. In short, Piper's work represents a popular way of enfolding concerns about race into justification of a narrow doctrinal system. Piper utilizes race to buttress his American Reformed tradition. Ironically, he proclaims an end to ethnocentrism through a "colorblind" appeal to the theological legacy of the Puritans. Piper's reflections on black flesh can be read as opportunities for theological self-defense. What appears to be anti-ethnocentric is in reality radically assimilationist.

The Theological Race Theory of Jennings and Carter

The theological race theory of Jennings and Carter was forged in a particular space. While Jennings reveals that the soil with which his mother worked is perhaps more constitutive for his understanding of place and race than is the academy of which he was a part for years,[34] it is not inconsequential

---

34. Jennings, *Christian Imagination*, 1.

that Duke is the space within which scholars such as Jennings, Carter, and Bantum were joined. It can be assumed that Jennings' interest in Jose de Acosta was influenced, at least in part, by his interactions with Walter D. Mignolo, the scholar of cultural studies at Duke who wrote the commentary on the new translation of Acosta's *Historia*, published by Duke University Press.[35] Additionally, it is probable that an environment in which questions are being asked about the centrality of Jesus Christ in a cosmopolitan milieu encouraged space for the theological race theory of Jennings and Carter to take root. These are the sort of questions asked by a wide range of prominent theologians at Duke, such as Stanley Hauerwas, Gregory Jones, and Richard Hays, although their answers differ from those of Jennings and Carter.

It is significant that Jennings mounts an implicit critique of the theological atmosphere of Duke in his critical read of Alisdair MacIntyre and "traditioned moral enquiry."[36] Given Duke's public reputation as a center for reconciliation studies, it is as if Jennings is suggesting that the "best" contemporary Christian talk about reconciliation often falls prey to objectifying views of the "other" made possible by supersessionist patterns of theologically imagining identity. Jennings is not singling out Hauerwas for criticism nor is he suggesting that Duke is susceptible to the racial imaginary to a greater degree than the Christian academy in general. Rather, he is demonstrating that a reclamation of the "tradition" in the face of liberalism is not free from being a carrier of the virus of racialization. Jennings' and Carter's thesis would grant Hauerwas, MacIntyre, and theologians such as John Milbank their conclusion that the language of liberalism is not the best way to describe reality. Stated differently, Jennings and Carter would agree that theology can make truth claims and that it is intellectually viable for divine revelation to be the epistemological center. In this sense, theologians who appreciate the role of tradition contra the hegemony of modern liberalism have been important voices in the conversation. However, Jennings' and Carter's contention is that the racial imagination was birthed from within the "tradition" during late medievalism, rendering a reclamation of scholastic orthodoxy a bit more problematic than originally supposed. Jennings and Carter are content with neither unqualified appeals to the "tradition" nor modern liberalism. Throughout this book I will describe this contention in detail before, in the Conclusion, moving to what I hope will be a more satisfactory way of imagining reconciliation along the lines of the theologies proposed by Jennings and Carter.

35. Acosta, *Natural and Moral History*.

36. Jennings, *Christian Imagination*, 71.

I will demonstrate that, unlike Cone and the fields of identity politics in general, Jennings and Carter more radically engage race through a more rigorous theological engagement than that employed by the available literature. This contention is substantiated by the key themes from their works which I have hinted at in my analysis of the murder of Trayvon Martin. At this point, I will briefly acknowledge several themes which I will develop throughout my treatment of each scholar. My aim, therefore, is to introduce my text around the structure of my introductory narrative.

First, the racialized scale inaugurated in the colonial period and maturing in modernity is identified by Carter through his interaction with the racialized architecture undergirding Kant's *Aufklarung* and by Jennings through his interaction with the racialized imagination of Acosta in his sixteenth century theological narration of the New World. It is this descriptive hierarchy that allows a white-Latino man to discern the morality and intentions of a black teenager with a glance. It can also be seen in my early struggle to theologically imagine black-white relations in a way that does not foreground assimilation.

Second, that the racialized scale is theological in nature is demonstrated by Carter in his close reading of Kant, whose rationalized "religion" was the engine of Enlightenment, and by Jennings in his careful analysis of four Christian thinkers engaged in intercultural interaction in a world re-shaped by colonization. These forms of "pseudotheology" find voice in Zimmerman's confession to a television news host that the purposes of God can be discerned in the killing of a non-white "other" and in the religious right who finds no discrepancy between the Way of Jesus Christ, Israel's Suffering Servant, and a legal system in which "Stand Your Ground" laws, funded by the gun lobby and justified by an anachronistic reading of the supposedly infallible Second Amendment, are upheld. I personally experienced the theological draw of supersessionism several years ago as I was writing a reflection on the second chapter of Ephesians, relating to Paul's invocation of Jesus as the peace between Jew and Gentile, making one new being out of the two,[37] as a way to narrate the reality of my ecclesial community. I ran up against my inability to biblically frame white-black relations as anything other than a hierarchical relationship between Jew and Gentile. It was at this point that I gave off writing because I intuitively recognized that this manner of framing the issue was inherently prejudicial. It was soon thereafter that I read Jennings' *The Christian Imagination* and Carter's *Race: A Theological Account* and understood the depth of the theological deformities I had inherited.

---

37. Eph 2:11–18.

Third, Carter finds whiteness to be the heretical *ordo* which, as a distortion of the Christian doctrine of creation, invites all being into its static ontological categories. Similarly, Jennings elucidates whiteness as the orienting structure behind the displacement enacted upon various peoples through the reordering of creation by colonization. The resultant static mode of being can be seen to have influenced Zimmerman's recognition of Martin as one who threatened him simply by being "a black male."[38] Blackness was the bottom of a static ontological structure into which Martin was escorted by Zimmerman's gaze. The static ontological designations assigned to various peoples by whiteness are also those which would keep me as pastor-scholar trapped within the bounds of my white male subjectivity. While I certainly cannot supersede my spatially-oriented status as a particular creature (which is a key element of Jennings' thesis), Carter suggests, through the work of Maximus the Confessor, that creation in the image of the One who is Trinitarian relationality, and recreation through the Jewish body of Jesus of Nazareth, renders *being* itself as *ekstasis*. It is this ecstasy of being that can be experienced through resisting the strictures of whiteness through a process of miscegenation in which non-white subjectivity is superabundant.

Fourth, Carter and Jennings both identify that the "best" of contemporary theological ways of imagining identity fall short of diagnosing what is most problematic about modern and early-modern Western theological anthropology. While Carter interacts with the Radical Orthodoxy of Milbank, and Jennings with the virtue ethic of MacIntyre and its theological deployment by Hauerwas, they are interested in the manner in which such ways of imagining Christian identity are refracted more broadly through intellectual and spiritual formation in the academy and church. Just as Jennings' and Carter's targets are not strictly Milbank and Hauerwas, but rather what they represent, so my aim in this text is not to discount the many positive contributions of each scholar. Rather, I am rendering explicit Jennings' and Carter's critique so as to censure myself and caution confessional Christians about the limitations of uncritical appeals to tradition or the narrative of the Christian West. I take Hauerwas' critique of modernity as a given—and as an important development—but suggest that moral formation in the academy and church has tended to introduce Christians into paternalistic ways

---

38. While this could be interpreted as a natural descriptor for the purpose of aiding in apprehension of the person Zimmerman perceived as being dangerous, such a reading may not take into account the full text of the 911 interchange. Zimmerman had already been asked earlier in the conversation to identify the race of the individual whom he decided to pursue and had responded by claiming "he looks black." It was not until Martin took notice of Zimmerman tailing him and ran away that Zimmerman categorized him as a "black male" and as one of "these assholes."

of pursuing reconciliation and pejorative patterns of imagining the "other." While I do not believe that liberalism has fared much better, I am suggesting that Jennings and Carter offer a way forward distinct from this gridlock.

Jennings' and Carter's analyses suggest that an emphasis on the church as radical counter-culture does not sufficiently take into account the ways in which whiteness was the outgrowth of the collusion of Christian theology and its attendant late medieval and early-modern politics. Just as it was not a "secular" Empire alone that instigated the racial imagination, so modern secularism should not be seen as the moral antithesis of the Christian tradition. While anti-modern polemics may serve to alert the novitiate to the problematic nature of moral modernity, they tend to retain white male subjectivity as the normalizing pole in aesthetics and ethics. Through appeals to "tradition," such accounts tend to reassert and reimagine Occidental prominence in the face of "multicultural" (or "pluralistic") contact. While I would not suggest that the responses I received to my reflections on the Martin-Zimmerman case were specifically influenced by virtue ethics, I am suggesting that both are invested in the maintenance of white subjectivity in similar and describable ways. Neither exhibits a fundamental openness to learning from those on the "underside of modernity."[39] This intransigence was exhibited in the resistance of Christians of "moral" character to recognizing the racial gaze within themselves when confronted with it in Zimmerman.

Fifth, Jennings and Carter both demonstrate that modern liberal discourse is not better at articulating a satisfactory analysis of race. Jennings and Carter identify the modern disciplines of cultural studies and religious studies as heirs of the racialized vision that took root within Western scholasticism as it engaged with colonization. While Carter offers a critique of the religious academy, Jennings presses beyond modern cultural studies to demonstrate the theological character of the origins of race. This methodology suggests that, while orthodox Christian belief has been a carrier of the virus of racialization, orthodoxy (as an expression of the particular salvation event centered in Jesus of Nazareth) is not to be jettisoned in favor of the humanistic spirit of the age. In this sense, the methodology of this book and that of Jennings and Carter (this is especially true of Carter) is not completely at odds with that of retrievals of orthodoxy. I contend that Jennings and Carter point to moments within the tradition that shed light upon a Faith more authentically Christ-like than the dominant narrative of the tradition. I will demonstrate several ways in which Carter and Jennings subvert the methodology of retrievals of tradition by radicalizing it.

39. Dussel, *Underside of Modernity*. Carter regularly utilizes this phrase in *Race*.

As the shared genealogy of their theses suggests, the problem is that the supersessionism maturing in Occidental hegemony was embryonically present in the early Hellenization of the Faith. Jennings and Carter read liberalism as a modern maturation of the tradition of Western philosophical rationality. One can see the inability of liberalism to sufficiently analyze this problematic legacy in the manner in which race is commonly framed within public discourse. As was demonstrated by the FBI report which attempted to find some evidence of "racial animus" or its lack in Zimmerman's past,[40] modern ethical discourse is characterized by an obsession about the will of the individual. Interestingly, the Christian right has imbibed the ideal of the autonomous moral agent, tending to argue ethical issues as universal moral imperatives (on this point, virtue ethics is to be preferred).[41]

As I discovered when criticizing the injustice of Martin's murder, it was not only the Christian right that defended the legal process and its outcome. As a friend committed to atheism in the face of the "irrationality" of the Christian faith commented, modern legal standards are the only thing keeping humanity from devolving into "angry mobs with torches and pitchforks."[42] Apparently, the irony of an armed vigilante being defended by the modern legal system was lost in this commenter's view. I could only suggest that optimism about "human progress" is misplaced. Jennings and Carter suggest that race has functioned precisely within this evolutionary logic. Anecdotally, most of my more "progressive" friends have not proven themselves more committed to a posture of humility in forming relationships of trust with others unlike them than have conservatives.[43]

Sixth, place is a primary theme addressed by Jennings and alluded to by Carter. While Jennings views the displacement enacted by colonization

---

40. See Robles, *FBI Records*.

41. Jennings and Carter are not content with either option. Carter, in his criticism of Kantian deontological ethics, tends to work within a modified virtue ethic due to his early affinity with Milbank (although he is not at home in this trajectory). Jennings, in his criticism of Aristotelian virtue ethics (and his recognition of the insufficiency of teleological ethics in general, including the utilitarianism of liberalism), tends to favor a modified Barthian divine command modality, albeit a divinity encountered in a new body politic forged by joining with the unlike other.

42. A militant posture against faith as irrational has been canonized in the works categorized as the New Atheism: See, among others, Hitchens, *God is Not Great*; Dawkins, *The God Delusion*; and Sam Harris, *The End of Faith*.

43. Much research suggests that more liberal communities are often some of the most segregated communities in the United States. Trends seem to suggest that there is a constellation of factors influencing these divisions, including socioeconomic status, educational affinity, occupational similarity, and cultural preference. The net effect, however, is that all the same people tend to cluster together, thereby reinforcing racialized identity. See, for example, Dahmer, "The Harsh Truth about Progressive Cities."

as the genesis of modern race as flesh was called upon to represent identity, Carter alludes to the necessity of the "impure" and scandalous sharing of space as the antidote to racialization. Place can be seen to be a factor in Trayvon's death as Zimmerman found it to be his duty to protect certain types of socialized space from the "other" assumed to be transgressing that space. As a "neighborhood watch volunteer" claiming spatial authority over a gated community, Zimmerman assumed that a young man of color walking to his family's house had no business being in that place. Modern space as private property is understood to be an ownable commodity appropriated for the use of some and the exclusion of others by the authority of "white" legal rationality. This contention warrants a brief excursus.

In *Christ, Power, and Mammon*, Scott Prather draws on the work of Jennings to explore the commodification of place in a "free market" system and its alignment along the lines of socioeconomic status and racial classification.[44] Prather contends that contemporary capitalism is driven not by a "free" market but by the collusion of various socio–political forces. Prather contrasts this market "freedom" with the Barthian notion of freedom as freedom for the "other," demonstrating that the concept of freedom employed by modern capitalist ideology is "a notion of independence through personal acquisition and upward mobility through social competition."[45] In this sense, "[t]he human condition presumed by capitalist freedom is socio–economic war." The work of Jennings aids Prather in exposing the connections between socioeconomic identity and racialized identity. Since Mammon and the racial gaze function in the modern world as mutually articulating realities, the existence of commodified space makes specific claims upon bodies. Rather than an organic connection between land and identity consonant with the Christian doctrine of creation, space as modern capital issues demands upon people, demands that illuminate race as "the primary matrix through which Mammon flexes its muscles of social division."[46]

When the boundaries policed by these demands are assumed to be transgressed, surveillance and disciplinary action are often the result.[47] Jennings demonstrates that the reordering of creation initiated by manifest destiny has reached its apex in the contemporary ability to keep the "other" out. When Trayvon as "other" transgressed the boundaries assigned by modern spatialization, his life became forfeit. Jennings' and Carter's in-

---

44. Prather, *Christ, Power, and Mammon.*

45. Ibid., 228–29.

46. Ibid., 232.

47. My thought in this regard has been influenced by Foucault, *Discipline and Punish.*

vocation of the scandalous sharing of place is an assault on racialization. I found that I had underestimated the power of scandalous space-sharing as on the Sunday morning following the Zimmerman verdict I again stood in awe at its healing work in my local worshipping community. Living where we should not, each in close proximity to the unlike other, we were together able to experience the theological promise of what Jennings calls the "transgress[ing] [of] boundaries of real estate."[48]

Seventh, while their language differs, Jennings' and Carter's accounts invoke ontological "impurity." What Jennings identifies by the term "joining" is similar to that which Carter calls "miscegenation" or "speaking in tongues." This mutuality, afforded by a vulnerability characteristic of the Incarnation, is best expressed in erotic imagery. Jennings' central image is two unlike bodies in desire for one another becoming one flesh in the body of God.[49] Remembering that miscegenation or intercultural joining was often occasioned by the rape of the non-white other,[50] these terms are being used to subversive effect. Aware that the "mulatto" child was the progeny of what was considered to be "impure" desire for the "other," Jennings and Carter are redeploying language of oppression to break "the pseudotheological backbone of whiteness."[51] Both theologians hesitate to use the term "reconciliation" because of its misuse in modern missiology and ecclesiology, beholden as they are to colonial-modern distortions. As Jennings explains:

> I could speak of this gift in terms of reconciliation. But I have purposely stayed away from the theological language of reconciliation because of its terrible misuse in Western Christianity and its tormented deployment in so many theological systems and projects. The concept of reconciliation is not irretrievable, but I am convinced that before we theologians can interpret the depths of the divine action of reconciliation we must first articulate the profound deformities of Christian intimacy and identity in modernity. Until we do, all theological discussions of reconciliation will be exactly what they tend to be: (a) ideological tools for facilitating the negotiations of power; or (b) socially exhausted idealist claims masquerading as serious theological accounts. In truth, it is not at all clear that most Christians are ready to imagine reconciliation.[52]

48. Jennings, *Christian Imagination*, 287.

49. Ibid., 288.

50. Ibid., 79–80.

51. Carter, *Race*, 156.

52. Jennings, *Christian Imagination*, 9–10.

"Reconciliation" in its extreme familiarity often supposes a motif of assimilation which reenacts relational dynamics similar to those experienced in the American slave plantation and the modern criminal justice system. However, for all its exploitation, a rich Pauline notion of reconciliation is that which Carter and Jennings are rearticulating as the antidote for racialization. In relation to Zimmerman, one cannot help but theorize what effect the racialized scale's resistance to "impure" relations may have had on the psychology of a person of mixed racial ancestry. As pastor of an "impure" community, I am existentially aware that it is necessary to consistently combat such a psychology.

The Structure of This Text

In the Conclusion, I will build on a sympathetic engagement with the works of Jennings and Carter as I flesh out some of the practical entailments of an ecclesiology of joining. The body of this text will exposit the works of Carter and Jennings by highlighting their positions in relation to two poles within the religious academy: a liberal relativizing and universalizing tendency in studies related to religion and culture and a conservative nostalgia for a virtue-based reclamation of Occidental subjectivity. Carter and Jennings read both of these trajectories as bound to the racial imagination of whiteness in important ways. Neither scholar is content with the identity politics of modern religious studies or the centrality of the European body in retrievals of virtue. I will analyze the works of Carter and Jennings in turn by positioning them between and beyond modern religious studies and Western "classical" scholastic theology.

I begin in chapter 1 with a brief summary of Carter's *Race: A Theological Account* before unpacking his central assertions in contrast with those of the modern religious academy. Through his interactions with Raboteau, Cone, and Long, Carter demonstrates the ways in which he is both heir and foil to the African American religious academy. Raboteau the historian, Cone the theologian, and Long the scholar of religion each contribute something to Carter's argument while Carter must ultimately disavow significant portions of their philosophical infrastructure as tending toward reification of race. Carter maintains that such essentialization tends to further harden the ontological categories of whiteness and renders static the anthropological designations introduced by it. I read Carter's ordering of his text as evincing increasing divergence with the black religious academy. While he borrows quite a bit from Raboteau in his shared interest in Eastern Orthodoxy and while Cone's volleys against whiteness have been helpful in allowing Carter to break a hole in the wall of racialized identity, Long's relativizing "universal religious primordium" does little more than reenact the objectifying gaze of whiteness. Throughout chapters 1 and 2, I also intimate Carter's relationship to early Afro-Christian sources, in whose autobiographical treatises he finds the intuitive moves necessary to undermine the anthropological objectifications perpetuated by European rationality through both cultural studies and theology.

In chapter 2, I position Carter in contradistinction to a popular contemporary way of theologically imagining identity. While I have noted Milbank's positive contribution in demonstrating the viability of theology over against sociology, I read Milbank's nostalgia for an Anglo-Catholic virtue ethic as a subtle reenactment of several characteristics of the theological architecture of British imperialism. While Milbank astutely diagnoses the impotence of liberal "secular" sociology to construct a satisfactory ethic, I read his revival of a "classical" Greek philosophical framework as suggesting insecurity about the decentering of the European tradition in the face of an ethic of "multiculturalism." Carter criticizes the soft imperialism of Radical Orthodoxy through his counterintuitive read of the similarities between Milbank's and Kant's theological anthropologies. Much like his read of Milbank, Carter reads the religious moorings of the Kantian Enlightenment project as grounded in Kant's insecurity about the relationship of white and non-white bodies vis-a-vis European conceptions of rationality and progress. Carter reads Kant and Milbank as constructing their systems out of their respective perceptions of the ascension or loss of white male subjectivity. While Radical Orthodoxy stands in explicit opposition to the Kantian project, it appears that the driving force behind both trajectories is the relation of the European subject to forces beyond that subject's control. As I close chapter 2, I briefly explicate Carter's invocation of Maximus the Confessor in order to demonstrate in concrete terms how he reads the Christian tradition against itself so as to offer a new way forward for theological discourse.

Chapters 3 and 4, in mirroring the treatment of chapters 1 and 2, present my argument in symmetrical fashion. In these chapters, I investigate Jennings' *The Christian Imagination* by structuring my analysis similarly to that which I performed in relation to Carter's *Race*. I first delve into Jennings' relationship to the discipline of cultural studies, of which he evinces several similar sensibilites, before finishing with Jennings' critique of a MacIntyrean virtue ethic.

In chapter 3, I begin with an overview of Jennings' key moves by locating them within the autobiographical narrative he offers in his Introduction. Jennings uses his own life story to introduce the themes he explores throughout his text. Because this methodology is unique, I spend a bit longer introducing

Jennings' argument than Carter's. Jennings' methodology has influenced my use of a similar structure in my Introduction. I have attempted to join with Jennings in exemplifying the sort of vulnerability needed to question the assumed objectivity of European subjectivity while not collapsing into a hermeneutic of suspicion. Jennings' use of autobiography as an opening to theological analysis suggests that a first step toward undermining whiteness is vulnerability through joining. In the body of the text, I do not overtly place my own experience into my analyses of Carter and Jennings because I recognize the importance of hearing their voices on their own terms as much as possible. It is not until the Conclusion that I again introduce several personal ecclesial experiences so as to theologically describe the practical entailments of an ecclesiology suggested by Jennings and Carter.

After explaining Jennings' thesis by analyzing his introduction, chapter 3 delineates Jennings' relationship to the disciplinary atmosphere of cultural studies. For each of the four historical characters Jennings utilizes (Jose de Acosta, Gomes Eanes de Zurara, Olaudah Equiano, and Bishop William Colenso), I choose several of the key scholars in cultural studies consulted by Jennings. While the literature surrounding each of these four figures is plentiful, the theological significance of each thinker has been largely overlooked. Jennings contends that this "oversight" is due primarily to the ways in which each figure exposes the imperialist grid of early-modern Christian theology.[53] Jennings largely accepts the narrative of events as chronicled by each scholar. However, his conclusions necessarily diverge from those of the ethnographic resources he consults. Whereas the disciplinary confines of historiographic treatments limit the scholar to conclusions little more revolutionary than a relativizing comparative analysis, Jennings as theologian is able to locate these seemingly disconnected narratives in a story of distortion, disconnection, and hope. Jennings retains hope that the Gospel, the story of YHWH inviting various particularities to join one to another in the particularity of Israel through the particular body of Jesus Christ, is neither an imperialistic nor assimilationist vision. He maintains that it is the Incarnation that allows for a new cosmopolitan body politic. I close chapter 3 with an intimation of what I call Jennings' Christology of joining. Jennings demonstrates the ways in which the philosophical infrastructure of the religious enterprise undergirds the modern missiology of Lamin Sanneh and Andrew F. Walls, who propose a "translation" of the universal Gospel message into various particularities. As Jennings demonstrates, this translation is a unilateral one that introduces the non-white body into the *ordo* of whiteness.

53. Ibid., 115.

In chapter 4, I turn to an in-depth analysis of Jennings' use of Acosta as the paradigmatic figure exhibiting early-modern theology's assessment of place and people (hence the title *A Theology of Race and Place*.) Jennings' choice of Acosta as primary interlocutor aids in understanding his criticism of the philosophical system of MacIntyre, its theological outgrowth in Hauerwas, and its inculcation through the theological academy. Whereas I read Radical Orthodoxy as buttressing European hegemony through its invocation of the "guiding virtuous elite," I read Hauerwas' anti-Constantinian ecclesiology as showing initial promise in transitioning the theological imagination from its collusion with Empire to embodiments of mutuality in local communities of faith. However, I contend that the initial promise of a Hauerwasian ecclesiology is limited by the manner in which it presents intellectual and spiritual formation within a MacIntyrean reclamation of virtue, thereby reenacting the pedagogical structures in which European colonialism flourished. Through Hauerwas' aesthetic, ethical, and liturgical vision, he tends to undermine the counter-cultural promise of his radical ecclesiology. After I detail Jennings' divergence from Hauerwas, I briefly align Jennings' theological anthropology with that of Barth and Bonhoeffer. I likewise demonstrate how Jennings' Barthian theological anthropology differs from that of the Aristotelian-Thomist tradition, the intellectual palette from which colonialism painted the world.

Jennings' "Christology of joining" is the starting point for my Conclusion, in which I expand upon the theological race theory of Jennings and Carter by proposing a consonant "ecclesiology of joining" oriented around the practice of eating together in shared space. This text ends in much the same way as it began, with an autobiographical narrative that proposes a way of life informed by Jennings' and Carter's theological visions. While the Introduction proposed an identification of the problem, the Conclusion proposes an account of reconciliation that aims to resist the distortions of the racialized Christian imagination.

Chapter 1: Carter and the Religious Academy

An Introduction to *Race*

I BEGAN THIS TEXT with an autobiographical narrative that demonstrated my difficulty in articulating how race functions within the modern imagination. It was in this difficulty that I encountered the works of Carter and Jennings. I will interact with each in turn, beginning with Carter's description of Enlightenment *as* architecture of whiteness. His theory purposes to explain why race is simultaneously a grid for interpersonal interactions in modernity and is invisible to those confined by it. In Carter's reading, modernity is not so much anti–religious as pseudotheological. The deformity of modernity is not that it is a secular alternative to the religious underpinnings of Western society, but that it is a maturation of the distortions of the theological problem of whiteness that were sown during the colonial period. Jennings delves more deeply into the planting of these seeds, and chapters 3 and 4 will engage his narrative of this earlier period. I will treat each author in the same sequence: First I will delineate the relationship of each theologian to the modern religious academy by way of the disciplines of religious and cultural studies. I will then articulate the radical nature of both theologians' critiques as I position them against a popular contemporary theological way of imagining identity. This first chapter will explicate Carter's relationship to the African American religious academy.

In *Race: A Theological Account*, Carter offers a theological analysis of the modern formation of the human as a racial being. In the contemporary academic landscape, he suggests, there have been a wide range of discourses about race in the social sciences and the humanities, but not in theology.[1] The few studies of race which do exist within the discipline of theology tend to reconfirm essentialized views of race by ontologizing it (e.g. "blackness") or being bound within some other version of identity politics. Such treatments tend to collapse under a hermeneutic of suspicion, and as a result are

---

1. Carter, *Race*, 3.

limited in their ability to offer a way forward out of the maladies and insular identity silos which whiteness has created. Carter maintains that in order to be resurrected into the new life offered to the world by the Incarnate God–man Jesus Christ of Nazareth, the pseudotheology of whiteness must be exposed in order to be resisted. Carter's work therefore aims to unmask whiteness, to identify what Michel Foucault has called the "order of things,"[2] thereby offering a more satisfactory account of the kind of emancipative discourse theology can be.

Given his contention that theology created 'man' as a racial being, Carter sets out to offer a genealogy of how this process took place. Additionally, he is interested in how theology itself as a descriptive method was transformed during the process.[3] His thesis is that "modernity's racial imagination has its genesis in the theological problem of Christianity's quest to sever itself from its Jewish roots."[4] In order to render itself a distinct religious construct, Christianity had to describe the Jewish people as a religion and as a race, in the process rendering them inferior to Europeans. The locus of theological authority was shifted from "Oriental" Judaism to Occidental power structures. Carter suggests that language of "Constantinianism" inadequately describes this process and offers "supersessionism" as a better descriptor.[5] Carter identifies two deeply interconnected steps in the development of supersessionism.

> Hence, the racial imagination (the first step) proved as well to be a racist imagination of white supremacy (the second step). Within the gulf enacted between Christianity and the Jews, the *racial*, which proves to be a *racist*, imagination was formed.[6]

Acknowledging that, in a post-civil-rights era, public discursive ethics both do and should hold racism to be improper, Carter believes that this limited diagnosis falls short of recognizing the more critical problem. By and large, ethics, the social sciences, the humanities, and theology still operate within a racial imagination while often explicitly denouncing racism, which Carter reads as the outgrowth of "man" being rendered a racial being. Carter contends that racism is an inevitable development of the

2. Foucault, *The Order of Things*.

3. Carter, *Race*, 3.

4. Ibid., 4.

5. Several clear examples of a critique of Constantinianism are to be found in Yoder, *The Politics of Jesus*; Hauerwas, *The Peaceable Kingdom*; and Hauerwas, *Resident Aliens*. Carter contends that these are truncated accounts that underestimate the racial character of the deformities they are observing.

6. Carter, *Race*, 4.

racial imagination, which reflects the key theological deformity of the West: supersessionism.

Carter's analysis of supersessionism and its dual offspring of racialization and racism (which he refers to together by the shorthand "the theological problem of whiteness"[7]) is presented in three distinct stages. First, he describes the Enlightenment as the maturation of the racial vision, interpreting the oft-identified philosophical distortions of modernity (Cartesian epistemology, decontextualized universalizing rationalism, secularism, the myth of human progress, among others) as the apex of whiteness as a substitute for the Christian doctrine of creation.[8] For Carter, many analyses of modernity's deformities leave intact its aberrant theological underpinnings. While many treatments of contemporary Christian identity or race may make important claims, most focus on symptoms alone. The core engine of modernity's "civilizing" project is the racial imagination.

Diverging from the common theological habit of describing modernity as "secular," Carter demonstrates why it is preferable to think of Enlightenment as inherently religious, or "pseudotheological," in nature. Carter's analysis suggests that the organizing motif (metanarrative) of modernity is whiteness as ground and *telos*, whiteness as beginning and end, whiteness as proton and eschaton. Many "postmodern" religious critiques of Enlightenment focus on the rationalistic tip of the iceberg while leaving the subaquatic theological body of whiteness intact. Carter buttresses this contention by utilizing Foucault's genealogy of race to identify how the formation of "man" as *homo sexualis* contributed to the conception of the human as the bearer of biological race as *homo racialis*. While Foucault's analysis is an important introductory move for Carter, the meat of his diagnosis is to be found in his presentation of Kant, which I will analyze in more detail in the next chapter. Engaging Foucault allows Carter to expose the racial character of the modern project while engaging Kant allows Carter to demonstrate the religious foundation of modern anthropology in the hope of whiteness as *telos*. The human as *homo racialis* is that which undergirds Enlightened humanity as *homo religiosis* and *homo politicus*.[9]

Second, Carter turns to reading the black religious academy's attempts at dislodging the racial imagination. He identifies important advances made by Raboteau and Cone while also demonstrating the ways in which they are beholden to, and in some sense trapped within, modernity's methodological, and thereby racialized, schemas. While Carter is sympathetic with both

7. Ibid., 4.
8. Ibid., 7.
9. Ibid., 59, 81.

scholars and acknowledges that his work would not be possible without theological pioneers such as Cone, he must ultimately disavow significant portions of their theses in order to more precisely aim at the racial imaginary that remains to influence their work. Specifically, Carter maintains that neither Raboteau nor Cone sufficiently theorize Gentile identity and its theological place within the Judaic salvation narrative. While Carter reads both scholars as making important steps in this direction (in Raboteau's iconic and thereby incarnational focus and in the early Cone's Barthian and thereby particularist Christology and theological anthropology), he interprets them both as collapsing into universalizing motifs characteristic of modernity qua whiteness. Raboteau's historiographic method tends to skip over the particular on its way to the universal, interpreting "faith" as an ahistorical primordium that must find particular historical "expression," while the later Cone's Tillichian insistence on a decontextualized "ground of Being" invites slippage into the universalizing abstraction of white theology. A third scholar with whom Carter interacts in this second section is Long, from whose program of "ontologizing blackness" he evinces the widest possible divergence. Carter reads Long's work as being inextricably bound to the presuppositions of modern religious studies, and thereby sharing little common ground with his own overtly theological (and primarily Christological) focus. While he identifies himself as an heir to the work of the black religious academy, Carter finds it insufficient to address the racial problematic.

Third, Carter moves to his constructive work. In so doing, he discerns a similarity between the "theological sensibilities" of New World Afro-Christian faith, as embodied in several writers of antebellum America, and that of certain pre-medieval Eastern patristic voices.[10] Carter excavates the writings of Briton Hammon, Frederick Douglass, and Jarena Lee in the third part of his book. By literarily positioning Irenaeus, Gregory of Nyssa, and Maximus the Confessor respectively as prelude, interlude, and postlude to the entire work, he points to an implicit connection between early Eastern Christian voices and early African American Christian voices. This methodology is wonderfully iconoclastic as Carter discerns in Hammon, Douglass, and Lee (voices whose theological sophistication is characteristically underemphasized by the contemporary religious academy) an embryonic intuition about the contrast between the Judaic nature of the Christian faith and the white supersessionist creation of the modern racial imaginary.

One final word must be said about how Carter uses terms such as *white* and *black* that are commonly associated with essentialized views of

10. Ibid., 7.

race. For Carter, "white" and "black" are not primarily designations of skin color. While whiteness certainly originated as the sociopolitical order of lighter, European peoples, and while blackness, as the photo negative for this order of whiteness, was a designation given to peoples of non-European ancestry on a hierarchical scale of civilizing potential evidenced by skin color, Carter defines the existence of whiteness and blackness as evidence of "a political economy, an *ordo* or a social arrangement . . . an *oikonomia*."[11] Restated, this means for Carter that the *ordos* of whiteness and blackness are anthropological distinctions that are distortions of the doctrine of creation. In contrast to this essentialization of identity, Carter contends that humanity was created with an intrinsic relationality as particular creatures in the Divine image.[12]

In redeploying the Christian faith to subvert the regnant religious and social order, Carter utilizes the voices of those on the "underside of modernity"[13] to criticize these modern anthropological tendencies while not dispensing with what he sees as the confessional center of Christian faith: the incarnation of Jesus Christ as a continuation of YHWH's covenants with Israel. Unlike the general methodological trajectory of modern religious studies, Carter does not throw the theological baby out with the racialized bathwater. In other words, while embarking on what is admittedly a sort of *anti–theology*, Carter is asking what he identifies as his "fundamental question": "What kind of discourse should Christian theology be?"[14] Carter does not position himself as a disinterested critic of theology, as would be the tendency of comparative religious studies. Rather, he intends to be only a faithful Christian theologian, acknowledging the missteps of modern racialized theology.

Carter and African American Religious Studies

In explicating Carter's relationship to the African American religious academy, no attempt is being made to present the "black" academy as monolithic. There are several influential and "canonical" scholars who represent various trends within the fields of African American cultural studies, theology, religion, and church history with whom Carter is well versed and with whose work he explicitly places his own in conversation. This is in large part due to his recognition that his own inquiry into a theology of race

11. Ibid., 8.

12. Gen 1:27

13. Carter, *Race*, 8.

14. Ibid., 9.

"proceeds with the acknowledgement that black theology sees beyond its predecessors only by standing on their broad intellectual shoulders."[15] He clarifies that, in choosing several key figures (such as Cone) as paradigmatic of larger trends within black theological thought, he is not attempting to "be reductive" but rather is acknowledging the role of such luminaries in defining a discipline. Carter will draw from his interlocutors while not being locked within the philosophical infrastructure undergirding the religious academy. Carter demonstrates the most convergence with Raboteau, from whose work he draws a theology of history that provides him with a proton and eschaton that will lead him to his Maximian view of dynamic identity. Carter progresses through Cone, the theologian of black liberation theology whose importance cannot be overstated, even as Carter takes issue with his "static" ontology. Finally, Carter ends with Long, the scholar of religious studies whose work is most congruent with the evaluatory stance of the modern (white) descriptive gaze and from whose work Carter most fully distances himself.

I read the structure of Carter's text as mirroring his relative level of convergence with, or divergence from, his interlocutors. Section One of Carter's text lays the groundwork for his inquiry by demonstrating the racialized religious underpinnings of modernity. Section Two begins in convergence with Raboteau and progresses through Cone to a quite stark divergence with Long. In contrapuntal fashion, Section Three of Carter's text is moving toward his constructive thesis of the genius of early Afro-Christian spirituality and its similarity to Eastern patristic theological anthropology. Therefore, Section Three demonstrates increasing convergence with antebellum African American authors, from Hammon, through Douglass, to Jarena Lee, with whom Carter is in closest agreement. Read in this way, Carter establishes the problem in Part I (the supersessionist Christology of Kant), before proceeding to trace a centripetal trajectory that begins with convergence (Raboteau), moves outward to divergence (Long), prepares to move inward again (Hammon and spiritual autobiography), and ends in convergence (Lee and Maximus). By structuring his text in this manner, the narrative construction of his text (centripetal convergence) mirrors his thesis (a retrieval of the centripetal narrative structure of a theological history centered on the scandalous particularity of the Jewish Messiah, Jesus of Nazareth).

One can sense a marked resistance in the works of Carter and Jennings to being classified as "black theology" (or, as Jonathan Tran has named it, "the new black theology."[16]) This is no doubt in large part due to the reality

---

15. Ibid., 159.

16. Tran, "The New Black Theology." The conclusion of Tran's article maintains that

that *being named* can render one an object to be classified and can reaffirm the distortion of creation that is whiteness as identity signifier.[17] Titles such as "black theology" are ironic given the stated intent of Carter to explode the false category of "the blackness that whiteness created," which he reads as little more than a settlement with whiteness.[18] Carter does not intend his resistance to "blackness" to be a cession to the neo-Gnosticizing claim of "colorblindness" prevalent in contemporary Western public discourse. Rather, Carter's particularist approach is geared toward maintaining the cultural integrity of various peoples without an accompanying essentializing or reductive impulse. Tran's title appears to be a subtle query about how effective Jennings' and Carter's theological race theory actually is in dislodging essentialized identity. I will examine Carter's relationship with the black academy so as to investigate this concern.

Albert J. Raboteau: Historicizing Race

Raboteau and an Iconography of Race

I now turn to investigating the connection between Carter's theology of race and the historiographic research of Albert Raboteau. In this section we will see how Carter borrows an iconographic focus from Raboteau while distancing himself from Raboteau's historiographic method. Raboteau, whose scholarly focus is religious history, including the history of American

---

"it was a mistake to call black theology 'black theology' in the first place. Consistency at least would have required that European theology equally bear the burden of qualifications ('colonizing theology') . . . Accordingly, the new black theology is best described as the new theology, no (dis)qualifying adjective necessary." However, the title of Tran's article appears to be sticking. A panel discussion at the 2012 American Academy of Religion annual meeting featuring Jennings, Carter, and Brian Bantum (the three theologians referenced in the *Christian Century* article), with Edward Philip Antonio and Joanne Terrell, likewise bore the name "The New Black Theology." I fear that such a designation insinuates that the theologies of Jennings and Carter are limited in their significance, appeal, and relevance. I also suspect that applying this title to the theological race theory of Jennings and Carter reinforces the demarcation between "insiders" and "outsiders" which Tran seems to wish to remove.

17. Cf. Gen 1:26, where Elohim, in creating 'man' (*ha adam*) in God's own image, is the One who grants identity and thereby is the One who names. The modern encyclopedic project of naming all of creation is therefore a fundamental distortion of the doctrine of creation, which is the point Carter makes when he explains that "whiteness came to function as a substitute for the Christian doctrine of creation" (Carter, *Race*, 5). See also page 49 where Carter utilizes Cornel West to identify that the scientific revolution, Cartesian philosophy, and the classical revival are all complicit in the formation of race.

18. Carter, *Race*, 190.

Catholicism, African and African American religious history, and Eastern
Christian spirituality, is Professor of Religion at Princeton University. Raboteau's landmark study *Slave Religion: The 'Invisible Institution' in the Antebellum South*[19] was published early in his career and became a benchmark in
the discipline. One of his later works, *A Fire in the Bones: Reflections on
African-American Religious History*[20], is a collection of essays that trace the
scope of his career. It is with this latter text that Carter devotes the majority
of his interaction as he maintains that it is in this work that Raboteau "makes
a signal contribution in showing how black religion generally and Afro-
Christianity particularly disrupt the logic of modern racial reasoning."[21]

Carter arrives at this conclusion by elucidating the relationship of
Raboteau to the cultural anthropology of the Boasian anthropologist
Melville J. Herskovits. Herskovits explored what he called the "genius" of
a people: that which is unique or distinctive about a particular people.[22]
Herskovits' innovation was that he began to speak of "cultures" as opposed
to a single monolithic "culture" toward which humanity was progressing.
Through interaction with thinkers of the Harlem Renaissance, Herskovits
had come to appreciate the specificities of a people's cultural memory and
therefore his thinking morphed into delighting in the particularities of "cultures," as opposed to the overcoming of "cultures" by human "culture" as
such. Carter maintains that this innovation by Herskovits and his teacher,
Frank Boas, was the birth of "a new method and practice of historical inquiry . . . ethnography, which through the analysis of language, aesthetic
and literary productions, folk artifacts, and religion in many ways does the
work of history."[23] Carter notes that it is this ethnographic analysis of cultural traits that so easily essentializes the concept of race, reifying identity
into a myriad of opaque, hard, static givens.

Carter reads Raboteau the historian as avoiding this essentialization
of race by pushing beyond a strict historical ethnography into a theology
of history. Carter does not maintain that this glimmer of hope amounts
to a complete disavowal, on Raboteau's part, of the modern understanding of the racialized being. As Carter contends, Raboteau is ultimately a
dialectical thinker who "remains within the gravitational pull of a racialized
understanding of identity."[24] Yet the glimmer of hope is Raboteau's serious

---

19. Raboteau, *Slave Religion*.
20. Raboteau, *A Fire in the Bones*.
21. Carter, *Race*, 126.
22. Ibid., 131.
23. Ibid.
24. Ibid., 137.

consideration of "the Christian element in antebellum slave religion,"[25] identified through his insistence on the significance of narrative and plot.[26] For
Raboteau, history and religion are both faith practices. While the historian,
through the priority she gives to various events, characters, and sequences, necessarily imbues history with a meaning and a structure, religious
faith contends that "salvation history," as understood within the "will and
providence of God," grants a continuity to the events of history.[27] Raboteau
identifies the historiographic method as "[reminding] Christian believers
of the scandal of the Incarnation, the historical specificity and contingency
of Jesus."[28] By reminding theology of the historical nature of salvation's narrative, history as such does the important theological work of preserving
the notions of the particular and the unique. As signposts of the Incarnation, the particular and the unique are iconographic in nature. It is through
the various particularities of being itself that divine being is seen; being is
therefore *ekstasis*. Carter finds hope in the realization that, for Raboteau,
history is not simply a causal sequence of seemingly random events but is
itself a window into the life of the Triune God. In this sense, Raboteau's
theology of history may more appropriately be termed an "iconography of
history."[29] It is this iconographic view of the historical salvation narrative,
and the plot structure that it bequeaths to all history, that Carter finds best
represented in the work of Maximus the Confessor and best intuited in the
work of Jarena Lee.

For Carter, Raboteau's "signal contribution" may also be identified in
his insistence on the importance of the narrative scope of history, specifically his recognition of the theological significance of the story of Israel for
understanding African American religious experience. It is the significance
of plot that allows Carter to maintain that "whiteness is the 'political unconscious' of false emplotment."[30] Because it is *A Fire in the Bones* that prompts
this important observation and because Carter finds it the most promising
of Raboteau's major works, I take it as the key text in analyzing Carter's
methodological relationship to Raboteau.

Raboteau was raised an American Catholic, but has since converted
to Eastern Orthodoxy. I take this journey to be archetypical of what I will
read as Carter's progression from the Anglo-Catholic retrieval narrative of

25. Ibid., 134.

26. Ibid., 144.

27. Ibid., 143–44.

28. Ibid., 143.

29. Ibid., 152–53.

30. Ibid., 146.

Radical Orthodoxy into an aesthetic sensibility akin to Eastern iconography. Carter's use of Eastern patristic theologians (e.g. the Cappadocians, Maximus) is implicitly subversive of the tendency of traditions of virtue to utilize classically Western theologians (e.g. Augustine, Aquinas). Carter finds Eastern theological anthropology to suggest a more dynamic conception of being than that of the Latin West. Carter proposes to "inhabit" the "aesthetic theory of iconic beauty" which Raboteau offers.[31] While he will offer black flesh as an icon of the divine, Carter will not be content with static identity but will construct an ecstatic aesthetic akin to that of Raboteau, who ends *A Fire in the Bones* by positing the "hidden wholeness" of the shared contemplative action of Thomas Merton and Martin Luther King Jr.[32]

Raboteau's Historiographic Method

Raboteau opens his text by relating a story of his childhood travels to Europe as part of a parish boys' choir. While his presence as a black chorister elicited all sorts of responses, including that of curiosity, the episode that most poignantly remains in his memory is that of being asked by a French monsignor to sing for them a "Negro spiritual" which, it was claimed, "we love."[33] This moment encapsulates for Raboteau the bewildering mix of thoughts and feelings he has experienced over the ensuing years surrounding the "complex relationship of race, religion, and national identity." He recognizes the somewhat paradoxical nature of his task as he offers his text as a "response to that French priest's invitation to sing 'one of your people's spirituals.'"[34] Raboteau implies a similarity between offering a scholarly work on race and singing for a European church leader. As he relates, "I also felt a vague unease about exhibiting something of my people for the enjoyment of white folks."[35] While the implication is that his work may be received in this fashion, Raboteau finds the experience of aesthetic mutuality worth the risk of misrepresentation. This position of vulnerability and its overture toward human connection moves beyond mere prosopopoeia and is methodologically akin to Carter's thesis. While Carter's posture is a bit more guarded, he nonetheless makes clear this dimension of his work by envisioning a scandalous miscegenation between peoples in which each learns the tongue

---

31. Ibid., 127.

32. Raboteau, *A Fire in the Bones*, 166.

33. Ibid., ix–x.

34. Ibid., xi.

35. Ibid., xi.

of another and receives her own being back from another in a process of mutual renaming.

Like Raboteau, Carter recognizes what he terms the "veritable conundrum of the black intellectual in modernity."[36] The postures of both Carter and Raboteau suggest that scholars of all people groups should experience humble awe at the complexity of the task of reflecting upon identity. This complexity is that which whiteness has attempted to iron out through colonial reorderings and the modern descriptive method. While religious studies has posited a relativist objectivity, Raboteau's posture demonstrates the possibility of an inter-human mutuality. While Carter is cautious as to the deployment of said mutuality given what he identifies as the racial legacy of coloniality-modernity, he nonetheless shares the same hope. We will see that this possibility is available only to lesser degrees in the works of Cone and Long.

The first two essays in *A Fire in the Bones* render apparent the ways in which Raboteau's iconography of history will be important for Carter. Raboteau overtly offers more than a simple historiographic enumeration of causal relationships.

> History, simply put, consists in telling stories about the ways that people lived in the past. Historians, as distinct from chroniclers, construct narratives that try to reveal the meaning of past events. Narration is of course already an act of interpretation. Events do not speak for themselves. In this very fundamental sense, history is based upon an act of faith, the faith that events are susceptible of meanings that can be described in narration.[37]

By recognizing that "Christian faith also asserts that the events of human experience have meaning, a coherent pattern, a *telos*," and by finding "the source of that meaning . . . in the will and providence of God," Raboteau holds in tension what he identifies as "the dialectical relationship" between "faith and the academic life."[38] Carter suggests the Incarnation as the cohesive structure in which Raboteau's dialectic could find synthesis. Raboteau maintains that "[t]he historian as historian" must remain "agnostic about such claims [of narrative meanings in history]," while as a "believer" he "cannot but hope that our history is touched by the providence of God."[39] The quest for "objectivity" in the historiographic enterprise discourages Raboteau from more fully developing his iconographic theology of history.

36. Carter, *Race*, 142.

37. Raboteau, *A Fire in the Bones*, 2.

38. Ibid., 2.

39. Ibid., 14.

Yet it is clear that Raboteau is moving in the latter direction. He utilizes a picture of former slave children "praying their ABCs" at a funeral as an "emblem" of the religious struggle for freedom through education.[40] It is Raboteau's use of "emblem" that Carter takes to be a vision of a material world imbued with iconographic Christian meaning. Because Carter finds the dialecticism of Raboteau's discipline to limit the analytical power of his history, Carter extends Raboteau's analysis into his own theology of race. Carter maintains that Raboteau is heading toward "an incarnational under-standing of faith and history" while still "continu[ing] to hold onto" a "dia-lecticism of faith and history."[41] Carter eschews dialectical tension through a Maximian account of the Incarnation, in which the world is inhabited as an "ensouled" reality by means of the *hypostasis* of "Jesus in his Jewish humanity."[42] As Carter explains,

> when Maximus says that "through the mutual exchange of what
> is related . . . the names and properties of those that have been
> united through love [are fitted] to each other," he is indicating
> that the same gesture of incarnation that fits divinity to human-
> ity and humanity to divinity so that they can take on each other's
> names, also refits human beings to one another so that they, too,
> can be named from one another. The latter intrarenaming of
> the human (and the history it opens) occurs inside of the in-
> terrenaming of the human that has taken place in Christ and
> that Maximus speaks about with recourse to the *communicatio
> idiomatum* of Chalcedon.[43]

For Carter, the theology of history that is opened in the Incarna-tion signals the death of dialectic. This is important for Carter because he contends that race functions precisely within the sort of Hegelian dialectic that is the posture of the modern academy. If thesis and antithesis must be had for synthesis to be achieved, then both whiteness and blackness as such are necessary for mutuality to occur. However, if, as Carter describes, being itself is not static but is translucent in an iconographic sense, then racial essentialization is not a necessary component of a proper relationality. Whiteness can no longer unilaterally name the other but must receive its own being in a mutual interrenaming of humanity within the space of the Incarnation. It is in this non-reified, ecstatic sense that Carter offers black identity as an icon of the divine.

40. Ibid., 1–2.
41. Carter, *Race*, 150–51.
42. Ibid., 150–51.
43. Ibid., 352.

What is most promising in Raboteau's work is that which Carter deems most properly theological. Carter fills out this theological framework with his thesis of the necessity of living into the salvific story of YHWH through his people Israel and her Messiah, Jesus of Nazareth, whose flesh is the particular ground of a new body politic. This is perhaps why, as Carter relates, religious scholar Donald H. Matthews accuses Raboteau of being a clandestine theologian and not confining himself to the historically "verifiable" ethnographic gaze.[44] It is this ethnographic gaze that Carter holds in suspicion.

Raboteau's Incipient Theological Trajectory

In the first two essays of *A Fire in the Bones*, Raboteau's theological trajectory comes to the foreground as he utilizes the story of Israel to locate the histories of various peoples. He relates that the key interpretative distinction between the myth of European America and the stories told by African American slaves is the manner in which they related to the story of Israel. Both groups recognized that meaning in history is to be found with reference to a particular center. In the American myth, America was the New Israel who had journeyed across the sea out of tyranny to inherit a land of promise, a land manifestly destined by God to be a light to the nations. For African slaves who had been brutally forced to journey across the sea, America was not a land of promise but a land of subjugation, violence, and forced servitude: "For African-Americans, however, the myth is inverted. For us, the Middle Passage was a voyage from freedom in Africa to perpetual bondage in an America that in biblical terms did not resemble Israel but Egypt."[45] In the next chapter, I will utilize a similar methodology as I invert common interpretations of the work of Milbank.

The centrality of Israel for a theology of history will be an important insight for Carter as he identifies supersessionism as the mechanism which generated modern race. In his subversion of Milbank's Anglo-Catholic counter-narrative, Carter will use Raboteau to suggest that early Afro-Christians "got the story right" in ways that the Anglo-Catholic tradition has not. While implicitly privileging theological history in his Judeo-centric narrative of the history of race in America, Raboteau tends to frame the matter in purely historiographic terms. He relates that history is necessarily perspectival and is imbued with meaning depending on the point of observation of the subject. He names historical research a relativizing pursuit that

44. Ibid., 136.
45. Raboteau, *A Fire in the Bones*, 4.

"offers us a salutary reminder that part of faith is doubt."[46] Yet Raboteau recognizes that such an understanding need not necessitate a pluralistic "crisis of faith," but rather a maturity consonant with "owning" a "set of values" and a "religious culture."[47] The historiographic enterprise can round off the contours of religious particularity in relativizing fashion or it can offer a humble maturity consonant with a theology of history. It is the tension between Raboteau's historiographic dialectic and his theology of history that Carter discerns. After Raboteau frames the manner as historical relativity, he moves into what he calls "a theology of history" or the study of "salvation history."[48] This transition within the first two essays of *A Fire in the Bones* is a microcosm of the development of his thought.

Carter, while distancing his project from the disciplinary confines of a history of religions, nonetheless finds Raboteau's historical research to be helpful in demonstrating the racial foundations of modernity. There are several places where Raboteau's research specifically points to the ways in which the philosophical presuppositions of Enlightenment were resultant from the reality of the slave trade and the related intellectual complexities surrounding the issue of race. Raboteau relates that from the beginning of the Atlantic slave trade in the sixteenth and seventeenth centuries, slavery was in large part justified in European nations by the conversion of slaves to Christianity.[49] This posed an immediate problem: How would the baptism of slaves, with its requisite elevation to status of "brother," affect the economics of enslavement? Would a slave cease to be property? If a slave was catechized in the Faith, how would education affect his "contentedness" with a subservient station? Both colonial legislation and church dogma performed calisthenics to ensure that "baptism did not alter slave status."[50] Raboteau relates that the *Anglican Church's Society for the Propagation of the Gospel in Foreign Parts*, founded in 1701 "to support missionaries to the colonies," had as its primary purpose guiding slave masters in their gospel instruction of slaves. A pedagogical mission could proceed without fear of the possibility of emancipation:

> In tract after tract, widely distributed in the colonies, officers of
> the society stressed the compatibility of Christianity with slav-
> ery. Masters need not fear that religion would ruin their slaves.
> On the contrary, Christianity would make them better slaves by

46. Ibid., 9.
47. Ibid.
48. Ibid., 12, 17.
49. Ibid., 18–20.
50. Ibid., 18.

convincing them to obey their owners out of a sense of moral duty . . . After all, society pamphlets explained, Christianity does not upset the social order, but supports it . . . The missionaries thus denied that spiritual equality implied worldly equality; they restricted the egalitarian impulse of Christianity to the realm of the spirit.[51]

Raboteau's research implies a causal relationship between the need to justify slavery and the neo-Gnostic spiritualization of much modern American Christianity. This causal relationship is buttressed by the reality that the slave masters had to be *taught* to interpret the Scriptures in a non-material fashion. Incidentally, the beginnings of the slave trade coincided with Descartes turning inward to the realm of the mind. Likewise, the rationalization of slavery in Western Christianity was taking place only decades before Kant would offer a rationalized reinterpretation of Christian faith as Western moral religion. While I am not suggesting that neo-Gnostic spiritualism and Cartesian rationalism are one in the same, I am drawing attention to the fact that a turn away from the material implications of the Gospel in the didactic pursuits of sixteenth- and seventeenth-century slaveholders and a rejection of realism through Kantian Idealism can both be read as influenced by fears of an elevated status for non-white peoples. I will fill out this claim in chapter 2 when interacting with Kant.

Another example given by Raboteau of a similar causal order of events is early American Evangelicalism's shift from a Gospel potent to change the social order to a Gospel that maintained the social order while changing only the spiritual destiny of converts. He relates the early and enthusiastic response of black Americans to the forthright preaching and experiential, ecstatic worship of revivalist groups like the Methodists and Baptists.[52] He paints a picture of an Evangelical revivalism that encompassed people from various ethnic and socio-economic groups. Black preachers were among those who exhorted the multiethnic crowds with the Good News of the Gospel. This reality influenced the strong abolitionism of late eighteenth-century Methodist conferences. Raboteau explains that, by and large, the denominations quickly retreated from abolition in the face of the "strong" and "immediate" pushback from aristocratic landowners. This resistance encouraged Evangelicalism to alter its early pronouncements by making slavery a matter of individual conscience that lay outside the influence of the Faith.[53] As a result of this turn away from the heterogeneity of its early com-

51. Ibid., 19–20.

52. Ibid., 21–28.

53. For a compelling argument that the later rise of the late-twentieth-century

munal makeup, Methodist and Baptist Evangelicalism became decidedly more rationalistic and aristocratic. For Raboteau, the characteristic marks of religious modernity are to be found in the problematic early-modern intersection of race and theology.

The early promise of Evangelicalism faded as two distinct and separate Christianities emerged. Black preachers

> mediated between Christianity and the experience of the slaves (and free blacks), interpreting the stories, symbols, and events of the Bible to fit the day-to-day lives of those held in bondage. And whites—try as they might—could not determine the "accuracy" of this interpretation.[54]

Segregated worship influenced a hermeneutical segregation not unlike the strict distinctions between disciplinary silos in the modern academy. Much like the creation of modern religious studies as a methodology detached from theology, "white" and "black" Christianity formed as separate traditions. Under the pressures of white discrimination and black self-determination, separate denominations were formed, such as the AME under the leadership of Richard Allen. While Raboteau is not decrying self-determination as a method of resistance, he is noting that such a necessity removes the possibility of mutual interpretation.

In such separate hermeneutical trajectories, the story of Israel took on quite distinct meanings. Identification with Israel became the point of departure for white and black Christians. White Christianity interpreted the Exodus as a spiritual liberation from sin, while black Christians emphasized the material significance of freedom in Christ.[55] These contentions on the part of Raboteau anticipate Carter's claim that the modern problem of race precludes both linguistic interpenetration and relational miscegenation. Raboteau's work illumines the fundamentally racial (and thereby racist) character of modernity while suggesting the perspicuity of Carter's development of this claim: the *Rassenfrage* is essentially the *Judenfrage*.[56]

American religious right was grounded in defense of segregation in education rather than the common myth of resistance to legalized abortion, see Balmer, "The Real Origins of the Religious Right." Balmer consults historical records surrounding this era in the life of Jerry Falwell's Liberty University and Bob Jones University to buttress this claim.

54. Raboteau, *A Fire in the Bones*, 24.

55. Ibid., 24–27.

56. Carter, *Race*, 121.

Raboteau's Dialecticism

Carter proposes an intellectual atmosphere that will "refuse dialectical intellectual arrangements altogether."[57] Despite their convergence, Raboteau-as-historian remains a dialectical thinker whose philosophical orientation feeds a racialized understanding of identity. Raboteau capitulates to the modern conception of a religious primordium that finds the apex of its expression in Western culture. This becomes evident in his optimism about the promise of America for the overcoming of racial divides.

Raboteau takes as his text the address of Puritan leader John Winthrop in his sermon "Modell of Christian Charity," in which Winthrop echoes the Sinaitic covenant and Moses' discourse of blessings and curses in Deuteronomy 30.[58] Raboteau reads Winthrop as proclaiming that "possession of the land is contingent upon observing the moral obligations of the covenant with God." Raboteau lauds Winthrop's address, which reads the Europeans' conquest of the New World as consistent with Israel's taking of the Promised Land. The "mark of the greatness of Winthrop's address" is that the virtues he extols are "justice, mercy, affection, meekness, gentleness, patience, generosity, and unity—not the qualities usually associated with taking or keeping possession of a land." It would be "later and lesser sermons" that would encourage the European inhabitants of America to "much more aggressive virtues." Raboteau is effectually reciting the traditional national mythology about the foundation of America being truth and justice and its continual progression toward a full incorporation of all people into its political commonwealth.

While Raboteau is uncomfortable with the "explicit notion of reciprocity between God's will and American destiny" inherent in Winthrop's theological exhortations, he remains hopeful that the promise of America will be made manifest in successive generations.[59] He maintains that it was through later perversions that the myth of the American New Israel took on a triumphalist tone. His example is the celebratory sermon of Ezra Stiles in 1783 soon after the success of the American Revolution. As opposed to Winthrop's invocation of the conditional election of the European pioneers based upon their adherence to God's law, Stiles proclaimed that the rise of the United States to "an acknowledged sovereignty among the republicks and kingdoms of the world" as "the vine which [God's] own right hand hath

57. Ibid., 156.
58. Raboteau, *A Fire in the Bones*, 28–29.
59. Ibid., 28–29.

planted" was secured.[60] Raboteau claims that it was not until this later "ex-aggerated vision of American destiny" that such "an exaggerated vision of human capacity" was expressed.[61] It is this later, more triumphalist move that Raboteau terms "God's New Israel becoming the Redeemer Nation." Raboteau implies that the anthropological problem of race was the result of later hubristic missteps not necessarily intrinsic to the original vision of Puritan America.

Raboteau contends that this later "exaggerated vision of American des-tiny" was belied by "the presence of another, a darker, Israel" in her midst.[62] The Afro-Christian counter-narrative of identification with Israel through the Exodus called into question the myth of America as carrier of "liberty and the gospel around the globe." Raboteau maintains that the Afro-Chris-tian counter-narrative authentically reclaimed the original promise of the theological vision of Winthrop. The paradigmatic moment of this reclama-tion was Martin Luther King Jr. echoing this "very old and evocative tradi-tion" in his final sermon at Mason Temple in Memphis, proclaiming, "I've been to the mountaintop . . . And I've seen the Promised Land. And I may not get there with you. But I want you to know tonight that we as a people will get to the Promised Land."[63] Raboteau reads King's exhortations as the culmination of the American project. Raboteau's methodology effectually de-radicalizes the resistance of revolutionaries like King, offering them as fulfillment of the noble impulses of American liberty and justice.

While Raboteau acknowledges that the people addressed by Winthrop "long ago took possession of their Promised Land" and that the people ad-dressed by King "still wait to enter theirs," he maintains that Winthrop's and King's versions of the Exodus "were not far apart."[64] They were both look-ing toward the "American Promised Land." While Raboteau is correct that King's rhetoric made extensive use of the promise of America,[65] Raboteau does not allow for the possibility that King was assuming the established terms of the debate as a means to subverting them. In other words, could King's rhetoric have been a way of proclaiming to white America, "this is what you say you believe but you yourselves are not living up to the promise of America"? During his 1963 speech at the march on Washington in which

60. Ibid., 30.

61. Ibid., 31.

62. Ibid., 31.

63. Ibid., 35.

64. Ibid., 35–36.

65. See Carson, *Autobiography of Martin Luther King, Jr.* A reading of this collection of Dr. King's sermons, letters, papers, and journals demonstrates his usage of language surrounding the potential latent within the as-of-yet unfulfilled promise of America.

Dr. King utilized the phrase "the true meaning of its creed,"[66] could he have been noting that the actions of white America belied the veracity of its own mythology? Carter's methodology suggests interpretations such as the latter as he maintains that the black intellectual in modernity often adopts the regnant terms of the argument in order to subvert the argument at the level of its own suppositions. Like Paul, whose use of the *haustafeln* can be exegeted as subverting the objectification of women, children, and bondservants in the household structures of ancient society, King can be read as adopting the ethical conventions of his day in order to shine a mirror of conviction upon their faulty deployment.[67] The linguistic structure of King's speeches, combined with Carter's method of interpretation, encourages this interpretive path. In this schema, the "true meaning" of the American creed is not the American creed itself, but the meaning which King's theology supplied. In his prophetic advocacy for justice, King utilized helpful rhetorical devices to subvert the established order.

Carter channels a tradition of reading that he maintains theologically exegetes Scripture against the grain of the social order.[68] It is this method of reading that Carter recommends as concordant with the genre of an Augustinian spiritual autobiographical "narration of the self."[69] It is this pattern of counter-exegesis which must be utilized in order to "read . . . inside the crease," particularly when interpreting African American autobiography against the dominant social order of whiteness.

This suggests that there is an inner logic and rationality peculiar to the Gospel itself that can work within the social reality dictated by the principalities and powers to present a *telos* divergent from that offered by the regnant system. I contend that it is this eschatological hermeneutic, and not the *telos* of modernity as religious political hope, that has enabled Christian activists to articulate the divine veracity of their causes. Raboteau's historiography does not satisfactorily distinguish between the two. Carter maintains that this is because Raboteau's discipline does not have the means by which to account for the type of tradition Christianity is. I am suggesting

---

66. Ibid., 226.

67. This rhetorical device can also be seen to operate as Paul assumes the terms of the arguments of his opponents (such as those of Philemon's "rights" in relation to Onesimus or the suppositions of the opponents of the doctrine of the resurrection who are nonetheless "baptized on behalf of the dead" in 1 Corinthians 15:29).

68. Carter, *Race*, 344.

69. Ibid., 266, 281. Carter uses the work of William L. Andrews (*To Tell a Free Story*), one of the primary scholars of black autobiography, to draw attention to the "seams or cuts [and creases] in these enclosed narratives," creases which often prove to be "subversive to the text."

that it is because of this lacuna that Raboteau has insufficiently theorized the relationship of King to America. As Carter explains:

> But there is the matter of Raboteau's early difficulty in historical-
> ly navigating Christianity as a living tradition. Doing so would
> have required engaging the question of what it means to speak
> of the hermeneutic encounter of traditions generally and, more
> specifically, the nature of that encounter when one of the tra-
> ditions is Christianity appropriated by those on the underside
> of modernity . . . Another way of handling the hermeneutical
> encounter of traditions would have been to give an account of
> the kind of tradition that Christianity is, such that it can receive
> the traditions of Africa (or the traditions of any people, for that
> matter) to re-tradition those traditions, and indeed, in the pro-
> cess itself be retraditioned. To account for this—or something
> like this—would have been to offer a historiographical method
> . . . [that] would have offered a more cogent account of Afro-
> Christian life as a *Christian* emergence.[70]

While the later Raboteau of *A Fire in the Bones* has discerned the significance of counter-narrative for African American Christians reappropriating the story of Israel, his historiographic method subtly reinscribes whiteness by being overly optimistic about the liberating power of modern civil religion.

Carter finds Raboteau to be most helpful when he is most theological. In his closing exposition of the "hidden wholeness" between the visions of King and Thomas Merton, who in the common year of their deaths (1968) were in the process of planning a shared retreat, Raboteau maintains that what unites contemplation and action is a kenotic, sacrificial love. It is this love that identifies with the oppressed, unites people "beyond barriers of race, nationality, and religion," and proclaims that "there are no aliens, no enemies, no others, but only sisters and brothers."[71] It is this latter observa-tion that Carter favorably appropriates as he emphasizes the kenotic love of the particular body of the Jewish Jesus of Nazareth.[72] It is this salvation narrative that offers an appropriate theology of history.

---

70. Ibid., 139.

71. Raboteau, *A Fire in the Bones*, 181.

72. Carter, *Race*, 155.

James H. Cone: Theologizing Race

Cone and Ontological Blackness

We now turn to analyzing Carter's relationship to James Cone, pioneer of black liberation theology and professor of systematic theology at Union Theological Seminary. The significance of Cone for theologies of liberation in the twentieth century cannot be overstated. Cone was actively involved in the struggle for civil rights in America in the nineteen-sixties, including drafting the 1969 public statement on "Black Theology," and his theology has been read by oppressed people groups around the world. Cone is a public intellectual whose work has profoundly shaped American civic discourse about race and has opened the door to considerations of the problematic theological posture of whiteness. In this section we will see that Carter draws on Cone in order to diagnose white theology as an abstracting system that undervalues particularity, while ultimately deeming Cone's oppositional dialectic insufficient for escaping the bonds of racial reasoning, bound as it is to the binary logic of whiteness.

While Carter favorably appropriates the early Cone's Barthian stress on the concreteness of being, he reads the abstraction of Cone's later, more Tillichian framework as problematic.[73] Carter finds Cone's early Barthian dialectic between God and creature to be replaced by a later Tillichian dialectic between being and nonbeing.[74] Black liberation from oppression becomes the "courage to be."[75] Carter maintains that Cone "remains, to the end, a dialectical thinker"[76] in that the "original, antisupersessionist promise" of Cone's Barthian focus on particularity has been replaced by "Christianity . . . as the answer to a singular, transhistorically existential and ontological situation: the struggle for being against the threat of nonbeing." It is this later move, referred to by Carter as a "nonhistorical, existential moment" of liberation over against the "privileging" of "a given history . . . as the dominant or unifying narrative,"[77] that Carter finds to be least sufficient for overcoming the strictures of racialized identity.

Carter is unconvinced of the necessity of dialectical intellectual arrangements. In suggesting a corrective to Cone's dialecticism, he offers a prolepsis of his own Maximian Trinitarian conclusion:

73. Ibid., 171.

74. Ibid.

75. See Tillich, *The Courage to Be.*

76. Carter, *Race*, 171. Carter reads both Barth and Tillich as being bound to dialectic.

77. Ibid.

[T]he dialectical gap between Christ and culture, between time and eternity, viewed in Christological and Trinitarian terms is really no gap at all. This is because the distance between them, the *diastema*, and difference between God and the creature . . . is always already traversed *within* the very person of the Logos and in the unity he has with the Father through the Holy Spirit. Indeed, the traversal of time by eternity—the idea at the core of a theological understanding of transcendence—is, in fact, what frees creation to be itself.[78]

Carter suggests that the early promise of Cone's work for "theologically disrupt[ing] modernity's analytics of race," recedes to a later ontology which "diasallows transcendence and thus recapitulates the inner logic of modern racial reasoning."[79] While Carter is not content with the end goal being a Barthian dialectic, which he reads as insufficiently acknowledging creation's—or cultures'—contributions to their relationship with the Father,[80] he prefers this particularizing dialectical arrangement to Cone's later universalizing dialectic. However, Carter finds hope for a way out of racialized identity in an eschewal of dialectic altogether in favor of a more classically Eastern incarnational Christology grounded in Trinitarian relationality.

While I find Carter's critique of Cone's ontologically racialized identity to be trenchant, I nonetheless fear that at certain points Carter has both exaggerated the lacunae in Cone's thought and underemphasized his own affinity with Cone's methodology. While affirming Carter's Maximian focus, I am wary of too easily proclaiming the death of dialectic. In the next chapter in our analysis of Milbank, we shall see how an emphasis on the Logos as collapsing the distance between God and culture easily slips into a far too cozy correspondence between Christ and culture.[81] I am not fully convinced that, from the point of view of the creature, some sort of dialectical tension can be fully done away with. While it is true that the gap between God and creation has already been crossed from the perspective of divine agency, dialectical tension is useful for the purpose of stressing the finitude and limitations of human agency and creaturely knowledge. As I see it, Cone's consistent usage of the rhetoric of dialectic is not so much a

---

78. Ibid., 166.

79. Ibid., 158.

80. Ibid., 178.

81. I have borrowed these terms from Niebuhr's classic *Christ and Culture*, which Cone also utilizes in his classic *God of the Oppressed*. My use of these terms is not a suggestion that Niebuhr's theological framework satisfactorily addresses the problems of race nor is it a suggestion that I am satisfied with Niebuhr's manner of framing the argument.

Christological misstep as it is a way to maintain epistemological humility. Cone reveals the motive behind this aspect of his theological methodology in *God of the Oppressed*:

> [T]he theologian must accept the burden and the risk laid upon him or her by both social existence and divine revelation, realizing that they must be approached dialectically, and thus their exact relationship cannot be solved once and for all time. There can only be tentative solutions which must be revised for every generation and for different settings. When theologians speak about God, they must be careful that their language takes account of the ambiguity and frailty of human speech through humility and openness. They can never assume that they have spoken the last word. But the recognition of the limitations should not lead to the conclusion that there is no word to be said. Indeed the clue to our word and God's Word is found in human history when divine revelation and social existence are joined together as one reality.[82]

Cone was attempting to combat the same problem that Carter would later address: the self-reflexive cataphatic anthropology of theological whiteness. While Carter acknowledges that his attacks on whiteness would not be possible without the preliminary volleys of pioneers such as Cone, I cannot help but wonder if dialectic (especially during the cultural milieu in which the early Cone was writing) is a helpful "epistemologically impoverished"[83] method of exposing the hubris of the pseudotheological tendencies of whiteness. I am not sure that Cone holds to dialectic solely because he is beholden to the binary logic of modernity. It seems more probable that Cone utilizes dialectic because of the paradoxical task of offering a counter-narrative from the perspective of the underside of modernity; Carter is engaged in a similar task.

Having made this brief caveat into Cone's use of dialectic, I still find Carter's argument quite compelling and believe that a reading of Cone demonstrates the limitations of his theological program as suggested by Carter. Carter distances himself from what he names the result of Cone's theological project: "ontological blackness."[84] Carter borrows this phrase from Victor Anderson, who diagnoses Cone's theology as a form of "cultural idolatry," a contention Carter engages in "filling out" through his own analysis of Cone.

---

82. Cone, *God of the Oppressed*, 89–90.

83. I am using Carter's own phrase here, albeit out of context: Carter, *Race*, 164.

84. Ibid., 159, 182.

The two primary texts of Cone that Carter interprets are his earliest monograph, *Black Theology and Black Power*, and *Risks of Faith*, his latest book at the time of the publication of Carter's *Race*. Carter utilizes both the earlier book (which, in 1969, was a version of Cone's doctoral thesis) and the later work (published in 1999) to demonstrate the trajectory of Cone's career and to highlight several distinctions between his earlier and later thinking surrounding theology and race. In order to adhere to this interpretive method, I take as my primary texts Cone's *God of the Oppressed* (1975) and his recent masterwork *The Cross and the Lynching Tree* (2011).[85]

I use these two texts for several reasons. One, since Carter has so thoroughly excavated *Black Theology and Black Power* and *Risks of Faith*, a fresh look at others of Cone's works will allow me to more adequately compare the two theologians. Two, in a move consonant with the hermeneutical paradigm Carter has established, taking these two texts together demonstrates the arc of Cone's career and Carter's increasing divergence from his work. Three, *God of the Oppressed* and *The Cross and the Lynching Tree* are the texts that Cone himself offers as representative of his career. In the preface to the 1997 edition of *God of the Oppressed*, Cone maintains that this text "represents my most developed theological position."[86] Likewise, Cone's Introduction to *The Cross and the Lynching Tree* names this text "a continuation and culmination of all my previous books."[87] Four, Cone overtly names his purpose in writing *God of the Oppressed* the utilization of the black church experience as his primary theological source. Responding to critics who accused him of relying too heavily on white, Western theological sources, Cone intentionally grounded this text in what he terms the greatest influence on his theological perspective and "the true source" of "the black theological enterprise": "the black community."[88] Cone uses a similar methodology in *The Cross and the Lynching Tree*. Carter makes a similar hermeneutical choice in his invocation of voices from antebellum African American Christianity. Cone and Carter both offer theological reflections that draw on African American theological thought and the black experience of race in America, while incorporating other voices from throughout the Christian tradition.

85. Cone, *God of the Oppressed*, and Cone, *Cross and the Lynching Tree*.

86. Cone, *God of the Oppressed*, ix.

87. Cone, *Cross and the Lynching Tree*, xv.

88. Cone, *God of the Oppressed*, xix.

Cone and the Christological Politics of the Oppressed

God of the Oppressed is the clearest expression of Cone's systematic theology. Cone later reflected on its writing: "Silence on both white supremacy and the black struggle against racial segregation made me angry with a fiery rage that had to find expression . . . I wrote because words were my weapons to resist, to affirm black humanity, and to defend it."[89] While attempts have been made to classify Cone as simply reactionary, a direct reading of Cone does not bear out this reductionism. Rather than muting his constructive theological insights, his understandable anger at centuries of brutal subjugation and murder often perpetrated in the name of "Christian" mission serves as a catalyst for his perceptive insights. What is surprising is not that anger finds expression in his work, but that this drive is so singularly focused toward a constructive theological vision for liberation and for race relations structured around justice.

I want to situate Cone as a scholar of his times without being reductive. My contention is that where Carter and Cone differ, it is largely due to the realities of the struggles for liberation faced in their respective cultural milieux. As Carter acknowledges, he has the benefit of writing in a theological atmosphere shaped by Cone. While I will read Cone as often collapsing into an ontology of identity that reinscribes the racial analytics of whiteness, and while I will read Carter's solution as a more sufficient theological rubric within which to consider questions of race, I do not read Carter as cancelling the trajectory of Cone. To the contrary, I maintain that Cone suggests many of the themes that Carter expounds upon, including the concreteness of being, the supersessionist impulse within white theology, and a just and liberating framework within which to imagine reconciliation. While I will read Carter as largely subverting the work of Milbank, I read him as entering into the legacy of Cone and redirecting it. In other words, taken together, the works of Cone and Carter are a "call and response" that, as in the ecstasy of worship, establishes new communal connections and initiates unexpected reflections on being. This non-Eurocentric method of discourse favors communal mutuality to unilateral agency. This aspect of the literary tenor of Carter's work converges with his thesis of ontological mutual transcendence as an icon of Trinitarian relationality.

Cone and Carter explicitly share the same dogmatic focus: Christology. While Cone names Christology "the starting point for Christian thinking about God,"[90] Carter recognizes that Christology is the "capstone of Chris-

---

89. Cone, *Cross and the Lynching Tree*, xvii–xviii.

90. Cone, *God of the Oppressed*, xiii.

tian thought"[91] and the "theological site of contestation, the site at which to engage modern racial reasoning."[92] Carter reads Cone's early phase as suggesting "a Christology that deals with the humanity of Jesus as a Jew."[93] Cone explains that "[t]he Jesus about whom I speak . . . is not primarily the one of Nicea and Chalcedon, nor of Luther, Calvin, and Barth . . . For christological reflections, I turn to the Jesus of Matthew, Mark, Luke, John, and Paul."[94] It is *this* Jesus who is "the Jesus of . . . the Spirituals and Gospel Music, Fannie Lou Hamer, and Martin Luther King Jr." The Jesus of "the biblical and black traditions" is "not a theological concept but a liberating presence."

Whereas Carter fills out Cone's Christology by focusing on the particular body of Jesus of Nazareth as the ground for the body politic, Cone's insights into the particularity of Jesus do not sufficiently present Christ's Jewish identity as encompassing, connecting, and reshaping all identity. Christ's Jewish identity as the liberator of the oppressed and as an impoverished member of a first-century minority (as Howard Thurman called attention to in 1949[95]), means little more for Cone than that he is the God of oppressed people groups everywhere, particularly African Americans. Cone does not explore how it could be that the particularity of Jesus' body redeems all particularities while simultaneously decentering European particularity-as-universality. Carter improvises beyond Cone in this regard, pointing toward a Christology of miscegenation that is both more radical than Cone's and more sufficient in decentering whiteness as orienting anthropological metanarrative.[96]

Carter present a scandalous "impure" confluence of particularities centered upon the particularity of the body of Jesus of Nazareth as the path forward out of the strictures of race and the white hegemony that created them. For his part, Cone has difficulty seeing beyond his recognition that the black struggle is a more authentic representation of the incarnation of the Suffering Servant than is the triumphalist rhetoric often characteristic of both white liberalism and orthodoxy. This leaves Cone with the risky proposal that "black people" are "God's Suffering Servant" for the "liberation of humanity."[97] While it is not my intent to debate the veracity of such a hermeneutical judgment, it does raise the question of the effects of "freezing"

91. Carter, *Race*, 162.

92. Ibid., 284.

93. Ibid., 170.

94. Cone, *God of the Oppressed*, xiii.

95. See Thurman, *Jesus and the Disinherited*, 15–19.

96. Carter, *Race*, 192.

97. Cone, *God of the Oppressed*, 178.

the status of "oppressed" and "oppressor" along racialized lines. If racialized identity is a product of the hierarchical evaluative scale of whiteness, then does not assigning divine election based upon such problematic ontological markers as race or socioeconomic status serve to reconfirm the identity categories of whiteness? At this point, Milbank's work could offer a salient reminder that theology cannot simply sanctify the conclusions of sociology. Cone lays out a narrative of liberation from material oppression as the sole interpretative framework within which to exegete the Scriptures:

> The hermeneutical principle for an exegesis of the Scriptures is the revelation of God in Christ as the Liberator of the oppressed from social oppression and to political struggle, wherein the poor recognize that their fight against poverty and injustice is not only consistent with the gospel but is the gospel of Jesus Christ. Jesus Christ the Liberator, the helper and the healer of the wounded, is the point of departure for valid exegesis of the Scriptures from a Christian perspective. Any starting point that ignores God in Christ as the Liberator of the oppressed or that makes salvation as liberation secondary is *ipso facto* invalid and thus heretical.[98]

While social liberation is no doubt an indispensable theme within the narrative of divine salvation, and while this motif has often been ignored within white Western theology, to narrow the scope of God's work in the world to competing hermeneutical frameworks is a distinctly modern technique refined in the white academy. This exegetical tendency is what Carter refers to as the "oppositional struggle for the right to be hegemon."[99] A polity in which "otherness" is the morally preferable position will be a polity in which more people will find ever new categories by which to define themselves as "other." As society increasingly splinters into competing groups staking this claim, it may relativize recognition of the evils perpetrated against those most often historically objectified. The problem of race, as the principal anthropological distortion in the history of the West, may not receive the careful and unique attention it requires.

A polity ordered around only a politics of identity cannot help but progress to an ever-increasing social splintering in which the only enemy is hegemony qua hegemony. Both the Christological category of Lordship[100]

---

98. Ibid., 74–75.

99. Carter, *Race*, 191.

100. I recognize that "Lordship" carries with it a lot of problematic historical baggage. Carter's work suggests a redefinition of "Lordship" not as a white patriarchal category but as a Christological category that refers to the Jewish Messiah and his Lordship

and a particular social ground of being are excluded in such a framework. "Unity" is this modern liberal polity is ordered around an assimilationist universality that Carter calls whiteness. This is why Carter's focus on the Jewishness of Jesus Christ as the ground for the body politic is so important and is preferable to Cone's Christological politics of the oppressed.

Cone's own hermeneutic often serves to relativize his conclusions. He states that we must recognize, as did Imamu Baraka, that "there is no objective anything," to which Cone adds, "least of all theology."[101] He recognizes the situatedness of all ethical and theological inquiry and utilizes several proponents of the "sociology of knowledge" school to insist upon recognition of "the social context of theology."[102] While this important insight should not be ignored, the significance for my current purposes is that this trajectory leaves him with only one option: "The dissimilarity between Black Theology and white theology lies at the point of each having different mental grids which account for their different approaches to the gospel. I believe that the social a priori of Black Theology is closer to the axiological perspective of biblical revelation."[103] While this is arguably true, this relativizing trajectory places the burden of proof within sociological disciplinary confines and outside the realm of theology. In other words, theology here becomes only a Tillichian "answering discipline."

> If the truth of the biblical story is God's liberation of the oppressed, then the social a priori of oppressors excludes the possibility of their hearing and seeing the truth of divine presence, because the conceptual universe of their thought contradicts the story of divine liberation. Only the poor and the weak have the axiological grid necessary for the hearing and the doing of the divine will disclosed in their midst . . . Since the gospel is liberation from bondage, and since the poor are obvious victims of oppression because of the inordinate power of the rich, it is clear that the poor have little to lose and everything to gain from Jesus Christ's presence in history . . . This difference in socioeconomic

---

over all creation. It is in this sense that I invoke Lordship: as the early Christian (and Pauline) confession that "Jesus is Lord." "Lordship" is *a priori* excluded from political arrangements that rely primarily on identity politics. In Western liberal democracies, for instance, "Lordship" has been refused in favor of a conception of "the people" as sovereign. Carter's work helps to expose how "the people" is a racial calculation.

101. Cone, *God of the Oppressed*, 15.

102. Ibid., 37–41.

103. Ibid., 41.

status between the rich and the poor affected the way in which each responded to Jesus.[104]

Cone's ontological freezing of the "difference in socioeconomic status" is further complicated by the fact that Cone calls "black people" "God's poor people."[105] In like terms, he names "the oppressed" "God's elect people."[106] And yet he maintains that "poverty is a contrived phenomenon, traceable to the rich and the powerful in this world" and that knowledge of this reality "requires that the poor practice political activity against the social and economic structure that makes them poor."[107] If poverty is described, I believe rightly so, as a "contrived phenomenon" perpetrated by the rich and powerful upon those who must struggle against it, would not that struggle, according to Cone's logic, entail a rejection of the very ontological designation by which the poor receive divine election? In a similar vein, if "poor," "black," and "oppressed" are used by Cone as functionally synonymous, would not overcoming poverty and oppression be an exercise in self-hatred as one seeks to overcome blackness? Here is a marked ambiguity in Cone's thought: he wants to explode oppression, poverty, and racist classificatory schemas while also privileging them within his hermeneutical framework. For Cone, the hopeful miscegenation envisioned by Carter could only breed a loss of election. The *telos* of Cone's framework is a reification of ontological blackness.

There is little room for the realities of ethical complication in a schema of static ontology. Cone finds it hard to allow for the possibility that the objectified "subjects" of whiteness could acquiesce to living out the politics of objectification or that members of the regnant social order could repent and call objectification into question by choosing to be identified with those objectified. While he does not negate the latter scenario, he declares it to be "the *rare* possibility of conversion among white oppressors."[108] He maintains that "it must be made absolutely clear that it is the black community that decides both the *authenticity* of white conversion and also the part these converts will play in the black struggle of freedom" and that "[t]he converts can have nothing to say about the validity of their conversion experience."[109] While he astutely diagnoses both the chronic resistance of white theology to submit to unlike others and its propensity to co-opt the struggles of

104. Ibid., 86–87.
105. Ibid., 125.
106. Ibid., 92.
107. Ibid., 115.
108. Ibid., 221.
109. Ibid., 222.

others in its own self-reflexive identity-struggles, the effect of redirecting the agency of reconciliation from the free work of God to the judgment of "the oppressed" is a weakening of the theological ground upon which the problematic patterns of white views of reconciliation may be criticized. While Cone's stated intention is to escape "a view of reconciliation based on white values,"[110] his solution is theologically problematic, based on his own insistence upon "the objective reality of reconciliation" as "an act of God."[111] Encouraging the passivity of whites in the process of reconciliation may also further encourage the problematic interior reflective patterns of whiteness. Cone recognizes this self-absorptive tendency in white theology, which he refers to as "a bourgeois exercise in intellectual masturbation."[112]

While I suspect that Cone is overstating his position a bit in order to make a necessary point about the objectifying nature of most white talk about "reconciliation," Carter reads Cone's work as not being sufficiently "trenchant" in diagnosing what makes white theology "white."[113] Cone's overstatement is displayed in his envisioning of a process of "reconciliation: black and white."[114]

> Whites must be made to realize that they are not only account-able to Roy Wilkins but also to Imamu Baraka. And if the latter says that reconciliation is out of the question, then nothing the former says can change that reality, for both are equally members of the black struggle of freedom. Unless whites can get every single black person to agree that reconciliation is realized, there is no place whatsoever for white rhetoric about the reconciling love of blacks and whites.[115]

While Cone's point is that if whites are "truly converted" to the struggle for liberation they will "know that reconciliation is a gift that excludes boasting,"[116] thereby precluding the possibility that "white converts" could use experiences in the "[black] community as evidence *against* blacks," it seems improbable that Cone actually desires a logistical scenario in which white people try to "get" (a word that invokes manipulation) "every single black person" to validate them in their desire for community. There is not much that could more effectively encourage the paternalistic and self-

110. Ibid., 207.
111. Ibid., 209.
112. Ibid., 43.
113. Carter, *Race*, 159.
114. Cone, *God of the Oppressed*, 215.
115. Ibid., 222.
116. Ibid.

obsessed psychology of whiteness than such a pursuit of reconciliation. Shifting the agency of reconciliation from the dominant social order to the objectified "other," rather than recentering it on the particularity of the divine work in human history through the Jewish Jesus of Nazareth, reconfirms the binary logic of whiteness. Cone more sufficiently summarizes his position when he notes that "liberation" is the "precondition for reconciliation."[117]

Cone appears to recognize that freezing ontological status based on relative sociological status may not be an entirely valid move, allowing himself several moments of vulnerability in reflecting on his contention that "Jesus is black":

> If Jesus' presence is real and not docetic, is it not true that Christ *must* be black in order to remain faithful to the divine promise to bear the suffering of the poor? Of course, I realize that "blackness" as a christological title may not be appropriate in the distant future or even in every human context in our present . . . But the validity of any christological title in any period of history is not decided by its universality but by this: whether in the particularity of its time it points to God's universal will to liberate particular oppressed people from inhumanity. This is exactly what blackness does in the contemporary social existence of America . . . To say that Christ is black means that God, in his infinite wisdom and mercy, not only takes color seriously, he also takes it upon himself and discloses his will to make us whole.[118]

This is the point at which Cone's argument gains the most traction and most clearly anticipates Carter's later conclusion. Further clarifying this contention he states:

> I realize that my theological limitations and my close identity with the social conditions of black people could blind me to the *truth* of the gospel. And maybe our white theologians are right when they insist that I have overlooked the *universal* significance of Jesus' message. But I contend that there is no universalism that is not particular . . . As long as they can be sure that the gospel is *for everybody*, ignoring that God liberated a *particular* people from Egypt, came in a particular man called Jesus, and for the particular purpose of liberating the oppressed, then they can continue to talk in theological abstractions, failing

117. Ibid., 210.
118. Ibid., 125.

to recognize that such talk is not the gospel unless it is related to the concrete freedom of the little ones.[119]

By insisting on theological particularity, Cone prefigures Carter's argument regarding supersessionism. Cone laments the divorce of theology and ethics, maintaining that this separation is a result of the Western imbibing of Greek philosophy rather than the Judeo-centric nexus of biblical revelation. This misstep has influenced the "exorbitant claims" Christian theologians have made regarding the "universal character of their discourse," which "was consistent with the God of Plotinus but not with the God of Moses and Amos."[120] For Cone, questions related to theology and race cannot be considered without recognizing the misstep the Church took in substituting Greek discourses of philosophical power for the biblical discourse of liberation. This disregard for situatedness carries with it a universalizing motif that finds expression in certain "cultural values."[121] These cultural values are named by Carter as *whiteness*.

While Cone's account of Jewish theological particularity prefigures Carter's theology, his disallowing of transcendence locks him in a static ontology. Whereas Cone freezes humans as either "oppressed" or "oppressor," Carter names them "Jews" and "Gentiles," thereby more sufficiently decentering the creature in light of the free agency of the Creator, rendering both oppression and objectification theologically untenable. While Cone should not be expected to bear the burden of reflecting upon white identity, Cone's theological trajectory tends to lock whiteness into a self-reflexive pattern that has trouble moving beyond "white guilt" into concrete work for justice, liberation, and relationship. If the white, Western worldview cannot be filled with a new spirit following the casting out of its demon, then it will produce little more than an "evil generation" filled with "seven other spirits more wicked than itself,"[122] a reality we are witnessing in the escalation of racial violence in "colorblind" twenty-first-century America. Static ontologies are unable to contend against this evil.

Cone and the Lynched Flesh of Christ

In his most recent work, *The Cross and the Lynching Tree*, Cone more strongly states the universal import of his theology, suggesting the redemption that

---

119. Ibid., 126.

120. Ibid., 181.

121. Ibid., 181–82.

122. Matt 12:43–45

is possible for all people as they are together identified with the flesh of the oppressed and crucified One. In *God of the Oppressed*, Cone held out the possibility of repentance from whiteness, referring to it as "white people becoming black."[123] This suggests that even in his earlier thought, his static categories of identity were a bit more permeable than he overtly allowed. Just as "white" and "black" are not for Carter about racial reification, so for Cone blackness may be more about the flesh of Jesus than about racial essentialization. "Becoming black" is akin to Carter's language of miscegenation, through which fictive blood lines are rejected in the desire of people for one another. If miscegenation threatens what Carter calls "the idolatrously false purity" of whiteness,[124] then it is not inappropriate to envision repentance as blackness. For Carter, this does not mean that the particularities of any one people should be unilaterally enthroned or rejected. What it does mean is that the particularity which masquerades as universality (read: "whiteness") is disavowed as various particularities together participate in the Jewish flesh of Jesus. Carter's language of miscegenation, or what he calls "a theology of participation" over against "an ontology of separateness," is a more precise formulation than Cone's.[125]

Drawing from the grammar of Chalcedon, Carter maintains that orthodox Christology must be understood as the life of YHWH being fully suffused with the life of the creature. This covenantal Christology "decenter[s] dialectic" by refusing "ontologized understandings of the person and work of Jesus":

> The problem with dialectical thinking and related forms of philosophical thinking is that they begin from closure and then have to negotiate passage through an "ugly broad ditch" between things that are closed . . . The covenant witnesses to the fact that for God, and only because of God's identity as God for us, there is no ditch to be crossed by us. God has from the first bound Godself to us in God's communion with Israel as a communion for the world. This is the inner logic of the identity of Jesus, the inner logic by which Israel is always already a mulatto people precisely in being YHWH's people, and by which therefore Jesus himself as the Israel of God is Mulatto . . . He is miscegenated, and out of the miscegenation discloses the God of Israel as the God of the Gentiles too.[126]

123. Cone, *God of the Oppressed*, 221.

124. Carter, *Race*, 192.

125. Ibid., 191.

126. Ibid., 191–92.

Because God is on both sides of the covenant, that of the Creator and that of the creature, dialectical frameworks such as Buber's *I-Thou* are "not radical enough."[127] While Cone has labored to transform the I-It relationship that whiteness maintains with the "other" to an I-Thou relationship in which the latter party is no longer objectified by the former, Carter contends that Cone's theology is ultimately unsuccessful in dislodging the "I" as the normalizing side of the equation. Carter explains that this formulation is "really only a settlement with whiteness, not its overcoming."[128] While it is "alluring" because it carries with it the benefit of a "settlement with blackness," a settlement with the "blackness that whiteness created" is only a settlement with whiteness "in the idiom of cultural blackness."[129] In that arrangement, the "I relates to the other but allows it a separate-but-equal status in relationship to itself as I."[130] Carter's analysis suggests the theological exhaustion that comes from the intellectual calisthenics necessary for the creature to attempt to fill the position of pseudo-creator as the universal "I." Carter suggests the redemption that can be found in the arms of "impure" relations:

> The conclusion to be drawn from my analysis is this: black liberation theology's refusal to see the I, and in fact all of creation, in gratuitous terms, that is, as a covenantal reality, leaves the problem of whiteness uncontested, insofar as at root it is a *theological* problem. As a theological problem, whiteness names the refusal to trade against race. It names the refusal to enter into dependent, promiscuous, and in short, "contaminated" relations that resist an idolatrously false purity. The blackness that whiteness creates names the same refusal, albeit cast as the photo negative that yet retains the problem. What is needed is a vision of Christian identity, then, that calls us to holy "impurity" and "promiscuity," a vision that calls for race trading against the benefits of whiteness so as to enter into the miscegenized or mulattic existence of divinization (*theosis*).[131]

As fraught with risks as this process may be, no less than this is at stake in the existence of a new body politic imaging Trinitarian mutuality. While a Conian ontologizing of blackness may be a helpful step out of objectifying relational patterns, a relationality of vulnerability and mutual dependance

127. Ibid., 192. See also Buber, *I and Thou*.

128. Carter, *Race*, 190.

129. Ibid., 190.

130. Ibid.

131. Ibid., 192.

cannot be envisioned within his framework alone. Carter's Christology more satisfactorily points to the beautiful messiness of the Incarnation.

I contend that, in *The Cross and the Lynching Tree*, Cone's sounding of several more hopeful and conciliatory notes about the relational possibilities within the body of Jesus Christ allows him to more satisfactorily frame his critique of whiteness. I read *The Cross and the Lynching Tree* as written, at least in part, in response to Carter's work. Cone is well aware of the work of Carter, about whom he has said: "I have nothing but praise for this work by a young African American scholar who must be reckoned with."[132] While I am not suggesting that Carter's work was the direct impetus for the authoring of *The Cross and the Lynching Tree*, it seems that there are several points within the text at which Cone implicitly responds to Carter's critique of him.[133] Since Cone offers *The Cross and the Lynching Tree* as a "culmination" of his career, he is no doubt interested in utilizing the utmost precision in his theological formulations as he further cements his legacy. While some of his prophetic fury has mellowed a bit, his articulation of the theological problem of whiteness has intensified. Perhaps counterintuitively, this increased theological precision allows him to utilize rhetoric that is less self-conscious.

One gets the strong impression in reading *God of the Oppressed* that, for all its fire, the book was in some sense an apologetic to make black faith more palatable to whites. While it made use of primarily African American ecclesial sources, it did so in a way that sought to explain their insights to those not versed in a "black" church tradition. While he explicitly disavows the necessity that his reflections be judged against "the theological treatises of Euro-American theologians,"[134] he nonetheless labors extensively to explain to the reader "why black people" utilize certain language or cultural forms in worship.[135] Rhetorical formulations such as "this is what black people are affirming when they say . . . " are presumably unnecessary for the very people Cone is describing. References to ecstasy in worship as "making it difficult for an observer to know what is actually happening," demonstrate an ambiguity in Cone's method. On the one hand, he wants to say that his

132. Ibid., back cover.

133. See, for instance, Cone's apologetic for the necessity of adult black males to assert their masculinity: "When an adult black male is treated like a child in a patriarchal society . . . proclaiming oneself a 'man' is a bold and necessary affirmation of black resistance" (Cone, *Cross and the Lynching Tree*, 17). This contention may be in response to Carter's critique of Frederick Douglass's overcoming of racial subjugation through assertion of masculinity and degradation of the "black feminine" (Carter, *Race*, 295).

134. Cone, *God of the Oppressed*, 224.

135. Ibid., 129–33.

utilization of black church traditions is in no way answerable to the white academy and, on the other hand, engages in describing what is "actually happening" in the worship of non-white bodies (as if the truth of the experience is found in an externally verifiable reality other than what the worshippers are themselves experiencing).

While this suggests that Cone is bound to presuppositions that favor white conceptions of rationality, in these moments one also feels that Cone is standing between two traditions and attempting to "translate" from one to the other. This proclivity in his work demonstrates both the paradoxical task of the black intellectual in modernity and, even in his early work, a marked desire to build connection and intimacy with others. Much in the same way as I interpreted Cone's use of dialectic as a way of maintaining epistemological humility, I interpret Cone's anger at subjugation as a deep desire for human connection and affirmation of the divinely-granted dignity of the creature. Rather than being committed to either dialectic or apologetic, Cone is defending people so as to establish non-objectifying connections between them. What I have characterized as Cone's "apologetic of palatability" can also be read as desire for mutual vulnerability. Even in *God of the Oppressed*, while stressing "self-determination,"[136] his goal was that "the neighbor [be] an end in himself or herself and not a means to an end.[137] This posture is a point of convergence between the works of Cone and Carter.

In *The Cross and the Lynching Tree*, Cone asserts the similarity between the instrument of the torture and death of Jesus at the hands of the Romans and the instrument of the torture and death of thousands of African Americans at the hands of white Americans. He asks how it could be that lynching has been so quickly "forgotten" in our collective memory and how it could be that the leading theologians of the late nineteenth and early to mid-twentieth centuries could have escaped the obvious parallels between them in their theological ethics. His contention is that white Americans would prefer to forget lynching because of the obvious Christological consequences of such a recognition, while black Americans have attempted to bury the memory because it is simply too painful to endure.[138] Cone again presents black existence as cruciform existence, which bears similarities to Carter's iconographic ontology. Whereas in *God of the Oppressed* the path

---

136. Ibid., 179. I am not suggesting that, in the face of white categorization of non-white peoples, "self-determination" is an altogether inappropriate task. What I am suggesting is that Carter would find it theologically insufficient for the creature to determine its own identity as "subject" or for any people group to be named in isolation from the mutual articulation of the body politic of Israel-Jesus.

137. Ibid., 214.

138. Cone, *Cross and Lynching Tree*, xiv.

from bondage to liberation was self-determination alone, in *The Cross and the Lynching Tree* the hope is that the demon of racism can be exorcised in part by white recognition of complicity in sin and a communal re-telling of the story of liberation. I will demonstrate several ways in which Cone's thought is moving in the direction of Carter's.

First, he states that his purpose in writing is that the "credibility and promise of the Christian gospel" would be maintained and that the hope of "heal[ing] the wounds of racial violence that continue to divide our churches and our society" would be realized.[139] While not being inconsistent with his earlier thought, the stated desire for the healing of ecclesial division is now presented in a different inflection. In his new preface to the second edition of *God of the Oppressed*, Cone invokes a desire to "make real the beloved community" and notes that:

> Human beings are made for each other and no people can real-
> ize their full humanity except as they participate in its realiza-
> tion for others. While some critics, shocked by my accent on
> blackness, missed this universal note in my theology, it has been
> there from the beginning. The end point of my theology is as
> important as the particularity out of which it was born.[140]

Second, Cone calls for black and white alike to retell the story of the lynching tree in their veneration of the cross, suggesting that whites can "separate themselves from the culture that lynched blacks" by "confront[ing] their history and expos[ing] the sin of white supremacy."[141] He acknowledges that "a host" of people, "black, white and other[s] . . . of many walks of life," "sacrificed their bodies and lives for . . . freedom."[142] This recognition, while perhaps being present throughout his work, has not been stated as clearly as it is now.

Third, in his criticism of Reinhold Niebuhr, Cone hints at the possibility that, in the ironic words of Niebuhr, "a fully developed interracial church" would be the "ultimate test."[143] Cone is not suggesting that Niebuhr's observation was wrong, but criticizing Niebuhr for not working to make this a reality at Bethel Church in New York, when two African American parishioners were opposed in seeking membership. Niebuhr had remarked that he "never envisaged" an intentionally interracial worshipping community, explaining "I do not think we are ready for that."

139. Ibid., xiii, xiv.
140. Cone, *God of the Oppressed*, xiii.
141. Ibid., xiii.
142. Cone, *Cross and Lynching Tree*, 92, 164–65.
143. Ibid., 43.

A fourth convergence with Carter is Cone's subversion of a prominent modern theologian. While Carter directs his critique against Milbank,
Cone explicitly calls Niebuhr to account for his failures to discern the
primary theological hypocrisy of his age and thereby personally combat
racial objectification. While Carter criticizes the Radical Orthodoxy of his
teacher, Cone reproves his predecessor at Union Theological Seminary, the
ethicist of "Christian realism" who has been a canonical source for much
contemporary thinking on social justice and a key influence on Cone. Like
Carter, Cone reveals how the "best" of "progressive" white theology often
falls short of adequately addressing the theological problem of race. Cone
presents Niebuhr as a Christian socialist who actively spoke out against
racism and waxed eloquent about the "terrible beauty" of the cross while
neither discerning the terrible irony of the lynching tree nor being able to
submit to learning from black subjectivity.[144] Niebuhr, whose social ethics
focused on justice rather than love,[145] demonstrated a "defect in the conscience of white Christians."[146] Niebuhr, while calling racism "the gravest
social evil in our nation,"[147] counseled gradualism in the struggle for black
liberation, unlike either King or Malcolm X. Cone maintains that Niebuhr
showed little interest in dialoguing with African Americans about racial
injustice, preferring instead to speak on behalf of them.[148] This critique is
all the more trenchant given Cone's personal story of joining the faculty of
Union Seminary and receiving Niebuhr's letter regarding his favorable, and
yet paternalistic, assessment of *Black Theology and Black Power*.[149] In contrast, Cone cites Bonhoeffer's involvement in an African American church
and his study of black theological and cultural resources during his time at
Union to demonstrate that, "it has never been impossible" "for white people
to empathize fully with the experience of black people."[150] While I will later
address what may be problematic about this latter formulation of Cone's,

144. Ibid., chapter 2.

145. Ibid., 33. This observation from Cone is quite interesting as he comments that
Niebuhr held that "the best that humans can strive for is justice, which is love approxi-
mated, a balance of power among competing groups." This is not dissimilar to Carter's
critique of Cone.

146. Ibid., 32.

147. Ibid., 38.

148. Ibid., 42.

149. Ibid., 59.

150. Ibid., 41. It would be interesting to ask Cone what he means by use of the word
"fully." For an account of the influence of Abysinnian Baptist Church in Harlem on
Bonhoeffer, an account that is more carefully nuanced than Cone's blanket assertion,
see Williams, *Bonhoeffer's Black Jesus*.

the point is that Cone suggests that Niebuhr failed to learn from King, although King explicitly cited Niebuhr as a primary influence. Cone laments that "[w]hite theologians do not normally turn to the black experience to learn about theology."[151]

Fifth, Cone is careful to qualify his invocations of mutual love by recognizing that reconciliation without liberation is empty.[152] In referencing the work of the literary giants of the Harlem Renaissance, Cone contends: "Artists recognized that no real reconciliation could occur between blacks and whites without telling the painful and redeeming truths about their life together."[153] Whereas in *God of the Oppressed* reconciliation had been impossible without the unanimous and unilateral consent of blackness, in *The Cross and the Lynching Tree* shared truth is the prerequisite for life together. The reason Cone is hesitant to speak of reconciling love is because "whites acted in a superior manner for so long that it was difficult for them to even recognize their cultural and spiritual arrogance, blatant as it was to African Americans."[154]

Sixth, Cone moves toward diagnosing what is faulty about the Christian imagination. He recognizes that the distortion of Christian identity runs so deep that "even in the black community the public meaning of Christianity was *white*."[155] He states that "the most 'progressive' of . . . white theologians and religious thinkers" have failed to recognize the distortion in the "American Christian imagination."[156] One cannot help but wonder if Cone has appropriated from Jennings this manner of phrasing the issue. Cone's purpose has been to explore how one can simultaneously be *black* and *Christian* when Christian identity has been defined by whiteness.[157] Cone's focus on the distorted imagination of Christianity as white intuits Carter's and Jennings' critique of supersessionism.

Seventh, in exploring what he calls the racialized scale of "white over black," Cone explains that the greatest fear of Anglo-Saxon civilization has historically been that of "race-mixing" or "mongrelization."[158] Even as sexual relations between the races were often consensual, miscegenation, or the perceived possibility of its occurrence, was the primary justification given

---

151. Cone, *Cross and Lynching Tree*, 64.

152. Cone, *God of the Oppressed*, 208–10.

153. Cone, *Cross and Lynching Tree*, 113.

154. Ibid., 11.

155. Ibid., xvii.

156. Ibid., 31–32.

157. Ibid., xvii, 149.

158. Ibid., 7–8.

for lynching. Protecting white women from the supposed "insatiable lust" of black men was the moral "duty" of white mobs.[159] This was in a climate where African American men desiring to protect their wives, daughters, sisters, and mothers from white male rape of black women often brought down "the full weight of Judge Lynch" upon themselves. If, as Cone maintains, the fear of miscegenation served as the ethical justification for the perpetration of one of America's greatest evils, then for Carter to identify this Christological and ecclesiological "scandal" as the greatest hope for resisting the false gospel of whiteness is all the more poignant.

Eighth, Cone gestures beyond ontological blackness by presenting black faith much like an "icon" for the salvation of all people: "I wrestle with questions about black dignity in a world of white supremacy because I believe that the cultural and religious resources in the black experience could help all Americans cope with the legacy of white supremacy."[160] Cone offers all people the opportunity to "step into black people's shoes" to realize that

> humanity's salvation is revealed in the cross of the condemned criminal Jesus, and humanity's salvation is available *only* through our solidarity with the crucified people in our midst. Faith that emerged out of the scandal of the cross is not a faith of intellectuals or elites of any sort.[161]

Against the self-assumed vocation of the "elite" (which we will see is characteristic of Milbank's ethics of virtue), Cone, like Carter, offers the historical and theological resources of black faith as a path out of the abstractions of whiteness.

In these ways, Cone, like Carter, presents the space of black-white relations as the space of the lynched body of Christ:

> Blacks and whites are bound together in Christ by their brutal and beautiful encounter in this land. Neither blacks nor whites can be understood fully without reference to the other because of their common religious heritage as well as their joint relationship to the lynching experience. What happened to blacks also happened to whites. When whites lynched blacks, they were literally and symbolically lynching themselves—their sons, daughters, cousins, mothers, and fathers . . . Whites may be bad brothers and sisters . . . but they are *still* our sisters and brothers . . . All the hatred we have expressed toward one another cannot destroy the profound mutual love and solidarity that flow deeply

159. Ibid.
160. Ibid., xix.
161. Ibid., 160.

between us—a love that empowered blacks to open their arms
to receive the many whites who were also empowered by the
same love to risk their lives in the black struggle for freedom . . .
We were made brothers and sisters by the blood of the lynching
tree, the blood of sexual union, and the blood of the cross of
Jesus . . . What God joined together, no one can tear apart.[162]

The Limits of Ontological Blackness

While I have listed eight themes in *The Cross and the Lynching Tree* which
demonstrate that Cone's thought is moving in the direction of Carter, I will
suggest that, for all its flourish, Cone's theology is in the end less radical than
that of Carter.

First, I am unconvinced by Cone's assertion, in relation to Bonhoeffer, that anyone can "empathize fully" with the experience of another. I am
likewise unconvinced that any person can "fully" understand his or her
own experience. While I appreciate the point Cone is making, *empathy* is
ultimately less radical than *participation*. "Empathy" names a quest to share
the feelings of another. "Empathy" alone can be as much an exercise in objectification as antipathy. It does not necessarily cross what Carter terms the
"ugly broad ditch" of dialectic; empathy does not exclude the possibility of
an "ontology of separateness"; empathy is less radical than mutual participation. Bonhoeffer, who is Cone's example of one who "fully empathize[d]"
with black subjectivity, demonstrates in *Creation and Fall* that he does not
trust even his own conscience.[163] In *Discipleship*, Bonhoeffer flatly declares
the quest for relational immediacy to be antithetical to the Gospel.[164] If
Jesus Christ is the sole mediator, then empathy, in addition to not being
"fully" possible, could provide a substitute for the path of the cross, through
which one receives the "other" back through the participatory mediation of
Christ's body. Perhaps this "forgetfulness" of self in the knowledge of God
is what enabled Bonhoeffer to more adequately respect, learn from, and be
immersed in nonwhite theological resources and ecclesial communities.
Carter's theology of "participation" moves the church in this direction. *Miscegenation*, as understood by Carter, names trading against race and becoming dependent upon the "unlike" other in order to enter divinization. This
mulattic participation is to be distinguished from empathy.

162. Ibid., 165–66.
163. See Bonhoeffer, *Creation and Fall*, 127–30.
164. See Bonhoeffer, *Discipleship*, 92–95.

Second, that Carter's vision is more radical than Cone's is seen in the paternalisms that plague Cone's work. Cone regularly speaks as if he were an outside observer categorizing those he desires to see liberated. For instance, while Cone confesses that he has been justifiably criticized for not satisfactorily listening to female voices in his work, when he does listen male paternalism sometimes creeps into even his most favorable assessments. In presenting Ida B. Wells' campaign against lynching as a prime example of theological integrity, Cone claims that "black women activists . . . did not need theological imagination to show [lynching to be wrong]."[165] Yet he has already labored to show that the lived experience of resistance produces theological imaginations that are profound in ways that more formal and detached reflections are not. Cone's implication that the experiential insights of women engaged in the struggle for freedom were less sophisticated theologically suggests that he maintains male subjectivity as the normalizing pole of the equation. Likewise, when referring to black ministers with "little or no formal training in academic theology," Cone claims that "they spoke from their hearts, appealing to their life experience . . . and the Spirit of God" while proclaiming "what they felt in song and sermon."[166] Yet again, why should "little or no formal training in academic theology" render someone unable to speak from the mind, as well as from the heart? Can those who have *not* been assimilated into white, Western theology *not* love God with all their *minds*? Is not Cone's appeal to "untutored" African American preachers' reliance upon their hearts and the Spirit very similar to those white authors like Piper who picture "the black experience" as adding a bit of soul or spirit to the Western tradition?[167] What does this have to say about Cone's views of what constitutes rationality and the "human"? As can be seen through these two examples, Cone's ontological blackness far too frequently produces objectifying classifications.

Finally, Cone's racialized ontology causes him to inadequately theorize Jewish identity. Whereas the early Cone suggested the particularity of the Jewish flesh of Jesus as the antidote to abstracting, white theology, in

165. Cone, *Cross and Lynching Tree*, 133.

166. Ibid., 74.

167. See Piper, *Bloodlines*, where he ends his text with a call (styled as "my dream") for the Reformed "sovereignty of God" theology of "dead white men" (which is alternatively glossed as "God-centered theology") and the "soul dynamic of the black experience" to flow together from two different "sides" (244, 255). Piper's vision of reconciliation is that there are "white people longing for the soul of black preaching and black people longing for the substance of classical preaching" (250). Accordingly, Piper lauds an African American pastor for "playing what may sound like white, Reformed God-centeredness . . . on his black instrument." Piper ends with, "Listen to him preaching!" (249).

The Cross and the Lynching Tree Cone several times equates Jewishness and whiteness. For example, he calls Julius Bloch both a "white artist" and a "Jew from Germany."[168] He paradoxically names Abel Meeropol, author of *Strange Fruit*, a "white Jewish school teacher" while attributing his sensitivity about racial injustice to being part of a "marginalized community who had a long history of suffering at the hands of white Christians."[169] While Jewishness and whiteness may be used interchangeably within modern, racialized identity reflections, Jennings contends that the colonial genesis of racialization was born out of a desire to extricate the Jewish contagion from European lands. This demonstrates that Cone does not conceive of whiteness as primarily a sociopolitical order but a skin color, which cannot but slip into essentialized conceptions of race. Carter maintains that Jewish flesh is covenantal, not racial flesh. We will see in the next chapter that race, in the modern era, was activated by distancing whiteness from Jewish flesh.

Although Cone has moved in the direction of Carter, his framework of ontological blackness complicates his many positive strides. Although Carter incorporates many aspects of the theological foundation laid by Cone, his relationship to Cone must be assessed as one of greater divergence than his relationship with Raboteau. We will now move to explicating Carter's relationship to the scholar from whose trajectory he most clearly distances himself.

Charles H. Long: Signifying Race

Long and the Religious Primordium

Charles Long is a celebrated historian of religions who retired from the Religious Studies Department of the University of California, Santa Barbara after teaching at both the University of North Carolina and the University of Chicago, where he earned his doctorate and worked closely with Mircea Eliade in establishing many of the parameters of their discipline. His work is representative of the manner in which modern religious studies tends to consider race. In this section I will show how Carter reads Long as more precisely recognizing the racial problematic than either Raboteau or Cone, yet more problematically imbibing the philosophical structure of Enlightenment than either scholar. Long's areas of expertise include creation myths, cultural contact in modernity (including cargo cults), and

168. Cone, *Cross and Lynching Tree*, 101.
169. Ibid., 134–35.

African American religious history.[170] His signature text is *Significations: Signs, Symbols, and Images in the Interpretation of Religion,* which is a collection of essays that probe the nature of "religion," cultural encounters, and the "symbols" of "Afro-American Religion."[171] In his treatment of the black religious academy, Carter substantively interacts with Long to demonstrate trends about which he has serious reservations. I will read Carter in contrast to Long in order to further explicate Carter's theology of race and to demonstrate the contributions Carter makes toward overcoming the modern problem of whiteness.

As he analyzes the problem of race in America, Long explores the meaning of the term "signifying" for African American communities. Signification is a way in which oppressed communities offer resistance against being signified by the oppressor; Long interprets African American religious history as little more than a complex system of signification. "Signifying," or "verbal misdirection," is a "very clever language game," not subject to "the rules of the discourse"[172] (rules that Carter identifies as being tied into whiteness). For Long, the significations of oppressed peoples must be analyzed so as to discern the "reality" underlying the mythology; he claims that this process is often "frustrating." Long explains that signifying creates, in the words of Saussure, an "arbitrary" bond between the "signifier and the signified,"[173] a relationship which is used to subversive effect by the community on the underside of the power structures.[174] Thankfully for Long, "all is not signification."[175] To the contrary, there is a "long tradition in the interpretation of symbol" that reveals an "intrinsic relationship between the symbol and that which is symbolized." It is this "long tradition," embodied in religious studies, that Long purposes to inhabit. Rather than "reduc[ing]" all hermeneutical decisions to the "problem of the sociology of knowledge,"[176] this tradition is able to offer an "archaic critique" sufficient to engage in "crawling back through . . . history" so that "the languages and experiences

170. The convergence of these three interests suggests the manner in which Long interprets African American religious history: as roughly equivalent with primitive religious myths.

171. Long, *Significations.*

172. Ibid., 1.

173. Ibid.

174. Long does not delve into the concept of signifying nearly as thoroughly as does Henry Louis Gates Jr. in *The Signifying Monkey.* Rather than exploring signifying as a practice, Long's goal is to get "behind" the significations to determine the inherent "archaic" religious meanings.

175. Long, *Significations,* 2.

176. Ibid., 2.

of signification can be seen for what they are and were."[177] "The religious experience" is the interpretive lens that is able to achieve this objectivity. For Long, the discipline of religious studies is able to get to the heart of the matter in ways theological studies is not. This claim on the part of Long is similar to Cone's project in describing "what is really happening" in African American worship. Carter reads both as being tied into the modern descriptive project and reinforcing the white gaze.

Long's trajectory displays key hermeneutical distinctions between his methodology and that of Carter. For Long, while the Enlightenment and colonial conquest are the "two critical issues" that have influenced Western descriptions of the "other," particularly as the West encountered heretofore "unknown" indigenous peoples, the Enlightenment itself offers the resources with which to interpret religion in a non-hegemonic fashion. Long's identification of colonization and modernity as the two points at which Western intellectual reflection created the "other" bears similarities to Jennings' and Carter's analyses, respectively. It is in this phase of his argument that Long, even more so than Raboteau or Cone, has his finger on the pulse of the problem as identified by Carter. Not unlike Long, Carter maintains that Christianity "betrays itself" by acting as "a universal, hegemonic discourse."[178] Carter states that Long's "challenge to the hegemony of (Christian) theology over other religions, and thus, over religion qua religion is rightly posed."[179] However, Long comes to widely divergent conclusions. Carter claims that Long's reduction of particular theological commitments to a universal religious "primordium"[180] misinterprets how Christian theology, at its best, should be understood. While Long is resistant to a Christianity that is seen as a religion crowning a hierarchy of religions, Long's *Religionswissenschaft* is not radical enough. Carter maintains that Long's science of religions renders Christian theology, and any theology for that matter, as little more than an "answering discipline" to the modern category of "religion."[181] In this manner, Long rounds off all particular theological commitments to a bland modern universal humanist religious impulse. It is this privileging of the "religious" as such that Carter will identify with the Kantian construction of race. Carter reads Long "as providing the philosophical orientation on the meaning of history that is ambiguously present in *Slave Religion* [Raboteau's early work]" and "as giving the philosophical infrastructure to James H.

177. Ibid., 9.
178. Carter, *Race*, 198.
179. Ibid., 202.
180. Ibid., 203.
181. Ibid., 195.

Cone's post-Barthian black liberation theology."[182] It is the Longian philoso-phy of religious studies with which Carter most clearly contrasts his own position:

> As one surveys the discipline of African American religious studies, from history to theology to philosophies of religious humanism, it is indisputable that Long's view of religion gener-ally and his view of black religion particularly is more or less the order of the day in the field of African American religious studies. Insofar as this is the case, Long and religious scholars who are heir to his general approach to religious studies would take African American religious thought in a direction counter to the direction I start to sketch at the end of the last chapter [Cone] and that I develop further in part III [Hammon, Doug-lass, Lee]. Indeed, it can be said that through his interpretation of black liberation theology as an opaque discourse, Long cul-minates the intellectual trajectory of black liberation theology as a pure science of religion: as *Wissenschaft* . . . My objective in this chapter is to raise a note of serious alarm regarding this direction of the field.[183]

While I will focus at the end of this chapter on Carter's alternative to this trajectory, I will first identify in Long that which so clearly troubles Carter.

Long's diagnosis of the racialized underpinnings of the Enlightenment is similar to Carter's:

> While the reformist structure of the Enlightenment had mount-ed a polemic against the divisive meaning of religion in Western culture and set forth alternate meanings for the understanding of the human, the same ideological structures through various intellectual strategies paved the ground for historical evolution-ary thinking, racial theories, and forms of color symbolism that made the economic and military conquest of various cultures and peoples justifiable and defensible. In this movement both religion and cultures and peoples throughout the world were created anew through academic disciplinary orientations—*they were signified*.[184]

In his most trenchant moments, Long utilizes language that hints at the theological distortions Carter identifies. When Long maintains that "peoples throughout the world were created anew," he gestures toward what Carter

182. Ibid., 196.
183. Ibid., 196–97, bracketed clarification mine.
184. Long, *Significations*, 4.

identifies as the distortion of creation that is whiteness, indicating the implications it had for anthropology and the natural sciences, with their evolutionary logic of human "progress" versus "primitivism." Long recognizes the problematic nature of the modern project, yet finds the path forward to be in the same methodological commitments. He imbibes the orientation of the modern religious academy in ways that neither Raboteau nor Cone did:

> I perceived that there was a structure for the universal in the human world that, though created from Enlightenment understandings of the human venture, expressed an opening for the authentic expression of others. Religion thus became the locus for a meaning that carried an archaic form; it was a root meaning and could thus become the basis for radical critical thought. The essays presented in this volume explore the possibilities of a form of thought that is rooted in the religious experience of black traditions.[185]

It is not so much the particularities of "black traditions" that are important for Long. What matters is the universal religious "root meaning"—the "primordium"—which the modern academy discerns within and through those traditions, or any traditions for that matter. While Long recognizes the problematic nature of modern classificatory schemas, he nonetheless finds hope for their overcoming through the "opening" the Enlightenment created: religion. Long defines religion as "orientation": "how one comes to terms with the ultimate significance of one's place in the world."[186] Longian religion is non-transcendent; it is a product of the human quest for self-situatedness. Long maintains that "the religion of any people is . . . experience, expression, motivations, intentions, behaviors, styles, and rhythms."[187] Black theology, or any theology, is nothing more than human self-actualization. The "archaic critique" of religious studies discerns what was "actually taking place" in the spiritual experiences of various peoples.[188] Instead of calling modern encyclopedic methodologies into question (as does Carter), Long has in effect upped the ante in their favor. For Long, the problem is not with the modern scholarly gaze, but that the intellectual quest has been distorted by what he calls "latent" power.[189]

---

185. Ibid., 8.
186. Ibid., 7.
187. Ibid.
188. Ibid., 9.
189. Ibid., 5.

> More often than not, the differences that bring a culture or a people to the attention of the investigator are not simply formed from the point of view of the intellectual problematic; they are more often than not the nuances and latencies of that power which is part of the structure of the cultural contact itself manifesting itself as intellectual curiosity.[190]

Long implies that if the power differential could be accounted for, the "point of view of the intellectual problematic" could produce a pure form of "cultural contact." This is epistemologically problematic to say the least. For Long, it is not the ability of the historian, scientist, anthropologist, sociologist, or religious scholar to arrive at a satisfactory observational knowledge of the "other" that is in question. Rather, the problem is that the "pure" empirical stance has not often been achieved because of the pursuit of power: desire for conquest was "masked by the intellectual desire for knowledge of the other."[191] Long maintains that by working to get behind "the creation of discourses of power," "what really happened" will be recognizable in the obvious "facts of history."[192] Carter's thesis suggests that Long's approach drastically underestimates the power that is wielded through the modern presumption of the ability to "know" and "describe."

Carter's vision of a Pentecostal re-ordering of language within "impure" relations calls into question the ability of the observatory stance of the modern religious academy to adequately discern the voice of the other. Carter's analysis suggests that the best that studies of "cultural contact" can achieve is a more "positive" evaluation of the particularities of the other (which is not a completely bad development). However, this reformist evaluative structure is less radical than mutual participation. The problematic nature of Long's descriptive tendencies can be seen as he reflects:

> For example, on the descriptive level, one cannot deny that there are peoples and cultures of dark-skinned, kinky-haired human beings who do not wear clothing in the manner of the cultures of the investigators, and, in addition, they express very different meanings regarding their orientations in their worlds. While this may be true on the descriptive and analytical levels, the fact that these characteristics were noted as the basis for significant differences is often unexplored. In other words, what leads one to locate the differences within what is the common?[193]

190. Ibid.
191. Ibid.
192. Ibid., 129.
193. Ibid., 5.

Long drastically under-emphasizes the significance of the comparative aesthetic judgments he is making. For Long, the evaluative ability of the observer is assumed; he sees the problem to be the assignation of comparative value. While he has a valid point regarding the problematic nature of maintaining a normalizing pole in cross-cultural encounters, what he takes to be analytically undeniable is itself an unrelenting aesthetic comparison that racializes the "other." For example, do not designations such as "kinky" or "dark-skinned" in and of themselves introduce the "other" into a linguistic world in which the assignation of comparative value is made possible? Surely calling hair "kinky" is itself a value judgment that assumes straightness of hair to be "normal." While descriptive words need not be as pejorative as "kinky," description as a form of analysis is not exempt from making aesthetic value comparisons. In the descriptive project, the self-articulation of the "described" person is necessarily muted. Carter's work leads to the conclusion that the discipline of religious studies would do well to recognize its limitations.

It is worth noting that Long's religious studies methodology seems to have begun from a posture of vulnerability. He reveals the situatedness of his own inquiry as he relates that his "concern for the meaning of the religious reality of black Americans" stemmed not only from his "scholarly discipline" but also from his "desire to make sense of my life as a black person in the United States."[194] He found the "history of religions" to be "the only discipline" that "responded to the . . . expressions of my origins." He purposed to "not begin with a methodology of pathology, one of the primary . . . cultural and social scientific languages about blacks." Yet Long's religious studies trajectory does not as sufficiently resist the problem of race as does Carter's theological focus. As a discipline, religious studies remains beholden to the modern methodological stance that introduced conceptions of pathology into the academy. While Long admirably laments that "the actual situation of cultural contact itself is never brought to the fore within the context of intellectual formulations,"[195] his epistemological humility collapses into the assumed objectivity of the disciplinary posture into which he is so clearly invested. Contrasting with Long, Carter presents a vision of mutual dependence in his language of miscegenation and linguistic interpenetration. Carter finds the methodological stance of religious studies to be central in the maintenance of the sociopolitical order of whiteness.

194. Ibid., 8.
195. Ibid., 5.

Long and the New God

Carter contends that Long's relegation of theology to the role of answering discipline does not decenter Western primacy. Rather than an Enlightenment schema in which Christianity is the apex of a hierarchy of religions, Long has substituted an Enlightenment schema which identifies a universal humanist religious impulse undergirding all cultural expressions. Longian religious studies has retained and redirected the rationalist aesthetic of modernity.[196] It is this stance that assumes a Kantian religious rationality which Carter will implicate in the construction of race. In this section, I will suggest that the religious studies enterprise is a reaction to deformities in the Christian tradition and offers a less satisfactory anthropology than Carter's invocation of theology done on the underside of modernity.

Gavin D'Costa's *Theology in the Public Square* is helpful in this regard.[197] While D'Costa's vision of a reenactment of classical "Christian culture"[198] is problematic in ways that Carter identifies in his treatment of Milbank, D'Costa's critique of secularization as the only acceptable public discourse is helpful in understanding Carter's critique of Long. It provides a way to understand how Carter can implicate both religious studies and virtue ethics in the maintenance of whiteness. D'Costa maintains that a post-Christian ethos of secularization is not more open to other modes of thought than is the Western rationalized Christianity of modernity.[199] Both are tied into the Enlightenment in ways that Christian theology need not be. D'Costa suggests that it is precisely *from* particular convictions devoutly held that genuine dialogue and mutuality can be had. It is genuine openness to the other in which true plurality is found, not in a universalizing religious impulse that rounds off the corners of religious doctrine in favor of a bland pluralism. What D'Costa defines as "the ideological nature" of "secularism" can be loosely correlated with how Carter reads Long's religious studies discipline. It suggests that pluralism as a dogma is static in ways that a thick theology of the Incarnation resists. D'Costa's recognition of the genuine encounter made possible within a Christian theology shaped by epistemological humility, over against the cultural imperialism of secular religious studies, bears similarities to Carter's invocation of Christian theology as a mode of "weak thought."[200]

196. See Carter, *Race*, 204, where he makes the connection between "various ways of expressing the religious primordium" and what he terms "rationalist aesthetics."

197. D'Costa, *Theology in the Public Square*.

198. Ibid., 1. D'Costa draws from Milbank, MacIntyre, and Hauerwas in this regard.

199. Ibid., 217.

200. Carter, *Race*, 369.

Carter reads Long's approach to religious studies as a reaction against a Christianity that had already long been distorted by supersessionism.[201] Long gives a genealogy of religious studies in which he traces the development of the discipline from Max Muller, the eminent linguist and progenitor of modern religious studies, through Rudolf Otto, Joachim Wach, and to Eliade (his colleague).[202] Long relates Max Muller's opposition to Adolf von Harnack, the influential modern liberal historian of dogma. Long extols Muller's approach and continues his criticism of Christian theology as unable to take seriously the study of other religions based on the merits of their own accounts. Long relates that Harnack was opposed to the establishment of the history of religions as a discipline because he "felt that such study would lead to dilettantism and that those who wished to study other religions should study them through Christianity."[203] Long maintains that Harnack viewed Christianity as "the absolute religion" by which all other religions should be evaluated. Long suggests that Muller's approach, which posits a *sensus communis* undergirding all linguistic forms, leading to an experience of the sacred known as the *sensus numinous*, was a liberating alternative to Harnack's absolutism.[204] Long presents his genealogy of religious studies as the progression from the *sensus communis* to the *sensus numinous*, "that capacity for the experience of the sacred that has always been the same for every human being."[205] For Long, Muller's quest for a "new primordium for Western culture" has now been realized in "the nature of experience itself as expressive of a primordium of human consciousness."[206] Long maintains that "religion is a practical social concern" whose "objective pole," while needing to "be validated by communal consensus," is "a mode of release from the entanglements of the social" and "the awareness of an objectivity that lies beyond the social and the existential."[207] Religious studies is a quest to ascertain the universality of the human spirit. In this quest, a transcendent god is irrelevant. A religious primordium is substituted for deity. For Long, it is the death of God[208] and his replacement by the universal

201. Ibid., 199–204.

202. Long, *Significations*, 20–21.

203. Ibid., 21.

204. Ibid., 20–21.

205. Ibid., 22.

206. Ibid., 21.

207. Ibid., 35.

208. Ibid., 193. See also Nietzsche, *The Gay Science*, where Nietzsche states, "God is dead. God remains dead. And we have killed him. Yet his shadow still looms. How shall we comfort ourselves, the murderers of all murderers? What was holiest and mightiest of all that the world has yet owned has bled to death under our knives: who will wipe

sensus numinous that Long celebrates as the rise of a "new god" who, while unable to be expressed in "the older theological languages," has evoked a "new beat, a new rhythm, a new movement."[209]

I have taken this brief detour through Long's approach to religious studies to demonstrate the perspicacity of Carter's critique of its disciplinary presuppositions. Carter maintains that "Long's vision of what ails theology may be overdetermined by the theological assumptions built into Harnack's resistance to *Religionswissenschaft*."[210] In other words, "Long seems to insufficiently acknowledge that Harnack's understanding of Christianity as 'the absolute religion' in many ways brings to culmination a deformation of theological reflection that has been some time in the making."[211] This deformation is Christianity's suppression of its Jewish center, or supersessionism. According to Carter, Harnack's resistance to the science of religions and his insistence upon the necessity of the refraction of religious reflection through the lens of Christianity was due to "a presumption of German cultural and philosophical superiority."[212] Carter concludes that Long has rightly discerned that there is something terribly amiss in the "intellectual colonization performed by Christian theology."[213] In this sense, religious studies as a discipline is a "politically counter-cultural enterprise."[214] However, Carter finds Long's account to be myopic in the sense that

> Long's reduction of Christian theology to its Harnackian or Harnack-like performances does not allow him to reckon with other types of Christian theological performances, both within and on the underside of the West, performances that might actually be consonant with and perhaps even radicalize his own brilliant insights into the poverty and wealth of existence.[215]

---

this blood off us? What water is there for us to clean ourselves? What festivals of atonement, what sacred games shall we have to invent? Is not the greatness of this deed too great for us? Must we ourselves not become gods simply to appear worthy of it?" (181).

209. Long, *Significations*, 197.

210. Carter, *Race*, 203.

211. Ibid., 201.

212. Ibid., 200.

213. Ibid., 201.

214. It is worth noting that Carter views both religious studies and Milbankian virtue ethics as counter-cultural. This suggests several similarities and limitations shared by both. These will become more apparent in the next chapter.

215. Carter, *Race*, 208.

If, as Carter maintains, a Harnackian theological approach "represents a deformation, a deradicalization, of Christian thought,"[216] then Long has an attenuated view of Christian theology. Carter claims that certain marginalized theological performances may more satisfactorily address Long's concerns than Long's religious studies approach. Carter maintains that, within its history of exegesis against the social order, Christian theology has often radicalized the sort of questions asked by religious studies. It is this history of exegesis-as-resistance that Carter finds in several antebellum Afro-Christian authors and Eastern patristics, of which Jarena Lee and Maximus the Confessor are preeminent. If as Carter maintains, Harnackian rationalized Christianity involved "a schematizing of religions such that religions were conceived as indices of humanity or its lack" and if this framework "was intent on suppressing . . . and ultimately stripping from Christianity what was Jewish about it," then "[t]his suppression . . . represents a suppression of the positivity of the eternal Word's relationship to the world's religions as so many expressions of what it means to be human."[217] In briefly summing up the direction his thought will take in claiming the body of Jesus Christ as the ground of a new body politic, Carter states:

> Long seems not to recognize that the twofold question (of other religions in relationship to Christianity and of religion in its own right) has been theologically radicalized in Christ . . . This is because the question and, in some sense, the reality of the religions and of religion in its own right are situated within the person of the eternal Word in his concreteness as Jesus of Nazareth, the Jew. This also means that both the reality of the religions of the world and the questions they pose, and the question of religion as such that only *Dasein* as homo religiosus can pose, are perpetually present in the eternal Word, Jesus of Nazareth, and therefore within the social or ecclesial field that he is.[218]

Whereas Muller and religious studies "celebrates the particular as a route to the universal" and whereas Harnackian rationalized Christianity "rides imperialistically, that is, roughshod, directly to the universal," Carter invokes the Jewish Jesus as the *concretum universale*.[219]

216. Ibid., 202.
217. Ibid., 201.
218. Ibid., 202.
219. Ibid., 203.

Long and the Polyglossia of Theologies Opaque

Carter's and Long's methodologies are placed in starker relief by investigating Long's perspective on "opacity of being" and what he terms "theologies opaque." Long travels the death of transcendence to its conclusion. He finds there an awesome silence in which a new ontology is born and the strength of the human spirit is affirmed.[220] He maintains that in finding the universal religious impulse running through the myths of various peoples, it is possible to move beyond the objectifying structure of theology and the conquest it influenced.[221] In this section, I will maintain that Carter's doctrine of the Incarnation is more effective than religious studies in addressing these concerns. Carter asserts that the Jewish Jesus, as the concrete universal, is the social field in which the particularities of humanity cohere. For Carter, religion is less about a universal impulse than about being drawn into the eternal Word that became flesh in particular space by in turn being particular humans in particular places.

Long reads particular human cultural expressions as manifestations of a universal religious primordium recognizable when various cultures come into contact with one another. Long, who was president of the American Academy of Religion in the early nineteen-seventies, finds, in the 1963 transition from the National Association of Biblical Instructors to the creation of the AAR, a newfound ability to move beyond the hegemony of white male Protestantism by affirming a *"polyglossia"* of cultural and disciplinary linguistic worlds in which, as in his treatment of the emergence of cargo cults in the face of unforeseen cultural contact, a "new form of humanity" is created.[222] Long's anthropology is built on the modern myth of human progress, through which he works to demythologize what he considers to be religious myths.

This "new" anthropology is realized as the "oppugnancy" or "opacity" of one being comes into contact with the opacity of another. Long maintains that the concept of "God," what Gerardus van der Leeuw called "the Object of Religion," was similarly created by humans as an oppugnant "Somewhat": an oppositional construct to the human.[223] For Long, human-human and human-divine relations are best understood as oppositional opacities. He sees the contemporary cultural contact between Western and non-Western religious discourses to be analogical to the contact between conquista-

---

220. Long, *Significations*, 59–62.

221. Ibid., 62–64.

222. Ibid., 64.

223. Ibid., 116–19.

dors and indigenes: it provides a path to the emergence of "a new human dimension" found through the coexistence of multiple opacities.[224] Long maintains that the "involuntary structure of the religious consciousness" is oppugnancy, which articulates itself in "the 'hardness' of life, whether the form of that reality is the slave system, God, or simply life itself."[225] As modern humans have recognized "the religious consciousness," the black community has moved from being "a vague 'Somewhat'" to an oppugnant "Other," thereby sharing in the progression of mankind "coming to terms with" its own opacity.[226] Carter contends that such an account does not take seriously the particular contours of faith, including the particular theological commitments of oppressed peoples.

Long's anthropology of progress operates within a modern evolutionary logic. He claims that "the study of non-Western and especially primitive religious expressions" has provided the academy with "an objective view of the life of others" that shines a critical light on the "inner life and subjectivity of the investigator."[227] For Long, demythologization of both traditions occurs through cultural contact.

> If the West demythologized and demystified the religious traditions of aboriginal cultures throughout the modern period, a proper study of these traditions might enable us to demythologize in turn our own discipline, and thereby extend our understanding of religion.[228]

Long reduces particularity to a religious universal, a least common denominator, so to speak. He hopes that "polyglossia" might further the study of religion qua religion, which for Long, echoing Eliade, becomes the "center" that is "the locus of revelation par excellence."[229] Long's ontology replaces the "old" center of theological revelation with a "new" center of religious opacity.

Whereas Carter favorably appropriates the overtly theological focus of the early Cone, Long approvingly reads Cone's work as "a religious valorization of color."[230] Long describes the works of Cone and Native American theologian Deloria Jr. as "opaque" theologies. He reads the statements "Jesus

224. Ibid., 124–26.
225. Ibid., 177.
226. Ibid., 178–79.
227. Ibid., 124.
228. Ibid., 94.
229. Ibid., 69.
230. Ibid., 185.

is black" and "God is red" as the same claim stated differently. He maintains that Cone and Deloria Jr. overcome the neutrality or meaninglessness of color, and thereby the transparency of the nonwhite body, by insisting upon the opacity of the people group being studied or signified. Long collapses the particularities of their projects into a general exercise of people speaking for themselves.

> Deloria and Cone join a group of intellectuals all over the world who have undertaken the issue of what I call the *opacity of reality*. Black is beautiful; God is red! These pronouncements by the opaque ones deny the methodological and philosophical meaning of transparency as a metaphor for a theory of knowledge . . . Protestant Christianity in implicit and unconscious ways has thought of deity as either white or transparent, so that the issue of color has been obscured.[231]

While Long's claim about the assumed whiteness of the "Christian" God is a point well taken, and while his resistance to "transparency" is a welcome development, he appears not to recognize the manner in which he objectifies the positions of Cone and Deloria Jr. by conflating them and reducing them to an impulse that squares comfortably with his religious studies program. In Long's view, the primary weakness of Cone's and Deloria Jr.'s works is that they are theological and, according to Long, theology is not the proper mode of discourse in which to consider issues of identity.[232] Long finds theology to be about power—the "power of God," the "hegemony of power," and the "power of specific forms of discourse about power." Long desires that "theologies opaque" would "undertake the destruction of theology as a powerful mode of discourse," replacing it with "a narrative of meaning . . . fired in the crucible of oppression."[233] I contend that Carter's account better accomplishes this goal than Long's account.

Long reads religion as "prior to theology"[234] and claims that it relinquishes power as it makes its observations. My preceding analysis has maintained that this is an underestimation of the power wielded by the descriptive process. Long finds the "narrative of meaning" of religious studies to be "part of the liberating thought structures of the Enlightenment heritage" that are the legacy of Freud and Marx, through which a "new primordium that is universal within the actualities of history rather than

---

231. Ibid., 193–94.
232. Ibid., 194.
233. Ibid., 195.
234. Ibid., 174.

mind is brought to the fore."[235] Quoting David Brion Davis, Long maintains that this new narrative of meaning does not need "the mercy of God or the mercy of those who exercise worldly leadership in His or other names."[236]

Long's conflation of the theological programs of Cone and Deloria Jr. to nothing more than a proclamation of opacity demonstrates a misunderstanding of both, particularly the latter. What Long calls "a religious valorization of color" is not what Deloria Jr. is after in his text *God is Red*. By contrasting Native spirituality with Western theological discourse, Deloria Jr. is attempting to overturn the very sort of comparative religious studies analyses in which Long is engaged. Rather than asserting something like the opacity of ethnicity, Deloria Jr. is presenting the importance of Native understandings of *place, land,* and *location* as constitutive of identity.[237] Deloria Jr. sets a spatially-constituted spirituality over against what he calls "a universal sense of religious feeling" that "replaced what had been rather precise formulations of religious beliefs."[238] Deloria Jr. criticizes Western reflection upon native peoples as creating "The Indians of the American Imagination."[239] Long's cursory treatment of Cone and Deloria Jr. does a disservice to the particular theological contours of each scholar's work and risks rendering nonwhite people an idealized object of religious study. This religious studies gaze is a key characteristic of whiteness.

Unlike Long, Carter offers a critique of modern theology's distortions *from within* the discipline of Christian theology. While Long recognizes that "[i]t is the intent and structure of theology as a mode of discourse that is at stake,"[240] he does not consider that theology could, often has, and often does, operate quite differently than his assessment of it. While Carter would agree that the nature of theology is at stake, he contends that Long's criticisms are directed at modern distortions of talk about the primacy of the Incarnate Word. Carter's plea for theology to become "a mode of 'weak thought'"[241] more effectively answers Long's concerns than Long's discipline does. Like Nietzsche, Long realizes that in the death of God something must fill the

235. Ibid., 196.

236. Ibid.

237. Deloria, *God is Red*, 61–75. See chapter 4, entitled *Thinking in Time and Space*, in which Deloria Jr. is contrasting the importance of temporal history for "religion" with the importance of place in native spirituality. It may be worth noting that the Christian doctrine of creation which Deloria Jr. criticizes is a much narrower understanding than that offered by Carter and Jennings.

238. Ibid., 37.

239. Ibid., chapter 2.

240. Long, *Significations*, 196.

241. Carter, *Race*, 369.

void. He offers religious studies, a projection of humanity's deepest desires, into the center left empty by deity. In Christian theological terms, this "new god," this "locus of revelation," echoes the "let us make" of Babel.[242]

Carter's Critique of Long's Opacity of Being

Long utilizes what Carter calls "the hermeneutical problem that is America" as a sort of case study to interpret cultural contact and, therefore, *being* itself. Carter relates that Long's study into how to narrate the reality of religious pluralism in effect asks the question: "How are existence itself and its meanings to be narrated?"[243] In this section, I will summarize Carter's critique of Longian ontology in order to present his alternative in the next section. Whereas Raboteau desired to incorporate non-European peoples into the historiography of the West and Cone enacted what Carter terms "a methodological inversion . . . in which black ideological values, or the values of whoever the oppressed group may be, dominate," Long probes the hermeneutical situation of cultural contact with a "history of religions-inspired philosophy of history" that hinges on "the notion of opacity."[244] This "notion of opacity" positions Long against "the iconic or incarnational theology and history that mark the writings of the later Raboteau,"[245] which, as we have seen, is the point of greatest methodological convergence for Carter with the religious academy. Long, in his rejection of the transparency of the non-white body, does not leave room for *being* as such to express a transcendent reality. Carter, on the other hand, rejects both opacity and transparency in favor of what he terms iconographic "translucency."[246]

Carter contends that, for Long, opaque theologies are not really theologies at all but are rather frameworks of opposition that arise from the "religious" as such.[247] In the words of Carter, only as "a species of negative theology" does Long view opaque theologies as valuable. Long finds opaque theologies to be problematic in that their "use of a Christian hermeneutic" necessitates suffering and assumes it to be transparently redemptive.[248] Long's view of black theology understands it to "fall from its deconstructive

242. Gen 11:4

243. Carter, *Race*, 213.

244. Ibid., 214.

245. Ibid.

246. Ibid., 154.

247. Ibid., 219.

248. Long borrows this formulation of the problem of suffering in Christian theology from William R. Jones, *Is God a White Racist?*

posture into the very mode of reflection and way of being in the world that it criticizes." Carter reads Long as questioning if "the structure of Christian existence is capable of defining or expressing freedom for those who suffer."[249] While Carter has clearly answered this query of Long's with a "no" inasmuch as the Christianity in question is Occidental rationalized "religion," he contends that there are other Christian performances in which Christianity is itself freedom for those who suffer. Carter finds in the incarnational theology of Eastern Orthodox patristics the rejection of Gnosticism, static anthropology, and all forms of slavery, and, in the early African American Christians whose autobiographical insights intimated these sensibilities, a faith whose structure is liberation of the self from static ontologies of tyranny into the dynamic life of the incarnate God. By postulating a supremely modern Christianity and then criticizing it with an appeal to the latent liberating potential of modernity, Long's project does little more than "fulfill the ambitions of the Enlightenment."[250]

Carter maintains that Long's commitment to "the religious Absolute" causes him to interpret the liberating legacy of Christian faith in Afro-Christian history as not arising from anything distinctly Christian. In Long's estimation, Hebraic and Christian imagery was used only because it was at hand and not because there was anything historical in New World black faith's encounter with God.[251] Long interprets the autobiographical comments of ex-slaves in *God Struck Me Dead*[252] in light of his account of the religiousness of consciousness and views conversion testimonies or accounts of prayer as projections of a Somewhat that "enabled them to maintain the human image."[253] Carter maintains that this hermeneutical decision introduces a positivism of history that prejudices Long's view of the first-hand accounts of African American slaves. This view disavows the possibility of "a positivity of difference" and entails an *a priori* decision that "the deity understood in Christian terms . . . does not positively and actually encounter the creature."[254] As Carter articulates in reference to Long's view:

> [T]he invocation of a Triune God, from his history of religions perspective, is an expression of the religious consciousness. For Long, therefore, black folks pray because they *have* to. They are

249. Carter, *Race*, 219.

250. Ibid., 220.

251. Ibid., 223.

252. Johnson, *God Struck Me Dead*. The volume to which I am referring was reprinted with a new introduction by Raboteau in 1993.

253. Carter, *Race*, 224.

254. Ibid., 225.

a "religious" people, and thus they pray because that's what religious people do: it is in their nature—their consciousness—to
do so. Stated differently, the aesthetic practice of prayer is but
a trace of the religious consciousness, as it were, realizing and
so fulfilling itself through its encounter with a Somewhat. This
Somewhat is the crisis situation that America presents to the
black religious consciousness. But is this not just another way of
saying that as a religious people, black folks remain in bondage,
that they are not free, being bound by the determinations of the
religious consciousness?[255]

In a Longian religious paradigm, it matters not to whom black folks
(or any folks for that matter) pray. Yet, as Carter explains, to "those who
are actually doing the praying" it matters quite a lot.[256] For those who are
oppressed, "prayer is a modulation or index of freedom; indeed, by virtue
of who it is to whom one prays, prayer *is* freedom."[257] The God of Israel
and Jesus is, in Carter's words, "not an-other either to history or to historically constituted beings in the way that oil is an-other to water."[258] Rather,
Trinitarian theology, in its acceptance of prayer as genuine encounter, draws
humanity away from human tyranny into the ecstatic life of God, thereby
creating new possibilities for historical creaturely existence. Because there
is neither genuine encounter nor a positivity of difference in the relations
between the human and the oppugnant Other in the religious enterprise,
there can be neither genuine encounter nor a positivity of difference in the
relationships between humans. In Longian perspective, the best that humanity can obtain is a coexistent opacity. Carter calls into question Long's
envisioning of encounter:

> Central to my first concern regarding how Long interprets
> existence under the rubric of encountering a Somewhat is the
> question of whether in such an outlook the other qua other re-
> ally appears in its own phenomenality and, therefore, in its own
> distinctness. But additionally, I question how the notion of 'en-
> counter' itself is being understood. For if the work of encounter
> is merely to bring the subject to self-realization in its opacity,
> then encounter, if it may be called this, amounts to a kind of
> solipsism between the subject as impoverished and the subject
> in an opaque orientation toward self-realization and thus to-
> ward fullness. In such a case, the Somewhat is but a cipher, a

255. Ibid.
256. Ibid.
257. Ibid.
258. Ibid., 226.

mediating moment, through which subjectivity must be passed on the way toward self-realization. This means that there really is not confrontation with the other as such; rather, the notion of the opaque represents a kind of reversal of the transparent gaze that structures modern racial reasoning and the forms of religious and theological thinking attending it. Both outlooks—the logic of the other in modern racial reasoning, and its logic in Long's theology of the opaque—share this problem; the other as other cannot be a positive, perduring, and irreplaceable reality for the I.[259]

As was the case in his study of cargo cults for the AAR, Long's opacity of being dissolves into an occasion for the subject's self-knowledge. Carter maintains that one's being can be received from another through a process of mutual rearticulation through joint participation in the life of the One whose Being superabounds into the being of the creature. Long's vision of oppugnant, dueling opacities precludes this type of participation.

Carter and the Poly-Glossalalia of Pentecost

Long utilized the concept of *polyglossia* to describe the coexistence of multiple linguistic structures that, in their own opacities, reveal the universal religious impulse underlying them all. In this section I will show how Carter proposes an exegetical interpretation of the coming of the Holy Spirit to the Jewish disciples of Jesus Christ on the day of Pentecost as the means to the speaking and understanding of languages not one's own. This is what I am glossing as Carter's *poly-glossolalia*, the gift of the Spirit of God for the mutual reception and articulation of the linguistic structures and thought-worlds of another. This concept is an explicit retort to Long's account of religion.

In Long's schema, projects involving linguistic interdependence are inherently suspect. Long has rightly observed that the default mode of reflection within the white Western academy has been an exercise in speaking *for* others. The non-white "other" is objectified through the gaze that the white subject trains upon the transparent object of its inquiry. To make visible those who were "invisible" (Raboteau) or to insist upon hearing the self-articulation of the oppressed (Cone) is an important step forward in dismantling the assessments of whiteness. The opacity of being (Long) is simply a stronger articulation of the philosophical assumptions undergirding these projects in self-articulation. However, remaining locked in opacity

259. Ibid., 222.

of being and its attendant monolinguistic structures effectively "freezes" being in an essentialized ghetto, thereby reinforcing modern racial logic. In the philosophical trajectory of the modern religious academy, other voices are introduced but are locked within their static subjectivity. White can speak only as white; black can speak only as black. While it is undoubtedly better to not speak *for* another, authentic speech *with* another or *through* each other is precluded by a predetermination of the relationship of various particularities to the religious universal.

The posture of the modern religious academy will allow neither white subjectivity nor black subjectivity to be converted into a shared subjectivity with another. For instance, the best the white male observer can achieve is a sort of voyeuristic empathy in which the object of study is now seen in a slightly more appealing light. This "progress" does not lessen the objectification of the non-white other. If anything, it carries with it the possibility of exacerbating the problem as it opens to the white observer an assumption of having "arrived" at a satisfactory intellectual assessment of the other, who is claimed and "mastered" for purposes of self-affirmation. The non-white other becomes what Carter has called a "cipher" that aids the observer in his own self-realization.[260] The *telos* of white subjectivity (and the blackness created by whiteness) is a cul-de-sac of static identity continually reinforced by hearing the opaque voice of the other. *Poly-glossolalia* is excluded.

Carter finds the path out of a tyrannical hierarchy of being in Maximus the Confessor's Pentecostal overcoming of a static ontology. In his exegesis of the *Mystagogia*, Carter explains that the "confusion of language and identity" inaugurated at Babel in Genesis 11 is overcome through the descent of the Holy Spirit in Acts 2. It is here that humanity finds "the Pentecostal reimagining and reordering of language and identity on the basis of a renewed auditory capacity."[261] While I will analyze Carter's Maximian vision in chapter 2 and suggest several aspects of its ecclesiological embodiment in the Conclusion, I will here intimate this trajectory through Carter's words:

> What is common to modernity's pseudotheological aesthetic of whiteness and to Long's aesthetic of the black religious consciousness is that neither aesthetic "speaks in tongues" (Acts 2), neither knows how to inhabit languages not its own, and thus both are, as Jacques Derrida might say, monolinguistic. Neither knows of the intercommunicability of all speech, thought, and existence, grounded as they are in the unity of the wealth (*simplex et completum*) and poverty (*non subsistens*) of being.

260. Ibid.

261. Ibid., 365.

Neither do those who operate out of the intellectual dispositions of whiteness or out of the dispositions of the blackness that
whiteness has created know how to probe the significance, for a
world religiously constituted through race and nation and now
through the stateless configuration of bodies in social space,
of the fact that being (*esse*) is always being-in-act . . . Failing
to reckon with this, Long's "negative theology" of the religious
consciousness figured through the significations of black religion forecloses the possibility of a Pentecostal overcoming of
whiteness . . . and a living into a new logic of existence.[262]

Contrary to the sort of monolinguism proffered by the religious academy,

[Maximus] is saying that there is an analogy between the work
that God does in making the many one with himself but without in the act of unifying them confusing what is distinctive
about the many . . . He attempts to imagine how God has no
stake in unredeemed ways of imagining homogeneity or diversity precisely because this opposition is ill framed. Rather, in
Maximian perspective, the scriptural narrative reimagines both
alternatives by calling creation into a different vision of itself as
both one and many. Pentecost enacts this alternative vision. As
he says commenting on Acts 4:32: "All [i.e., many] had but one
heart and one mind [i.e., one]."[263]

The theological distortion that is race exists in a postlapsarian world,
awaiting the consummation of a new order which has been inaugurated
through the person of Jesus of Nazareth and the body politic which bears
his image. This theological perspective takes the reality of sin seriously.
Yet it does not accept that the Fall has the last word. Carter suggests that
the ontologization of racialized identity in the religious academy is a way
of allowing sin to define *being*. Whereas Carter maintains that evil and
nothingness become "the ultimate horizon of experience" for Cone,[264] he
maintains that Long's opacity of being does not allow for being as such to be
"structurally open" or "more than any 'sinful' determination of history—be
that determination slavery in America, Auschwitz in Europe, or Apartheid
in South Africa."[265]

In a comparative religious studies paradigm, and in a modern
public square shaped by these patterns of interaction with the "other,"

262. Ibid., 227.
263. Ibid., 364–65.
264. Ibid., 167–68.
265. Ibid., 226.

communicative speech becomes a sort of dialogical "crossfire." Bodies become locked in essentialized dueling opacities. The predictable response is violence. The George Zimmermans of the world assume knowledge of the "other" as a static type; they stop their ears to languages not their own. In the United States, a nation whose consciousness and notion of "peoplehood" was forged in a racialized scale, the "other" is who Katheryn Russell–Brown has named the "criminalblackman."[266] Police forces profile and target this sociological "type;" black bodies are gunned down. The words "I can't breathe"[267] fall on deaf ears.

While gleaning important insights from Raboteau, Cone, and Long, Carter breaks with the philosophical infrastructure of the religious academy. He offers the body of Jesus Christ as the ground for the body politic. The broken and bleeding body of the Suffering Servant is the representative flesh for the bleeding bodies of African American men lying in America's streets. The resurrected and glorified body of the risen Lord gives the lie to the essentialization of bodies, whether white, black, or brown. The communal body of Christ activated by the Spirit of God binds the bodies of humanity together and causes them to hear and speak in tongues. While Carter resists the religious studies trajectory with his iconographic Christology, he is not content with theological traditions that reenact whiteness. We now turn to Carter's subversion of the Anglo-Catholic retrieval of Radical Orthodoxy. While Carter draws from Milbank in his resistance to modern social theory, he subverts Milbank's nostalgia for classical virtue and the way identity is imagined in such a tradition. Carter deploys a subversive tradition of Scriptural counter-exegesis found in the Christological reflections of Eastern Orthodoxy and the autobiographical anthropologies of antebellum African American Christianity.

266. Russell-Brown, *The Color of Crime.*

267. The dying words of Eric Garner, uttered eleven times as he was strangled to death on a sidewalk by white police officer Daniel Pantaleo.

Chapter 2: Carter and Radical Orthodoxy

John Milbank: The Revival of the Elite

IN THIS CHAPTER I will more thoroughly excavate Carter's theological analysis of the modern formation of "man" as a racial being by placing his work in conversation with a contemporary way of theologically imagining identity. In contrasting his position with both liberation theology (as exemplified by Cone) and retrievals of virtue (as exemplified by Milbank), Carter is attempting to demonstrate that Christianity is a way of life that is continually "re-traditioned" as it is connected to the living Christ and the neighbor. To this end, Carter is reclaiming a subcurrent of the tradition he finds running through classically Eastern iconography and early Afro-Christian autobiography. He envisions how this counter-cultural narrative presents an authentic contemporary way of living into the communal life of Christ:

> The question that remains . . . for all intellectuals—black, white, and others besides—who care about these matters, is this: What would it mean to refuse dialectical intellectual arrangements altogether, arrangements that allow us to neatly but insistently sequester the dispositions of faith from the dispositions of the modern academic, and then rewrite history, do literary criticism or philosophy or sociology or political science or what have you as Christian intellectuals? What would the intellectual life look like then? . . . But more to the broader issues of this book, how much more would the pseudotheological backbone of whiteness be broken for the sake of the redemption of us all, were we to escape the intellectual dispositions of whiteness and the ambiguities of blackness that it creates?[1]

This resistance to dialectic can be traced to one of Carter's teachers at the University of Virginia: John Milbank, the progenitor of Radical Orthodoxy,

1. Carter, *Race*, 156.

who was a member of Carter's doctoral committee. I read Carter's *Race*, which began as his doctoral thesis,[2] as a study in distancing himself from the trajectory of Milbank after initially imagining the racial problematic primarily within a retrieval of Western orthodoxy. While I read Carter's theology as consonant with the sensibilities of a broad tradition of orthodoxy, I suggest that he is not comfortable with the cultural hegemony and aesthetic elitism that comes along with many attempts to imagine Christian identity primarily as a recovery of Western orthodoxy. Carter does not discount the value of voices that have gone before us but is also not comfortable with the manner in which many revivals of the tradition tend to silence non-Western voices. While Carter is well-versed in traditions of theological orthodoxy, he reads Radical Orthodoxy as carrying forward the theological architecture undergirding British imperialism (whether or not this is the intent of its spokeswomen and spokesmen). I maintain that it is most effective to read *Race* as a transitional work in which Carter both deploys the methodological sensibilities of Radical Orthodoxy and evinces profound divergence from what he interprets as imperialistic overtones in Milbank's work.

Carter presents his divergence from Milbank by implicitly and provocatively aligning Milbank's incipient Christology with the rationalized Christ-figure of Kant's modern religious project. At the same time, through his use of Raboteau, Carter has invoked a counter-narrative of antebellum black voices that he reads as most authentically embodying the narrative of Israel. This counter-methodology bears similarities to Milbank's theological program. In this chapter, I will demonstrate Carter's divergence from Radical Orthodoxy (through his use of Kant) and his convergence with Milbank (through his use of Raboteau), while maintaining that his convergence is finally an exercise in subversion of Radical Orthodoxy's methodology. I read Carter's account as both more "radical" and more broadly "orthodox" than that of his teacher.

Milbank and Carter are both critics of the Enlightenment. However, whereas Milbank tends to be in agreement with those scholars who locate the lacunae in modernity in a Cartesian epistemology, a Smithian capitalist order, a Lockean political autonomy, and a Constantinian state-church order, Carter diagnoses the deformities of modernity as racialized maturations of early-modern theological and religious supersessionism. Carter maintains that the formation of man as a rational, autonomous citizen at the helm of the expanse of "civilization" is fundamentally a racial vision. As he puts it: "Thus, with the advent of modernity, the problem is no longer simply Constantinianism or even neo-Constantinianism . . . Rather, it is now

2. Ibid., v.

the problem of what I would like to call the color of Constantinianism."[3] Carter views many contemporary attempts at reasserting the centrality of the Christian *polis* in a "secular" milieu as evincing insecurity about Occidental self-identification. In other words, how is the white male subject to envision his existence in relation to others as he is experiencing the vertigo of being decentered? While Carter reads identity politics as falling prey to a hermeneutic of suspicion, he reads Milbank's philosophical theology as a reassertion of Western hegemony. Carter is not content with either answer and offers a theology that takes the problem of race seriously, treating it as *the* problem of modernity. Carter suggests that Radical Orthodoxy, which ironically refers to itself as "a new theology,"[4] reenacts the racially-charged vision of Kant even as it seeks to distance itself from the philosophical legacy of *Aufklarung*.

Carter maintains that Milbank's "overall claim" about modern secularism parasitically feeding on "Christianity's narrative of the meaning of the world by taking over and distorting it" must be "reckoned with."[5] Carter's critique of the religious academy can be read as a critique of the philosophical architecture of modern secularism. Yet Carter reads Milbank's project as heir to the production of the modern racial being through its aesthetics, ethics, and ontology. This is why Carter refers to Milbank's philosophical theology as an "important influence" with which he has "developed an ambivalent, if not now distanced relationship." I read Carter as resisting the pull of Radical Orthodoxy by offering a more theologically satisfactory account of what is at stake in modernity's totalizing vision. If, as Carter suggests, Radical Orthodoxy is a repristination of the theological architecture of British imperialism, it is unsurprising that he has become increasingly unsatisfied with it. Reclamation projects like Radical Orthodoxy tend to operate out of a melancholia about the perceived deposition of the Occidental subject and tend to encourage paternalism in relations with others. Such theological frameworks cannot long be satisfying to persons not of European ancestry nor persons engaged in miscegenistic ecclesial communities. While Carter's implicit critique of Milbank in *Race* is clearly present, one can only assume that he will stress this distinction even more strongly in future works.

My task will be to demonstrate how Carter is positioning himself as heir to the tradition while distancing himself from a contemporary redeployment of the tradition. My read of Milbank is admittedly counterintuitive. I do not

---

3. Ibid., 230.
4. See Milbank, *Radical Orthodoxy*.
5. Carter, *Race*, 388 n. 5.

intend these reflections on Milbank to be a totalizing assessment of the value of his theology. I take it for granted that Milbank's assertion of the value of theological speech in the face of secularism is a good thing. However, the manner in which Milbank makes this assertion (with a retrieval of Western philosophical virtue and a reassertion of an Anglo-Catholic *polis*) betrays a glaring blind spot about the problem of race. It is because my ears have been attuned to listening to white Christian talk through the ears of my African American sisters and brothers that this lacuna in Milbank is so obvious.

I must also note that I do not intend to collapse all accounts of virtue ethics into one. While I do not find virtue ethics to be the most compelling way to think about living a moral life (because it tends to underemphasize the work of the Spirit in bearing the fruits of virtue in the lives of those joined with Jesus Christ), I suggest that some accounts are better than others. In my treatment of Jennings, I will maintain that Hauerwas' account of virtue more satisfactorily incorporates biblical conceptions of virtue than does Milbank's. The primary limitation in Hauerwas is his over-incorporation of MacIntyre's account of Aristotelian virtue as Christian virtue. In this section, I will claim that Milbank's account of virtue is little more than a means to support his reassertion of the primacy of the Western elite. The problematic position in which Milbank's schema places the non-white body calls into question the tenor of his project.

Self-Centered Theological Discourse

Theology and Social Theory is Milbank's systematic theology in answer to the secularizing morass of "liberal" modernity. This influential text can be read as the culmination of a theological trajectory begun in several papers written early in his career and published more recently in *The Future of Love: Essays in Political Theology*.[6] While I will arrive at placing Carter's *Race* in conversation with *Theology and Social Theory*, first I will read several essays in *The Future of Love*, united under the heading *Theology and English Culture*, as offering the clearest picture of Milbank's reassertion of the prominence of Western Christendom. In this section, I suggest that Milbank's opening comments hint that he imagines theology as an Anglo-centric exercise.

In presenting his theological method, Milbank envisions a center-periphery trajectory extending from Europe (and more specifically, Great Britain) outward to the world. In introducing, in September 2008, "eighteen essays . . . written over roughly the past twenty-five years,"[7] Milbank claims

6. Milbank, *The Future of Love*.

7. The beginning of the composition of these essays is coincident with the

that his political theology, "written from a British perspective . . . opens itself out to Continental and North American intellectual influences, as well as to global concerns."[8] I maintain that Milbank's choice of language suggests that he thinks of theology as a British enterprise that, while addressing global concerns, does so from a unilateral perspective and not as a mutually-articulating discourse. It is not inconsequential that Milbank's British theology "opens itself" instead of "being opened" (or some similar action) and even then primarily only to other European sources. While these formulations may seem incidental, Milbank's later invocation of a cultural "elite" spreading aesthetic and ethical formation around the world will buttress my interpretation.

Milbank shifts from situating theology as a geo-inclusionary British project to a self-reflective stance through which he attempts to demarcate his own identity. In self-deprecative fashion, Milbank uses the comments of the "late Texan theologian John Clayton" to fully situate himself within the English theological tradition while simultaneously positioning himself as an "outsider" competent to offer critiques of his tradition. Milbank reminisces:

> He had finally worked out what was "weird" about me: "Most of us, John, are trying to combine German theology with Anglo-Saxon philosophy. A few trendy people go for Continental philosophy as well. But you're doing the opposite—with utter perversity you're trying to combine *British* theology (of all things!) with Continental philosophy—and what is worse, with *French* stuff!"[9]

Milbank's choice of descriptors signals what may be a common contemporary insecurity among theologians of European ancestry and those within Western academic discourse: How can one situate himself as an heir to the tradition while still being appropriately self-aware (a "self-conscious" reading[10])? In Carter's view, this self-reflexive stance is not a position from which the core problems of modernity can be addressed because, due to its supersessionist tendencies, it is fundamentally closed to the influence of others. If Milbank imagines Christian identity as European rather than being tied to Jewish history in a thick sense, it would explain his calisthenics over self-identification. Milbank's work implicitly asks: How can Western theol-

---

Thatcherite-Reaganite conservative resurgence, which may bear important sociological implications for how Milbank views his own theological project to function.

8. Milbank, *The Future of Love*, ix.

9. Ibid., ix.

10. For a definition of a "self-conscious reading," see Brock, *Singing the Ethos of God*, chapter 1.

ogy be self-critical without deposing itself from power? Milbank responds that while Clayton's adulation "is by no means altogether true . . . it contains a grain of truth."[11] This has the net effect of entrenching Milbank in what he calls a "minority report" within "British intellectual history." He belongs to a prophetic minority able to offer an outsider perspective from within.

Milbank subsequently locates himself in an Anglo-Catholic strand of Christian socialism, which he distinguishes from "secular socialism and Hegelianism-Marxism."[12] This approaches the center of Milbank's interests: political and economic theory from an ideological position other than what he deems the modern liberal consensus, whether "right" or "left." He understands his vision of Christian socialism to cut across this polarity by embracing the broad Catholic tradition of economic teaching, thereby being "orthodox" and yet "radical."[13] His concerns are theological only inasmuch as they necessitate an alternate polis in which to enact his sociopolitical vision. This alternative polis is the church (which, in Milbankian discourse, does not reflect the Jewish character of the Faith in any substantive way). As Milbank introduces his "theopolitical" interests, the sole theological category he proposes is "ecclesiology," preceded by "culture and cultural pluralism, government, economics, history" and followed by "pedagogy."[14] If, as Carter will propose, ecclesiology on its own is a dangerous category within which to imagine issues relating to "culture and cultural pluralism," then Milbank's invocation of "pedagogy" as the primary outgrowth of his *polis* may be cause for alarm. In Carter's view, this may be shorthand for imperialism. Carter's reading is further borne out by Milbank's later contention that "what ecclesiology is really all about" is a "structural logic for human society."[15]

Kant and the Modern-Racial Project

If ecclesiology alone is inadequate to challenge race in any significant way, then what doctrinal category should provide the ground for theology as it relates to cultural studies (with which Milbank and Carter are both concerned)? Carter offers Christology as a theological point of reflection sufficient to address the core questions of cultural pluralism. In this section,

11. Milbank, *Future of Love*, x.

12. Ibid., x.

13. Ibid., x–xii.

14. Milbank, *Future of Love*, x. See also Milbank, *Theology and Social Theory*, 382, where his constructive vision of the *altera civitas* is described as being "first and foremost an *ecclesiology*" that is its own "sociology."

15. Milbank, *Theology and Social Theory*, 410.

we will see that for Carter, Kant's rationalized religious Jesus (as ground for modern moral autonomy) functions similarly to Milbank's "virtuous elite" (as ground for the body politic). I read Carter's critique of Kant, the architect of *Aufklarung*, as being his most trenchant diagnosis of modern racial reasoning. In the *Prologue* to *Race*, Carter identifies the Kantian vision of Enlightenment, in which the white body is the teleological "type" of the human, as the soil in which the colonial construction of man as a racial being took root.[16]

Through a close reading of Kant's oeuvre, Carter identifies Kant's central concern as that of philosophical anthropology, or in the words of Kant: "What is man?"[17] While I will later engage Kant directly, at this point I am interested in Carter's reading of Kant. In answer to his own question, Kant proposes to engage "the great drama of religion" by locating an ideal religious figure, the "one shepherd" who will stabilize the cosmopolitical order as an ethical community, a figure who, in the words of Carter, will be "a representation of the species as a whole and thus . . . a cultural reflex, a symbol of its moral development."[18] Drawing from his pietistic Lutheran background, Kant identifies this person as Jesus Christ. In order to claim Christ as the ur-human, and thereby the cultural property of the West, Kant deposes the Judaic Jesus in favor of a rational figure leading a purely moral religion. In the words of Carter: "Kant's language reveals that the modernity he envisioned is not areligious. Nor is it inimical to Christian thought forms. Rather, it redeploys Christian thought forms inside of, indeed, as a cultural reflex of Western civilization."[19] It is with this end in sight that Kant develops his scientific theory of race, which will be the infrastructure buttressing his philosophical anthropology. To square this with our earlier summary of Carter's Foucaultian conclusions, the Kantian vision of humanity as *homo*

16. Carter, *Race*, 5. Carter is clearly referencing knowledge of Jennings' argument, made explicit in *The Christian Imagination*, that the modern conception of biological race had its genesis in the colonial moment as Europeans sought to both describe difference among peoples and to maintain cultural, financial, and political superiority over other peoples. The racialized scale was theologically afforded Europeans by supersessionism, as "the church" (as Western cultural construct) replaced the covenantal reality of Israel and Israel's God, YHWH. Carter accepts this thesis and is concerned with pinpointing the maturation of the racial imagination in modernity, which he finds particularly well–displayed in Kant. While Carter's text was published in 2008 with Jennings' following in 2010, Carter's nod to the day "not too far off" when the pre-Enlightenment matters would be given their due theological consideration shows knowledge of Jennings' thesis and his forthcoming publication. Therefore, the question of which text is genetically first, while remaining open, leans toward Jennings.

17. Ibid., 80.

18. Ibid.

19. Ibid., 81.

politicus and *homo religiosus* is founded upon the conception of humanity as *homo racialis*.[20]

In an essay entitled *Of the Different Human Races*, Kant provides his scientific theory of race, which ends in an improvisation that will prove particularly important for our analysis. Through empirical data resultant from his own powers of observation, Kant informs the reader that there are four race types: white, Negro, Hun, and Hindu.[21] However, two of these race types are the polarities from which all other races are derived. According to Kant, "Negroes and whites are the base races." This ontology is obtained through a rationalistic epistemology intrinsic to white modern man's powers of observation. As Kant would have it, the existence of base races is so profoundly clear that the "reason for assuming [it] is self-evident."[22] What disturbs Kant is that the natural sciences, while being able to discern the way things are through their encyclopedic methodology, cannot provide a *telos* for their observations. They can describe *how* reality is ordered but not *why* it is so. We shall see that one of Milbank's core concerns is a search for a teleological orientation for the *good*, apart from the rationality of the social sciences. This shared question, which is properly a theological question, is that which Kant improvises upon and proceeds to answer through his systematic philosophy.

Kant embarks upon what Carter identifies as the quest for "a teleological orientation of the species."[23] While that teleological orientation is ostensibly toward *Aufklarung*, or Enlightenment, Kant provides clues that his philosophical and sociopolitical order is grounded in a racialized anthropological vision. Kant identifies in the human species certain inner "purposive causes" that are leading humanity to its perfection.[24] While he conjectures that climate may be the means through which racial characteristics are produced, the "purposive" cause for raciation is teleological. Through an evolutionary logic, Kant theorizes that the "lineal root genus" for the species of humans is the white race and that humanity is progressing by, in effect, working out or "spinning off" its imperfections by producing darker races. In the words of Kant as quoted by Carter:

> If we ask with which of the present races [*Rassen*] the first human stock [*Menschenstamm*] might well have had the greatest similarity [*die meiste Ahnlichkeit*], we will presumably—although

20. Ibid.
21. Ibid., 84.
22. Ibid.
23. Ibid., 86.
24. Ibid.

> *without any prejudice* because of the presumptuously *greater perfection of its color* when compared with that of the others [emphasis added]—pronounce favor on whites.[25]

For Kant, Enlightenment is a process of the human species reclaiming its prototype—the white body—and achieving purity through the process of expelling darkness through raciation.

In order to substantiate that this horrific logic is in fact what Kant actually intended, Carter refers to one of Kant's private fragments, the *Reflexionen 1520*. In it, Kant suggests that

> All of the races will be stamped out (Americans and Negroes can't rule themselves. They serve therefore only as slaves), but never that of whites. The stubbornness of the Indians in how they use things is at the root of their problem. This is the reason why they do not melt together with whites. It isn't good that they are interbreeding. The Spaniards in Mexico.[26]

Carter, attending to the German syntax, carefully exegetes this list of propositions. He relates that the term for "stamped out" (*ausrotten*), denotes an internal annihilation, destruction, elimination, or eradication resulting from "limitations that arise from within those races themselves, limitations that cannot be overcome."[27] Carter notes that the phrase "but never that of whites" demonstrates that whites are not subject to the inner decay which is intrinsic to the "races" and which springs from an imbalance of passions. Therefore, for Kant, whites are not properly a "race." Whiteness is both the prototype and the *telos* (theologically speaking: the first and the last, the proton and eschaton) of the human species. Whiteness is that which is universal and is not limited by its own particularity. Blackness, or that which is brought about by the raciation process (and is therefore antipodal to Enlightenment), is that which cannot overcome its own particularity and its own inherent limitations. It is through the process of raciation that whiteness reclaims the teleological orientation for the species. The philosophical and anthropological underpinnings of Enlightenment are fundamentally a racial logic. As Carter explains,

> Consequently, they [the "races of whites"] are not a race in the same way that the other human races have become races. The other races have become races in such a way as to be held hostage to their own particularity. Their particularity as race

25. Ibid., 87.
26. Ibid., 92.
27. Ibid.

groups is excessive or out of balance inasmuch as it aims at only its own particularity. Indeed, they suffer under the entropy of their own particularity: they can't get over themselves. Thus, the racialization process has occurred for the darker races in such a way that their racial existence is an impediment to their human existence, where "human" here stands for the universal.[28]

This is why the prospect of miscegenation so concerns Kant in his private reflections. Interbreeding, blood mixing, and "impure" reciprocity all threaten the progress of the species toward overcoming its limitations, triumphing over its hindering particularities, and achieving universal reason. For Kant, the goal of universality will be achieved primarily through aesthetic and moral education. In *Anthropology from a Pragmatic Point of View*, Kant maintains that human beings must be "educated" into a vision of "the good" society. By being educated into "the arts and sciences," human beings will transcend their material impulses through a process of "self-cultivation," "self-civilization," and "self-moralization," resulting in the ability of the human to climb out of the "crudity of his nature" and into the "progressive organization of citizens of the earth into and toward the species as a system that is cosmopolitically united."[29]

Kant's vision necessitates the leadership of an "elite" group qualified to train others into the aesthetic sensibilities and virtues concordant with such a sociopolitical order. Presumably, this is why Kant identifies the task of "molding and governing human beings" as existing alongside that of "observation" of the way things are.[30] In the *Menschenkunde*, Kant makes clear that while the Americans (Natives) lack passion and cannot receive education, while the Negros (sic) are overcome with passion but can receive training for service, and while the Hindus can be educated in the arts but not the sciences and therefore cannot progress, the "Race of Whites contains within itself all motivations and talents."[31] Enlightenment depends upon a social and vocational "elite" who take it upon themselves to educate the "races" into aesthetics and morality. According to the logic of *Aufklarung*, the great modern drama is that the whites, who embody universal morality and rational religion, will be of service to the rest of humanity by pedagogically aiding in either their progression to subservience or their eradication and decay due to internal imbalance.

28. Ibid., 89.

29. Ibid., 100.

30. Ibid., 98.

31. Ibid., 91.

While Carter's reading of Kant is perhaps unconventional, it seems thus only because the mainstream body of literature surrounding Kant does not seriously probe the racial underpinnings of Enlightenment, preferring instead to focus on philosophical technicalities. Carter is aware that "some will attach different significance to the fact that Kant left these most extreme views out of print and even out of the classroom."[32] Carter admits that it may be tempting to read Kant's personal journals as evidence that his most racist views were tentatively held. However, Carter is persuaded that Kant was quite clear as to the racial nature of his modern philosophical program. Carter cites the Italian political philosopher Domenico Losurdo, who draws attention to Kant's words in a letter of 1766: "Indeed I believe, with the firmest conviction and the utmost satisfaction, many things that I will never have the courage to say, but I will never say anything that I do not believe."[33] And in 1794, Kant reflects that, although authorities may be able to forbid him from "fully revealing his principles," he does not regret "in the least" what he had been "doing thus far."[34] Carter theorizes that Kant's "conclusions . . . regarding the darker races and the vision he has of the destiny of whites" may be "what he was hiding all along, only to be spectrally present in what he publically said."[35] Either way, I am persuaded, given Carter's thesis concerning the racial imagination as existing at some basic level independent of the will, that the intentions of Kant are not of utmost importance. It remains the case that Kant's program, and that of the philosophical project of modernity in general, operated (and continues to operate) within a racialized imagination, even if said imagination has not been consistently expressed in such an overtly racist manner.

Seen in this light, I read *Religion within the Boundaries of Mere Reason* as the elevation of particular cultural ideals over all others.[36] If the power and danger of the sociopolitical order of whiteness is that it masks its own particularity by elevating itself to rational, moral, and aesthetic universality, then limiting religion to reason alone presupposes a particular cultural appropriation of the divine. This is not because Occidental forms of thought are somehow more "rational" than others, but because hidden in language about "rationality" are suppositions about what constitutes rationality. In *Religion*, Kant's philosophical anthropology is on display as he finds the distinction between the "animality" and the "humanity" of a human being

32. Ibid., 401 n. 29.

33. Ibid.

34. Ibid.

35. Ibid.

36. Kant, *Religion within the Boundaries of Mere Reason*.

to be in "rationality."[37] Kant finds that a "savage" and "bestial" nature exists in humanity which must be overcome through "personality." Given Kant's treatment, in the *Menschenkunde*, of the "base races" and their respective "vices" or "virtues," the racialized hierarchy at work in *Religion* begins to be apparent. Kant assigns relative rationality, and thereby humanity, along a racial continuum. He uses the "savagery" of the natives of "New Zealand," the "Navigator Islands," and parts of "America" as the comparative counterweight to the "civilized state" of Europeans.[38] While Kant's point in this passage is that all people, including "civilized" peoples, have a "propensity to evil," he nonetheless makes this point by utilizing the trope of native savagery as the antithesis to European civilization.

In *Religion*, Kant exegetes biblical texts about Jesus Christ as symbolizing the moral advancement and self-actualization of the human subject. In this sense, Kant's program is an anticipation of the modern discipline of religious studies and has significant resonances in Milbank's "elite." For Kant, Jesus Christ is not Savior in any thick sense of the term, but is rather the "prototype" for emulation.[39] It is the "universal human duty to *elevate* ourselves to this ideal of moral perfection." Kant's ethics do not leave room for grace. On the contrary, "it is essential to know *what a human being has to do himself* in order to become worthy" of divine "assistance."[40] For Kant, the idea of "another being above" man is unnecessary, as it is "morality" itself which "inevitably leads to religion."[41] Hence, ethics is understood as the human ability to attain a virtuous ideal, a trajectory not dissimilar to certain strands of virtue ethics. While it is beyond the scope of this chapter to comment upon all the threads I have identified in Kant, several of these themes were hinted at in chapter 1 in my analysis of Carter's relationship to Long. Several more loose ends will be tied up as I engage Carter's critique of Milbank's Anglo-Catholic retrieval. In short, Kant's anthropology bears striking similarities to the rationalistic conception of the *imago Dei* within the Anglo-Catholic tradition. In addition, Kant's ethic of emulation, his invocation of virtue, and his role for the aristocracy in aesthetic and moral education are echoed in the virtue ethic of Radical Orthodoxy. Kant maintains that "only common morality is needed to understand the essentials of [his] text."[42] However, as has been noted in critiques of natural law tradi-

---

37. Ibid., 50–51.
38. Ibid., 56–57.
39. Ibid., 80.
40. Ibid., 72.
41. Ibid., 33–35.
42. Ibid., 41.

tions, "common morality" is very rarely "common" outside of a particular cultural milieu.

In contending that Kant's philosophical anthropology is dependent upon Christ as "cultural reflex," Carter's theological diagnosis of the supersessionism of modernity becomes apparent. Kant explicitly decouples Jesus Christ's identity from his Jewish personhood. As Carter relates, Kant traverses several steps in achieving this goal. First, Kant identifies his perfected white race with the term "remnant race," evoking recognition of the Pauline language of Romans 9–11, thereby casting whites as the new Israel, the new chosen people.[43] Second, Jews become the contagion within (as contrasted with the contagion without, i.e. the darker peoples who become colonial subjects), a "negative racial other" that stands in for all nonwhite flesh.[44] What began in Kant as a white/black racial binary ends in his *Anthropology* as a white flesh vs. Jewish flesh opposition. Third, because of his linking of race and religion, Kant (like Dohm, a compatriot *Aufklarer*) must sever Christianity from its Jewish roots in order to preserve it as European cultural property. As Carter relates, the "rationalization" of Christianity means its "dejudaization."[45] Kant proffers a Marcionite view of the God of Israel as a petty tyrant and the Jewish law as a heteronomous force standing opposed to the autonomous reasoning subject. He suggests a rational reinterpretation of the Law (Torah) into laws of *virtue* and a transmutation of Jesus into a figure who represents what humanity "can or should make of itself."[46] As Kant reads it, Paul was able to transcend his covenantal (racial) being through an application of the autonomous and transcendental spirit of the law of reason as opposed to the heteronomous letter of the law of YHWH. Fourth and finally, in *Religion*, Kant completes his supersessionist project by identifying Jesus as, in Carter's summary quotation of Kant, "'the personified idea of the good principle' that has 'come down to us.'"[47] By presenting Jesus as an idea for "emulation," the scandal of his particularity has ceased,

43. Carter, *Race*, 81.

44. Ibid., 104. Within this white/Jew binary, Kant parses the "white type" by suggesting that among the European races, Germans are the perfect balance between the warring French and English and are therefore positioned to lead the way to the perfection of the race. This is in part because of their "modesty" (102). In this sense, Kant provides an early impetus for the binary "contagion" logic deployed almost two centuries later by the Third Reich. His definition of the *Volk* as being characterized by the "innate, natural character" of their "blood mixture" is a philosophical systematization which bears certain resonances with Spanish *limpieza de sangre* laws from several centuries earlier.

45. Ibid., 106.

46. Ibid., 107.

47. Ibid., 114.

his covenantal heritage has been severed, and his co-option as white religious property has been completed.

The final piece in the puzzle is for Kant to graft Jesus into the Western classical tradition. He accomplishes this in *Religion* by explaining that the Jews had recognized within their own people "all the evils of a hierarchical constitution," a recognition that was afforded by their interaction with "the Greek sages' moral doctrines on freedom," resulting in their ripeness for the arrival of Jesus Christ, whose wisdom embodied an even higher form of purity than "the previous philosophers."[48] Kant goes so far as to maintain that the Jews were not "capable" of being motivated by anything other than "the goods of this world," wishing "to be ruled by rewards and punishments" related to "external compulsion."[49] It was the "sudden . . . appearance" of Jesus Christ-qua-philosopher, coupled with the preparative work of Hellenistic philosophy, which had "gradually gained influence over them," challenging the Jewish "slavish mind." In the Kantian moment, Christ's Jewish flesh is superseded and his divinity is interpreted as his continuity with the Greek tradition of moral inquiry. Kant's ethics have no room for obedience to a living Word, instead emphasizing participation in the Western classical tradition of virtuous philosophical reflection. In modernity, Jesus is no longer Jewish; he is Greek. In his own words, Kant's project is complete: "The euthanasia of Judaism is pure moral religion."[50]

The Guiding, Virtuous, Elite

In this section, I will demonstrate similarities between Milbank's and Kant's ethics and their reflections on identity. Again, while this reading may seem counterintuitive, I am considering how the non-white body is marginalized in similar ways in the works of each scholar. While Milbank does not approach the bald racist rhetoric of Kant, his reflections on the pedagogical mandate of the Occidental elite is degrading to non-white modes of being. By recognizing these similarities, I do not intend to overemphasize their convergence; there are important differences between the two. Whereas Kant's deontological ethic focuses on the moral autonomy of the individual, Milbank criticizes the manner in which modernity is disconnected from a communal ethical tradition. Whereas Kant's philosophical idealism leads him to posit the existence of propositional universal moral imperatives, Milbank is a theological realist who is attempting to reclaim something

48. Ibid., 116.

49. Kant, *Religion*, 95.

50. Carter, *Race*, 119.

akin to a Thomist account of virtue. Whereas Kant had recreated Jesus as the Western ur-human, Milbank offers a group of Occidental elites for emulation. While these differences are not inconsequential, I propose that Milbank's solutions are little better than Kant's in addressing theological questions related to race in the modern world. Carter's work suggests that Kant's Jesus and Milbank's *ecclesia* are best understood as cultural reflexes that reassert the prominence of the European subject.

At the helm of Milbank's *ecclesia* is the "guiding virtuous elite,"[51] whom he refers to as the "'guardians' of virtue, the virtuosos of *charisma*."[52] Milbank identifies the elite as chivalrous "heroes" who are both "Christian 'pastors'" and Platonic shepherd-guardians. Milbank contends that such "sacramental ordination and anointed monarchy" is for the sake of "equity," albeit an equity monitored by the "guardians." Milbank's elite follow the pattern of Jesus Christ, who rules at "the summit of the *ecclesia*" like "Richard the Lionheart in Sherwood Forest."[53] This Jesus sets the "pattern that is followed by the Church hierarchy which mediates his authority."[54] I contend that Milbank's Jesus is similar to Kant's Jesus in that he is reclaimed as a Western hero. Neither the Kantian nor the Milbankian Christ is Jewish in a significant way. In other words, the particularity of Jesus is underemphasized in order to assert his universality. In doing so, Jesus is grafted into Western narratives; he becomes Western property and is offered back to the world as such. In *Theology and Social Theory*, Milbank will later maintain that the "very essence" of Christianity is found in its "break with Judaism," making possible its universal scope.[55]

The contemporary hero-type that Milbank utilizes to illustrate his virtuous church leader and guardian is Batman, the *Dark Knight*.[56] Milbank contends that in a contemporary "secular" milieu, the pastor-guardians may be "mocked and invisible," lacking the "glamour of obvious 'honor,'"

51. Milbank, *The Future of Love*, xii.

52. Ibid., xi.

53. Ibid., xiii.

54. Ibid.

55. Milbank, *Theology and Social Theory*, 390. Making such a strong distinction between Israel and the Church leads Milbank to conflate Christianity as a "religion" and "social grouping" and to measure other forms of human expression against it: "Christianity's universalist claim that incorporation into the Church is indispensable for salvation assumes that other religions and social groupings, however virtuous–seeming, were, in their own terms alone, finally on the path of damnation. In this fashion, a gigantic claim to be able to read, criticize, say what is going on in other human societies, is absolutely integral to the nature of the Christian Church, which itself claims to exhibit the exemplary form of human community."

56. Milbank, *The Future of Love*, xiii.

and acting as "hidden 'outlaw[s].'"[57] Milbank's characterization of the "elite" tends to invoke the masculine European archetype of chivalry, honor, and service who, in the face of the forces of darkness, benevolently gives of himself for the salvation of others. Whereas the Dark Knight is a vigilante who sacrifices himself in what Milbank calls the Platonic "noble lie," the "guiding elite" serve by offering instruction in the virtues of the Anglo-Catholic theological and Greek philosophical traditions. Milbank defines his *ecclesia* as "human society" and "eschatologically the entire human race" while calling for it to be governed by elites inculcated in Western virtue.[58]

Milbank's assumption that the "guiding elite" will be Occidental figures tasked with engaging the world can be clearly demonstrated in his appropriation of Samuel Coleridge. According to his essay *Divine* Logos *and Human Communication: A Recuperation of Coleridge*, the significance of the Incarnation is that the divine *Logos* is continually communicated through the "development of human civilizations" under the tutoring of

> a class of inspired people who can be variously considered as poets, prophets, philosophers, or legislators; a class which existed most perfectly in antiquity in the times of a precise coincidence of all these roles, but a class whose function must be constantly revived if true human culture is to continue.[59]

It is this "class" of "philosopher-poets" who "establish a process of communication, of human interchange" that ensures "the cultural becoming of the human race."[60] Milbank maintains that through "Coleridgean aesthetics," a "providentially guided process leading to the highest possible knowledge" will encourage "primitive human beings" to freely respond to "a primary divine language" which will enable "their future growth."[61] The philosopher-bards, whether the leaders of "the Christian Church" or the "secular prophets, the clerisy . . . the learned class," must bring "all wealth-producing and technologically innovative processes . . . under a paternalist surveillance," thereby reducing the market "to the minimum."[62] The learned class must consider education to be "the most primary political dimension," a dimension more important than democracy because "free agreement" is

57. Ibid., xiii.
58. Ibid., xiv.
59. Ibid., 4–5.
60. Ibid.
61. Ibid., 5.
62. Ibid., 21.

inadequate in the face of the need for "the constant inheritance of patterns of life and thought that are not, in the first place, chosen."[63]

Milbank finds the genius of Coleridge in that he "sought a single doctrine embracing both a metaphysical theology and a theory of language and literature."[64] For Milbank, this means that "communication" is a "political matter" that is in a state of "constant interweaving" with "aesthetic-cultural and philosophical-cum-religious" concerns. Milbank's *Logos* is a universalizing order encompassing aesthetics, linguistics, philosophy, theology, politics, and religion. It is this sociopolitical order which Carter refers to with the shorthand "whiteness."

It is hard to escape the implication that Milbank envisions a semi-Charlemagnian social order:

> The earthly city is valid insofar as it serves the heavenly, and from the outset Christianity has modified the role of the political ruler in a "pastoral" direction (sometimes for ill as well as good). He becomes more a kind of ecclesial pastor of material affairs—which always have an implication for our salvation.[65]

While Milbank recognizes that such a political order has often been problematic, he nonetheless envisions a social order in which Western Christian leaders will assume theological and political leadership for the purpose of the aesthetic and ethical progress of the world. Milbank's incipient Christology becomes visible as he explicates his ecclesiology. Milbank's Christ functions much like a Kantian *universal religious figure* to be emulated by the "guiding elite" in their governance of human affairs.

Whereas Kant's Christ displayed a universal moral ideal for emulation, Milbank's Christ is the universal *Logos* incarnated through Occidental aesthetics and ethics. While a living deity is not necessary in Kant's schema, Milbank's system affirms active divine agency but binds it to a particular group of people charged with the expanse of human civilization and the cultural development of "primitive" peoples. Kant's Enlightenment purposed to direct the races to maturation; Milbank's Anglo-Catholic retrieval promises to "guide" the "human race" to its "cultural becoming." For Kant it was the "race" of whites that were the teleological ordering for the "species"; for Milbank it is the Anglo tradition which provides a theological *telos* for all peoples. While important philosophical differences remain, the Christologies assumed in both Kant and Milbank are supersessionist; both function

63. Ibid., 21–22.
64. Ibid., 3.
65. Ibid., xv.

so as to deny the covenantal particularity of Jesus by co-opting him as the ideal Western figure. Milbank's Christology is more Kantian than Nazarene.

Milbank proposes a threefold vocation for the "guiding virtuous elite," motivated by what he calls beneficence and love: One, Milbank suggests that the "aristocratic"/"monarchic" class assume the education of others. Two, Milbank envisions the ruling "elite" as the stewards of economic resources, tasked with ensuring just and charitable distribution to the "lower" classes. Three, Milbank explains that the elite will "naturally" be the determiners of the historical record. This threefold vocation will ensure that the most virtuous (the "few") will be the guardians of "the real universal . . . 'the common good'" on behalf of the "many."[66] Modeled on the Levitical ruling class, the "historians" will "naturally" be designated "the legislators."[67]

The paternalism of Milbank's early positions will be seen to operate in more muted fashion throughout *Theology and Social Theory*. In the preface to *The Future of Love*, written in late 2008, Milbank states that he has "deliberately eliminated all that [he] would now renounce" from his essays so that the corpus of his thought is able to stand as a unified whole.[68] Milbank attempts to blunt the imperialist overtones implied in his writings by proclaiming that "[any] atavistic dangers in this form of thought are, at this stage, obviated by the eschewing of nationalism, the political state, and all forms of violent coercion."[69] Milbank's rejection of the violence of the nation-state gives way to a "peaceful" aesthetic and economic order into which all peoples may be assimilated. For Milbank, if the "Protestant" nature of the contemporary *ecclesia* and *politia*, with its "opposition to high culture," can be resisted, the "suppressed British Catholic past" will be resurrected.[70] His vision of economics is much like his *ecclesia*: "the corporation based upon Christian principles" must be "like the units of 'feudalism' . . . in the Middle Ages."[71] While Milbank recognizes that his account is "bound of course to raise charges of fascism," he explains that "fascism involves a secular cult of state, race, or military power."[72] If Milbank defines fascism as a *secular*

66. Ibid., xii.

67. Ibid., 6.

68. Ibid., xi.

69. Ibid., 8.

70. Ibid., xix.

71. Ibid., xvii. After he envisions "Christian principles" creating economic entities that "must" function like the feudalism of the Middle Ages, he attempts to temper his forthrightness with the parenthetical phrase: "though that is a mis-description." But even it the "units of 'feudalism'" is an inelegant way of phrasing his vision, he can think of no other description to more accurately convey his nostalgia.

72. Ibid., xviii.

cult of race, then Radical Orthodoxy could be read as something akin to a *religious* cult of race.

A close read of Carter encourages the interpretation that Radical Orthodoxy's tendency toward nostalgia could be, at least in part, a lament about the demise of the Church-State order, which is tied into whiteness in the ways I have enumerated. While Milbank's reclamation of theological orthodoxy over against an ideology of secularism is a welcome development, his theology's reenactment of whiteness raises more problems than it solves. I read Milbank's reclamation of the theological underpinnings of Anglo-Catholic society as evincing anxiety about the position of the white male body in a climate of "secular" multiculturalism.[73] This theological vision renders Anglo and Christian functionally synonymous and implies that nonwhite and secular are functionally synonymous. In light of Carter's identification of the link between *homo religiosus* and *homo racilias*, Milbank's use of "secular" may function much like "heathen," "benighted," or "dark" did in time past. Milbank's theology, while correctly questioning the philosophical basis of secularism, encourages a paternalistic soft imperialism by reenacting a peaceful regime of whiteness extended through aesthetics and ethics.

Breaking Free

Divergence and Convergence: The Non-White Intellectual in Modernity

The analysis I have offered so far interprets Carter as offering a strong, albeit somewhat implicit, critique of Milbank's counter-narrative to modernity, which Carter reads as reinscribing British aesthetic, ethical, and pedagogical imperialism. In addition to this divergence, I have also hinted that Carter's account converges methodologically with Milbank's in several ways, primarily through the use of counter-narrative and his resistance to dialectic. In this section, I will suggest that this methodological convergence is due to what Carter calls the "veritable conundrum of the black intellectual

---

73. This reading is buttressed by the reality that the Church as body of Christ worldwide is by not under threat of fading away. Rather, the Western church is losing control of the political levers of power. This does not mean that the West as Empire is declining. Overt monarchical power structures have simply morphed into what Foucault calls "biopower," becoming more effective in surveillance, discipline, and punishment exerted constantly upon the most minute dimensions of human existence. See Foucault, *Discipline and Punish*, or his many essays and lectures on power/biopower. For a popular contemporary read of how overt systems of social control have morphed into less visible disciplinary power structures, see Alexander, *The New Jim Crow*.

in modernity."[74] While I read Carter as redeploying the anti-modern polemic of Radical Orthodoxy, I interpret this move as a subversion of the methodology that shaped his earlier theological thought.

I suggest that Carter's trajectory is related to Milbank in three interconnected ways: One, Carter is breaking free from the intellectual gravitational pull of Radical Orthodoxy; two, he finds aspects of Milbank's methodology to be useful for his own counter-narrative to white modernity; and three, he is intentionally utilizing the retrieval sensibilities of postmodern white theology to subvert its nostalgia. It is as if Carter is employing the Pauline technique of assuming the terms of his interlocutor in order to call opposing assumptions into question on the basis of their own internal logic.[75] While engaging in an anti-modern polemic, Carter is shining a mirror on Western virtue-based reclamation projects to demonstrate that there are marginalized groups who have better enacted an *ecclesia* potent to subvert the regnant sociopolitical order. Carter finds early Afro-Christian autobiography to be an authentic mimesis of the Judaic story of liberation from oppression and a more faithful retelling of Christian history than the triumphalist rhetoric connected to narratives of manifest destiny. By using the shape of black American Christianity as a counter-narrative to white stories of America as the New Israel, Carter is utilizing, to subversive effect, methodology akin to Milbank's. Whether or not this methodology holds the fullest promise for rendering whiteness impotent will become clearer as differences between the arguments of Carter and Jennings are enumerated. While I will contend that Jennings' narrative of joining more fully resists whiteness than Carter's counter-narrative of the iconographic nature of black flesh, I maintain that Carter successfully exposes the pseudotheological machinations of whiteness, thereby setting the stage for further conversations to be had and further study to be completed in line with the genetic tale he and Jennings are telling.

Like Milbank, Carter identifies a counter-culture who walks in the footsteps of prior theological sensibilities retrieved from other points in Christian tradition (e.g. Milbank's invocation of a modern Augustinian *Civitas Dei*). Unlike Milbank, for whom this counter-society is best embodied in contemporary Christian socialists who adhere to a broad tradition of Catholic economic and social teaching and classically Western philosophical virtue, for Carter this group is antebellum African American Christians whose theological sensibilities intuit the anti-gnostic treatises of Irenaeus, the abolitionist theological anthropology of Gregory of Nyssa, and the "anticolonialist" Incarnational theology of Maximus the Confessor. Carter's

74. Carter, *Race*, 142.
75. See 1 Cor 15:29.

intellectual vision, like Milbank's, shuns modern dialectical intellectual arrangements for a retrieval of a Christian counter-narrative. Carter does not
read the "tradition" as a unified whole; he contends that many of the identity formulations suggested by both pre-modern orthodoxy and modern
liberalism must be thought beyond. I suggest that Carter is perhaps more
indebted to the "tradition" than he would like to admit. However, I am also
persuaded by him that there is a problematic tendency in retrieval projects
to read the tradition as a monolithic whole. He reminds us that such a view
tends to silence other voices, both historical (Eastern iconography) and
contemporary ("black" theological thought).

I suggest that the dual nature of the relationship of Carter's work to
that of Milbank (divergence and convergence) is in large part due to the
time lapse between the publication of his doctoral thesis (2001) and the
publication of *Race* (2008), which Carter explains was "literally rewritten,
as they say, from the ground up" over a "long evolution."[76] Carter's thought
is progressing away from that of Milbank, whose intellectual universe was
that in which Carter initially attempted to imagine the theological problem
of race. This evolution leaves the reader with the task of "reading between
the lines" in excavating Carter's argument, which is the interpretive method
prescribed by Carter as he approaches Hammon, Douglass, and Lee.[77] While
I am not contending that Carter's work has been subject to the same level of
"white" censorship encountered in antebellum African American autobiography, I am suggesting that the nonwhite intellectual in modernity is often
forced to be multilingual in ways that the white intellectual is not. Whereas
the white intellectual has often assumed a perspective from "above," it has
often been necessary for the nonwhite intellectual to be well-versed in both
regnant discourses and marginalized linguistic worlds so as to offer an alternative (thus the multilingual character of "blackness" as opposed to the
more monolinguistic nature of "whiteness"). There is often a need in the
academy to package the "black message" (read: any reading that subverts
whiteness) in a "white envelope."[78] It is reasonable to assume that Carter
is existentially aware of the difficulties intrinsic to this requisite theological improvisation. The interpreter of Carter would do well to employ this
methodology of subversive reading in interpreting Carter (as he utilizes this
methodology himself).

The purpose of this brief excursus is neither to attempt an "historical-
critical" analysis of Carter's text nor is it to psychologize Carter's reflections;

76. Carter, *Race*, v.
77. Ibid., 257–73.
78. Ibid., 267.

my assumption is that we must take the text as we have received it. At the same time, Carter's text reveals that his thought has evolved, and a read of his doctoral dissertation suggests several ways in which that evolution has taken place.[79] This evolution will be explored throughout the next two sections.

Raboteau and "Pushing Beyond" Milbank

I have maintained that Carter finds the modern philosophical infrastructure of the religious academy complicit in the construction of race. At the same time, because Carter agrees with Jennings that late medieval scholasticism provided a theological impetus for colonization, he is wary about theological projects that center on retrievals of the Anglo-Catholic tradition as reclamations of orthodoxy. In other words, Carter is an heir of both orthodoxy and liberation theology but finds neither alone sufficient to address the modern problem of race (nor does he necessarily find them to be dialectically oppositional). This is why Carter, like Milbank, uses an anti-modern polemic against the religious academy while, like Cone, he criticizes theology for its failure to discern the tragedy of racialization. In this section I will demonstrate Carter's convergence with the methodology of Milbank through his use of Raboteau while in the next section I will demonstrate Carter's divergence with Milbank through his use of Cone. At the same time, I am pushing toward Carter's constructive account of the Jewishness of Jesus presented through his iconographic Christology and Maximian ontology of love. Carter's constructive account "pushes beyond" Milbank.

As I explicated in chapter 1, Carter reads the later Raboteau's "theology of history"[80] as his "signal contribution in showing how black religion generally and Afro-Christianity particularly disrupt the logic of modern racial reasoning."[81] Raboteau (and by appropriation Carter) maintains that it was identification with the Exodus of biblical Israel that empowered early Afro-Christians to resist the mythology of Manifest Destiny in which America was the New Israel, the "Promised Land of milk and honey."[82] It is here

79. See Carter's University of Virginia PhD dissertation of the same name, "Race: A Theological Account." Carter appears to have been initially more optimistic about "patristic Christology" alone being able to criticize "a distressing aporia in African American religious studies and theology" (iv). While neither renouncing orthodoxy nor Chalcedon, Carter has since recognized the ways in which both orthodoxy and liberalism have been carriers of the modern virus of racialization.

80. Carter, *Race*, 149.

81. Ibid., 126.

82. Ibid., 147.

that Carter's counter-narrative most closely resembles the methodology of Radical Orthodoxy: The reclamation of the Christian story, embodied in a particular faith community *as the people of God*, is the answer to resisting the dominant social order. We shall see that while Carter does not end with such a unilateral formulation, he utilizes this methodology to subvert the Anglo-Christian narrative.

Carter momentarily appears to vacillate between denouncing the supersessionism of whiteness and canonizing a similar (albeit arguably more authentic) impulse in early black Christian faith. He does so by acknowledging that "differences of interpretation" about historical material are "always filtered through the consciousness (and unconsciousness) of the specific intellectual."[83] As Carter quotes Raboteau, "The conflicting claims upon history made by the search of different communities for meaning raises the issue of whose story it is that history tells."[84] As Carter puts it, white America told "the story of Israel . . . so badly" so as to "constitute itself as a nation, as a body politic . . . to the exclusion of others . . . chiefly to the exclusion of those raced as non-white generally and black particularly."[85] Carter's argument is that black Christians of early America told the story of Israel in a more authentic fashion. It could be contended that in much the same way as Milbank's Anglo-Catholic retrieval is an insufficient substitute for a theology of the proton and eschaton, so Carter's retrieval sensibilities problematically substitute antebellum Afro-Christianity for the theological centrality of the people of Israel as *the* people for all peoples.

At the same time, however, as has been noted by Thurman and Cone, it is reasonable to contend that there are certain communities which more faithfully embody the narrative of Christological (and thereby Judaic) existence, namely those of the oppressed and subjugated. In reference to early African American Christians as Israel, Cone has noted,

> Like white American theology, black thought on Christianity has been influenced by its social context. But unlike white theologians, who spoke to and for the culture of the ruling class, black people's religious ideas were shaped by the cultural and political existence of the victims in North America. Unlike Europeans who immigrated to this land to escape from tyranny, Africans came in chains to serve a nation of tyrants.[86]

83. Ibid.
84. Ibid., 147–48.
85. Ibid., 148.
86. Cone, *God of the Oppressed*, 49.

Carter is undoubtedly correct that the reality of African slaves in cruciform bondage more authentically exhibits the soteriological trajectory of YHWH and his Messiah than does the existence of slave-masters particularly and the objectifying sociopolitical order of whiteness generally. Yet it remains the case that such a distinction necessitates a continuous struggle to determine whose historical mythology best tells the story of Israel, a struggle Carter has called the "right to be hegemon." As dubious as the founders of the United States' claims to be the New Israel may be, especially in the light of their subsequent subjugation of peoples of color and genocide of the natives of the land, my analysis in chapter 1 suggested that the *telos* of African American slaves *as* the biblical Israel may have contributed to an essentialization of blackness as oppressed and impoverished flesh (as can be seen in Cone), and thereby *subject* of whiteness. If that is the case, competing mythologies surrounding unilateral identification with Israel may define blackness vis-à-vis whiteness. While a counter-identification with Israel may help render apparent the falsehood of whiteness, Carter's counter-genealogy is not the theological *telos* toward which his work is pointing.

Carter's counter-culture methodology is strikingly similar to Milbank's four-fold emphasis, in *Theology and Social Theory*, on "counter-history," "counter-ethics," "counter-ontology," and "counter-Kingdom."[87] The problem with such a way of framing community is that a counter-culture can be categorized as *counter* only inasmuch as it takes its identity cues from a dominant culture. "Black" faith as "counter" faith leaves whiteness as the normalizing pole. If Carter's thesis of *being* as iconographic is appropriated and lived into, it will be recognized that, while certain communities may be comparatively better incarnations of the salvific trajectory of Israel, the modern racial imaginary will be resisted only through a realization of God's election of the particular people Israel, whose story is the theological center of history into which all peoples (including black, white, and brown) are grafted.

Carter seems to anticipate the difficulty his counter-narrative presents for his central claim as he maintains that "[t]he identification between persons of African descent in America and the people Israel avoids the modernist problem of supersessionism because that identity is mediated through the worship of the Jew, Jesus of Nazareth."[88] The immediacy of whiteness with Israel is supersessionist while the immediacy of early African American Christianity with Israel is not. This places Carter in the position of having to explain how persons of African descent were worshipping Jesus as a

---

87. Milbank, *Theology and Social Theory*, 383.
88. Carter, *Race*, 148–49.

Jew while white worship was directed toward a different Christ: the "cultural reflex" Christ. While Carter neither explicitly responds to these apparent difficulties, nor offers particulars as to how the worship of Jesus by "persons of African descent in America" is to be understood as Jewish, he does give a promising hint as to the political shape of a non-supersessionist ecclesiology. Carter suggests that both struggles for liberation and the contours of worship provide an opportunity for living into the life of the Jewish Jesus. Carter's first answer (liberation) is more typically Conian while his second answer (worship) is more typically Milbankian. Therefore, he is pushing beyond both.

It is in "pushing beyond" Milbank that Carter aligns himself with Raboteau, offering the "ecstasy of worship" as a paradigm for a satisfactory political ecclesiology.[89] Raboteau maintains that it was in the ecstasy of worship that black Christians made a "connection so immediate" that they "became the children of Israel" and thereby "traveled dry-shod through the Red Sea," witnessing Pharoah's army drowned and entering into the promised land of freedom and deliverance. Carter presents the power of the worship experience as connecting peoples with the God whose saving acts in history liberate the oppressed and the oppressor and draw them toward each other as formerly racialized and oppositional bodies are grafted into the non-racialized flesh of the Jewish Jesus. It is this experience of which I have been given the grace to have a foretaste in my local community. It is this experience that Carter offers for all people, as they together constitute the body of Jesus Christ, who "in his particularity is a communal person, the ground of a full-orbed body politic."[90] While modernity created a Jesus-as-Western-cultural-reflex, oppressed black Christians lived into the story of God's oppressed chosen people by ecstatically identifying with Israel through worship of her Messiah. It is this worship, and not the worship of whiteness, into which the biblical narrative invites all peoples. In this sense, authentic Christian worship is "black" worship. By using Raboteau's historical analysis, Carter redirects a Milbankian counter-culture sensibility toward realization in a cosmopolitan community.

Another methodological tendency of Milbank's that Carter utilizes and subverts is his proposal to "inhabit" an "aesthetic theory of iconic beauty."[91] Carter's aesthetic offers "black existence and black faith" as an icon for "the eternal Logos" and a "disruption of the colonizing gaze of race."[92] Whereas

89. Ibid., 148.
90. Ibid., 154.
91. Ibid., 127.
92. Ibid., 127, 152.

Milbank's Christology led him to posit a universal *Logos* communicated in a Coleridgian aesthetic embodied in Occidental elites, Carter's Christology offers an aesthetic of iconographic and translucent blackness as a path out of racialized identity. Thirdly, Carter utilizes retrieval sensibilities as he draws parallels between the Christocentric shape of early Afro-Christian faith and "the vibrancy of Christian communities in Africa in the apostolic and patristic epoch of the church."[93] Carter appropriates Raboteau's contention that "African spirituality *foreshadowed* ancient Christianity," making it later possible to, in the words of Carter, "reclaim . . . Christianity itself as an African religion." As Raboteau frames it, this reclamation was accomplished through an "[i]dentification with Israel" that "gave the slaves a communal identity as special, divinely favored people."[94] Carter's iconographic aesthetic and his reclamation sensibility demonstrate similarities with the theological methodology of Radical Orthodoxy. Whereas Milbank's aesthetics reenact Occidental hegemony, Carter's aesthetics attempt to disrupt the regnant order through the iconic significance of the black body.

Milbank and Carter both articulate an iconographic theory of aesthetics that challenges modern dialecticism through reclamation of patristic Christian theological insights by a counter-cultural ecclesial group most faithfully embodying the biblical narrative. The decisive difference is that Carter more effectively identifies Israel, not the Gentile church, as the center of God's saving activity in the world. Whereas for Milbank the "Christian counter-history . . . fulfils a counter-history and counter-ontology already in part imagined by Plato and Aristotle,"[95] for Carter early African American spirituality "entered into the body of Israel and into Israel's covenant with YHWH," in order to "imagine and live into a history of Exodus."[96] Carter's analysis suggests that reclamation projects are only a first step in disrupting the order of things, which is why he closes his reflections on Raboteau with an eschatological vision of unity in the body politic of Jesus Christ. Carter employs retrieval methodology as a reminder that Christian mutuality cannot be achieved through the theological imagination of whiteness, which

93. Ibid., 151.

94. Ibid., 148, 151, 152.

95. Milbank, *Theology and Social Theory*, 326, 390. While Milbank does not fully equate his "Christian counter-history" with heroic Greek society, the distinction is quite minor. Milbank claims that, in addition to "fulfill[ing]" and "perpetuat[ing]" the Greek philosophical legacy, his Christian counter-history "breaks with" it. Nonetheless, he lauds this joint legacy for being "a single *Western* history of 'ethics'" and an "'aristocratic' republic" to which we must "return . . . in the first place" before we can return to "the *Civitas Dei*."

96. Carter, *Race*, 149.

tends to separate the universal Christ of faith from the particular Jesus of salvation history. Carter suggests that the "now and not yet" of salvation history must look something like the tenacious biblical faith and ecstatic worship courageously embodied in the mothers and fathers of New World Afro-Christian faith. This allows him to subvert the whiteness of Radical Orthodoxy and present black faith as an icon of the divine. It is this faith which holds the promise of rendering "the pseudotheological backbone of whiteness . . . broken for the sake of the redemption *of us all*."[97] It is this vision that Carter concludes is properly theological:

> Here is the moment of transformative possibility ensconced within New World Afro-Christian faith. The borders of its Christological and Trinitarian economy of being in the world are made to embrace, engage, and thereby transfigure through struggle the political economy in which it found itself. In so doing, faith began to weaken modernity's discourse and pseudotheology of race. It opened up a new disposition on history. Thus, far from being anti-historical, faith became history's *telos*—or better, a realization, even if not yet a thoroughgoing one, of the eschaton. Faith bears the fullness of history and is shown to be fraught with burden, struggle, and fulfillment in its participation in the fullness of time. Faith, thus, "confirms and completes the experience [of history] by reminding us that there are no aliens, no others, but only sisters and brothers." The journey of history and faith . . . is the search for transformed social relations, the anticipation of and yet continued quest for a different way of being in the world.[98]

While Carter's counter-narrative of Afro-Christian faith suggests a lingering Milbankian tendency, his constructive eschatological and ecclesial vision maintains hope for a new body politic that affirms the various particularities of Gentile existence while uniting them together to the Jewish body of Jesus Christ. Carter's use of Raboteau's historical method and his methodological convergence with Radical Orthodoxy are employed subversively for the purpose of pushing beyond Milbank.

Cone and the *Particular* Ground of Being

I have suggested that Carter's appropriation of Raboteau's historical narrative demonstrates convergence with Milbank and subverts Radical

97. Ibid., 156, italics mine.
98. Ibid., 155.

Orthodoxy's counter-history. In this section, I contend that Carter's use of Cone most clearly demonstrates his divergence from Milbank. Cone's concrete Christology allows Carter to offer a critique of Milbank's incipient abstract Christology. Carter read Kant's rationalized religion as exhibiting a similar Christological abstraction.

As I maintained in chapter 1, Carter draws on the early Cone's Barthian notion of the concreteness of Being, which Cone refers to as "the categorical . . . absolute, qualitative difference between God and the creature."[99] Cone's dialectical account is held in tension by his focus on the Incarnation, which he reads as a particular revelation of divine universality. As Carter quotes Cone:

> Christianity begins and ends with the man Jesus—his life, death, and resurrection. He is the Revelation, the special disclosure of God to man, revealing who God is and what his purpose for man is. In short, Christ is the essence of Christianity . . . In contrast to many religions, Christianity revolves around a Person, without whom its existence ceases to be . . . According to Barth, all theological talk about God, man, church, etc. must inevitably proceed from Jesus Christ, who is the sole criterion for every Christian utterance. To talk of God or of man without first talking about Jesus Christ is to engage *in idle, abstract words which have no relation to the Christian experience of revelation.*[100]

Carter reads Milbank's implicit Christology as overly abstract and as minimizing the concrete Jewishness of Jesus. By engaging ecclesiology, political theory, economics and pedagogy without satisfactorily stressing the particularity of Christ, Milbank's Christology tends to collapse into the sustenance and furtherance of particular forms of white culture. I have maintained that tendencies like these are often motivated by self-reflexive white anxiety about identity in a modern pluralistic milieu. While striving to reassert the centrality of the Christian faith in the wake of secularism, Milbank reinscribes the intellectual atmosphere of imperialism because of his inability to conceive of Anglo identity as Gentile identity. As Cone's theology implies, if Christian identity is grounded in the concrete being of Jesus Christ, then Christian identity is necessarily that of being grafted into the Judaic salvation narrative without superseding it. The abstraction of Radical Orthodoxy is tagged by Carter as existent in white theology on the whole.

---

99. Ibid., 160.

100. Ibid., 161.

Cone is acutely sensitive to the problem of abstraction in theology. He understands it to be the perennial problem of white theology and Euro-American racism as a whole. Indeed, as he sees it, a commitment to thinking and acting abstractly is central to why neither white theology nor the white church authentically expresses the Christian faith. White Christianity does not entail concrete living, though it passes itself off as doing so. As such, white theology is neither a practice of reflecting on God's concrete relationship to humans nor a concrete reflection on how humans relate to one another. Rather, white Christianity is an abstract mode of life, and white theology is an abstract mode of thought.[101]

To interpret Carter as making a judgment about a particular theologian's motivations or as saying that persons of European ancestry cannot engage in theological reflection without succumbing to abstraction would be to miss his point. It is important to remember he is summarizing Cone in this regard. Additionally, Carter's point is that theological reflection, when undertaken as *white* theological reflection (that is, reflection that imagines itself as the authoritative ground), of necessity eschews the particularity of YHWH's covenantal work and collapses into abstraction. In Carter's account, for the reasons made explicit in his reading of Kant, any theology which works to relativize or transcend the scandal of particularity can reasonably be called "white." Because of the totalizing influence of whiteness, theology done by persons of any ethnic group can easily defer to these hegemonic tendencies. Carter's theological program is paradoxically an anti-theology, which must to some extent subvert regnant modes of discourse to re-center theology upon the centripetal motion of YHWH's covenant for the whole world through the chosen people of Israel and her Messiah, Jesus. "White" theology often attempts to sidestep this covenantal trajectory. The melancholia of Milbank's theological program, as it attempts to reassert Western centrality, falls short precisely at this point.

For reasons discussed in chapter 1, Carter is not entirely content with Cone's dialecticism. However, his use of Cone represents his most clearly formed divergence with Milbank. In a Conian move, Carter grounds his theological program in what (or more accurately, whom) he recognizes as the *concretissimum*—Jesus of Nazareth.[102] Carter contends that whiteness as a substitute for the *concretissimum* is that which paved the way for American racism, which, in the words of Carter, is a "kind of 'natural theology' run

101. Ibid., 160.
102. Ibid., 162.

amok."[103] It is revealing that Radical Orthodoxy finds the Anglo-Catholic "natural theology" tradition so appealing. This trajectory tends to favor cataphatic theological formulations, which can easily buttress a relationship of epistemological hubris to the divine and to humanity. Carter suggests that Cone's emphasis on relationality serves as an important reminder that "just as human concepts of God always stand in a relationship of epistemological impoverishment to God their referent, so also human concepts about the human being are epistemologically impoverished."[104] Therefore, "positive or cataphatic anthropology . . . requires a negative anthropology."

Milbank's reassertion of the prominence of the elite as a reflection of the *Logos* and his invocation of the universal transcendence of aesthetics and ethics mimes the surety and systematic comprehensiveness of the natural theology tradition, which arguably influenced the modern construction of objectifying anthropologies (more on this in my interaction with Jennings). The political ecclesiology of Radical Orthodoxy is insufficient to resist this objectification and abstraction. A concrete Christology along the lines of what Carter is proposing promises to be the beginnings of a vaccine against the virus of racial reasoning.

> In Christ, identity is instituted afresh in the covenantal humanity of God in Christ. Such a view of things entails thinking of Jesus in his particularity as the *concretum universale*, the concrete universal, the one in whom all being is embraced. Conceiving Jesus of Nazareth in this way takes us beyond the Kantian moment and its conception of Jesus Christ as the abstract universal that religiously sanctions an oppressive conception of human existence and an oppressive vision of the sociopolitical order of things.[105]

Although Milbank is a critic of the Enlightenment, his theology has important similarities to the abstraction of Kantian rationality. After initially utilizing aspects of Milbank's methodology, Carter's theology turns an important corner in breaking free from the sway of Radical Orthodoxy by stressing the concrete particularity of the body of Jesus Christ.

103. Ibid., 160.
104. Ibid., 164.
105. Ibid., 256–57.

Radical Orthodoxy

The "Externality" of Whiteness

So far I have summarized Milbank's vision of an Anglo-Catholic revival and suggested that the Christ of Radical Orthodoxy bears certain similarities to the Kantian rationalized Jesus. I have also demonstrated the ways in which Carter utilizes a similar counter-narrative methodology to distance himself from Milbank. I now turn to demonstrating the maturation of Milbank's vision in *Theology and Social Theory* and the ways the racially-charged atmosphere surrounding his invocation of the "elite" has been carried forward by various proponents of Radical Orthodoxy.

In *Theology and Social Theory*, Milbank maintains that theology must be reclaimed as a metadiscourse.[106] Social theory, operating in the domain of the "secular," is a belief system that had to be imagined. "Once, there was no 'secular' . . . Instead there was the single community of Christendom."[107] According to Milbank, the problem which came into being in late medievalism, exacerbated by the Protestant revolution, was a belief in human autonomy as opposed to the heteronomy of Catholic tradition. This matured into the skeptical epistemology of the Cartesian era, with Kant at its helm. A proper Augustinian *telos*, theologized by Aquinas and mediated by the church hierarchy, was lost as a new anthropology of individualism won the day.[108] Individual autonomy was canonized in the political structures of the early-modern and modern West through Hobbes and Locke. Modern politics were buttressed by a new biblical hermeneutic which forsook the authority of a "*tradition* of reading" and, through the confluence of Lutheran *sola scriptura* and the modern critical method, desacralized the text into a narrative of autonomy and freedom.[109]

While Carter acknowledges that Milbank's thesis "must be reckoned with," he reads Milbank's self-described "archeological"[110] account as telling a truncated tale. Carter offers the reader a variant genealogy in which Milbank insufficiently theorizes the ways in which the Western "tradition" aided in the creation of racialized humanity. For Carter, this is because Milbank

---

106. Milbank, *Theology and Social Theory*, 1.

107. Ibid., 9.

108. Ibid., 10–16.

109. Ibid., 18–20.

110. Ibid., 3.

has neither a theological account of race nor a narrative of his own formation as a British theologian who is heir to colonialist uses of both theological orthodoxy and liberalism, nor, finally a theological accounting of nineteenth-century and twentieth-century British imperialism as a religious, political, and cultural process.[111]

Carter's analysis suggests that Milbank's theology includes a reenactment of important aspects of the theological architecture of the *Pax Brittanica*, the early-modern Empire which controlled almost a quarter of the Earth's land mass and counted a fifth of the world's people as its subjects. Milbank does not evaluate the significance of his own theological school coming of age in the era of the Thatcherite/Reaganite conservative resurgence within the culture wars of the mid–twentieth century. Rather, Milbank cites as examples of his theopolitical vision such figures as Matthew Arnold, who he presents as advocating against "philistinism" through a return to a "common notion" of "character" for "British subjects," a reclamation of Hellenic philosophy, and an emphasis on reason over revelation.[112] He also favors John Henry Newman, a leader in the Oxford Movement from whom Milbank wants to borrow a resurgence of British Catholicism, an insistence on "common" sense and imagination, an invocation of "the concrete co-belonging of the true, the good, and the beautiful," and a reclamation of Aristotelian *phronesis* and Thomist virtue.[113]

For these reasons, Milbank's lament about the decline of Christianity as a metanarrative seems to be coupled with an anxiety about the loss of white subjectivity. Milbank's "ontology of peace," as opposed to what he calls the secular domain's "ontology of violence," can be read as evincing a *melancholia* about the loss of a unified and manageable Occidental description of a complex world and a variegated human history. While Milbank recognizes the problematic nature of modern autonomy, his work seems to be nostalgic for the early-modern theological architecture that advocated a return to classical virtue as a means of organizing the intricacies of a "new" world. Carter contends that this theological atmosphere was the climate which would allow for the flourishing of British imperialism.

---

111. Carter, *Race*, 388.

112. Milbank, *Future of Love*, 26–27.

113. Ibid., 36–59. See Milbank's ironic question: "Was Newman therefore simply overwhelmed by his own inherited habits of mind, combined with a fear of an irreversible decline of Christianity?" (56). While Milbank laments the "inconsistent" nature of Newman's vision, he nonetheless lauds him as "a most remarkable heir" of "authentic Britishness" (59).

While Milbank's motivations are not the point of contention for Carter, he finds Milbank's manner of theologically imagining identity dangerous because it is couched in a vision of assimilation to the Western tradition as the means to reconciliation and peace. Milbank's own framework should place him in a position of being open to this charge, given his invocation of classical Christian right action as an "externality" opposed to a modern retreat to the internality of motivations:

> The depth that can be reported does not really arise from diving expeditions into the soul, but, on the contrary, from an indefinite hermeneutic endeavour which constantly delivers new judgements upon one's external attitudes and emotions. The pernicious effect of the rhetoric of depth . . . is indeed to encourage us to ask 'but is my motivation *really* pure' and to seek out an insincerity more 'real' than our apparent good faith . . . Unlike the stoic inwardness, which does indeed concern pure 'attitude,' Christian inwardness is opened up by a revisability that accompanies all external modes of expression. Thus, the 'depth' revealed in Augustine's *Confessions* is the effect of his reflections on past actions, of the realization that they might have been different, that they can be totally re-read in the context of the more general story of the Church, and that he can transform himself in the future.[114]

Like Milbank, Carter is interested in evaluating what Milbank calls "external modes of expression" rather than rendering judgments upon intentions or "internality." I suggest that a brief summation of the aesthetic and ethical theories and practices of Radical Orthodoxy (i.e. its "externality") will demonstrate its problematic ecclesiological vision. Is Radical Orthodoxy a tradition that is open to being, in Carter's phrase, "re-traditioned"? Can diverse peoples be incorporated into its *ecclesia* in a way that respects their various particularities? Carter finds Radical Orthodoxy to be insufficient for a theological account of race or an ecclesiology marked by difference.

A New Song?

I propose that several examples from the text *Radical Orthodoxy: A New Theology* will confirm Carter's concern that the elasticity of Milbank's system is severely limited. The aesthetic theory of Catherine Pickstock and the Eucharistic imagination of Graham Ward provide examples of the problematic "externality" of Radical Orthodoxy. Pickstock reads Augustine's invocation

114. Milbank, *Theology and Social Theory*, 291–92.

of the intrinsic relationship between aesthetics and ethics as evidence that what is most needed in our current climate of "secularization" is

> a restoration of the integrity of the Western tradition concerning musical theory, which is an appeal for a restoration of the Western (Platonic-Christian) tradition as such. For against fashionable invocation of the non-Western . . . this essay has sought to show . . . exactly why only this Western musical succession foreshadows a possible future political 'equality' or harmony.[115]

Pickstock's appeal to Western musical theory-qua-Christian unity is in agreement with Milbank's declaration that "ethics is only a sub-sphere of aesthetics, governed by criteria of good taste," which dictates that "manners" and "style of behavior" as well as "buildings and furniture" are subject to "moral criteria."[116] In analyzing "*all* cultures," Milbank contends that "[t]he ethical only arises, as a local sphere, because certain continuous aesthetic performances are regarded as highly desirable for all." Does Milbank really believe that ethics is little more than "good taste" and "desirable" aesthetic performances? Has Pickstock considered the implications of claiming that "only" Western musical progressions point toward the sort of harmony God desires for humans to experience with one another? Pickstock's and Milbank's vision for political and ethical harmony appears to be assimilation to Western criteria of beauty.

Radical Orthodoxy offers an important narrative of resistance against the modern secular state. However, Carter's thesis suggests that this narrative of resistance foregrounds Western aesthetic assimilation. For Radical Orthodoxy, "classic" Western aesthetic practices constitute the seditious counter-culture that questions the power of the State over all flesh. For Ward, the aesthetic act that generates sociopolitical revolution is the Eucharist. While I agree that practices of eating together carry important significance for the body of Christ, marked as it is by difference, I read Ward's Eucharist as primarily a formal liturgical act imagined in terms that devalue a diversity of aesthetic expressions being realized in one body. For Ward, the Eucharist is the displaced body of Jesus Christ that, due to its breaking, is now "transposable" in crossing boundaries of "place and space," thereby "incorporat[ing] other bodies" into its own.[117] While Ward presents a Eucharist that binds people one to another, he tends to imagine this unity as constituted in non-centripetal fashion. Ward's Eucharist hinges on the "displacement of the physical body" in which "place and space . . . are redefined

---

115. Milbank et al., *Radical Orthodoxy*, 268.

116. Milbank, *Theology and Social Theory*, 360.

117. Milbank et al., *Radical Orthodoxy*, 167–68.

such that one can be a body here and also there." [118] Rather than a focus
on something akin to Carter's miscegenation between bodies sharing particular space, Ward's Eucharist underemphasizes the significance of place
and particularity. It gravitates to the universal, assuming that its aesthetic
contours will have universal import. Radical Orthodoxy tends to imagine
union among various people as standing in contradistinction to a movement of convergence toward a center. Reconciliation that is "centripetal" is
explicitly described as belonging to the "state *mythos*." [119] This suggests that
Radical Orthodoxy does not imagine the particular people of YHWH as
occupying a central place in redemption. Carter's scandalous corporal imagery more adequately describes the convergence that takes place in the love
feast than do the "center versus periphery" schemas of Radical Orthodoxy's
Eucharistic imagination.

As Milbank expounds his aesthetic vision, he contends that, in the *Logos*, "the unity of the all [is] present in every particular." [120] This position may
allow various particularities to remain separate while independently imaging the divine. While gesturing toward incorporation of diverse peoples and
socioeconomic groups in their anarchic sacrament, the proponents of Radical Orthodoxy propose a theological framework impotent to overturn the
sociopolitical logic of "separate but equal." The contemporary fetish with the
Eucharist as the automatic cure for ecclesiological ails runs aground on the
recognition that proper liturgical enactment alone has not served to create
local bodies of mutuality throughout history. Western liturgical enactment
has not been missing from the colonial-modern project; it has often been
co-opted to sit at its helm. In the Conclusion, I will offer an ecclesiology
consonant with Carter's and Jennings' theologies of race by suggesting a
political shape for ecclesial practices that resists the aesthetic elitism of
whiteness.

The aesthetics and sacramental theology of Radical Orthodoxy are at
variance with the iconographic anthropology and miscegenistic ecclesiology of Carter. Radical Orthodoxy's "ontology of peace" and "eschatology
of reconciliation" are characterized by aesthetic imperialism. The "external
modes of expression" of this theological school buttress Carter's suspicions
about the racially-charged atmosphere of Milbank's invocation of the

---

118. Ibid., 167–68.

119. Ibid., 194, 197. This contention is from an essay by William T. Cavanagh, who,
while perhaps not being most accurately described as belonging to the school of Radical Orthodoxy, has included an essay in this collection. While Cavanagh's theopolitical
insights are helpful in resisting the principalities and powers, his Eucharistic reflections
here may unwittingly reenact the social imaginary of the power structures he criticizes.

120. Milbank, *The Future of Love*, 17.

"guiding elite." In Radical Orthodoxy, the convergence of all flesh in the particularity of Jesus is underemphasized and replaced by the non-centripetal movement of bodies toward each other, rendering unnecessary the risky and vulnerable particular sociopolitical manifestation of diverse bodies being drawn together in what Carter calls a new "body politic." The centrality of the Jewish flesh of Jesus Christ provides Carter with a way to imagine the coexistence of the universal and the particular without enacting either assimilation or separatism.

I will also utilize *Theology and Social Theory* to further demonstrate that Milbank's vision of reconciliation is marked by Eurocentric assimilation. Milbank deems "political and liberation theology . . . guilty, for all its protestations, of reducing the content of salvation to a quasi-Marxist concept of liberation."[121] While Milbank's contention may sometimes hold true (as we saw in aspects of Cone's program), the alternative he proposes does not adequately reflect the radical nature of the body politic shaped by the Gospel. Rather than suggesting something along the lines of a theology concerned with both the centrality of Jesus Christ in the work of reconciliation and a just mutuality among neighbors that includes liberation from material oppression, Milbank's answer is an Aristotelian "charity as friendship." To this Aristotelian *philia*, Milbank adds the Thomist supposition that there is no *vera virtus* without *caritas*, no "true virtue" without "charity." For Milbank, "charity . . . transcends the perspective of doing exact justice."[122]

What takes the place of justice in Milbank's schema is "tact": "Prudence concerns moral tact, the giving of everything its due in the right place and at the right time, and charity must still be exercised with tact if it is to be a proper care."[123] Milbank pictures the church as the giver of charity and creates the "other" as its object. His schema undervalues the agency of the recipient of "charity" and does not allow room for a relational structure in which the "virtuous" Christian may be the recipient of such charity from another. He states that "[i]n striving to *bring everyone into this mutuality, we* will remove all difficulties in *their* path."[124] Milbank's charity operates within an I-thou framework in which the "other" exists as recipient of the virtues of the Occidental subject and in which a subject-object distinction flourishes. No such "difficulties" or barriers appear to exist for the one "bringing" the other into "mutuality." Milbank affirms that the "ontologically ultimate" in

121. Milbank, *Theology and Social Theory*, 234–35.

122. Ibid., 234.

123. Ibid.

124. Ibid., emphasis added.

the Gospel is "intimate communication and mutuality,"[125] yet he envisions reconciliation as unilaterally extending from the "elite" to the one in need of tactful charity. Milbank's "mutuality" and "intimacy" are quite different from the mutual articulation and re-traditioned tradition envisioned by Carter.

For Milbank, "our judgement of the 'truth' of events . . . is essentially an aesthetic matter," in which "the measure of truth is likeness to the form of the divine beauty of which our soul has some recollection."[126] Therefore, "truth, for Christianity, is not correspondence, but rather *participation* of the beautiful in the beauty of God."[127] Over against sociology's "ontology of violence," an ontology that requires every "difference" to be "an event of war,"[128] Milbank proposes an ontology in which other traditions are incorporated into "the tradition" of Christianity through a "peaceful transmission of difference" that expresses itself in an aesthetic of "differences in a continuous harmony."[129] Yet this harmony is to be understood as dissimilar to the "impure" mutuality envisioned by Carter. While Carter would agree that *participation* is constitutive of the body politic, he would ask what tune is being sung in Radical Orthodoxy's ecclesial song.

For Milbank, "difference and harmony" mean that all join together in a "'Baroque' hierarchy" in which "each individual can contemplatively and actively rise" to the "summit . . . of a full participation in the suspension downwards of hierarchies (the aiding of others by charity)."[130] Milbank's aesthetic schema is hierarchical, allowing for the recipients of charity to learn the tune so as to ascend to the status of full participant. Through a process Milbank calls "self-realization," those who are hierarchically lower are invited to add their own "ornamentation" to the "Baroque" progression.[131] The reference to a particular European musical style and historical era should not be read as incidental. Several decades after the tectonic shifts of the Reformation and Counter-reformations, in the midst of Western colonial expansion into the New World, the Baroque era offered a unified and ordered aesthetic account of the complexities of a world theretofore unknown. Milbank's reconciliation can be read as a nostalgia for a world able to be comprehended and ordered by the West. It does not encourage "a new song" in which the peoples

125. Ibid., 233–34.
126. Ibid., 434.
127. Ibid.
128. Ibid., 290.
129. Ibid., 422.
130. Ibid., 434, 436.
131. Ibid., 436.

of the world together improvise on a melody sung over the people of God by YHWH.[132] Milbank's "peaceful transmission of difference" invokes an imperialistically-tinged "peace."

Milbank defines reconciliation as "an invitation to the other to embrace this difference because of its objective desirability."[133] It is not the other who is desirable; it is that the other should desire the objective beauty of the aesthetic performance on display. If Milbank's contention that truth is participation in a shared divine harmonious endeavor is granted, then should it not be that a convergence of diverse aesthetic traditions requires the singing of "a new song" shared by "every tribe and language and people and nation" together praising the "Lion of the tribe of Judah"?[134] This latter vision is an ecclesiology anticipated by Carter in his Pentecostal *poly-glossolalia*.

Ecclesial Coercion, Ontological Peace

Milbank envisions his hierarchical polity as extending through both Church and State. In this section, I will demonstrate how the implicit imperialism of Milbank's early essays builds to a crescendo in *Theology and Social Theory*. Building on his contention that "what ecclesiology is really all about" is a "structural logic for human society,"[135] the denouement of his sociopolitical vision is revealed: "The Church, in order to be the Church, must seek to extend the sphere of socially aesthetic harmony—'within' the State where this is possible."[136] While he alludes to the problematic character of exercising religious virtue through the apparatus of the State, whose "formal goals" consist of "*dominium*," he concludes that the "tragic . . . resignation" of the ecclesia to "this *dominium* can also not be avoided."[137] In contrast to his aforementioned obviation of the dangers of elite governance through the rejection of nationalistic violence, at this point Milbank's "safety valve" is something he calls "good motives": "violence as such delivers no dialectical benefits, of itself it encourages only further violence, and it can only be 'beneficial' when the good motives of those resorting to it are recognized and recuperated by a defaulter coming to his senses."[138]

132. See Zeph 3:17.

133. Milbank, *Theology and Social Theory*, 290.

134. Rev 5:5–10

135. Milbank, *Theology and Social Theory*, 410.

136. Ibid., 428.

137. Ibid., 428–29.

138. Ibid.

Milbank acknowledges that violence may be necessary to sustain this "peace." It is in this sense that he offers something called "ecclesial coercion,"[139] a redeployment of the Augustinian *civitas Dei* through the exercise of the *dominium* of the *civitas terrena*.[140] Milbank explains that a "legitimate, non-sinful, 'pedagogic' coercion" is the duty of the Church, whose authority is centered in a "Christian emperor" who "exercise[s] a pastoral rule."[141] For Milbank, the problem with Empires such as Rome is not primarily their exercise of *dominium*, but its basis in ontological antagonism instead of ontological peace. Milbank contends that an ecclesiological navigation of difference takes place best through a "socially aesthetic harmony" peacefully extended through the apparatus of the State.

Milbank reveals the anthropological assumptions within which his pedagogical vision operates:

> For a polity based on virtue, the goal of authority is not simply an effective peace and order . . . nor the liberty and equality of individuals, but rather the education of individuals into certain practices and states of character, regarded as objectively desirable goals for human beings as such. The possibility of such a politics depends upon the acceptance of the view that there is . . . a 'natural' way for human beings to be . . . [A] politics of virtue . . . assumes that humans stand at the apex of a natural order, and that there is an objectively right way to be human.[142]

Milbank utilizes the natural law tradition to claim objective purchase on what it means to be human. He maintains that he is attempting to "radicalize" the Hellenistic philosophical virtue ethic of MacIntyre by extending its reach into theology.[143] As we study Jennings in the second half of this book, we shall see how colonization operated within precisely this sort of theopolitical framework.

Love and Repentance

I shall close my analysis of the conversation between Carter and Milbank by contrasting their ideas of love and repentance. Milbank concludes that the contemporary Church "has become a hellish anti-Church" and that a

139. Ibid., 424.
140. Ibid., 392–93.
141. Ibid., 425–26.
142. Ibid., 327–28.
143. Ibid., 328.

"vision of ontological peace" is the only thing standing between a "paradisal community" and a "hellish society."[144] While I agree that there are aspects of secular liberalism that are more harmful than helpful (as demonstrated in chapter 1), I do not agree that a reclamation of the theological under-pinnings of Christendom would be an altogether positive development. Carter's analysis demonstrates that modern liberalism is an outgrowth of (and reaction to) a "Christian" society which often created living hells for its oppressed masses. For instance, surely it would not be desirous to in-clude the era of the Middle Passage in a return to the "Christian" values of the West. While Milbank admirably warns against modern society as a sort of humanistic Babel, his language reflects theological sentiments that have contributed to the creation of all manner of modern Christian em-pires. Carter claims that there are better ways of theologically imagining the centrality of Jesus Christ, chief among them the centrality of YHWH's people Israel.

Even though Milbank laments the state of the modern Church, he maintains that "the emanation of harmonious difference"[145] is still pos-sible if it is enforced through "loving discipline."[146] In his view, love is "a highly complex, learned practice" that is neither "obvious" nor dependent on "motivation,"[147] but has a teleological orientation toward the "common good."[148] This vision of "love" as operating through the mechanics of in-fluence and as oriented toward conceptions of the common good is quite different from the definition of love offered by Carter. As Carter explains, love is "the risky exposure and vulnerability" that, grounded in Trinitar-ian mutuality, "lies at the ground of creaturely being."[149] For Carter, love is that which resists static identity structures through mutual vulnerability, not elitism or dominion. In this light, Milbank's invocation of love bears similarities to Carter's definition of sin: "the tyrannical exploitation of the exposure and risk of love, the positive nihil."[150]

As we saw in chapter 1 through Carter's interaction with Cone, Carter presents whiteness as an abstracting, universalizing way of being which requires continuous *metanoia* to maintain. It is a sociopolitical *ordo* into which humans are born again and within which they are discipled. I have

144. Ibid., 442.

145. Ibid., 440–42.

146. Ibid., 411.

147. Ibid., 240.

148. Milbank, *The Future of Love*, xii.

149. Carter, *Race*, 165.

150. Ibid.

contended that whiteness is, in Milbank's words, an "external mode of expression"[151] from which Carter suggests a Christian can repent. Whereas Milbank identifies Hellenic philosophical and Anglo theological traditions as encompassing the central story of Christian history, Carter offers YHWH's work through his people, Israel, and her Messiah, Jesus of Nazareth, as creation's orienting narrative. Carter suggests that by recognizing its peripheral, gentilic identity, the Christian church will assume its proper, chastened place. Milbank maintains that, as the "story of the Church" is "re-read," one finds that he can be transformed, that his trajectory might have been different, and that his manner of being in the world is subject to a certain "revisability."[152] If Milbank is correct that repentance accompanies hearing the story anew, Radical Orthodoxy would do well to listen to Carter retell it.

Carter's Constructive Vision

An Iconographic Christology

So far in my analysis of Carter's *Race* I have contended that Carter began his theological inquiry seeking to imagine the problem of race largely along the lines of the anti-modern polemic of Radical Orthodoxy but found that system lacking in its ability to sufficiently diagnose the theological genesis of racialization, which Carter reads as undergirding the formation of modernity itself. At the same time, I have submitted that Carter inhabits a kindred methodological sensibility to that of Milbank in order to subvert and retell the retrieval narrative of white theology. I have likewise suggested that the keys to recognizing this program are to be found in the ways in which Carter relates the subversive renarration of modernity by early Afro-Christian voices as they intuit the anti-gnostic, abolitionist, and anti-colonial theological moves of Eastern patristics. It is through this renarration that Carter communicates the risky move antebellum black Christians were making as they attempted to walk the line of renarrating the supersessionist theology of whiteness without simultaneously translating their bodies into the racialized anthropology of modern man. It is this process which Carter names the "veritable conundrum of the black intellectual in modernity."[153] In this way, Carter's entire text can be read as the struggle of the black intellectual, as theological heir to colonialist uses of both orthodoxy and liberalism,

151. Milbank, *Theology and Social Theory*, 291–92.
152. Ibid., 291–92.
153. Carter, *Race*, 142.

to narrate the body over against the pseudotheological architectonics of whiteness. Carter narrates the black intellectual as reclaiming the subversive potential latent within the tradition and redirecting it toward breaking the backbone of whiteness. This struggle is Carter's struggle. In the final reading, the black intellectual subverting the genealogy of whiteness for the sake of reclaiming the promise of Pentecost is himself.

In concluding this chapter I will conclude where Carter concludes. In this section, I will briefly relate several key elements of his interaction with Jarena Lee, in whom he finds the most propitious framework for a fully developed theological anthropology, while in the next section, I will analyze Carter's utilization of Maximus the Confessor, whose iconographic Christology is strikingly similar to the theological intuition of Lee. Lee, like Hammon and Douglass, employs the genre of spiritual autobiography in order to renarrate the self, outside the strictures of modern gendered, racialized existence.[154] In so doing, Lee's vulnerable self-narration runs the risk of being interpreted as capitulation to the *ordo* of whiteness. Carter conveys that it is common to read the accounts of authors such as Lee as completely constricted by the demands of the era in regard to black autobiography.[155] In this hermeneutic trajectory, Lee's truncated account of her "pre-Christian" childhood is interpreted as the triumph of "Christian" (read: white) anthropology over pre-Christian modes of being, signaling the triumph of modernity over uncivilized human nature. According to this framework, while Lee gained literacy, it was at the cost of being translated into a Christianity that degraded her flesh. Black identity, particularly the

---

154. I am not suggesting that "gender" is an inappropriate theological category. Rather, I am sensitive to Carter's concern that "modern" gender has often been an essentialized concept, much like race. I am also sensitive to Barth's attempt (in *Church Dogmatics III.4*) to maintain the validity of gender as a theological concept (drawn from the creation account in Genesis 2) without succumbing to "natural" typologies that say more about gender than Scripture is willing to say. I am concerned that perhaps Carter's account does not sufficiently distinguish between gender and race as theological categories, a concern I have reframed in several ways throughout this analysis. Whereas gender is "something" from a biblical standpoint (although, like Barth, I suspect that attempts to define in what that "something" consists are not properly theological and often devolve into prejudicial hierarchical constructions), race is not a theological category grounded in creation. "Race" is a distortion of creation (as Carter maintains). In the second half of this book, I am sympathetic with Jennings that understanding race in connection with place is a better way into the problem. I maintain that if race and gender as theological categories are not sufficiently distinguished from one another (and "gender" is not preserved as an appropriate theological distinction), the ability to criticize race as a distortion of creation will be weakened.

155. Carter, *Race*, 317.

black feminine, found a voice "only as it [was] inserted into the narrative of Euro-American civilization."[156]

While Carter does not disagree that this line of criticism makes a valid point, particularly that nonwhite self-articulation is often translated into the regnant discourse of white modernity, he offers a different, more hopeful interpretation of Lee's (and, by implication, his own) project.

> Yet, such a reading, as important as it is, does not tell the whole story, for it also can be said that Lee employs the genre of the American spiritual autobiography to subversive effect. The question is not only *what* remains, but equally *what she does* with what remains . . . It is precisely here that Lee's literary subtlety, especially in its function of engaging the very white Christianity that sanctified her subservience within an economy of whiteness, must be reckoned with. I argue that Lee's *disremembering* of her childhood and, by metaphoric extension, the *disremembering* of a black past that is violently brought into the New World, is a peculiar *remembering* or reconstituting of it as well.[157]

While Lee seeks to overcome the denigrating racializing anthropology of modern Christianity by enacting a retrieval of the self within the covenant of Zion-Israel, Carter seeks to overcome the story of modernity by retelling it as the story of the racial project. I read Carter as enacting a similar "literary subtlety" to Lee in his subversion of Radical Orthodoxy's retrieval methodology as he constructs his own narrative of theological retrieval. Like Lee, Carter *remembers* black existence within the narrative of Christianity in such a way as to *reconstitute* it within YHWH's narrative of creation-redemption. Likewise, Carter *remembers* the Christian tradition in order to *reconstitute* it as a trajectory of liberation and reconciliation for all creation.

Lee reconstitutes identity by explicitly situating her own identity within an *inclusio* of Mary the mother of God and the Easter preacher Mary Magdalene, thereby inhabiting a mariological ecclesiology consonant with the classical Eastern doctrine of the *theotokos*. In so doing, Lee is able to rearticulate the self as being received from a whole Christ, divinely birthed through the womb of Mary-Israel.[158] It is this classically orthodox theology of the sacred feminine, as necessitated by the scandalous particularity of the Incarnation and the Athanasian logic that helped interpret it,[159] that

156. Ibid., 317.
157. Ibid., 318.
158. Ibid., 339–41.
159. See Athanasius, *Against the Arians*, 3.29, where he argues for the orthodox

initiates an assault on the racializing (and by extension, gendering) anthropology of modernity. Carter finds the theological moves undergirding such
an assault to have taken place twelve hundred years earlier in Maximus the
Confessor's explication of the *communicatio idiomatum*. By explicitly offering a retrieval of Eastern patristic sources, and by examining the ways in
which Lee's anthropological assumptions intuit quite similar sensibilities,
Carter is utilizing and subverting the methodology of Radical Orthodoxy.
Carter favors a *retrieval* of classically Eastern Christian dogmatic sources
as a *reclamation* of the liberating power of said sources. Carter's project is a
counterexegesis of the "tradition." He is reading the tradition against its use
as the machine of colonization-modernity.

> My claim is that a particular way of reading Scripture—read-
> ing against rather than within the grain of the social order—is
> the hinge holding together these two theological visions, the
> Maximian one formed before the advent of the modern/colonial
> world and the Afro-Christian one arising in its wake and as a
> response to it.[160]

Carter is not engaging an anachronism here:

> My point in all of this is not to make the historically unsustain-
> able claim that early Afro-Christians read Maximus the Confes-
> sor (or Nyssa or Irenaeus for that matter). Rather, it is to note
> the symmetry between their respective ways of understanding
> both the self and the task of theology in a world marked by tyr-
> anny, the tyranny structured in terms of some figured as obedi-
> ent bodies and others as bodies to be obeyed.[161]

Carter's analysis of Maximus the Confessor's incarnational Christology
causes his disagreement with Milbank to reach a crescendo and further
clarifies their points of distinction. This analysis, the finale to Carter's work,
serves to conclude my second chapter.

An Ontology of Love

Carter introduces his interaction with Maximus the Confessor with an
epigraph in which Maximus maintains that "the three greatest, primordial

---

doctrine of the *theotokos* based on the divinity of Christ and his "taking on" flesh from
the virgin Mary.

160. Carter, *Race*, 344.

161. Ibid.

evils" are "ignorance . . . self-love and tyranny."[162] Carter's presentation of
Maximus focuses on how Maximus' doctrine of the Trinity and his Christology combat the latter two: tyranny and self-love (*philautia*). Carter
describes *philautia* as the posture that maintains one's own subjectivity at
the expense of another. Therefore, *philautia* and tyranny are interrelated.
Tyranny as self-love is "the disposition that orders the world and the things
of the world as the possession, as Kant might say, of the mature (as opposed
to immature and hence childlike) self-constituting I or the *autos*."[163] Tyranny as self-love (as opposed to *philadelphia*, the love of others) is "the basic
structure of colonialism" in which "the self-constituting I creates a reality
and draws all else into it by making it utility or assigning it a use value in the
world of the I."[164]

It is here that we gain a glimpse of how Carter understands the task
of theological ethics to function: "When human beings live in accordance
with love, and thus in accordance with the Triune God who is love and
from whose will creation arises, they live virtuously."[165] The virtuous life
comes from being joined to the life of God (much like the Eastern concept
of *theosis*, or divinization). Therefore, the virtues are not something to be
had; they are not standards to be attained; they are not the possessions of
mature (Kant) elites (Milbank) who have a responsibility to inculcate a culture of virtues in all flesh. Rather, it is in the vulnerability and dispossesive-
ness (Maximus' asceticism) of divine love that the life of the Triune God
is made manifest in the life of the creature. Love, therefore, is the supreme
theological virtue. Attainment of this virtue operates oppositionally to the
manner in which virtue-ethics projects tend to function.

Rather than love being foremost a learned pattern of behavior (Milbank), love is a posture of impoverishment to the divine and a posture of
kenosis to the other. Love is that which allows the subject (the "I") to pen-
tecostally hear the promises of YHWH spoken to itself from another (the
"thou"), thereby collapsing the distinction between subject and object. This
is why Carter maintains that "theology must rediscover itself as a suffering discourse and relinquish its identity as a discourse of possessive power
through which class consciousness and racial sensibilities still work."[166]
Theology must be radically "poor," "kenotic," and "weak."[167] In my treat-

162. Ibid., 343.
163. Ibid., 345.
164. Ibid.
165. Ibid.
166. Ibid., 368–69.
167. Ibid., 369.

ment of Jennings, I will contend that such an understanding of poverty is to be distinguished from the "radical" poverty that is the fetish of much contemporary "white" theological thought (in which poverty is often used as a field upon which to narrate the virtues of the subject). Rather, according to Carter, the "form of the slave" which theology must assume resists its being "an activity of mastery and thus of control."[168] Carter reads theological systems such as Radical Orthodoxy as functioning more like discourses of scholastic control and mastery than invocations of the kenotic reality of Trinitarian love. In this Maximian-Carterian vein, love becomes more than a theological virtue; it is the supreme ontological reality.[169]

It is this "ontology of love" that Carter juxtaposes with Milbank's "ontology of peace." As I have already maintained, Carter reads Milbank's ontological peace as an imperialistically-tinged assimilation to the dominant cultural values of whiteness. Carter instead proposes the ontological priority of love. Improvising on Maximus, Carter maintains that divine love within the relationship of the Trinity produces the "many": the "difference that has contained within it the possibility of all other differences."[170] In this sense, Maximus' theological anthropology is one of *ecstatic* identity. This ecstatic identity is twofold: the ecstasy of Trinitarian mutuality is superabundant, producing the ecstasy of creation, which is the ecstasy of the many.[171] The *communicatio idiomatum* holds together the divine and the human so as to maintain joining in difference through a process of mutual exchange. This reality is made manifest in Christ's body, thereby drawing up human identity and relationships into a community of mutual exchange and reciprocity. The *hypostasic union* opens human nature not only to God but back to itself. This mutuality and openness between human and human is much more than a modern relationality in which autonomous individuals "will" to be in voluntary contract with one another. In addition to allowing a reciprocal naming between the divine and the human, the mutuality concordant with the *communicatio idiomatum* dictates that humans receive their identity from one another. As Carter explains:

> Whiteness functions in modernity as a substitute for the doctrine of creation in its quest to create a reality into which all else must enter. Maximus saw in Christ the solution to the many violent and tyrannical divisions that could arise from a vision of creation that functions in this way. In Christ, the gesture of

168. Ibid.
169. Ibid., 349.
170. Ibid., 349–50.
171. Ibid.

ecstatic openness to God in human self-fulfillment, which is the gesture to receive oneself from God, is necessarily a gesture of openness to all created beings as revealing God. "To be" ecstatically is to receive oneself from other human beings precisely as the receiving of the self from God. Hence, being named from God entails being named from other human beings. In undoing whiteness as a theological problem, Christ leads human nature out of this disposition.[172]

This trajectory points to a "peaceful difference" that "refuses anything like a logic of 'separate but equal'" and "resists all political and cultural nationalisms."[173]

Ironically, Carter's use of "peaceful difference" is the language at which Milbank arrives in his constructive ecclesiology.[174] Milbank also utilizes Maximus as one who identifies God as "the distinction of the different."[175] This shared language between Carter and Milbank is another instance of Carter's subversion of whiteness. As Carter reveals in the footnote to his striking use of this contested language:

> The language of "peaceful difference" risks sounding a lot like John Milbank's "ontology of peace" . . . While there may be some affinities between our languages, it would be a mistake to interpret my proposal in strictly Milbankian terms, for, in fact, the theological program I am initiating here calls Milbank's program into question precisely to the extent that it still, in my view, intellectually enacts a strong, colonialist Christianity. In contrast to what I propose here, Milbankian "radical orthodoxy" . . . has yet to reckon with the ways they perform theology in continuity with Catholic and Protestant theology's racial-colonialist past. That past articulated itself in terms of theological orthodoxy and presented itself in terms of a sacramental and liturgical imagination.[176]

Carter adds that "one would be equally mistaken to reduce the program of intellectual reflection being initiated here to a species of theological liberalism" of the modern sort. He maintains that there is a direct lineage of "racial-colonial theological continuity" from fifteenth-century orthodoxy through modern liberalism. In this sense, "theological liberalism is not an

172. Ibid., 352–53.
173. Ibid., 351–52.
174. Milbank, *Theology and Social Theory*, 366–67, 382, 422–23, 429.
175. Ibid., 429.
176. Carter, *Race*, 462 n. 17.

aberrancy, but rather, the culmination of modern theological orthodoxy as the discursive space within which the modern world as we have come to know it was forged."[177] The poles of colonialist orthodoxy and modern liberalism "form a single reality that must be thought beyond." It is between these poles that "whiteness as a theological problem oscillates and within which Christian identity remains tyrannically and grotesquely distorted."[178] My analysis in chapters 1 and 2 has positioned Carter as combatting whiteness by moving beyond these poles through reclaiming important aspects of patristic thought in order to counter modern distortions.

The "peaceful difference" to which Carter refers is an "intrarenaming of the human."[179] The problem with whiteness is that, instead of viewing itself as a particularity in need of the mutual articulation of various other particularities in a shared experience of divinization, it "philautically" masquerades as divine universality: "The distortion lies in the fact that the pseudotheological identity of whiteness exports itself but never receives itself."[180] As we have seen, Radical Orthodoxy functions in much the same way: as educator of many, student of few. While Carter recognizes that Maximus knew nothing of modern colonization or racialization, he maintains that Maximus "foresaw how theology could be complicit in this fashion [as a racial-colonialist way of ordering the world] precisely through the rhetorics of orthodoxy."[181]

A direct read of Maximus' texts bears out this contention. Maximus does not explicitly juxtapose Israel's story with a supersessionist Christian narrative.[182] Carter recognizes that it would be anachronistic to suggest that, on the face of it, he and Maximus are dealing with the same problem.[183]

---

177. Ibid., 462.

178. Ibid.

179. Ibid., 352.

180. Ibid.

181. Ibid., 345.

182. For recent critical translations of Maximus' primary writings (including *Epistle 2* and *Ambigua 10*), as well as an excellent analysis of Maximus' theology, see Louth, *Maximus the Confessor*.

183. See Carter, *Race*, 345, where he maintains that "On the one hand, *Ep.* 2 then becomes an interesting and unexpected resource for probing whiteness as a racial-colonialist way of ordering the world that, in fact, deploys the discourse of Christian theology to do its work. What is interesting about Maximus is that he foresaw how theology could be complicit in this fashion precisely through the rhetorics of orthodoxy. *Epistle 2* constructs an alternative vision of theology, what can be called 'difficult orthodoxy' or, as he himself might have no doubt preferred, ascetical (*askesis*) or spiritual theology. The alternative vision he proposes turns on the link between Abram–Abraham and Jesus of Nazareth." See also 352: "While Maximus knew neither the history of modern

While Carter highlights the Maximian narrative of YHWH's salvific work in the world by contrasting it with the mythologies of late medieval theology and philosophical modernity, Maximus was not at all aware of these distinctions. Carter's interpretation is compelling precisely because Maximus would not have found it revolutionary to connect the narrative of Christ's salvation with the womb of Israel. It is because it was instinctual for Maximus to theorize theological anthropology within the identity of Abram-Israel that the distortions of modern Christianity are all the more apparent. Carter's analysis of the rabbinical style of Maximus' exegesis, coupled with Maximus' tendency to exegete texts from the Hebrew Bible (Abram) or ones that specifically connect Jesus to the Judaic covenant (the Transfiguration), demonstrates how foreign the modern critical method finds this style of theological exegesis to be. While a direct reading of *Epistle 2* and *Ambigua 10* does not in itself produce a diagnosis of modern Christianity as supersessionist and modern anthropology as essentialist, it further illumines the distinctive character of Maximus' exegesis in contrast to modern exegesis, thereby further buttressing Carter's conclusion that something is radically amiss in our modern racialized understanding of personhood. Carter is suggesting that Maximus' way of theologically theorizing the self/flesh provides a way to escape modern racialized identity.

Maximus' theological anthropology, found primarily in his *Epistle 2* (*"On Love"*) and *Ambigua 10*, is rooted in his theological exegesis of the Scriptures, through which he locates the world inside the story of Israel.[184] These texts are oriented around exegesis of two stories: YHWH's call to Abram while in Ur of the Chaldees and the Transfiguration of Jesus. Maximus unpacks his understanding of identity as *ekstasis* through his interpretation of Abram's call to sojourn in a land as yet unknown. In the words of Carter, "[Abram's] identity is not something he constructs. It always lies ahead of him."[185] Abram's name would come only through his descendent Jacob (Israel). Therefore, neither should Jewish identity be parsed as that of "hermetically sealed" modern racial identity nor should it be seen as

conquest nor its internal racial dimensions, nor that it would be Christian theologians who were most responsible for making arguments in justification of all of this, he did have insight into the root of the problem. Its root, as he sees it, lies in created nature's self-enclosure: the transformation of the one-many structure of creation into the tyranny of division through the agency of humans in their quest to be 'gods' (in replacement of God the Creator) and thus to 'create' their own reality."

184. Louth, *Maximus the Confessor*, 84–154.

185. Carter, *Race*, 354.

operating within a "fortress mentality."[186] Jewish identity is an open, ecstatic identity received in following the call of YHWH.

According to Maximus' interpretation of Jesus' Transfiguration, Christ's garments are the dual revelations of Scripture and creation as well as revelations of the divinity and humanity of Christ. In this sense, the garments Christ wears are his very flesh, his means of mediating his divinity to humanity. Maximus contends that the appearance of Moses and Elijah on Mt. Tabor are the legal and prophetic words of YHWH's covenant, *logoi* that aid in understanding divine revelation in creation, adhering in the *Logos*, Christ the Word. Christ's flesh, therefore, is necessarily Jewish flesh which cannot be superseded by "natural" revelation. The disciples' understanding of creation and flesh is mediated by Jesus' particular covenantal flesh.[187]

In relating that Maximus wrote *Ambigua 10* to a group of Origenist monks who were prioritizing the immaterial (spiritual) over the material (flesh), thereby "seeing the latter as in need of being overcome," Carter contends that Maximus offers a corrective for modern anthropological tyranny.[188] Maximus' Christology finds "the fleshly and the material" to be "vehicles to encounter God." The posture encouraged by this Christology is one of "dispossessive love," arrived at through "ascetic struggle."[189] Carter understands proper aesthetic perception to come about by viewing the world not through a lens of possessiveness (the tendency of whiteness), but through a lens of reception as God's gracious gift in creation. It is this reception of identity-as-gift in which all flesh is together transformed in the *ordo* of Christ's flesh. Rather than flesh being overcome, flesh itself is transfigured in the transfigured body of Jesus of Nazareth. For Maximus, it is not the flesh that is problematic but the will to possess. It is this "will" that Carter parses as "the will-to-power as the will-to-possession," a will that "distorts the meaning of embodiment."[190] It is in this sense that Carter reads Maximus the Confessor as an "anticolonialist intellectual."[191]

As we saw in chapter 1, this does not mean that Carter capitulates to the static identity structures often assumed in modern ideas of liberation. Carter maintains that a Maximian vision of mutual participation in divine love, with its concomitant reciprocity of intranaming among the members of Christ's flesh, is "more radical" than "liberation theology [as a] discourse

186. Ibid., 366.
187. Ibid., 361.
188. Ibid., 359.
189. Ibid., 358.
190. Ibid., 359.
191. Ibid., 343.

of modern academic theology."[192] Carter's Maximian vision of Pentecost provides him with the exegetical framework in which to articulate this ecclesial intranaming. In the *Mystagogia*, Maximus interprets the coming of the Spirit upon the disciples in Acts 2 as the drawing of all beings away from the periphery of "the myriads of differences" into the common center of Jesus Christ's body. This convergence is one in which He who is the "center" effects by "his unique, simple, and single cause and power" a circumscription of all those who are "different . . . in such distinctives as language . . . where they are from . . . and manners and customs."[193] In this manner, "the holy Church of God is an image of God" in that it does not "confus[e]" but rather "bring[s] together their distinction." The Church's nature is that of the union of natures in Jesus Christ, in whom difference is joined without confusion. This Christological insight simultaneously resists essentialization, segregation, and assimilation.

Carter's work is more radical than a "preferential option for the poor,"[194] which tends to be the common default of liberation theology. Because divinity and humanity are joined in the poor flesh of Jesus of Nazareth, divinity has taken on poverty so that poverty now "articulate[s] the wealth of divinity."[195] It is this mutual articulation which allows "the poverty-wealth binary and the class consciousness and racial sensibilities that function within this binary" to be "broken down and reordered in Christ's flesh." In this way, the "poor" are divinized within the kenotic flesh of Jesus while "poverty" is neither essentialized nor aligned with racial classifications (as was the tendency for Cone). A communal *theosis* takes place in the space of Jesus' body, a space in which the "auditory capacit[ies]" of peoples are "renewed" so that a "Pentecostal reimagining and reordering of language and identity" takes place.[196] I contend that this mutual convergence and radical sociopolitical unity in the space of Jesus' flesh is the sign of a new *ordo* in which, rather than either liberation theology's *preference for* the poor or Radical Orthodoxy's *concern for* the poor, impoverished humanity in all its various particularities enacts the most radical and revolutionary work of all: it experiences mutual *friendship*. This friendship is not one which is antipodal to liberation nor is it antithetical to social justice. It is rather one in which the *other* is neither objectified nor essentialized. This friendship is

192. Ibid., 367.
193. Ibid., 362–64.
194. Ibid., 367.
195. Ibid., 368.
196. Ibid., 365.

indispensable, as it is the process by which one receives her own identity. As Maximus maintains:

> The clear proof of this grace is the voluntary disposition of good will toward those akin to us whereby the man who needs our help in any way becomes as much as possible our friend as God is and we do not leave him abandoned and forsaken but rather that with fitting zeal we show him in action the disposition which is alive in us with respect to God and our neighbor . . . For if the Word has shown that the one who is in need of having good done to him is God . . . on God's very word, then, he will much more show that the one who can do good and who does it is truly God by grace and participation.[197]

Both the one who gives and the one who receives are together divinized in Christ's flesh. As the lines between giver and recipient are blurred in the reciprocity of centripetal convergence, the essentialized identities that dictate "who is who" are no longer clear.

In this manner, mutuality gives the lie to essentialism. As I have found in surprising ways through unlikely relationships in a local church community inhabiting shared space, the beauty of ethnic difference can be maintained while racial typologies are resisted. Until intentional relationships of difference marked by intimacy and trust are common, there will not be a serious challenge to the racial typologies that find expression in the racial violence plaguing America, nor will there be a communal discourse potent to challenge our Western racial imagination. As particular lives are bound together across ethnic and socioeconomic lines, those lives are drawn up into the life of Christ's body. In the Conclusion, I will suggest several ways this mutuality can take shape, including forms of eating together that resist conceptions of Eucharistic liturgical and aesthetic "purity." Nostalgia for a more unified "Christian" way of describing the world is often a cheap and easy alternative to the hard work of being identified with unlike others so as to be identified with Christ. The former tends to operate from a position of control, the latter from a position of fragility.

Carter's theology of race proves to be an example of the sort of discourse he contends that theology should be: a suffering and kenotic form of "weak thought."[198] It is from this posture that he is able to contend that theology "can no longer do its work . . . as an enterprise of the religious elite functioning in the interests of power."[199]

197. Ibid., 367.
198. Ibid., 369.
199. Ibid., 372.

Chapter 3: Jennings and Cultural Studies

An Introduction to the *Christian Imagination*

I INTRODUCED THIS TEXT with a narrative that demonstrated my difficulty to theologically diagnose the problem of race in the modern world. I related that Jennings and Carter, who I read as together offering an emerging school of theological race theory, offered me a framework in which to more satisfactorily consider racial reconciliation. While Carter deals with the racial logic of Enlightenment, Jennings offers an account of the ways in which this racial logic was forged in pre-modern colonization. Having demonstrated in chapter 1 that Carter is not content with the dialectical atmosphere of the religious academy, in chapter 2 I presented Carter's interpretation of Radical Orthodoxy as a repristination of the theological architecture of British imperialism. I now turn to performing a similar analysis with the work of Jennings. In this chapter I will elucidate Jennings' relationship with the discipline of cultural studies, while in chapter 4 I will deal with Jennings' critique of a MacIntyrian virtue ethic. I will then build on Jennings' argument as I conclude with a consonant constructive ecclesiology.

In chapter 1, I began with a summary of Carter's work before describing his relationship to the works of three scholars of religious studies. In this chapter, I will summarize Jennings' argument before placing him in conversation with the cultural studies literature surrounding four historical Christian figures utilized by Jennings. Whereas Carter presents his thesis in a linear argument, Jennings utilizes a sustained historical narrative to weave his thesis throughout his text. To more fully explain this latter approach, I offer a more detailed analysis of Jennings' work before explicating his relationship to the discipline of cultural studies.

Jennings' Story and Method

Jennings opens *The Christian Imagination* with an autobiographical narrative which succinctly encapsulates his central argument. While some form of identity confession is a common introductory move throughout much modern writing on identity issues,[1] such confessions are not often in the form of a tightly woven autobiographical tale that summarily integrates the author's core concerns. Identity confessions can tend to either distance the reader through use of a self-conscious hermeneutic or invite the reader to a shared proximity through self-revelation. I interpret Jennings' autobiographical narrative as belonging to the latter. Through disarming vulnerability, Jennings hints that his central theological framework will be an invitation to radical joining. He introduces himself as descendent of a northern migration from the Jim Crow South, the son of parents deeply connected to the land. It is clear from the first words of his theological autobiography that place will play a central role in his exposition of the formation of racial identities by theology locked inside colonial sensibilities.[2]

Jennings resists the classificatory nature of encyclopedic inquiry by building his case through sequential discussions of historical narratives. While Jennings' personal genealogy is the canvas upon which he introduces the story he will tell, his broader genealogical method highlights a hidden narrative of deep distortions that have occurred within the Western theological imagination, thwarting the deepest desires of intimacy that lie dormant within the Christian faith. He suggests that, "like a film director," he will "take the reader on a journey" by focusing in on a few particular people in particular places, times, and contexts, so as to "paint a portrait of a theological problem in order to suggest a way forward."[3] Jennings implies that the first story thus engaged will be his own.

Jennings references three episodes in his life that illumined barriers to unlike people sharing an intimate knowledge of each other. He begins with what is fundamentally an epistemological question: "Why did they not know us?"[4] This query is in reference to two white men from the stately Christian Reformed Church located within the neighborhood in which the Jennings family lived, several blocks away from their home. On what the two men must have assumed to be a missionary venture, they approached Mary Jennings and her son Willie, while they were gardening on their plot of land, and launched into what appeared to be a formal, rehearsed speech extolling the activities afforded the neighborhood residents by their church. Having called this community home for many years and being the son of prominent members of a local Missionary Baptist church, the young Jennings could not but be confused and surprised by this behavior. "Why did

1. See Patte, *Ethics of Biblical Interpretation*, 1–2.

2. Jennings, *Christian Imagination*, 1.

3. Ibid., 9.

4. Ibid., 3.

they not know us? They should have known us very well."[5] What Jennings is articulating here is not that these particular men and the Jennings family were unacquainted, but rather how it could be that the white congregants of a church in Jennings' own neighborhood, bearers of an orthodox theological tradition, could be so profoundly unfamiliar with the community of black residents in proximity to their church building.

Even more so than this missiological blunder, how could it be that there was so deeply ingrained in these men an assumed knowledge of the identity of the family whom they were attempting to proselytize? How was it that the men could so clearly gesture toward intimacy and belonging while so plainly locating the Jennings family on the periphery of the soteriological hope which they held out? And perhaps in the most grotesque malformation of all, how could they stand in a position of inherent condescension toward a woman who was a devout Christian and pillar of her local church? How could Christianity be at the same time an invitation to intimacy and a perpetuator of classificatory schemas?

Ironically, the second episode Jennings relates took place during his days as a student at Calvin College, "the very college founded by that church and that denomination."[6] Jennings tells the story of being asked, at the last minute, to preach in chapel because of a cancellation by the speaker for the morning. While the precise content of the sermon has long since been forgotten, what is emblazoned in his memory is what happened immediately following his oratory. A line of his Dutch Reformed professors formed in order to thank him for his proclamation of the Word of God. The countenances and embraces of these reserved white men exuded a warmth and familiarity normally lacking in their classroom demeanors. While their "fatherly love and appreciation" could in hindsight be interpreted in problematically paternalistic ways, nevertheless, Jennings again experienced, albeit for a fleeting moment, the capacity of the Christian faith to enact "a sense of connection and belonging and of a freedom to claim, to embrace, to make familiar one who is not."[7]

Third, Jennings relates that in his current experience within the academy he has observed the moral formation of students as they are ushered into similar postures as the missional parishioners of his youth and the theology professors of his undergraduate education. As a professor and academic dean at Duke Divinity School, Jennings "watched with a sense

5. Ibid., 3.
6. Ibid., 5.
7. Ibid., 6.

of melancholy the formation process of Christian intellectuals."[8] According to Jennings, the theological academy produces theologians who display a "resistance . . . to think[ing] *theologically* about their own identities."[9] This is indicative of

> the negation of a Christian intellectual posture reflective of the central trajectory of the incarnate life of the Son of God, who took on the life of the creature, a life of joining, belonging, connection, and intimacy. Such a posture would inevitably present the likelihood of transformations not only of ways of thinking but of ways of life that require the presence of the risks and vulnerabilities associated with being in the social, cultural, economic, and political position to be transformed.[10]

Jennings here suggests a diagnosis that he will elaborate in detail in the body of the book: the malady underlying this thwarted intimacy is Christological in nature. He does not suggest that the Western tradition has explicitly embraced a heterodox Christology, but that its patterns of social embodiment belie heretical Christological habits of mind.[11]

Jennings will utilize his entire treatment to explore how it could be that such thwarted patterns of intimacy, specifically across lines of ethnic difference, are far too often the norm within Christian experience. If, as Jennings contends, these dysmorphic ecclesial practices are rooted in theological distortions, he will investigate how it could be that such distortions are thoroughly enmeshed in the theological imagination of Christianity. Why, within a way of life that holds out the promise of reconciliation to the God who "surprises us by love of differences,"[12] are diverse peoples not often joined to each other without their relationality being marked by assimilation or subjugation?

In a world shaped by the contorted theological suppositions of colonization, a theologian who as a young man was driven by questions which were unanswerable by his pastor sought "imaginative possibilities" that would lead him beyond "the cultural nationalism, or the conservative theo-political ideologies, or the crass materialism that would beckon" to "a generation of postmigration black children who tore large rips in the garments of racial and denominational identity" worn "out of respect" for their elders.[13]

8. Ibid., 7.

9. Ibid.

10. Ibid.

11. Ibid., 166–67.

12. Ibid., 9.

13. Ibid., 5.

In much the same way that his Dutch Reformed professors' gestures of joining exhibited a "stark contrast" with their "proper pedagogical form," Jennings claims that Christian theology cannot see the "profound connections
between an embrace by very different people in the chapel and theological
meditations articulated in the classroom."[14] It is this embrace which holds
out the hope that we as Christians can "find together . . . a life already prepared and offered for us."[15] Jennings' story has provided a hermeneutic lens
through which to interpret my own experiences in compelling ways.

Stories of Hope Deferred

Jennings utilizes four historical Christian figures engaged in theological
reflection in the midst of cross-cultural interaction. The primary historical
figure he references is Jose de Acosta, the colonial Spanish Jesuit missionary
to the New World. I take Jennings' interaction with Acosta to be paradigmatic of the method of genealogical inquiry he pursues throughout his four
interconnected narratives. While each figure has been previously utilized in
cultural studies literature, one is hard pressed to find *theological* analyses of
these persons, although each understood himself to be a faithful Christian
engaged in theological narration of his cultural milieu.[16] Jennings maintains
that this "oversight" has taken place because serious interaction with these
thinkers reveals the distorted theological architecture undergirding both
modern orthodoxy and liberalism.[17] Jennings draws attention to the fact
that four Christian figures who have long been recognized as significant for
cultural studies and ethnography have largely been disregarded by Christian theology.

   In each story, Jennings finds moments of hope as possibilities for
intimacy, belonging, and mutuality appear before being swallowed up by
hubris, categorization, and subjugation. In the moments where some level
of vulnerability and reciprocity is achieved, it is due to a hemorrhaging of
the Christian tradition of which each character is both recipient and participant. Jennings maintains that the Christian imagination of each individual
has been stunted by theology's role in the colonizing and descriptive processes instigated by Europeans in late medievalism and continuing in the
racial imaginations of moderns.

   14. Ibid., 7.
   15. Ibid., 11.
   16. This is similar to Carter's complaint about the lack of theological accounts of
race.
   17. Jennings, *Christian Imagination*, 115.

In the first chapter, Jennings begins with the story of Gomes Eanes de Zurara, the Portugese Infante Henrique's royal chronicler, who describes in a theological narrative the arrival of a "cargo" of African slaves. Zurara cries out to God in pity at the pathos he is observing, linguistically embedding the Africans in a Christological trope while succumbing to an explanation of this act as proof of the workings of divine providence in white dominance over nonwhite flesh.[18] Zurara's description of the suffering of the Africans as chattel is a well-known passage often referred to within cultural studies literature and will be referenced in some detail later. Jennings' innovation is that he mines the story of this familiar character for the theological legacy of Christian reflection initiated by such categorization. Jennings finds the descriptive projects undertaken by each thinker to narrate racial existence into and from a theological trajectory of which much contemporary identity reflection is heir.[19]

In the story of Acosta, who assumed leadership of the Spanish mission to Lima, Peru, in coordination with the colonizing efforts of the Viceroy Toledo, Jennings likewise offers a glimpse of a moment of hope which is quickly drowned in hubris. Acosta laughs (as recorded in his journals)[20] in his epistemological uncertainty upon encountering the new and unexpected.[21] In the space between the known and the unknown, as he journeyed by ship to the New World, Acosta confessed that he "laughed and jeered at Aristotle's meteorological theories" when experiencing different conditions than had been expected.[22] Here is a moment of pause; a breath before the storm. The hope that he will approach his epistemic crisis with humility, evidenced by a desire to listen to and learn from the self-articulation of the indigenous people, is swallowed up as he subsequently embarks upon a project of theological description that would buttress the project of political subjugation in which Spain was engaged. Acosta was unable to imagine "a theological appropriation of native knowledge as an act of theological reflection itself."[23] He sliced the geographic sensibilities out of his tradition so as to maintain the systematic integrity of the discursive practices of Aristotelian Thomism. He utilized his late medieval scholasticism to narrate the natives rather than allowing his tradition to be shaped by the other.[24] While

18. Ibid., 17–18.

19. Ibid., 8.

20. Acosta, *Natural and Moral History*, 88–89.

21. Jennings, *Christian Imagination*, 84–85.

22. Ibid.

23. Ibid., 91.

24. Ibid., 86.

Acosta's journey presented numerous radical possibilities, including submission to native understandings of the place into which he travelled as guest, he carried forward the resources of his exhausted theological imagination, joining himself to the colonizing project rather than the people with whom he interacted. Jennings' subtle use of erotic metaphors communicates the deeply corporal nature of the Incarnational imagery he employs. Jennings' main conceptual task is to show us why it is helpful to understand Acosta, the neighborhood outreach duo, and contemporary theological formation to be unwittingly engaged in similar projects.

Jennings' third chapter tells the tale of John William Colenso, the Anglican Bishop who oversaw the British colony of Natal in South Africa. In working closely with the people of the land, Colenso's story displays new possibilities for mutuality. Engaged in the work of Bible translation, and partnering with William Ngidi, a Zulu man who assisted him in his linguistic work, Colenso initially utilized the existence of Ngidi in a way that narrated his own soteriological concerns.[25] As a modern liberal and romantic thinker, Colenso's reflections upon Ngidi influenced his embrace of a soteriological universalism and a higher critical perspective toward Scripture, which led to him being ousted as a heretic by the Anglican Church.[26] In order to engage in relational intimacy, Colenso could only imagine jettisoning the orthodoxy he had inherited. His Christian imagination was unable to envision radical inter-cultural joining as drawn from the historic life of Christ and his body in any thick way. Jennings maintains that Colenso's tradition did not provide him with an understanding of covenantal history within which to conceive a nonsupersessionist salvific trajectory.

Jennings' fourth chapter offers the ultimate character in his literary progression: a man who falls chronologically before but theologically later than Colenso.[27] Olaudah Equiano, the famous author and freed slave who argued for the abolition of the slave trade, is a bearer of the promise and limitations seen in the lives of the previous three individuals. From the cover of his autobiography, Equiano stares directly at the white reader, denoting "equality through connection."[28] He is an entrepreneur who uses his copious skills in self-promotion, fundraising, and political lobbying to advance the abolitionist cause. Yet as a Christian the most Equiano can imagine is an "economic confraternity" with his white brothers.[29] The Christianity

25. Ibid., 150.
26. Ibid., 148–49.
27. Ibid., 171.
28. Ibid., 189.
29. Ibid., 184.

bequeathed to him was an individualistic form of personal piety characteristic of consumerist relationships shaped by capitalist markets. As with the
other protagonists, either subjugation or assimilation were the only options
available to him.

In telling these four stories, Jennings clearly has in mind various
contemporary ways of theologically imagining identity within the space of
multicultural contact; these implications will be suggested throughout this
chapter and chapter 4.

Hope Anticipated

Through the stories of each character, and the ramifications of those stories
as corroborated by his own experience, Jennings has located his critiques
under the headings of *displacement* and *translation*. Jennings subsequently
turns his constructive theological vision to the space of *intimacy*. Considering together a wide breadth of resources, Jennings' work suggests a myriad
of implications for inter-disciplinary analysis. While I will deal with some
of his conclusions more fully in chapter 4 and the Conclusion, they should
be hinted at now.

In the fifth chapter of his text, Jennings demonstrates how vernacular
translation of the Scriptures had the accompanying effect of serving nationalist interests by renarrating indigenous worlds into the European linguistic
universe. Through translation, the pedagogical and catechetical functions of
the church also formed the nonwhite novitiate in the ethical and aesthetic
systems of the Occident. The creation of universal vernacular literary space
was mirrored by the creation of vernacular physical space through the im-
position of the Western economic concept of "private property."[30]

In the New World of the United States, the vernacular translation impulse was coupled with prohibitions against literacy for African slaves.[31] In
the rare event that slaves received education for literacy, it was done so as to
fully encapsulate African Americans within hermeneutical space in which
slavery and white supremacy were due to the providence of God and the
correct interpretation of Scripture. On the other hand, as slaves were forced
to obtain literacy by their own means, separate paths of biblical interpretation emerged, which in turn added to the segregated nature of ecclesial
gatherings and corporate worship.[32] Jennings maintains that this segregated
liturgical reality continues to be painfully apparent in contemporary eccle-

30. Ibid., 220–33.
31. Ibid., 234.
32. Ibid., 240.

sial embodiment. Finally, Jennings notes that much as the slave plantation revolved around and was constituted by the body of the white landowner, so American society in particular and Western society at large has been formed around an evaluative framework of whiteness extending its reach through "the true . . . the good . . . and the beautiful."[33]

In his sixth and final chapter, Jennings articulates his hope that, through recognition of the colonialist missteps of Christian theology, Christianity itself will be reclaimed as "an alternative form of cultural joining and interaction."[34] For this to happen, however, will require a much more robust doctrine of creation, which is fundamentally about place and people.[35] Jennings draws on Barth's trajectory of *Near and Distant Neighbors* in the *Church Dogmatics*[36] as he offers a biblical exposition of the relationship between the *ethnos* (Gentiles) and the covenantal history of Israel.[37] Barth tells a narrative in which the saving action of God extends, through Israel and her Messiah Jesus Christ, to all peoples from the particularity (place and space) of its Judaic center. Jennings refers to Israel as both biblical Israel and living Israel ("the people of God"), as opposed to Israel as a modern racial construct.[38] I will later clarify these definitions of Israel as I interact with research specifically related to supersessionism, which I have left heretofore largely undefined. Jennings' language of supersessionism is meant to invoke a Gentile remembrance that we have been written into someone else's story—that we have been invited to someone else's table—through the Jewish Messiah Jesus Christ. Jennings maintains that the body of Jesus Christ is the scandalous particularity that opens up new ways of being that transform all without denying the particularity of any.

A vision of creation connected to land requires the tangible joining of lives through the "transgress[ing] [of] boundaries of real estate" as people intentionally live where and with whom they should not.[39] This mutual identification in real space across ethnic and socioeconomic lines is the disruption, to the remade world of nationalistic identities and capitalist logics of exchange, that enables the creation of a new body politic in Jesus Christ. The accompanying necessity to "speak in tongues" creates the space where

---

33. Ibid., 277.
34. Ibid., 247.
35. Ibid., 248.
36. Barth, *Church Dogmatics* III.4, 305–23.
37. Jennings, *Christian Imagination*, 286.
38. Ibid., 254.
39. Ibid., 287.

vulnerability, humility, mutuality, and rebirth can flourish.[40] As Jennings holds forth:

> Imagine a people defined by their cultural difference yet who turn their histories and cultural logics toward a new determination, a new social performance of identity. In so doing, they enfold the old cultural logics and practices inside the new ones of others, and they enfold the cultural logics and practices of others inside their own. This mutual enfolding promises cultural continuity measured only by the desire of belonging. Thus the words and ways of one people join those of another, and another, each born anew in a community seeking to love and honor those in its midst.[41]

Jennings and Self-Revelation

Before I turn to an analysis of Jennings' central argument in conversation with the discipline of cultural studies, a few preliminary comments about Jennings' technique need to be made.

While Jennings' work is a work of theology, its style and pacing differ in several ways from common disciplinary modes of inquiry such as systematics, ethics, and exegesis. While his work navigates the intersection of these disciplines, he is "attempting to do theology in a different modality."[42] To use a musical analogy, he is improvising on familiar chord changes in order to reveal unforeseen possibilities in their progression. At the same time, he is attempting to identify the dissonance which imperialism introduced into Christian theology. In these ways, his work does not fit neatly into any of the "three rival versions of moral inquiry" offered by a MacIntyrian framework.[43] While Jennings is constructing a genealogical account of the missteps that gave rise to the racial imagination within the Christian tradition, I do not read him as calling confessional Christianity into question. In fact, I maintain that he is doing the opposite—presenting devout Christian life as an invitation to joining with God and with others. He is not claiming that imperialism is the necessary outgrowth of early Christian orthodoxy but rather is drawing attention to the ways in which a heavy reliance upon Western philosophical categories and an increasing split with Judaism paved

40. Ibid., 266.
41. Ibid., 274.
42. Ibid., 10.
43. MacIntyre, *Three Rival Versions*.

the way for the supersessionist theological imagination active in coloniza-tion. For instance, while he seems to find Chalcedonian Christology to be a faithful contextual expression of the person and work of Jesus Christ, his thesis suggests that its capitulation to Platonic modes of thought may have unwittingly served to distance the Christ of faith from the Jewish Jesus, thus preparing the way for the supersessionism of late medievalism. This leads to the conclusion that, while orthodox Christology has safeguarded impor-tant mysteries about the Incarnation, it nonetheless served to systematize, rationalize, and Westernize reflection on God becoming flesh.[44] The early development of Christology was coincident with increasing anti-Jewish rhetoric, rhetoric that would be fertile ground for later more tragic develop-ments. It is the multi-disciplinary scope of Jennings' work that allows for these conclusions to be made.

The literary progression of *The Christian Imagination* is supportive of its thesis. By weaving his account through his own story and several his-torical narratives, Jennings is able to tie together seemingly disconnected concerns in order to arrive at unexpected conclusions. By dealing primar-ily in sources related to cultural studies and history rather than theology, Jennings' theology has interdisciplinary ramifications. His text itself is an invitation to joining: the meshing of disciplines, the connection between author and reader, and the joining of diverse peoples.

Cultural Studies and Theology

As with my analysis of Carter in chapter 1, I now turn from summariz-ing Jennings' text to placing him in conversation with the cultural studies literature he consults. In this section, I will elucidate Jennings' methodologi-cal relationship to the discipline. Jennings engages thinkers such as Acosta, who was by training and practice a theologian, but have been "relegated to missionary texts, or mission or inter-cultural studies texts, or even early ethnography or anthropological texts, not, as it should be, to standard texts on the performance of theology in the New World."[45] He maintains that this is "not because of simple intellectual oversight, but because he exposes the

44. In addition to Jennings, my thinking on this point has been influenced by Justo L. Gonzalez's *A History of Christian Thought*. I find Gonzalez's thesis of the develop-ment of orthodox Christology as both necessary and yet problematically reliant upon Hellenistic philosophy to be concordant with Jennings' thesis. At the same time, I am convinced by Gonzalez's assertion that such rationalization was a faithful buttress against the even more speculative and philosophically systematic heresies against which orthodox doctrine was developed. (See particularly volumes 1:394–395 and 2:88–89.)

45. Jennings, *Christian Imagination*, 115.

imperialist matrix within which orthodox Christian tradition continues to exist."[46] Until moderns "reckon with his laugh," we will not be able to "make sense of Christian theology or Christian intellectual life since colonialism."[47] In our current reality, Jennings writes, the practice of teaching systematic theology as a distinct discipline disconnected from missiology or intercultural studies is "immoral."[48]

It will become apparent throughout this analysis that the methodologies of Jennings and the cultural studies scholars with whom he interacts do not share the same *telos*. Yet Jennings takes their historical accounts basically uncontested, demonstrating that he does not find historical knowledge to be antithetical to the Gospel, but rather material to it. Here is one of Jennings' key hermeneutical distinctions: he appears to be more interested in disciplinary joining than academic segregation or disciplinary "purity"; he takes cultural studies seriously while holding contemporary theological virtue ethics at a distance. As Jennings' Barthian methodology suggests, the knowledge of the world is not something *other* than the knowledge of God.[49] Divine revelation meets us in the mundane details of human existence, which can be seen most clearly in the Incarnation. The practice of history or other sciences with methodological integrity can be a means to better understanding God's revelation in creation. Jennings is not positioning himself against cultural studies, but is conducting a pre-theological reading of the literature. Similar to the manner in which, in *The Politics of Jesus*, Yoder was not attempting to work primarily within the disciplinary confines of biblical studies but rather to build the connections between that scholarship and theological ethics,[50] Jennings is not setting out to recreate the historical record but to locate this record within the theological history of YHWH. Jennings' work is for church and academy, which are both ecclesiological in that Jennings' interest is the joining of particular people in particular space.

I will demonstrate the manner in which Jennings utilizes the historical record relating to each character while briefly indicating the ways in which his conclusions differ from those of the discipline of cultural studies. While in turn examining the body of literature surrounding each character, I will elucidate the theological categories Jennings utilizes to locate the significance of each figure for the Christian imagination. I will also intimate what

46. Ibid., 115.

47. Ibid., 115–16.

48. Ibid., 115.

49. Barth, *Church Dogmatics* I.1, 6–8.

50. Yoder, *The Politics of Jesus*, preface.

appears to be the contemporary significance of each of Jennings' analyses. Following my analysis of the treatment of Acosta, I will provide a brief excursus into Jennings' theological method as compared with that of modern historiography and an explication of several of the keys terms Jennings employs. I begin with Acosta because he will serve as Jennings' paradigmatic figure in his analysis of a tradition of virtue.

Jose de Acosta

Three of the scholars Jennings consults for the historiographic significance of Acosta are Sabine MacCormack, Walter Mignolo, and Tzvetan Todorov. While interacting specifically with Acosta, MacCormack also more generally enumerates the religious implications of the collision between colonial Spanish Catholicism and native Peruvian spiritual frameworks. Through an analysis of Acosta's evaluation of native communication, Mignolo elucidates the ways in which European linguistic conceptualities eclipsed indigenous views of history. Todorov, while referencing Acosta, focuses more generally on a philosophical examination of the implications of cultural contact with an unlike "other." While their analyses are crucial for Jennings' investigation into the theological moves underpinning colonialism, their delineation of causal relationships is not interested in (and perhaps is insufficient to the task of) locating each historical character within the overarching narrative of theological history. This limitation in the sociohistorical methodology of cultural studies becomes apparent as the Christian theological categories invoked by each character (each of whom viewed his own work *as* Christian theological reflection) are underemphasized in favor of historiographic interests.

We begin with the work of MacCormack, professor of history with a specialization in Latin American studies at the University of Notre Dame. In *Religion in the Andes: Vision and Imagination in Early Colonial Peru*, MacCormack demonstrates several ways in which Acosta's religious and descriptive framework was beholden to the Aristotelian-Thomist tradition as refracted through Spanish colonial Catholicism.[51] As she notes, the psychological categories of Aristotle were adapted by Aquinas into a Christian framework and utilized by the colonial missionaries to categorize the natives. By holding to an Aristotelian schema in which the perception of the five senses produced a *common sense* which was translated by the *imagination* in the form of *phantasms* or *images* into the *intellect* and subsequently stored in *memory* in the back of the brain, colonial Thomist classifications

51. MacCormack, *Religion in the Andes*.

produced a "cultural hierarchy under the guise of cognition."[52] The missionaries therefore conjectured that while the sense perceptions of the indigenes may have been the same as those of the Europeans, the natives had undisciplined imaginations, thereby producing inferior intellects. Acosta, following Aquinas, affirmed that intellect is "the highest, most noble part of the soul" and is therefore immortal.[53] While the significance of Aquinas' conception of the *imago Dei* as found in reason will be evaluated in chapter 4, it is important to recognize here that Acosta followed Aquinas in equating the Aristotelian intellect with the immortal soul of humans, which aided in his evaluation of the natives as anthropologically inferior.[54]

While Aristotle's psychological categories allowed him to posit an anthropological distinction between Greeks and non-Greeks, Acosta expanded Aristotle's designation of the latter group as *barbarians* into three distinct classes. Whereas Aristotle had simply assumed the inferiority of non-Greeks, Acosta now transmuted that classification into subgroups along ethnic lines. This racialized scale pitted Europe as, in the words of Acosta, "the better and more noble part of the world," a place in which, as MacCormack relates of Acosta's worldview, "human knowledge and institutions . . . had reached their most perfect state."[55] The peoples of the Americas and Africa became the counterweight to the virtuous Europeans. The darker peoples were held to be the epitome of inferiority while the comparatively lighter Asians, who were discerned as being more highly civilized and more receptive to the Gospel, were placed in between.[56] Because it was held that the capacity to be higher-functioning was intrinsic to Europeans and lacking on the part of Native Americans and Africans, the latter peoples needed to be governed by European Christians who could, in the words of Acosta, "enforce their continued adherence to Christianity" whereas Asian peoples could be converted by "reasoned teaching" as had been done to the Greeks and the Romans by the apostles.[57]

MacCormack explains that Acosta was firmly opposed to the idea of *accommodation*, in which any sense of native religious understanding could be preserved within a Christian framework. Rather, Incan and Andean religious, and thereby cultural, frameworks had to be *extirpated*.[58] Acosta

52. Ibid., 24–26, 225.
53. Ibid., 280.
54. Ibid., 16–17.
55. Ibid., 266.
56. Ibid., 264–67.
57. Ibid., 267.
58. Ibid., 263.

interpreted the customs and religious practices of the natives as idolatrous and maintained that the Quechua vocabulary was inadequate for Christian teaching.[59] Because of the "slow intellect" of the natives, extreme patience was required on the part of the missionary. The most convincing witness comparatively simpleminded indigenes could grasp was the virtuous life of the clergy.[60] Acosta held that because of native inferiority, the miracles performed by the early Christian disciples were not necessary for the conversion of the native peoples (as they had been to convince the comparatively superior Greeks and Romans), which provided an explanation for the vexing problem of the colonial missionaries' inability to work the miracles accomplished by the apostles.[61] Apparent lack on the part of the carrier of the message was due to the ineptitude of the recipient of the message.

While Jennings accepts these observations as he forms his thesis, he does not end where MacCormack does, confined within her disciplinary mode of inquiry. While MacCormack's explanation of Acosta's worldview informs Jennings' theological analysis, her modern cultural studies framework encourages her to find in the beginnings of the Enlightenment the antidote for colonial cultural hierarchies. The hero of MacCormack's analysis is Baruch Spinoza, whose break with Orthodox Judaism in favor of modern higher criticism is seen by MacCormack as the groundwork for the beginning of religious studies as a discipline.[62] For MacCormack, it is in the study of religion, rather than in antiquated theological pursuits, that respect for a plurality of cultures is to be found. It is in this vein that she invokes Spinoza, who rejected Aristotelian psychology and Thomist theology (which had been used to discern the demonic in the indigenes) because, in his universe, "the devil did not exist."[63] Rather than undertaking theological criticism of specific aspects of Thomism, Spinoza rejected theology out of hand precisely because it did not conform to his modern suppositions. MacCormack favors what she relates as Spinoza's read of the Scriptures: a treatise "on the pursuit of a virtuous and pious life" rather than a narrative focused on "the true nature of God."[64] She maintains that Spinoza did not find Israel's election to be related to God's revelation to them which he saw as being "very ordinary," but rather because of their "ordered polity" and

59. Ibid., 264.
60. Ibid.
61. Ibid., 267.
62. Ibid., 448, 454–55.
63. Ibid., 443.
64. Ibid., 445.

"attainment of temporal security and well-being."[65] In this fashion, God would choose other nations in the future based upon their adherence to these ideals. MacCormack explicitly views Enlightenment as the undoing of a colonialist posture rather than its maturation. While Jennings finds MacCormack's analysis of Acosta useful, he disagrees with the conclusion that modernity stands in liberating opposition to colonization. This is not to deny that there have been important liberating strides in modernity, such as abolition of the transatlantic slave trade, (which, incidentally, was largely accomplished by Christians such as Equiano). Rather, Jennings' genealogy of colonialism-modernity reminds us that slavery, economic exploitation, violence, and racism (and the racialized imagination undergirding them all) are still very much alive in modernity.

In much the same way that MacCormack identifies Acosta's disdain for Quechua linguistic structures, Mignolo deals at length with the subject of vernacular translation. Mignolo is professor of literature specializing in cultural anthropology and romance studies at Duke University, where Jennings was tenured. The influence of Mignolo's work can be discerned as Jennings builds upon it with his discussion of the theological significance of vernacular translation of the Bible by colonial powers.[66] Mignolo appears to understand the theological significance of Acosta more than MacCormack does. Presumably, Acosta becomes Jennings' paradigmatic historical figure in large part due to the academic space he has shared with Mignolo. In chapter 4, I will further intimate the significance of this relationship as I directly consult Acosta's writings and Mignolo's commentary on them.

Mignolo provides more nuance to Acosta's accounts of the languages and historical records of the peoples of Peru than does MacCormack. As he relates, while Acosta did not consider the quipus (beaded knots of rope) to be a valid system of writing, Acosta nonetheless conceded that through their use "the Indians of Peru . . . conserved no less the memory of ancient lore, nor did they have any less account of all their affairs of peace, war, and government."[67] Acosta weighs the means of record-keeping of the "other" against that of his own people and finds it lacking because it does not fit his definition of writing. Yet he observes that through the use of quipus, the Indians did not keep any less of an adequate account of their history, being able to maintain "as many differences as we have with our twenty-four letters" and producing "an infinity of words" and "innumerable meanings

---

65. Ibid., 451.

66. Jennings, *Christian Imagination*, chapter 5.

67. Mignolo, *The Darker Side of the Renaissance*, 84.

of things."[68] What can be implied from this analysis is that Acosta does not seem to have been consciously utilizing theology as an instrument of oppression. Rather, his particular vein of late medieval/early-modern virtue ethics inculcated him into a classificatory structure within which he was unable to conceptualize the Amerindian outside of a framework of European supremacy.

Acosta was left in the awkward spot of postulating, as in the case of the Aztecs, how a native people could maintain such formal oratory without letters.[69] Mignolo presents Acosta as arguing that the Amerindians were in fact intelligent human beings, but that they simply lacked letters.[70] For Acosta, this presented quite a conundrum, which he resolved by concluding, in the words of Mignolo, "that anybody can keep records of the past, but history can only be written with letters."[71] These viewpoints were grounded in the works of classical Greco-Roman culture. The specific theory of writing developed by Acosta was based on Aristotle[72] while his view of what constituted history was rooted in the works of Cicero and Quintilian. Quintilian had distinguished *historia* (the true narration of past events) from *fabula* and *argumentum*, which applied to feigned narratives or those far from the truth.[73] Perhaps this is why Acosta, in his aptly-named *Historia*, declared that "it is easier to refute what is false about the Indians' origins than to discover the truth, for among them there are neither writings nor any certain memories of their first founders."[74]

Identifying a lack of writing (as European cultural construct) as indicative of a lack of truth in native self-articulation, Acosta was led to judge both the aesthetics and ethics of the Peruvian people. Not only would joining to the other no longer be a necessity, it would be fraught with danger and moral compromise. Evaluation, categorization, subjugation (and instruction) of the "other" would become morally incumbent upon "Christian" nations and peoples. Thus the Franciscan and Jesuit educational programs in the New World consisted of "making Castilian available to the Amerindian and, together with teaching how to read and write in Castilian, transmitting Castilian values and manners."[75] Translation functioned in service to

68. Ibid., 84–86.
69. Ibid., 110.
70. Ibid., 133.
71. Ibid., 134.
72. Ibid., 133.
73. Ibid., 134.
74. Jennings, *Christian Imagination*, 91.
75. Mignolo, *Darker Side of the Renaissance*, 65.

"the numerous edicts and mandates published by the Crown."[76] Whereas MacCormack's thesis found theology itself to be the problem, Mignolo's analysis more precisely discerns what was problematic about the particular theological trajectory Acosta inherited. In other words, Jennings is not dismissing theology as a mode of discourse but is rather criticizing particular presuppositions that led to theology becoming a discourse of power, control, classification and universal education.

A third scholar Jennings consults is Todorov, a Franco-Bulgarian philosopher who has written extensively about literary theory and cultural criticism. His primary research interests have included totalitarianism and the history of the conquest of the Americas. In *The Conquest of America: The Question of the Other*, Todorov uses the heuristic device of encounters with the "other" to narrate the tragic legacy of colonialism. While his discourse with Acosta specifically is somewhat limited, his framing of the typology of Acosta's mode of interaction with the "other" bears similarities to Jennings' analysis of Acosta. Todorov identifies that because of his theological worldview, Acosta held that something as important as the discovery of the Americas must have been foretold in the Scriptures and, to that end, labored to elucidate the connection.[77] Todorov notes that by attempting to conform the other to his orienting framework, Acosta "neglect[ed] the interhuman dimension" and failed to recognize the other "both as equal and as different."[78] While these observations are similar to those Jennings makes about the difference between translation and joining, Todorov concludes that because Europeans created "otherness," the antidote is an inherent perspectivism in religion.[79] Jennings alleges that Todorov "overreach[es]" in his conclusions, thereby distancing himself from Todorov's modern comparative analysis. Jennings does not appropriate Todorov's "equal" and "different" logic, which does not require joining and therefore does not necessarily resist the logic which animated legalized American racism. In this sense, Todorov's research informs Jennings' analysis while Todorov's thesis provides a clarifying contrast to Jennings' stress on joining in the particular body of the Jewish Jesus Christ.[80]

By not sufficiently evaluating the theological significance of Acosta, the cultural studies literature does not pinpoint the supersessionist distortions Jennings identifies in the late medieval and early Renaissance theological

76. Ibid., 65.

77. Todorov, *The Conquest of America*, 75.

78. Ibid., 76.

79. Jennings, *Christian Imagination*, 58, 101.

80. Ibid., 58, 101.

frameworks about which it is concerned. MacCormack does not recognize that Spinoza's modern humanistic divergence from Orthodox Judaism is, according to Jennings' analysis, a maturation of colonialist sensibilities rather than their undoing. In this way, the cultural studies discipline is unwittingly beholden to the colonial legacy. Jennings' work suggests that Christianity qua early-modern religious construct represents a distortion of Christian faith. In much the same way that Muller criticized modern Harnackian rationalized religion *as* Christianity, the cultural studies literature criticizes a faith already distorted by supersessionism and colonial grabs for power and land. This faith is a deviation from a lived hope in the Incarnate Jewish Messiah's life as constitutive of the interconnectedness of humanity.

Rather than focusing on these methodological divergences, Jennings theologically renarrates the analyses provided by the cultural studies literature. The title *The Christian Imagination* appears to be a clever subversion of the Aristotelian conception of *imagination* utilized by the colonial missionaries to denigrate the natives. Ironically, the process of discernment that MacCormack relates the Europeans used to classify the "undisciplined imaginations"[81] of the natives becomes for Jennings the "diseased social imagination" characteristic of "Christianity in the Western world."[82] The analyses of MacCormack, Mignolo, and Todorov together constitute a backdrop upon which Jennings' central theological concerns become apparent.

I will conclude this treatment of Acosta with the theological significance Jennings finds in the historical narratives offered by these scholars and suggest the contemporary significance of Jennings' assessments. The racialized scale catalogued in the work of MacCormack is described by Jennings as residing in a distorted view of creation resulting from displacement as a theological act.[83] The subsequent supersessionism and relentless comparative schema of whiteness can be seen displayed in the words of another Jesuit missionary as he gazed over the Amazonian jungles of Peru and "yearn[ed] to journey among those *gentiles* in their unknown land."[84] Second, Mignolo's description of the vernacular translation efforts of the colonial missionaries grounds Jennings' identification of the transference of European aesthetic hegemony through Bible and devotional translation and the hymnic work of Isaac Watts, among others.[85] Finally, Todorov serves to

---

81. MacCormack, *Religion in the Andes*, 26.

82. Jennings, *Christian Imagination*, 6.

83. Ibid., 31.

84. MacCormack, *Religion in the Andes*, 280, italics mine.

85. Jennings, *Christian Imagination*, 210.

provide a structure of cultural anthropology with which Jennings compares his invocation of joining as reflective of the Incarnation.

Through his use of Acosta, Jennings is targeting contemporary incarnational postures that imagine intellectual formation along the lines of retrievals of Western virtue. Such systems tend to form Christian scholars and ministers in patterns of intellectual dominance. The bulk of my analysis in chapter 4 will be employed in filling out this claim. The primary spokesperson for a contemporary Aristotelian-Thomist virtue ethic is the Catholic philosopher MacIntyre, who is named by Jennings in his reflections on Acosta.[86] While being named by Jennings in a footnote rather than the body of the text, its primary theological proponent is Hauerwas, the public theologian to whom Duke Divinity School owes much of its exemplary reputation.[87] Jennings interacts with MacIntyre's thesis and references several of Hauerwas' primary interlocutors.[88] In this sense, *The Christian Imagination* can be read as an indirect critique of Hauerwas' central claims about the moral formation and education of Christian intellectuals, as summarized in *The State of the University*.[89] While sharing the communitarians'[90] recognition of the problematic nature of modernity, Jennings peers back further to identify the diseased imagination of colonialism and the patterns of theological reflection it has influenced. Jennings suggests that anti-modern polemics often offer superficial analyses stemming from the fact that "Western Christian intellectuals still imagine the world from the commanding heights."[91]

> My claim here would seem to fly in the face of a number of theologians and philosophers who believe that societies have now entered a post-Christian or post-establishment Christian reality in the Western world in which the easy alignment of Protestantism with the quasi-religious sensibilities of the nation-state has vanished. Whatever the claimed cause of this situation for the church in the modern "post-Christendom" world, the conclusion is the same: Western Christians are a minority, an exilic people in a strange land . . . [S]uch readings of the reality of Christian existence in the West are painfully superficial. They

86. Ibid., 68–72.

87. Ibid., 307.

88. Ibid., 296.

89. Hauerwas, *State of the University*.

90. I have borrowed this term from Brian Brock, (*Captive to Christ*), who uses it to describe scholars, such as Hauerwas, whose primary theological focus is the historic and contemporary ecclesial community as radical counter-culture.

91. Jennings, *Christian Imagination*, 8.

bypass the deeper realities of Western Christian sensibilities, identities, and habits of mind which continue to channel patterns of colonialist dominance.[92]

Hauerwas is the theologian who has most clearly articulated claims about Christians being an alien and exilic people in modern society.[93] These claims are deeply compelling and deserve to be taken seriously from a biblical and theological standpoint. I will interact with these claims in some detail in the next chapter. Suffice it to say that I am persuaded by Jennings that such a manner of imagining Christian peoplehood owes more to supersessionist notions of peoplehood (developed in concert with the idea of "peoplehood" articulated by the modern nation-State) than the communitarians may care to admit. In the next chapter, I will suggest that, of Milbank, MacIntyre, and Hauerwas (who each offer subtly different accounts of virtue), Hauerwas most satisfactorily resists such pitfalls. However, to the extent that he rearticulates MacIntyrian conceptions of virtue, Hauerwas reenacts problematic patterns of intellectual formation. While a MacIntyrian virtue ethic is not Jennings' only target, his familiarity with the sorts of relationality constituted by such a tradition (and its ubiquitous nature in contemporary Christian life) encourages him to contrast his reflections with it.

Methodological Excursus

Having seen the manner in which Jennings utilizes the scholarly historical consensus surrounding Acosta as paradigmatic of his interaction with the discipline of cultural studies, we are better positioned to further differentiate Jennings' theological focus from the historiographic enterprise.

Jennings offers a theological account of history rather than a distinctively modern philosophy of history. As such, it is an account of God the Creator's activity in space and time, according to the Barthian logic that the only properly historical account is that revealed by the One in whom history coheres: "The judgement of God is the end of history . . . the negation under which all flesh stands, the absolute judgement, which is the meaning of God for the world of men and time and things . . . also the crimson thread which runs through the whole course of the world."[94] Biblical history is neither another discipline alongside modern historiography nor an "interpretation" of

---

92. Ibid., 8.

93. Hauerwas and Willimon, *Resident Aliens.*

94. Barth, *Epistle to the Romans*, 77.

secular history. Both trajectories place the revealed Word of YHWH under the authority of the human apprehension of knowledge. If theological history is that in which humanity's various histories find their cohesion, it is neither subservient to naturalistic sources nor apprehended without faith. As Barth states:

> Unless, quite apart from the study of documentary sources, there exists a living perception of the one constant significance of all human occurrence, history becomes merely a sequence of epochs and a series of civilizations; elements, of separate individuals, ages, periods, relationships, and institutions; it teems with phenomena which charge about in all directions . . . To call it 'interesting' is not the equivalent of saying that it is full of meaning. A past, marked by a chaos of faces, is not an eloquent, understood, and apprehended past. If history can present no more than this, it is trivial. Be the material never so carefully and critically brought together; be the devotion in delving into the past never so great, and the accuracy of the scholar never so precise; be the understanding of an ancient culture and manner of life never so sensitive, and the sympathy with different points of view thrown up by the past never so delicate—yet this, for all its competence, is not history: it is photographed and analysed chaos . . . In times of spiritual poverty, historical analysis is a method we are bound to adopt. But one day it will itself reach its limit . . . and then it too will stand before the same commanding necessity of a synthesis which is the starting-point of the book of Genesis . . . We have no desire to fetter or to cast suspicions upon the critical method. But it also cannot in the end survive the KRISIS, the sickness unto death, under which we stand. Indeed, in its own fashion it hastens the process . . . And just in so far as it comes to this conclusion, it opens the road to . . . the necessary synthesis, and finally to the impossible possibility of which we must sooner or later dare to take stock, namely—our faith.[95]

While Barth's account of history has often been accused of being fideistic,[96] and while Jennings does not take a strictly Barthian tone in his text, it is nonetheless helpful to identify a Barthian influence in Jennings' work. Jennings' theological use of cultural studies literature is an attempt to join that which has been "[k]ept separate in conventional analyses" and has

---

95. Ibid., 145–48.

96. While I do not claim that Barth's work is completely immune to such criticisms, I contend that they do not take into account the manner in which Barth believes that there is a rationality peculiar to faith, one that proceeds from it.

produced a "natural, almost evolutionary character."[97] By joining a theological account with the available historical record, Jennings is able to suggest a theology of history unavailable within the sharp disciplinary distinctions of modernity. Jennings locates the various histories of the historical figures and peoples he examines within *the* revealed history of God's work of re-creation through his people, Israel, and her Messiah, Jesus.

While MacCormack describes the manner in which Acosta privileged his own *historia* at the expense of the indigenous peoples' *fabula*, and while Mignolo relates Acosta's prejudices regarding native record-keeping, neither scholar offers a compelling and competing vision to Acosta's methodology. This suggests that modern historiography is heir to the colonialist patterns of reflection inaugurated by early-modern encyclopedic observation. Cultural studies must necessarily content itself with suggesting causal relationships as constituting the force of history. Jennings as theologian effectually "undoes" the work of Acosta by suggesting another manner of viewing history. In the light of God's revelation in the incarnation of Jesus Christ, history itself becomes a vehicle for divine revelation.

Particular *joining* between peoples cannot be the main problematic of the cultural studies authors Jennings utilizes. The vulnerability of joining renders the historian's observations suspect and questions her academic objectivity. The contemporary historiographic enterprise necessarily maintains a distinction akin to Acosta's *historia* and *fabula*. Jennings' historical methodology is more sensitive to the sort undertaken by Deloria Jr., who proposes taking the creation stories and mythologies of the world's peoples at face value.[98] Deloria Jr. finds the modern tendency of Christian theology to "demythologize" theological history to be a capitulation to a naturalistic methodology that misunderstands the nature of religion.[99] Jennings' analysis suggests that the cultural studies enterprise devalues the claims about revelation made by people of faith. Additionally, his theological historical account attempts to avoid what was one of Barth's gravest concerns about the historiographic enterprise and its attendant forms of natural theology (the sort employed by German National Socialism): Naturalistic analyses

97. See Jennings, *Christian Imagination*, 220, where he interacts with Adrian Hastings' account of vernacular biblical translation and the rise of cultural nationalisms. Jennings concludes by noting that the best Hastings can offer is a causal sequence which Hastings suggests demonstrates that "the correlation between biblical translation and what one may call a national awakening is *remarkably close* across most of Europe and, quite often, for other parts of the world as well" (italics mine). Hastings' method suggests correlations based on observations but cannot offer a metanarrative in which to locate those observations.

98. Deloria, *God is Red*, 113–32.

99. Ibid., 115–19.

can easily presume that particular cultural perspectives are universally normative, that it is "obvious" that things are as one wants them to be. Jennings' account suggests that what is "self-evident" may not remain so when particular lives are joined together in Christ.

As with orthodox theology's relationship to the sometimes suspicious tendencies of modern critical methodology, Jennings' relationship to cultural studies diverges methodologically while still drawing from the discipline. While much can be learned from critical studies related to the Scriptures or to human cultures, the theologian cannot take wholesale an account of reality centered on anything other than God's own self-revelation. Modern historiography tends to place human empirical observation in the seat once held by divine revelation.

Race and Place

Before analyzing Jennings' interaction with his remaining three historical Christian figures, it is necessary to further probe the theological significance of several designations Jennings utilizes, designations I have heretofore left largely undefined. In this section, I will probe what Jennings calls the theological "density of effects"[100] taking place in colonization by explicating his terminology of *place*, *race*, and *supersessionism* and demonstrating how the terms are interconnected.

For Jennings, *place* is a means of getting into the particular significance of the doctrine of creation: "Belief in creation has to refer to current real-world places or it refers to nothing."[101] For Jennings, place cannot be generalized or universalized; it has to do with particular spaces in the created order and their defining characteristics.[102] The various characteristics of particular places are identity signifiers that constitute the people of the land and shape that people's self-understanding; they are the means by which created beings participate in their creatureliness. Trees, vegetation, contours of land, climate, animals, bodies of water, seasonal patterns, movement of solar bodies, and weather systems are all aspects of the created order manifested differently in various places; they serve to establish particular peoples as members of the created order. If creation is the action of God in space, time, and history, and if humanity is intrinsically bound to the created order by obtaining sustenance from it and by serving it through cultivation, then identity is best understood with reference to place. Identity

100. Jennings, *Christian Imagination*, 24.
101. Ibid., 85.
102. Ibid., 40ff.

as spatially-constituted is neither an essentialized designation nor an essentially movable schema (like that of race).

This is not to imply that a particular people and a particular location are divinely connected in the sense of a definitive *ordo* of creation. To say such can lead into theories of place as motherland, which feed conceptualities of blood purity, thereby reinforcing modern national borders and racial anthropological classifications. As Barth recognized: "This is the *cul-de-sac* into which we can be betrayed if we do not think out critically this question of near and distant neighbors, but obliterate the distinction between creation and providence, between the divine command and the divine disposing."[103] Jennings' identification of the sixteenth-century Spanish obsession with "blood purity" (*limpieza de sangre*) as being formed out of fear of the Jews (and inaugurating the conception of modern race) finds important parallels in Barth's identification of twentieth-century German National Socialists' invocation of the "motherland" as arising in response to the *Judenfrage*.[104] Both diagnoses are born out of the scholars' recognitions of the theological importance of place and the ways such theological import has been distorted.

In contrast to a hardening of place or an essentialization of race, Jennings is simply acknowledging that identity is shaped by place, that we are organically connected to the created order. Place is the conduit by which we participate in our creaturely reality; we necessarily exist as members of a particular spatially-constituted people. That a human exists in a specific place communicates that she is a creature and, more specifically, that she is this creature and not another. Even though Cartesian epistemology would imply otherwise, humans are material beings who are incapable of floating disembodied in empty space. Place does the doctrinal work of combating all sorts of neo-Gnostic tendencies. In the same sense that a thick Christology invokes the scandal of particularity, a theologically-centered anthropology recognizes human existence as spatially-oriented. Place identifies us as creatures rather than the Creator, necessitating that the vulnerability of mutual joining in the body of the Incarnate One requires sharing of space. "Place-sharing" confirms us together as one new person in place of the two.[105]

While place is constitutive of a people's identity, identity is tied to place in a relationship that can be either concordant or discordant with the purposes of God. In the creation of man and woman in the garden, YHWH

103. Barth, *Church Dogmatics III.4*, 309.

104. See Jennings, *Christian Imagination*, 79–81 and Barth, *Church Dogmatics III.4*, 309.

105. Eph 2:15. See Root, *Relational Youth Ministry*, 124–65, where he translates Bonhoeffer's *stevelltretung* as "place-sharing."

bound their self-understanding as creatures to the specific landscape of Eden. In exilic punishment resultant from their transgression of the spatial boundaries God had assigned for them,[106] man and woman became in some sense an ever-exilic people, always experiencing the punishment of their displacement as a fundamental opposition between them and the land.[107] As Walter Brueggemann notes in *The Land: Place as Gift, Promise, and Challenge in Biblical Faith*, land is at the center of both divine blessing and divine judgment and is that which grants a continuity to history: "Land-loss means the end of history."[108] Likewise, displacement "is experienced like the empty dread of primordial chaos."[109] Throughout the biblical narrative, humanity understands its identity in relationship to place, which can include experiences of being aliens and strangers.[110] The promised hope of the eschaton is a particular place with specific describable characteristics.[111]

In addition to the divine work in creation being made manifest in and through particular space, God's work in redemption likewise claims place for his purposes. In YHWH's election of Israel, he chose for himself a people taken out of a particular place and the peoples of that place (as opposed to Israel being a "pure" race in the modern sense of that term). For Abraham, it was a call to travel from Ur of the Chaldeans to a land that would be revealed to him.[112] For the nation from his loins, it was deliverance from the place of their oppression and bondage.[113] Egypt had become a place of identity-constitution for the Israelites. Their greatest temptation was to return to the land of their slavery.[114] The judgments of YHWH upon the gods of Egypt were therefore judgments upon the physical characteristics of that specific place.[115] The land of promise to which Israel was led was a particular place, identifiable by its material realities.[116] Throughout

106. See Gen 2:15–17, which offers a topographical description of the garden by assigning to the humans boundaries for action which, when transgressed, would constitute a misappropriation of land use.

107. Gen 3:17–19, 22–24.

108. Brueggemann, *The Land*, 105.

109. Ibid., 28.

110. 1 Pet 2:11.

111. Rev 21, 22.

112. Gen 11:31—12:3.

113. Exod 3:16–17.

114. Exod 16:2–3.

115. Exod 12:12.

116. E.g., "A land flowing with milk and honey" (Exod 3:8), a land known for its produce (as in the great cluster of grapes of Num 13:23–24 and the place that bore its name), and the eventual land divisions situated along natural spatial boundaries and given to particular tribes (Josh 13–21).

theological history, the identity of the people of YHWH and the identity of their Creator was tied into the divine acts among that people in identifiable places at particular times. YHWH would be revealed to his people through the midst of a sea, in fire on a mountain, in the smoke of glory in a tabernacle, and in the suffering of a lamb. YHWH's acts of salvation and deliverance were connected to particular topographies and were recalled with monuments, songs, writings, and narratives that became part of the landscape and served to reinforce who the people were. Names and meaning were attached to mountains, rivers, seas, trees, deserts, and animals. These designations served to reconfirm the people in their identity when collective amnesia occurred. In the same way that the land of their slavery had become for the Israelites an idolatrous temptation away from their identity in YHWH, the physical specificities of the land of promise likewise became the markers by which the descendants of the people would be catechized into the life of the community.[117]

In the Scriptures, divine judgment often resulted in displacement. Both the people of Israel and the "nations" (*ethnos*) often were punished through removal from land. Exile can signify a loss of cultural identity, manifested in a reeling lack of self-awareness resultant from disconnection from place. As can be seen in the exilic Psalm 137, to be removed from Israel's land was to risk cultural dissolution and ambiguity of identity. While not being the center of the redemptive story, the *ethnos* are seen throughout the Scriptures as having similar identity-connections with their lands. For the "nations" as such, removal from their lands was often a result of divine judgment, as was revealed to Abraham in relation to the Amorites who occupied the land of Canaan.[118] It must be clearly stated, however, that, for Jennings, divine warrant for the forced displacement of peoples from their lands is never something a people can claim for themselves.

Jennings finds the divine command to Israel for the destruction of the people of Canaan to be a punctiliar, non-repeatable act given to a particular chosen people for the sake of all peoples. Jennings references the narrative of the Israelite conquest of Canaan as God's election of a people in a place for the sake of invitation to the world. It is in this sense that "[t]he theological justification for conquest was an unrepeatable act" grounded in "the divine demand of obedience."[119] While distinguishing this action from both

117. See, for example, Josh 4:5–7, where the stones taken from the middle of the Jordan (the land boundary) are used as a memorial to cause the children of Israel to ask their meaning and the elders to re-tell and pass down the story of YHWH's acts of salvation in that place.

118. Gen 15:16.

119. Jennings, *Christian Imagination*, 257.

"the workings of statecraft" and "the ideological justification for conquest," Jennings acknowledges that it is a scandal:

> However, the deepest aspect of this scandal received scant attention in the history of the church's theologies: Gentiles may never claim for themselves what was true only for Israel . . . What was repeatable, however, was the clear implication for Gentiles: YHWH announced divine claim from the land of Israel on all land and all peoples.[120]

Because the displacement enacted upon the powerful and fortified *ethnos* by the nomadic and vulnerable people of YHWH was a divine command, the early-modern colonization enacted by powerful empires claiming their own divine prerogative becomes a particularly despicable act. The recognition that it was only by divine command that Israel was justified in displacing the Canaanites may explain the invocation of "Manifest Destiny" by modern Empires engaged in military expansionism (as well as contemporary assertions of God's blessing in modern warfare against "evil" nations.)[121]

Distinguishing the actions of biblical Israel from those of the modern nation-state, Jennings maintains: "God stood between them and the land, forever reordering their connection to place."[122] In the Hebrew Bible, when Israel forgot her God, forsook her identity, and committed the despicable practices of the *ethnos*, she too was removed from the land of her identity-constitution. Referring to the problematic equation of divine election with modern statism, Brueggemann notes:

> The outcome of [the] merger of old traditional claim and contemporary military capacity becomes an intolerable commitment to violence that is justified by reason of state . . . [I]t is clear that the same ideology of entitlement has served derivatively the Western powers that are grounded in this broad ideological claim and that have used that claim as a rationale for colonization of other parts of "the earth." That is, *land entitlement* leads to *earth occupation*. There is no doubt that such land entitlement has functioned as a warrant for European seizure of what became the United States with a brutalizing dismissal of Native Americans, who are regarded as an inconvenience for the arriving entitled Europeans . . . No doubt these cases can

120. Ibid., 257.

121. Consider George W. Bush's famous post-9/11 claim that Iraq, Iran, and North Korea were an "axis of evil" requiring American military intervention.

122. Jennings, *Christian Imagination*, 256.

be replicated in many other places concerning Western colonization under the guise of an entitlement rooted in biblical tradition.[123]

Whether enacted by YHWH in the establishment of a theological center for history (as in the case of Israel), or by humanity in an idolatrous grab for divine authority (as in the case of colonization), displacement is a theological act with far-reaching implications for an anthropology grounded in creation theology.

Ted A. Smith's book *Weird John Brown: Divine Violence and the Limits of Ethics* is helpful in understanding what Jennings is getting at in his treatment of the conquest of Canaan.[124] Smith offers a theological appraisal of John Brown, the famous abolitionist who, in 1859, led a raid on the federal armory in Harpers Ferry, Virginia, and was subsequently sentenced to death by hanging. Smith offers an ethical appraisal of Brown that differs from the tendencies to present Brown as either mentally unstable or as a martyred servant of an immutable "higher law."[125] Smith maintains that no attempt should be made to justify Brown's actions. In fact, according to ethical categories, Brown's violence was wrong, even considering the horrendous nature of the legalized violence (slavery) he was combatting. Smith takes an ethical approach akin to Kierkegaard's consideration of Abraham's sacrifice of Isaac in *Fear and Trembling* in which he understands ethics to function not as eternal moral principles but as obedient response to the free command of God.[126] Smith contends that to justify Brown would demonstrate what Charles Taylor calls "code fetishism"[127] and would simply reconfirm the state's criteria for (and monopoly on) "legitimate" violence.[128] Rather, Smith suggests seeing Brown's actions as in need of "pardon"—an act akin to the grace of divine forgiveness.[129] In this sense, invoking the need for "exceptions" to the rule acknowledges the rule as a necessary, if imperfect, reality of a fallen world.[130]

For Smith, the Word of God encounters the world as "divine violence," as a negation.[131] Smith is asking how John Brown's violence witnesses to the

123. Brueggemann, *The Land*, xv–xvi.
124. Smith, *Weird John Brown*.
125. Ibid., 86–108.
126. Kierkegaard, *Fear and Trembling*.
127. Smith, *Weird John Brown*, 52.
128. Ibid., 36–38.
129. Ibid., 123.
130. Ibid., 60–62.
131. Ibid., 118.

way God's word comes to the world, in effect leaving open the interpretation that Brown was in a sense an instrument of divine violence.

> I try to show the ways that an ethics of universalizable immanent moral obligation, when taken to be sufficient in itself, distorts and limits our abilities to understand situations and act in relation to them. I try to show some of the visions that a richer kind of practical reason might make visible and some of the actions that it might make thinkable. I argue that we need to cultivate the ability to reason about situations in ways that leave room for exceptions, that do not reduce all goods to moral obligations, and that cannot fit within an immanent frame. In particular, I argue that we need some notion of divine violence.[132]

Much like Bonhoeffer's refusal to justify his participation in a plot to assassinate Hitler,[133] Smith (and arguably, Brown himself) refuses to justify Brown's actions. It is in this vein that Jennings refuses to justify the violent conquest of Canaan; he does not claim that it is an ethically "good" thing (or much less an example to be followed), but rather that it signals humanity's position under divine judgment.

For my purposes, it is worth noting that when arguing from code understandings of ethics, rarely do people ask why it is that a person commits certain actions. According to Smith's account, asking such a question does not necessitate a capitulation to some version of ethical relativism, utilitarianism, or "situational" ethics. By not claiming that Brown was a holy crusader in service to an unchanging moral principle, we are left free to ask why Brown led a violent uprising.

> Seeing the raid as a fallen, faithful witness to the messianic fulfillment of law shows its continuity with other parts of Brown's life. He lived outside the laws of his day not only in his acts of violence but, perhaps even more radically, in his daily relations with African Americans. In a time when few whites had much to do with African American people who were not serving them, Brown stayed in the homes of Stephen Smith . . . Frederick Douglass . . . and many others. He sought advice from Harriet Tubman. He did not hesitate to trust his life to fellow raiders Oswald Anderson . . . and Dangerfield Newby. He was a treasured neighbor of Lyman Epps, who sang at his funeral. As W.E.B. DuBois wrote, Brown "worked not simply for Black

---

132. Ibid., 8.

133. See Bonhoeffer, *Ethics*, 67, where he says, "What is worse than doing evil is being evil."

Men—he worked with them; and he was a companion of their daily life, knew their faults and virtues, and felt, as few white Americans have felt, the bitter tragedy of their lot."[134]

Asking why Brown led a violent raid in resisting slavery, or why a Baltimore neighborhood would riot in response to contemporary unpunished violence against black men, or why I find it impossible to interpret the deaths of unarmed African Americans as resultant from anything other than a racialized vision, comes close to the heart of Jennings' invocation of joining. Encountering Christ in relationship with others often leads us to action, even if that action is imperfect. It is this sense of "divine violence" that Smith contends is better considered under a politics of "pardon/grace" than a politics of "justification."

Smith's final question is whether, according to a similar logic, slavery can finally be pardoned or "gotten over" (often an implicit query of many contemporary white folks when discussing race). Smith's answer is "No."[135] To do so would be to offer what Bonhoeffer called "cheap grace."[136] The reason for this refusal to pardon is that, unlike the treason committed by the Confederacy or the murder committed by Brown, slavery was not against the law; on the contrary, it was written into the laws of the United States.[137] How can something be pardoned that was not against the law, that was not legally acknowledged as wrong? Even when slavery was outlawed, the nation was expected to continue on as if it had never happened. (It is historically demonstrable that the refusal to offer some sort of reparations or reconstruction [such as Special Field Order #15: forty acres and a mule] to African Americans—as was offered to the Confederate states—contributed to post-slavery realities like sharecropping and the eventual Jim Crow). A pardon for slavery would, in effect, be given from the nation to the nation (from "above"). As Smith eloquently states, any sense of pardon in this case would have to come from "below":

> If pardon for slavery could be given, it could be given only by a sovereign power that had the standing that came from suffering. If we dare to hope that God might have the power to offer such a pardon, then we commit ourselves to a distinct vision of God. For pardon could only be given by a God who had been seized in the night, chained in the hold of a ship, sold at auction, separated from family, raped at gunpoint, worked to death, and buried in

134. Smith, *Weird John Brown*, 123.
135. Ibid., 150–52.
136. Ibid., 152.
137. The 3/5ths compromise of 1787 demonstrates this contention.

an unmarked grave. It could be given only by a God who had
found ways to survive, even to thrive, when these things were
impossible. It could be given only by a God whose law was broken by every moment of the slave system. It could be given only
by a God bound so closely to all those who suffered that it would
not compound the sin to say that God endured the suffering in
God's own flesh. And if such a God decided to offer pardon, it
could come only by God's free decision in God's own time.[138]

Smith's eloquent conclusion demonstrates his affinity for Jürgen Moltmann's
vision of divine suffering, a trajectory with which Jennings is also sympathetic. Forged in a Lutheran *theologia crucis*, a horror at the evils of Nazi
Germany, and an openness to theologies of liberation, Moltmann revisits
the radical conception of a human God on a cross, while remaining thoroughly Trinitarian and avoiding the difficulties of patripassianism.[139] This
Moltmannian convergence between Smith and Jennings demonstrates why
it is helpful to utilize *Weird John Brown* as we consider Jennings' invocation
of the theological significance of place.

In relation to the divine violence of the conquest of Canaan by
YHWH's people, Jennings notes that God "draws death and violence into
the divine sphere of influence," entailing "the encircling of violence" in "an
ever-tightening sphere of divine sanction." In this sense, "YHWH is seizing
the reins of violence and bringing it into subjection to the divine word."[140]
Not only is the justification of violence outside the purview of humanity,
but God's work in salvation history is one of constraining violence to the
purposes of redemption, ultimately triumphing over violence through the
cross of Christ. To claim violence in service of the divine is to claim the
epistemological privilege of the knowledge of good and evil.[141]

The second term that would benefit from additional analysis is *race*.
Jennings is interested in demonstrating how modern "race" (as a static anthropological designation) follows from the loss of place. In the Introduction, through the work of Prather, I suggested that the organic conjunction
between people and place assumed in the Christian doctrine of creation
stands in marked contrast to the modern capitalist conception of private
property, which treats land as an essentially malleable and redefinable

138. Smith, *Weird John Brown*, 153–54.

139. Moltmann, *The Crucified God*.

140. Jennings, *Christian Imagination*, 257.

141. Gen 2:17. Bonhoeffer deals with this theme in *Creation and Fall*, which I will
reference later.

commodity and encourages an ethic of exclusion.[142] The modern conception of land is tied into a Lockean assignation of value according to human
labor and the myth of human progress.[143] Jennings maintains that in the
wake of colonial displacement, skin color, flesh, and body were called upon
to do what they were never intended to do: reveal identity.[144] The eventual
development was racial essentialization, a modern static ontology in which
specific traits are held to be naturally and self-evidently intrinsic to a people.
The early colonial *limpieza de sangre* scale, rooted in hatred of Jews, was an
influential schema which filled in the void left by the disconnection of the
identity of peoples from place.[145]

> This effect begins with positioning Christian identity fully with-
> in European (white) identity and fully outside the identity of
> Jews and Muslims. The space between these identities, Christian
> on the one side and Jews and Muslims on the other, became
> the space within which one could discern authentic conversion.
> This discernment constituted an ecclesial logic applicable to the
> evaluation of all peoples.[146]

The result was what Jennings calls a "pigmentocracy."[147] One of the
most insidious effects of the *limpieza de sangre* system was the promise of
"becoming white" through the dilution of non-European blood over several generations of "inter-breeding" (often occasioned by the rape of native
women by European conquerers).[148] Jennings' analysis suggests that many
contemporary experiences of reconciliation are powerfully and obliviously
indebted to this psychology. Additionally, many popular accounts of reconciliation attempt to transcend the category of race by reading the Jews as an
example of ethnic closure that has been overcome through the "multiethnic" body of Christ (thereby "racializing" the Jews in the process).[149]

142. Consider several pre-modern-capitalist ways in which Christendom provided
for common usage of land, such as the "commons," and considered land boundaries to
be permeable, such as "right of passage" laws.

143. See Locke, *Two Treatises of Government*, 294–96, where "ninety-nine hundredths" of the value of land comes from labor. This is how Locke justifies Europeans
seizing native lands, which he views as "uncultivated wastes."

144. Jennings, *Christian Imagination*, 59.

145. Ibid., 79.

146. Ibid., 33.

147. Ibid., 79.

148. Ibid., 79–80.

149. See Piper, *Bloodlines*, where he maintains that the Gospel marks the end of
ethnocentrism in a way that relativizes the Jewishness of Jesus (115ff, 147ff). Jesus' Jewish flesh is superseded by a spiritualized personal salvation narrative in which divine

The desacralization of place actuated race. Rather than the created order shaping a people's self-understanding, the observatory powers of whiteness categorized the traits of various people groups along a comparative continuum that assigned inalienable attributes to particular peoples. The colonial appropriation of new lands and unfamiliar peoples presented a "need" to categorize: to judge identity. Jennings maintains that the doctrines of *creatio ex-nihilo*, with its view of the instability of creation, and the Incarnation, with its location of the Creator in time and space, were manipulated in an assumption of Christological authority for the reordering of place as an act of *creatio continua*.[150] The racialized scale is therefore a distortion of the doctrines of creation and Christology.

This is the force of the third term we will explore: Jennings' diagnosis of *supersessionism*, which he describes as "the most decisive and central theological distortion that exists in the church" and loosely defines as the belief that "the church replaces Israel in the mind and heart of God."[151] He promises to take his "entire treatment, each chapter adding layers to [his] account of this decisive distortion, to describe the awesome effects of this way of thinking on the imagination of Christians."[152] Jennings' interest is not primarily in offering a doctrinal treatment of supersessionism but in describing how the Christian imagination has been affected by reading itself into the place of Israel in Scripture and reading non-white peoples as Gentiles. For this reason, "supersessionism" remains a somewhat amorphous classification throughout his text. Jennings' work should not be read as a systematic treatment of supersessionism but a historical account of the way it shaped the racial imaginary. Rather than a strictly dogmatic account, Jennings is working in the realm of theological ethics.

Perhaps the most thorough treatment of supersessionism from a doctrinal and exegetical standpoint is Tommy Givens' *We the People: Israel and the Catholicity of Jesus*.[153] While I will point to several key differences between Givens' and Jennings' conclusions, Givens' work is helpful in clarifying what we are talking about when we talk about supersessionism. Much like Jennings, Givens is not as interested in refuting what he calls "traditional supersessionism, wherein the Christian church is understood to have replaced the Jews as Israel because the Jews refused to become

---

election applies to individuals rather than a people (for the sake of all peoples). Piper's views on racial reconciliation become a means to reaffirming his TULIP doctrine of individualistic approbation and reprobation.

150. Jennings, *Christian Imagination*, 28, 186.

151. Ibid., 32.

152. Ibid., 33.

153. Givens, *We the People*.

Christian"[154] as he is in describing the manner in which supersessionism affected notions of peoplehood, especially the "non-religious" shape it has taken in the modern nation-state.[155] I contend that Givens' account of supersessionism is helpful in its doctrinal precision even if it sometimes seems to slip into imagining the church as the central point of reference, most notably in its tendency to speak of the Christian need to "remember" the Jews as "our own."[156]

Givens works primarily from Yoder's account of Christianity as Jewish in Yoder's *Jewish-Christian Schism Revisited*.[157] While he applauds Yoder for recognizing that the Christian tendency to see itself as non-Jewish has animated much of the Church's historic tendencies toward violence, Givens claims that Yoder sees the Jewish-Christian continuity mostly in terms of an ethical correspondence.[158] Therefore, Yoder's invocation of Christianity's Jewishness tends toward a self-determining voluntarism. Givens maintains that Yoder's interest in articulating the Jewish nature of Christian faith is centered around a reclamation of Jewish peoplehood as typological of Yoder's own nonviolent radical reformation tradition (i.e. Yoder reclaims the Jews as his own, even if he prefers to speak of being claimed by historical Judaism, which is, ironically, my basic hesitancy about the tendency of Givens' account).[159] Interestingly, for the purposes of this treatment, Givens suggests that accounts of virtue and invocations of the people of God as "an independent political entity" tend toward a similar ethical voluntarism and thereby reconfirm autonomous and self-determining notions of peoplehood rooted in the modern nation-state.[160] This is similar to my claim about the limitations of the communitarian account of the church as a radical counter-culture.

Givens recognizes that such self-determinative forms of Christian identity tend to play into racial conceptions of peoplehood. Therefore, Givens asks what sort of people Israel is. If Israel is neither a voluntary association nor a modern ethnic group, how are we to understand the peoplehood of Israel? Givens, following Barth, prefers to speak of election. In this manner, Givens maintains that Israel and the church are one because of God's

154. Ibid., 93.

155. Ibid., 118–24.

156. Ibid., 411.

157. Ibid., chapters 1 and 2.

158. Ibid., 49–53.

159. Ibid., 83–84.

160. Ibid., 88, 417. These are similar to the basic contentions I read Jennings as having with Hauerwas.

gracious election and only secondarily in any sense of human subjectivity.[161] Givens is clear that election means not simply good news as opposed to damnation (as in many individualized Calvinist accounts of election), but includes judgment for the people of God: "the elect people is only itself as the judged people."[162] Givens' only hesitation with Barth's account of election is that, in his view, Barth's overly formal Christology collapses Israel *into* the Church[163] and does not maintain Israel as a "living . . . Israel in the flesh" in any thick way.[164] At the same time, Givens does not intend his invocation of "living Israel" to be interpreted in terms of "ethnicity," which he maintains is "an accretion of the modern discourse of peoplehood."[165] Because of these reasons, Givens is resistant to identifying biblical Israel with the modern nation-state of Israel.[166]

Givens wants to avoid communicating that Israel is a "pure" race in the manner in which such concepts were imagined in the age of early-modern exploration and have been continued today through national discourses of "peoplehood." Much like historic colonial supersessionism, these modern discourses function by determining who is "in" and "out" based on characteristics of who "the people" are—characteristics that dovetail neatly with conceptions of race.[167] Contemporary echoes of this discourse can be heard in much of the "white" national commentary surrounding violence against African Americans. As will be seen below, I maintain that Givens' account is not as effective in resisting modern notions of ethnicity as is Jennings' account because Givens does not draw the link between place and race as clearly as Jennings does.

At the same time, Givens' doctrinal account does pose several important questions for Jennings' historical treatment. By not defining supersessionism in detail and not clearly explaining how it relates to the modern state of Israel and to ethnic Israel, Jennings risks leaving himself open to

161. Ibid., 187.

162. Ibid., 215. This flows from Barth's famous assertion that Jesus Christ, as God's elect, is also the reprobate.

163. Ibid., 231ff.

164. Ibid., 183.

165. Ibid., 244.

166. Ibid., 118. I suspect that Jennings would not have a problem with some sense of land–sovereignty for the modern people of Israel. Particularly after the Shoah, the need for a people to be safely located in their own homeland should be recognized. While aggressive Israeli militarism should be resisted, a position of opposition to Israeli self-defense begins to look fairly anti-Semitic. While Givens does not explicitly fall into this latter camp, he does not clarify what he means by being resistant to Israel as a modern nation.

167. Ibid., 118–24.

the criticism that he is reclaiming Israel for his Christian account of race in a similar manner to Yoder's ethical affinity between the radical reformation and what he reads as post-exilic Jewish nonviolence. In other words, in what specific ways does Jennings suggest that Gentile joining in Jesus Christ is to be understood as connected to Jewish history and the Jewish people? This is further complicated by the fact that Jennings closes his text by picturing specific Jewish and African American artists living and working together in early twentieth-century America without exploring how various Gentile peoples today might enter into this sort of community in a meaningful way (i.e. How can non-Jewish peoples come together to constitute Jewish flesh?).

However, these issues are quite minor; Jennings' interest is not in delineating between various doctrinal shades of supersessionism but in weaving together a tale that demonstrates how a supersessionist way of *imagining* identity has led to viewing the world through the lens of whiteness. Jennings wants the Church to have a simple Gentile remembrance—to read itself into the biblical text and the "tradition" as those on the outside being drawn in by grace. I contend that, for Jennings, supersessionism is not as much a problem of "doctrine" (in a technical sense of that term) as it is a distorted way of viewing the world that has theological roots. I suggest that, while Givens' account is not primarily about race (although it is one of his themes inasmuch as he finds race to be connected to modern discourses of peoplehood), Jennings' account more adequately discerns the problematic optic characteristic of whiteness.

There are several limitations that become apparent in Givens' treatment as it is compared with Jennings' account. For instance, Givens resists describing Israel as "ethnic" but has a hard time determining *how* she is constituted as a people. While Jennings also resists ethnicity as a means of identifying people, he nonetheless acknowledges that Israel must be thought of as an "ethnic" group in some sense (in addition to what he calls "biblical" and "living" Israel).[168] While Givens' answer to Israel's non-ethnic constitution is "election," he recognizes that such a concept can be nebulous and therefore strives to offer several tangible aspects of Israel's constitution as a people. He points to what he calls the "minutiae" of Israel's life (story, sexual relations, food . . . a list with "no end") as a "stream of contingencies" that make up her communal continuity.[169] For Givens, because language of "ethnicity" does not account for the various peoples who trace their family lineage to a descendent of Abraham, Isaac, or Jacob and yet are not considered "Israel" (e.g. Ishmael and Esau), Israel's identity must be understood

---

168. Jennings, *Christian Imagination*, 254.
169. Givens, *We the People*, 284–88.

according to factors other than ancestral lineage.[170] Givens maintains that the Mosaic laws against intermarriage had little to do with "ethnicity" and more to do with prohibitions against idolatry.[171] While these are all points well-taken, I am not convinced that it is possible to entirely escape identifying Israel as an "ethnic" people, even with all the necessary qualifications to distinguish how Jewish "ethnicity" is to be distinguished from modern notions of racialized "ethnicity." I suspect that this is why Jennings has retained language of ethnicity in his text. He defines ethnicity with regard to place more so than cultural continuity.

Since, for Jennings, people are constituted primarily by place, he can speak of "ethnicity" in non-racialized terms: as a spatially-oriented peoplehood. While Jennings is resistant to modern biological race, he recognizes that to locate a people's constitution in various "minutiae" or "contingencies" is to have too cozy a relationship with the sort of observational categories of which modern religious and cultural studies is composed. Perhaps the key distinction between Givens and Jennings is that Givens foregrounds "time" in the constitution of the people of Israel (as opposed to Jennings' invocation of "place"): As Givens maintains:

> Israel has never been "an ethnicity," whatever its participants may believe along the way . . . Merely bringing children into the world guarantees nothing about Israel's future, for Israelite children can be born into an Israelite society riddled with idolatry and injustice, a life already in the throes of assimilation by surrounding gentile peoples . . . For children born to Israel to continue Israel's promise in the flesh, they must be born into a time in which God has provided for Israel's remembrance of its God and forestalled absorption into gentile societies . . . Thus, what conceiving and bearing children means for Israel is contingent on the time in which children are born . . . That particular time is more determinative of the shape of Israel's life in that time than the way particular Israelite communities then choose to live in that time . . . Thus, by God's election the people is not determined by the way it lives in time, but by the time in which it lives.[172]

Givens' purpose is to find a basis for the life of the community other than ethical self-determination. While time is undoubtedly a key biblical component of Israel's identity (i.e. feasts and festivals, Sabbath), Jennings demonstrates that place is the more crucial category (i.e. slavery, promised

170. Ibid., 252.
171. Ibid., 251.
172. Ibid., 281–82.

land, exile, return). Additionally, place is the category that has been more distorted by the West than time (e.g. the West enacted colonial displacement while retaining a chronologically-oriented liturgical "Church year"). Therefore, time should be understood as making sense of the people's relationship to place. Israel's marking of time is related to the seasonal cycles of the land: the land producing its fruits as gifts of divine blessing and animals being the proper age for sacrifice (e.g. First Fruits, Passover). Conceptions of time are possible only because humans are created beings located in specific space.

Givens' and Jennings' biblical interpretations are also inflected differently. As Givens turns from his doctrinal work to his constructive exegetical work, he interprets one of the passages used by Jennings: the story of Jesus and the Canaanite woman (Matthew 15:21–28). While I will reference Jennings' interpretation of this story in greater detail in the Conclusion, it is insightful to draw a distinction between Givens' and Jennings' readings of the story. Jennings' interest is that Christians read themselves into the position of the Syrophoenician woman in the story: dogs at another people's table.[173] Givens, however, runs the story in another direction. He maintains that it is primarily about "how Israel's history of enmity with the Canaanites is coming to an end in and through Jesus."[174] While he stresses that Gentiles obtain salvation "only at the table of Israel," he tends to view the story as a generic invocation of reconciliation in Christ more so than a caution about how reconciliation is to be understood. In other words, he tends to move toward the universal import of reconciliation without first properly centering it on its particular locus. I suggest that such an interpretation may stem from imagining oneself "above" (the place of Jesus) rather than "below" (the place of the woman).

Through his exegesis of Romans 9–11, Givens frames his work as a plea to Christians to not "disown" or "treat as foreign" their spiritual parents, the Jews, but instead to "remember" them "as our own."[175] While these word choices may seem like minor details, they suggest that Givens retains an imagination in which Christians extend hospitality to the Jews (as opposed to the other way around). Again, my interpretation of Givens' exegesis flows from listening to how the Church's language about reconciliation and peoplehood affects (and is heard by) those marginalized by whiteness. Givens presents a meticulous nonsupersessionist theological account but does not as sufficiently deal with what Jennings identifies as the key problem

173. As I have heard a pastor fittingly remark: "I don't care what you call me, Jesus, as long as you call me." Or, "The crumb of cake on the floor is from the same piece they are eating on the table."

174. Givens, *We the People*, 322–23.

175. Ibid., 395, 410–11.

of supersessionism: the racial imagination. As a doctrinal treatment of supersessionism, Givens' work is an important contribution; as a work about
"peoplehood," it is not as effective as Jennings' genealogy. Givens' text is an
important companion to Jennings' work.

This brief excursion into Givens' work helps to clarify why Jennings is
less interested in a doctrinal treatment of supersessionism than a historical
treatment of its theological import. In analyzing the racial imaginary, Jennings does not offer an explicit and detailed definition of supersessionism.
Similarly, Jennings is less concerned with evaluating the systematic integrity of various theological traditions than he is in investigating the ways
in which these traditions have been deployed to subjugate or marginalize
people. For instance, Jennings agrees with the center of orthodox Christology (e.g. his continued resistance to Docetist and adoptionist tendencies)
but maintains that a racialized imagination has often flourished alongside
an "orthodox" Christology.[176] For Jennings, one's supersessionist "habits of
mind" are perhaps most telling of how one imagines the Incarnation.

Jennings presents the Jews as a people called out *from the nations* (the
ethnos) by YHWH. Abraham was taken *from his country and kindred* so
that *all nations* would be blessed through him.[177] YHWH created for God-
self a people whose borders and boundaries were pervious to include other
peoples in its lineage, claiming Israel's God and YHWH's people as their
own, thereby being grafted into salvation history. This joining culminates in
the person of Jesus Christ, from the loins of Abraham by way of the tribe of
Judah, himself carrying the identity of other peoples in his ancestral blood-
line.[178] He is the One for the many, who in his very Jewish, covenantal, and
even "ethnic" flesh subsumes all flesh into his own Body. Just as Jesus is
the One human for humanity, the Jewish people are the one people for the
many peoples. Theologically speaking, Israel is the only people. The *ethnos*
are those who "were not a people," those who were "far off" strangers to
YHWH.[179] The *ethnos* are those brought near through Jesus Christ as guests
at another people's table.

---

176. As I suggested earlier in my consideration of what I read as Justo Gonzalez's
and Jennings' central agreement with the theological intuition of Chalcedon, I am not
claiming that Jennings finds the capitulation of Chalcedon to Hellenistic terminology
to be free from difficulties. Rather, I am claiming that, by recognizing the historical and
contextual situatedness of Chalcedon, Jennings finds the early church's orthodox sensibilities to be a faithful example that confessional Christians would do well to remember.
This position is similar to Barth's confessional reworking of Chalcedonian grammar.

177. Gen 12:1–3.

178. Matt 1:1–17.

179. 1 Pet 2:10; Eph 2:11–22.

While doctrinal critiques of supersessionism go a long way toward resisting modern notions of race, critics of supersessionism (who are becoming a larger camp as the distortions of supersessionism are more widely recognized) would do well to follow Jennings in retaining some sense of a spatially-oriented ethnicity. This is where Jennings' account of supersessionism is the most trenchant: he recognizes the link between race and place.

Gomes Eanes de Zurara

Having further explicated Jennings' thesis by explaining his terminology of place, race, and supersessionism, I now turn to briefly interacting with Jennings' utilization of Zurara, Equiano, and Colenso along the lines of inquiry I have pursued in reference to Acosta. This advances this chapter's discussion by further demonstrating Jennings' pre-theological reading of cultural studies literature, his disciplinary joining, and the manner in which he extends historical treatments into theological analyses. Three scholars who are critical for understanding Jennings' use of Zurara are Hugh Thomas, David Brion Davis, and Robin Blackburn. The work of each scholar focuses on New World slavery, primarily the Atlantic slave trade. They share an effort to demonstrate the historical sequences through which such atrocities were perpetuated by humans upon their fellow humans. For each author, Zurara plays an important role in the early-modern racialization of slavery, which had been a ubiquitous institution throughout human history. Because Zurara framed his observations in the form of Christian reflection and because deployments of Christian theological categories and the Scriptures played such a vital role in the legitimization of this institution, each scholar's treatment necessarily interacts with Christian conceptualities. As with the works about Acosta, the primary purpose of the scholarly literature is not to provide a theological account of racialization but to trace historical causal sequences. Jennings' innovation is treating these theologians as theologians.

The cultural studies' treatments of Zurara characteristically find the slave trade to be grounded in the heteronomy of the Judeo-Christian tradition as opposed to the autonomy of modern natural law, which is suggested as the ideal toward which humans are progressing. The discipline of cultural studies tends to view itself as fulfilling the most radical ideals of the Enlightenment. One example will suffice to demonstrate Jennings' theological divergence from the cultural studies enterprise. Davis, in *The Problem of Slavery in the Age of Revolution*, concludes by invoking a Hegelian ideal of "man" as an "autonomous value."[180] Davis maintains that the

---

180. Davis, *Problem of Slavery*, 563.

quest to "recognize other men as autonomous values," a quest that bears only "a superficial resemblance" to "the ideal of Christian brotherhood," is the difficult work toward which humanity must press in order to overcome the ideal of "lordship." It is this hope toward which the cultural studies enterprise strains, as evidenced by the closing words of Davis' text:

> Above all, Hegel bequeathed a message that would have a profound impact on future thought, especially as Marx and Freud deepened the meaning of the message: that we can expect nothing from the mercy of God or from the mercy of those who exercise worldly lordship in His or other names; that man's true emancipation, whether physical or spiritual, must always depend on those who have endured and overcome some form of slavery.[181]

While Jennings also listens to the voices of those experiencing oppression, his thesis suggests that Davis' position does not take seriously the identification of the oppressed with the liberation of YHWH. Davis makes the hermeneutical choice to preclude divine agency from his explanation of history. Jennings' theological method listens to the available historiography while not privileging a modern observational stance. He suggests that there is more going on than the cultural studies literature allows.

At the same time, Jennings liberally draws from the cultural studies literature surrounding Zurara. For instance, each scholar demonstrates the manner in which Aristotelian anthropology and political philosophy contributed to the development of proto-racial classifications. Thomas, British historian, author, and honorary fellow at Queen's College, Cambridge, notes that in the sixteenth century, during the age of imperial conquest, "Aristotle was looked upon as the guide to almost everything."[182] Thomas suggests that Aristotle's anthropological designations were not peripheral to the rationale for slavery within the classical Greek *polis* and its legitimization in the New World in the age of European conquest. As he quotes Aristotle:

> Humanity is divided into two: the masters and the slaves; or, if one prefers it, the Greeks and the Barbarians, those who have the right to command; and those who are born to obey.
>
> A slave is property with a soul.

---

181. Ibid., 564.
182. Thomas, *The Slave Trade*, 28.

> The use of domestic animals and slaves is about the same; they both lend us their physical efforts to satisfy the needs of existence.[183]

Aristotle's anthropology is marked by a determinism which invokes naturalistic caste distinctions within a hierarchy topped by Hellenism. While not being properly about modern race, a proto-racial sensibility can be seen in the works of Aristotle. We shall see in chapter 4 how contemporary accounts of virtue ethics attempt to reclaim the centrality of Aristotle's aesthetic and ethical Hellenism while exculpating it from its more "unsavory" aspects.

Blackburn, British historian and Professor of Sociology at Essex University, similarly assesses Aristotle's anthropological contributions to colonialism and the sowing of the seeds of racialization:

> Aristotle had developed a doctrine of 'natural slavery' which wrapped together class-like and ethnic features. The 'natural slave,' according to Aristotle, was a barbarian whose inclination was to defer and who was distinguished by brawn, not brain; the 'natural slaves' needed the direction of those who were gifted with independence of character as well as intelligence and civilization.[184]

Blackburn quotes Aristotle as maintaining that "warfare which is just" is that which "must be used both against wild beasts and against such men as are by nature intended to be ruled over but refuse."[185] Aristotle grounds his teleological account of natural law in the proposition that everything is ordered with an "end in view," which designates that Nature "made all of them for the sake of man." [186] In chapter 4, I will explore the ways in which both late medieval Christian Thomism and modern Lockean political theory appropriated these views. Aristotelian anthropology and natural law theory were dominant in the thinking of Zurara, who concluded that enslavement was beneficial to the Africans because they were ignorant of the Gospel, lived "like beasts," did not have "decent clothing or housing," existed in "ignorance of who they are," and had "no knowledge of what is right."[187] Having discerned the ethics, aesthetics, and identity of the African, it became the moral responsibility of the Western elite to instruct and rule him.

---

183. Ibid., 28.

184. Blackburn, *Making of New World Slavery*, 35.

185. Ibid.

186. Ibid.

187. Ibid., 105–6.

In an account quoted at length by both Blackburn and Jennings, Zurara is moved by the plight of a "cargo" of African slaves newly acquired by Portugal, invoking divine providence as ordaining the hierarchical arrangement of peoples:

On the next day . . . those captives . . . placed all together in that field, were a marvelous sight; for amongst them were some white enough, fair to look upon, and well proportioned; others were less white like mulattoes; others again were as black as Ethiops [Ethiopians], and so ugly, both in features and in body, as almost to appear (to those who saw them) the images of a lower hemisphere. But what heart could be so hard as not to be pierced with piteous feeling to see that company? For some kept their heads low and their faces bathed in tears, looking one upon another; others stood groaning very dolorously, looking up to the height of heaven, fixing their eyes upon it, crying out loudly, as if asking help of the Father of Nature; others struck their faces with the palms of their hands, throwing themselves at full length upon the ground; others made their lamentations in the manner of a dirge, after the custom of their country. And though we could not understand the words of their language, the sound of it right well accorded with the measure of their sadness. But to increase their sufferings still more, there now arrived those who had charge of the division of the captives, and who began to separate one from another, in order to make an equal partition of the fifths; and then was it needful to part fathers from sons, husbands from wives, brothers from brothers. No respect was shown either to friends or relations, but each fell where his lot took him. O powerful fortune, that with thy wheels doest and undoest, compassing the matters of this world as pleaseth thee, do thou at least put before the eyes of that miserable race some understanding of matters to come; that they may receive some consolation in the midst of their great sorrow. And you who are so busy in making that division of the captives, look with pity upon so much misery; and see how they cling one to the other, so that you can hardly separate them. And who could finish that partition without very great toil? For as often as they had placed them in one part the sons, seeing their fathers in another, rose with great energy and rushed over to them; the mothers clasped their other children in their arms, and threw themselves flat on the ground with them; receiving blows with little pity for their own flesh, if only they might not be torn from them. And so troublously they finished the partition.[188]

I quote this oft-utilized passage from Zurara at length because it clearly and succinctly demonstrates multiple theological operations that Jennings identifies throughout his work. Zurara frames his descriptions of nonwhite flesh as a Christian prayer to the Father of Nature, who working through the Portuguese monarch Infante Henrique, has worked "the salvation of those souls that before were lost."[189] In the words of Jennings, Zurara "invokes the idea of divine providence, of which he is a firm believer" and "anchors human beings in the actions of . . . God" through the doctrine of "divine immutability."[190] For Zurara, the moral uprightness of the Portuguese conquest of nonwhite peoples is not in question, it is the problem of how to locate the suffering he is witnessing within the unchanging plan of God. It is at this point that Zurara inadvertently describes the Africans in the Christological trope of the Suffering Servant.[191] In attempting to assuage his own conscience and in praying for a revelation from God to the slaves about divine purposes in this matter, Zurara is doing theodicy "bound to the colonialist project."[192] It is ultimately Prince Henry, Christ's representative by the authority of Nicholas V, who, in an incarnational pattern reflective of papal doctrines surrounding the "transferability of [Christ's] authority to humans,"[193] including power over space and bodies, provides the divine stability and hermeneutic lens through which the suffering of the Africans is interpreted:

> The Infante was there, mounted upon a powerful steed, and accompanied by his retinue, making distribution of his favours, as a man who sought to gain but small treasure from his share; for of the forty-six souls that fell to him as his fifth, he made a very speedy partition of these for his chief riches lay in his purpose; for he reflected with great pleasure upon the salvation of those souls that before were lost. And certainly his expectation was not in vain; for, as we said before, as soon as they understood

188. Jennings, *Christian Imagination*, 18–19.

189. Ibid., 19.

190. Ibid., 18.

191. Ibid., 22: "[I]n telling the story of Portugal's rise, Zurara joins the slave body to the body of Jesus. He would not have done this on purpose, as he seems unaware of the immense tragedy of the moment he has entered. But Zurara also reveals he is not innocent. He knows—behold the man!"

192. Ibid., 18.

193. Ibid., 28.

our language they turned Christians with very little ado; and I
who put together this history into this volume, saw in the town
of Lagos boys and girls (the Children and grandchildren of those
first captives, born in this land) as good and true Christians as if
they had directly descended, from the beginning of the dispen-
sation of Christ, from those who were first baptized.[194]

In this account, the white body is that which orders chaos. Translation into
European-qua-Christian identity justifies all manner of atrocities. Divine
providence is discerned in Western enculturation; Christological authority
is mediated by the Church; the problem of evil becomes a key concern for
those reflecting on the suffering of others.

While slavery had been a ubiquitous institution throughout human
history, all three scholars contend that ancient old world slavery was not
based upon racial classifications. Respectively, they relate that Roman slavery was "comprised of a multitude of ethnicities,"[195] that "human bondage"
in "biblical and early antiquity . . . carried no racial implications,"[196] and that
"the Greeks and the Romans were unprejudiced on grounds of race: they
were quite insensible as to whether someone with black skin was superior
to someone with white, or vice versa."[197] While these observations may be
overstated, given the proto-racial classifications at work in Aristotle, the
point is that the modern racialized scale was not quantifiable as such until
the marriage of theology and exploration in late medieval scholasticism.
The shared contention of the cultural studies literature is that the existence
of the black Atlantic slave trade was the hermeneutic determinative for racialization. In the words of Davis:

> This circularity points to an actual causal sequence in the ori-
> gins of antiblack racism: The very presence of increasing num-
> bers of black African slaves, first in the Islamic world, fused the
> ancient stereotypes of slaves (regardless of ethnicity), and the
> negative symbolism of "blackness," with the physical features of
> sub-Saharan Africans.

While Davis suggests a causal sequence of events, Jennings' thesis fills out
his account by suggesting that contemporary theological ways of imagining identity often operate within a similar circularity: White male subjectivity positions the nonwhite body as inferior within a Western aesthetic

194. Ibid., 19.
195. Blackburn, *Making of New World Slavery*, 34.
196. Davis, *Inhuman Bondage*, 68.
197. Thomas, *Slave Trade*, 27.

and ethical scale and then utilizes that comparison to demonstrate that its judgments of aesthetic unsophistication are correct. Many tendencies in contemporary ethical reclamations of some sort of Aristotelian virtue can be read as evincing a similar circuitous insecurity.

Early-modern biblical hermeneutics often operated according to this circular logic. Crucial for the colonial fusing of blackness with forced servitude were interpretations surrounding the so-called "curse of Ham" in Genesis 9:18–27.[198] Linking the "curse of Ham" with blackness in general and the enslavement of Africans in particular was in large part a product of the necessity of justifying the African slave trade throughout the sixteenth, seventeenth, and eighteenth centuries.[199] This trajectory continued through interpretations that found the "mark of Cain" to be dark skin and the Mormon belief, championed by Brigham Young, that blackness is a curse.[200] The scholarly consensus in this regard reinforces Jennings' conclusion that modern racial classifications had their genesis in early-modern theological suppositions.

Jennings' contention that supersessionism is the animating force behind the racial imagination is buttressed by the cultural studies literature. Davis concludes: "There is much evidence that the Christians' growing fears and anxiety over the mass conversion and intermixture of Jews in late medieval Spain gave rise to a more general concern over 'purity of blood'— *limpieza de sangre* in Spanish—and thus to an early conception of biological race."[201] Jennings restates this position theologically: "This effect beg[an] with positioning Christian identity fully within European (white) identity and fully outside the identities of Jews and Muslims."[202] Jennings recounts from the historical treatments the terms utilized to classify "suspicious" converts: *moriscos* (converts from Islam/Christian Moors) and *conversos* (converts from Judaism/New Christians).[203] Fear of a convert with a single drop of "non-Christian" (read: non-European) blood drove Christians to search out Jews and Moors and bar them from positions of leadership in the

---

198 The designation "curse of Ham" reveals an ideological position in itself. In the passage in question, Noah curses Canaan, not Ham. However, in order for the curse to reach the supposed black African Cush, the curse was read as pronounced upon his father, Ham. Zurara explicitly makes this judgment. Contrary to this colonial exegetical move, early rabbinical explanations were that the curse extended to the "light-skinned Canaanite foes" of the Jews (Davis, *Inhuman Bondage*, 68, 72).

199. Davis, *Inhuman Bondage*, 69.

200. Ibid.

201. Ibid., 70.

202. Jennings, *Christian Imagination*, 33.

203. Ibid.

church.[204] According to Davis, the Spanish Inquisition tortured and burned thousands of *conversos*, translating fear and jealousy of the success of Jewish converts into racialized terms.[205] Davis' historical research indicates that "Christian anti-Semitism developed into a racist ideology."[206] For Jennings, theologically speaking, Israel's election was replaced by "that new elected body, the white body."[207] Davis states that "much is yet to be learned"[208] about the relationship between hatred of Jews and the construction of the classification of race. Jennings engages this pursuit by calling supersessionism "the most decisive and central theological distortion that exists in the church."[209]

Through his use of Zurara, Jennings is developing his contention that theology and racialization must be considered together, while also laying the groundwork for his subsequent historic accounts. He is combating essentialist theories of race, which characteristically do not take into account specific geographies or theological specificities. At the same time, he acknowledges that "antiessential, antirace positions . . . are spiritually vapid" and that "[n]o easy answers follow."[210] Strategies such as "resistance to racial identity," "racial improvisation," or renunciation of "white privilege" are no more effective than an attempt to move a mountain "by turning one's face away from it." Jennings concludes that racial identity is "reflexively calibrated

204. Ibid.

205. Davis, *Inhuman Bondage*, 72. Davis notes that "the *limpieza* movement appealed to demagogues of lower backgrounds, who celebrated their own purity of blood while revealing the contamination of the elite." Similarly, in the words of Blackburn, "The pressure to establish the principle of *limpieza de sangre* came mainly from plebian Spaniards who employed it against what they saw as an aristocratic/*converso* alliance" (Blackburn, *Making of New World Slavery*, 48).

206. Davis, *Inhuman Bondage*, 72.

207. Jennings, *Christian Imagination*, 33.

208. Davis, *Inhuman Bondage*, 72. See also Thomas, who cites a law under Constantine that said that no Jew could own a Christian slave. Later Roman law refined it to state that no Jew could *buy* a Christian slave and that if one were inherited, the Christian would be set free if attempts at conversion or circumcision were made. While this is not the modern racial scale as cited by Jennings, it does point to the fact that when Christianity came to be articulated fully within European ethnic boundaries, the connection between Jewishness and race began to emerge (Thomas, *Slave Trade*, 31).

209. Jennings, *Christian Imagination*, 32.

210. Ibid., 63–64. Jennings' discussion at this point is directed toward both theology and critical race theory: "Thus the freedom to renounce race is a direct descendent of the theological power to deny and undermine geographically sustained identities . . . At this point my concern is to illumine an intensely tangled mistake that cannot be improved by race-antinomian intellectual forays . . . The way forward, if there is a way forward, will involve several more conceptual steps before a future of communion might be envisioned."

to the turnings of spatial habitations" and that race and place must be considered together.[211] Jennings resists both essentialist and race-antinomian intellectual arrangements by connecting identity to the doctrine of creation through an emphasis on place.

Olaudah Equiano

Jennings' inquiry into the theological significance of Olaudah Equiano is best understood against the backdrop of his utilization of the historical works of Marcus Rediker, William L. Andrews, and Vincent Carretta, who I will here consult to further elucidate Jennings' relationship to cultural studies. Rediker traces the horrific journey of the Middle Passage of the Atlantic slave trade, while Andrews delves into the literary significance of Equiano's autobiography, and Carretta offers a compelling biographical portrait of Equiano. Jennings utilizes the historical accounts related to the life of Equiano to suggest the theological dangers of treating economic assimilation as relationship.

Rediker, Distinguished Professor of Atlantic History at the University of Pittsburgh, has authored several social histories dealing with justice issues including *The Slave Ship: A Human History*, which Jennings references. Rediker uses Equiano's autobiographical account of his time aboard a slave ship to allude to the significance of the Middle Passage for many developments, including the implications of spatial displacement, the genesis of ethnography, and the galvanization of resistance. He observes that, through the slave ship, Equiano's "alienation from kin and village was complete," noting the identity challenges constituted by displacement,[212] that "ethnogenesis was happening on the ship," recognizing the comparative descriptive project initiated by the age of exploration and colonization,[213] and that "a culture of resistance" formed among those enslaved,[214] expressed through refusal to eat, study of the innerworkings of the ship in order to discover details about one's captivity, and occasional suicide.[215] Because the contact between diverse peoples was initiated by and forged in imperial conquest,

211. Ibid., 60–64. Jennings utilizes Barth's conception of God as "the One whose *being* is revealed in divine action" and who is "unconditioned by us" (60) to explicate how whiteness, in "acts of breathtaking hubris" (61), took upon itself the organizing attributes of deity. Land and place became malleable and no longer an "articulator of identity," resulting in "human skin" being "asked to fly solo and speak for itself" (64).

212. Rediker, *The Slave Ship*, 114.

213. Ibid., 118.

214. Ibid., 121.

215. Ibid., 118–21.

black-white relational dynamics became locked in a struggle between resistance and market assimilation.

Jennings, in turn, articulates the journey of the slave ship as a theological act.[216] The "brutal march" to the sea is a "demonic reversal of a pilgrimage," escorting people into a Christianity marked by alienation and competition,[217] while the slave ship, floating on the sea and "suspended between worlds" becomes the middle space which announces "the recreation of the world," a distortion of the Christian doctrine of creation,[218] and the voyage across the sea inaugurates a twisted relationality in which peoples are interlocked in a cosmopolitanism characterized by "the one reality of violence," a "common [economic] journey and mission," and a subordination of various tongues to a shared language of commerce and exchange as a parody of Babel and Pentecost.[219]

Andrews, professor of English and comparative literature at the University of North Carolina at Chapel Hill, sustains a succinct discourse with Equiano in his *To Tell a Free Story: The First Century of Afro-American Autobiography, 1760–1865*. Compared with other African American autobiographical narratives of its time, Equiano's *The Interesting Narrative* is a work apart, "more than quadruple the size of any other slave narrative of its era."[220] Andrews notes that, due to a lack of editors, Equiano's work was both an authentically-researched document and a highly personal story of African experience in the New World.[221] Jennings locates both realities theologically: that by writing without his self-articulation being refracted through a white editor, Equiano could refer to himself as "the African," writing both for and to the many as the second Adam.[222]

Andrews also eloquently pens Equiano's relationship to both acculturation and the economics of the West:

> Having been initiated into the wonders and terrors of the Euro-Christian world order, he could not blink away the material and technological advancement of that civilization over the one from which he had been kidnapped. Unwilling to deny his affinities with either civilization, Equiano designed an autobiographical persona that embraced both. Unwilling to hymn a testimonial

216. Jennings, *Christian Imagination*, 174.
217. Ibid., 174.
218. Ibid., 175.
219. Ibid., 171–72, 178.
220. Andrews, *To Tell a Free Story*, 57.
221. Ibid.
222. Jennings, *Christian Imagination*, 187.

to the blessings of acculturation, he paid special attention to the processes of acculturation, noting what was gained and lost as the African outsider took up a new role within the Western world order. Most important, Equiano structured the development of his own bicultural perspective in his narrative so as to conduct his white reader along the same path of psychic evolution.[223]

Jennings likewise makes the risky choice of utilizing his own story in order to draw the reader to his central thesis related to joining. Rather than utilizing a stale self-conscious hermeneutic that distances author from audience, he makes the decision to navigate multiple linguistic worlds to allow others to take his journey with him. Like Equiano, he is "unwilling to hymn a testimonial to the blessings of acculturation" but instead "not[es] what [is] gained and lost" within a "bicultural perspective."

However, unlike Equiano, Jennings does not settle for an assimilationist relational structure characteristic of Western commodity exchange. Jennings recognizes the problematic theological moves narrowing Equiano's view of relationship to the market. He does so by referencing Joseph Calder Miller's *Way of Death: Merchant Capitalism and the Angolan Slave Trade*.[224] Jennings contrasts traditional African economies of exchange based on an "indissoluble association of a person with the thing he or she had created" with the exchange value of the West, in which "the potential worth of an object" is achieved by "definitively separating oneself from a product of one's personal labor."[225] By considering together Andrews and Calder Miller, the latter of which does not specifically reference Equiano, Jennings is constructing a vision of the pseudotheological economics of relationship within modern capitalism in order to contrast it with his vision of mutual joining within the body of Christ.

Finally, Andrews illumines the analogous relationship Equiano postulates between Africans and Jews. As "the African," Equiano places his people in a "complex relationship to the Euro-Christian scheme of things" in which Africans "both partake of and stand apart from the Western Christian tradition" as they "still await their 'land of promise'" as "descendants of Abraham."[226] The African-Jewish relationship postulated by Equiano suggests that he intuitively ascertains that a supersessionist impulse is at the heart of the subjection of Africans by Europeans. Jennings examines

223. Andrews, *To Tell a Free Story*, 57.
224. Miller, *Way of Death*.
225. Jennings, *Christian Imagination*, 171–72.
226. Andrews, *To Tell a Free Story*, 58.

this analogy of relationship as Equiano "suggest[ing] a reorientation for his white readers—toward kinship."[227] In the constructive portion of his text, Jennings offers several examples of relations between blacks and Jews that signify "the space of struggle for the overturning of the racial imagination and the reassertion of the theological framework necessary for the generation of an authentic Christian social imagination."[228]

Jennings maintains that Equiano's vision of kinship is necessarily hindered by the lack of relational potentiality within the strictures of commercialized life. Reborn into a Christianity in which neither conversion nor baptism were efficient to change the social order,[229] and introduced into "the increased commercialization of black life"[230] within an economy in which exchange networks substitute for "abiding kinship relationships,"[231] the best Equiano can imagine is an "economic confraternity."[232] Within this new world, Equiano achieves intimacy by becoming a businessman.

> He will offer himself for relationship by offering himself for purchase, not from the hold of a ship but from the free market in a text. Equiano is caught up in the trajectory of English commerce, which was becoming the currency of relationship.[233]

While Jennings in no way faults Equiano for being a "shrewd businessman" and "owning his literary self,"[234] he nonetheless points to the "poverty of desire"[235] that is regnant in imagining intimacy within this truncated framework. Theologically speaking, the best that this model of reconciliation can offer is "an eschatology of assimilation."[236] The Christianity Equiano claimed was quite real; Jennings cautions that it is far too easy to dismiss it as "simply psychologically forced faith."[237] However, communion was not a necessary component of Equiano's Christianity. The best it offered him was a relational structure constituted by the market and afforded to him as a self-made man.[238]

227. Jennings, *Christian Imagination*, 190.

228. Ibid., 277.

229. Ibid., 182, 196.

230. Ibid., 173.

231. Ibid., 181–82.

232. Ibid., 184.

233. Ibid., 188.

234. Ibid., 189.

235. Ibid., 202.

236. Ibid., 200.

237. Ibid., 201.

238. In my own community, engaged as we are in economic development and educational initiatives, I often recognize the paradoxical nature of our work. When

In Carretta's classic study *Equiano, the African: Biography of a Self-Made Man*, there are several key concepts which Jennings re-articulates within a theological framework. Carretta's analysis describes the consumerism of the Christianity that Equiano inherited. After "shopping for religion"[239] among various expressions of faith, Equiano's conversion came with nothing but his Bible and a revelation of the crucified Jesus Christ as his companions.[240] Ironically, his conversion took place within the cabin of a ship, the first recipients of his newfound witness being the captain and the crew, to whom "he sounded like an incomprehensible 'barbarian'" as he "tried to share his joy."[241] Jennings articulates the theological implications of this individualistic experience of salvation:

> His spiritual quest with its salvation episode also pointed to a sense of belonging that normalized loss . . . The loss here is an absence of Christianity constituted in community, a Christianity that joins all the people who claim to be Christian . . . Equiano entered a Christianity constituted without belonging. So he was left to perform a Christian life filled with the surrogates for that loss, God and the Scriptures . . . It may seem counterintuitive to suggest a relationship with God and a strong desire for the Scriptures as surrogate forms, given their constituting centrality for the Christian life. But here one must grasp the deepest tragedy for the formation of Christianity in the racial West: belonging was racialized. Equiano could not overcome this and therefore imagined Christian belonging along the only lines of thought available to him: he belonged to God, and the Scriptures belonged to him. The true worth of his soul was established between those boundaries.[242]

---

working to collapse socioeconomic distinctions through the market (employment, entrepreneurship, education, housing, etc.), one is necessarily engaged in the maintenance of what have come to be forms of social control. While attempting to turn those historical forms of exclusion into contemporary forms of inclusion, empowerment, and redistribution, one is often unwittingly engaged in assimilation to market sensibilities and identities marked by economic value. If not attended to carefully, the pursuit of justice can easily mimic modern forms of social tracking such as those undertaken by the criminal "justice" system. This is why it is of utmost importance to, as Jennings suggests, be joined one to another across ethnic and socioeconomic lines so that solutions can be borne out of shared relationship rather than paternalistic attempts at "charity" or "development." Such are the realities of navigating the social and relational implications of living in a community marked by difference for the sake of the Gospel.

239. Carretta, *Equiano*, 162.

240. Ibid., 174–75.

241. Ibid., 175.

242. Jennings, *Christian Imagination*, 198–99.

Carretta relates that while Equiano's "religious rebirth had happened suddenly," his conversion to the abolitionist cause was gradual.[243] This is not surprising, given the truncated and socially impotent form of Christianity into which Equiano was initiated during his spiritual formation. However, this "secular conversion" was every bit "as significant as his spiritual conversion."[244] It was this "secular conversion" that enabled Equiano, who as a "free African" could now be "more economically productive than enslaved Africans," to find "a mission that would enable him to do very well by doing good."[245] Jennings observes that, rather than conversion or baptism, it was Equiano's newfound ability to be an autonomous agent establishing his own economic independence on the free market that constituted his entrance into Christian relationship. An *ecclesia* constituted by commerce was the substitute for cultural joining.

Jennings' analysis of Equiano suggests several contemporary ramifications. He demonstrates the impoverished theological trajectory bequeathed to nonwhite peoples through colonization, specifically the uninviting Christianity offered to peoples of African descent, characteristic of the formation of "Black Atlantic Christianity."[246] Just as whiteness gave to Equiano an attenuated religion, limited in its communal scope and crippled in its imagination of relational possibilities, so the "unappealing" Christianity offered to black intellectuals has resulted in a sterile experience for many African American theologians and church leaders.[247] It has forced many promising thinkers into the disconnected intellectual silos characteristic of the disciplinary confines of white rationality, encouraged the exodus of many black scholars from the church itself, and silenced others through disregard and requisite assimilation.[248]

The best relational posture imaginable for many nonwhites is an "economic confraternity" in which they are invited to ascend the ladder of Mammon alongside their white counterparts. This "crass materialism"[249] is often the means by which relationship is constituted in the West, even as the insufficiency of the eschatological hope of capitalism is being experienced by the whites who have constructed it and the nonwhites who bear the greatest burden of its collapse. Jennings contends that authentic ecclesial

243. Carretta, *Equiano*, 237.

244. Ibid., 237.

245. Ibid., 236–37.

246. Jennings, *Christian Imagination*, 202.

247. Ibid., 202–3.

248. Ibid., 203.

249. Ibid., 5.

intimacy cannot be forged primarily around relationships of commerce.[250] While colonialist Christianity certainly carried within it the seed of a new communal life, its growth was inhibited. Jennings' analysis suggests that a vision of simply "making it in the new world" through pietistic personal hygiene and financial self-sufficiency is not a sufficient Christian hope. Ideologies of uplift have contributed to the "increased commercialization of black life" and encouraged people to "offer [themselves] for relationship by offering [themselves] for purchase."[251] While the path to social structures that do not perpetuate injustice upon nonwhite peoples certainly welcomes a process of economic advancement as a means toward the ability to make one's own choices in freedom, Jennings offers a critique of the assumption that this path constitutes an acceptable relational structure within which the vulnerability of joining reflective of the Incarnation can occur. Those engaged in contemporary forms of "social justice" through economic and community "development" would do well to recognize the complex dynamics associated with what Jennings names "the poverty of desire" inherent in post-colonial Christianity.[252]

This "poverty of desire" cannot be overcome through the evaluations of cultural studies. For instance, the most radical vision available to Rediker, in closing his text *The Slave Ship*, is the possibility of economic reparations to the descendants of the victims of slavery from the descendants of those who perpetrated the slave trade.[253] While Jennings would not suggest that Western governments should not seek a just economic distribution or that some form of reparations or reconstruction should not be procured for black Americans (who, as a group, still face an overwhelmingly uphill battle in economic advancement compared to their white counterparts and yet are disproportionately overrepresented in underfunded and failing schools, the prison industrial complex, etc.), his point regarding the limitations of "economic confraternity" as the *telos* of relational structures can be demonstrated in Rediker's conclusion.

While Rediker admits that "justice cannot be reduced to a calculus of money," he makes this observation simply because he doesn't trust that those who "spawned the slave trade in the first place" would "play by the rules of the game" in rendering reparations.[254] While this may be an accurate observation, it remains that the most that Rediker-as-historian can

250. Ibid., 171–73.
251. Ibid., 188.
252. Ibid., 202.
253. Rediker, *The Slave Ship*, 353–55.
254. Ibid., 355.

hope for is that "the legacy of slavery" would be "overcome" by allowing "the price of exploitation, of unpaid labor, [to be] computed" so that the descendants of those who were enslaved might receive "the full and just value of their labor."[255] The sheer unlikelihood of accomplishing such a task notwithstanding, Rediker's comments do not appear to be forged through substantive interaction with communities who would qualify for said reparations. If Rediker truly believes that the economic system is set up in such a way that those receiving reparations would not be treated justly in the distribution, would not those in power exploit all means necessary to quickly regain the money through the market? Perhaps Rediker's lack of proposing a workable solution is due to the fact that unspeakable evils cannot be extricated by economic repentance alone. At best, Rediker's conclusion tends to function as a moralistic exercise tacked on to the end of an otherwise insightful study. At worst, such an exercise subtly exculpates the bearer of such opinions from having to engage contemporary manifestations of the racial imaginary in specific situations "on the ground." Such a conclusion effectually proposes "paying off" the nonwhite "other," affording the severing of relational ties after having "washed one's hands" of one's neighbor and having declared proximate "justice" achieved. Equality in Rediker's schema appears to encourage separation. By contrast, Jennings predicates work for justice upon the necessity of lives being joined together in physical space.

In a section entitled *Living in the White House*, Jennings articulates that whiteness has become "the *arche* of . . . universal values."[256] Racial comparison has become "the only conceptuality strong and wide enough to anchor in a comprehensive way the many identities of people in relation and interaction."[257] The "always present but unspoken facilitator" for the discursive practice of racial classification is whiteness.[258] To illustrate this point, Jennings utilizes examples from American athletics, the entertainment industry, and advertisements characteristic of "aggressive capitalist-generated media."[259] In each one of these instantiations, whiteness is the norm by which the ability, value, or appeal of people of other ethnicities is evaluated. Whether in sports, where whiteness signifies the "fundamentals," discipline, and "hard work" of the game, in entertainment, where nonwhite characters are escorted in and out of the narrative plot of the "social and moral landscape" of white characters, or in advertising, where nonwhite

255. Ibid.

256. Jennings, *Christian Imagination*, 246.

257. Ibid., 247.

258. Ibid.

259. Ibid.

models are used inasmuch as they display the closest approximation of European features, whiteness is the evaluative standard by which nonwhites are judged.[260] In such a framework, the most a people can hope to achieve is the status of "commodity fragment."[261]

By referencing both the advancements made by Equiano as "a man ahead of his time,"[262] and the inherent limitations of the world he imagined, Jennings seems to be spinning a cautionary tale for contemporary generations of African Americans who would follow Equiano's example of locating identity and relational hopes in the market. Whether this be in business, entertainment, commerce, athletics, advertising, or the insatiable quest of career advancement, "cultural dissolution" is the greatest danger to modern peoples caught in the web of the global economic order.[263] Jennings' response is to ask "whether there is a form of cultural joining and cultural interaction that does not depend on or enact the dissolution trajectories of modern global economies and cultures or set in place desperate and destructive xenophobic responses to these overwhelming forces."[264] The answer that Jennings gives is that Christianity is "just such an alternative form of cultural joining and interaction."[265]

In order to perceive the Gospel as constituting such a joining force, Christians must recognize the distortions inherent in theology bound to market interests inaugurated in colonialism. This recognition includes decrying the false gods of nationalism and Mammon through shared space and shared experiments in reimagining economies of exchange along the lines of an economics of justice. The result will be an ecclesiology constituted not by commerce, assimilation, or racial or national identity, but by a full Christology reflected in a new body politic. In short, both the promise and limitation of the life of Olaudah Equiano must be remembered.

John William Colenso

I will now bring my consideration of Jennings' relationship to cultural studies to a close by explicating his analysis of the literature surrounding the life of Bishop Colenso. Unlike the three aforementioned characters, Colenso has been studied by ecclesiastical historians. While Acosta, Zurara, and Equiano

260. Ibid., 246–47.
261. Ibid., 247.
262. Ibid., 203.
263. Ibid., 247.
264. Ibid.
265. Ibid.

are each common figures within cultural studies, analyses of their theological significance have been limited. By way of contrast, Colenso's historical significance is explicitly framed as religious, albeit given little treatment because his theological vision is assessed as relatively insignificant in the scope of nineteenth-century liberalism. Drawing heavily on the romanticism of Samuel Taylor Coleridge and Frederick Denison Maurice, Colenso is remembered primarily for his universalistic soteriology, as evidenced by his commentary on the book of Romans, and his modern critical biblical hermeneutic, as evidenced by his commentary on the Pentateuch, both of which led to the Anglican Church dismissing him as a heretic. In the historical judgment of religious studies, neither of these trajectories is especially innovative or uncommon. I will contend that, much like the question of "why" John Brown engaged in armed revolt, Jennings is interested in "why" Colenso found his orthodoxy to be exhausted. While Jennings will not suggest that this was a "necessary" development for Colenso, he will demonstrate that joining led him to places his theological systems could not.

The standard treatment of Colenso is either by religious studies as a modern liberal or by historical studies as a political activist on the side of the Zulu people against the British colonial powers. As Peter Hinchliff, a leading Anglican historian in South Africa and professor of ecclesiastical history at Oxford, concludes: "Colenso may be considered as important in Church History in two ways: as one of the protagonists in the constitutional struggle which took place in South Africa; or as representative of 'liberal' Anglican theology in the mid-nineteenth century."[266] In a similar way to that in which we have seen Jennings' theological method differ from modern historiography, Jennings' theological interest in Colenso diverges from these comparatively reductive accounts.

Jennings maintains that, while shaped by modern liberalism, Colenso's theology was forged primarily in the fires of interpretation wrought by dialogue and communal life with William Ngidi, the Zulu man who was Colenso's partner in translation.[267] Neither Hinchliff, nor Jeff Guy, former Professor of History at the University of Natal, the two standard biographers of Colenso, sufficiently consider the impact cultural joining had on Colenso's theology.[268] In commenting on the charges of heresy brought against Colenso, Jennings contends: "Absent from every official engagement and assessment of Colenso's thought by his initial accusers was any consideration

---

266. Hinchliff, *John William Colenso*, author's note.

267. Jennings, *Christian Imagination*, 131.

268. Guy, *Destruction of the Zulu Kingdom*.

of why he came to his theological positions."[269] Like Colenso's prosecutors, historical studies has largely overlooked the significance of the relationship between Ngidi and Colenso. While Hinchliff recognizes that Colenso's views on the historicity of the Pentateuch were developed, at least in part, in response to Nigidi's inquiries while they together translated Genesis and Exodus, he mentions Ngidi only three brief times in his entire biography of Colenso, at each point referring to Ngidi to illustrate an aspect of the life of Colenso.[270] Likewise, Guy mentions Ngidi by name only twice in his work *The Destruction of the Zulu Kingdom*, both times referencing the same quote from Ngidi about the European role in inciting civil war among the Zulu for the purpose of conquest.[271] In one other place, he refers to the "'intelligent Zulu' whose penetrating questions were the origin of Colenso's notorious biblical criticism."[272] Here we see the methodological posture of white modern historiography at work: Both Hinchliff and Guy demonstrate that they are aware of the formative relationship between Ngidi and Colenso but do not consider it to be important enough to warrant sustained engagement.

Hinchliff and Guy demonstrate the limitations of their methodology as they laud Colenso for fighting "for the African people of Natal"[273] by preaching against the destruction wrought by the British invasion of Zululand[274] without considering the significance of the relationships between Colenso, Ngidi, Magema Fuze, and Ngidi's brother John, or the courageous work undertaken by the Zulu people on behalf of their own land. As Jennings maintains, the process of becoming "attuned to the concerns of native voices" caused Colenso to join the Africans in advocating for indigenous freedom against the dehumanizing forces of imperialism. This stance ended Colenso's lifelong friendship with Theophilus Shepstone, the British co-

269. Jennings, *Christian Imagination*, 149.

270. Hinchliff, *John William Colenso*, 88, 151, 190–91. The first is this point about translation, the second a reference to the "famous William Ngidi, who was supposed to have been responsible for starting Colenso's Old Testament criticism," and the third to Ngidi running the local parish church and preaching "simple little critical sermons."

271. Guy, *Destruction of the Zulu Kingdom*, 67, 245–46.

272. Ibid., xx. While the text I am referencing is not Guy's biography of Colenso (*The Heretic*), the lack of mentioning Ngidi's name on the part of Guy is startling, given his unknowingly ironic observation of the instrumentalist use of the South African natives: "the nature of the Zulu people and their history has been transformed to fulfill particular needs among widely differing groups of people, thousands of miles away from Zululand" (xx).

273. Hinchliff, *John William Colenso*, 193. Hinchliff indicates that, before his death, Colenso "planned to become official 'protector' of the Africans," a designation that, in hindsight, can be interpreted paternalistically.

274. Guy, *Destruction of the Zulu Kingdom*, 92.

lonial agent in charge of Natal, a man who, "obsess[ed] with creating his own black kingdom in Zululand," had overseen the seizure of native lands and animals, the capture of indigenous people, and the deposition of the Hlubi chief Langalibalele.[275] In what Jennings calls "the end of translation," Colenso "chose to listen to his cotranslators: not Shepstone, but Fuze and Ngidi."[276] Unable to adequately summarize the beauty of where Colenso's path led him, I quote at length from Jennings:

> From the Langalibalele affair forward all the intellectual, po-
> litical, social and ecclesial tools he had honed in defining and
> defending his theological positions were placed in the service
> of the black body. His unrelenting advocacy for the chief and
> his people opened up the world he thought he knew into the
> world he would now understand . . . Colenso turned down an
> opportunity to preach at Westminster Abbey to press his theo-
> logical positions out of concern that it would detract from the
> Langalibalele situation. Again, Colenso chose the African. His
> actions were certainly consistent with his theology . . . As is al-
> ways the case, however, theological beliefs are always more than
> one imagines. Whether those beliefs are weak or strong, they
> leave open a door, and through that door came collectors on
> those beliefs, demanding a life consistent with that confession.
> For Colenso, the voices he had heard carefully year after year in
> translating were now speaking to him in a new way, and now
> that he had chosen the African he had new ears to hear . . . This
> was a place his theology could not take him, but precisely where
> the Africans drew him . . . His translated life was of a world
> forming, moving inextricably toward binding, toward commu-
> nion. His life and his work were of one piece.[277]

Jennings suggests that while Colenso's written theology may not in itself be interesting, his lived relational theology became revolutionary as his relationship with Ngidi developed. Being joined with Ngidi renewed Colenso's auditory capacity.

Jennings maintains that, because of his relationship with Ngidi, Colenso recognized the inherent chauvinism in European soteriology but was unable to reimagine God's saving work in the world in a way that both respected the "other" and maintained the particularity of the Christian salvation narrative. Colenso's joining tested his Christology; the Christianity he had inherited rendered him unable to conceptualize joining within

275. Jennings, *Christian Imagination*, 161–62, 164.
276. Ibid., 163.
277. Ibid., 163–65.

the body of the Jewish Jesus.[278] Jennings maintains that Colenso labored to overcome the particularity of Israel and the historicity of the salvation narrative because he saw no other way to respect the particularity of his Zulu brothers.[279] Colenso could not embark on a joined way of life without imagining Israel as a theologically exhausted construct. He had no theological framework within which to envision mutuality with those on the fringe of white soteriology. Trapped within a distorted yet orthodox imagination, Colenso opted for a modern liberal universalism that posited Christian faith as the revelation of a universal inherent righteousness.[280] By reducing divine presence to a universal light of love, "Colenso's vision evacuated Christian identity of any real substance," in effect rendering it "the moral universal inherent in all people."[281] Colenso's limited theological vision was not dissimilar to the Kantian moment and the modern presuppositions of cultural and religious studies.

Jennings contends that modern missiology, in its attempt to more satisfactorily conceptualize the non-European "other," is subject to the same limitations as Colenso. In order to demonstrate the supersessionist theological imagination at work in Colenso and in modern missiology, Jennings analyzes the works of missiologists Andrew F. Walls and Lamin Sanneh, with whose Christology of translation Jennings contrasts his Christology of joining.[282] By offering a critique of Sanneh, a missiologist favorably appropriated by Hauerwas,[283] Jennings hints that he distinguishes his Christology of joining from both the cultural studies enterprise and a theological tradition of virtue. Jennings reads Sanneh as positing a universal revelation of God in all peoples in a way that underemphasizes the particularity of the Jewish Jesus, leading to a thoroughly modern relativity foreign to the biblical narrative. While admirably striving to avoid ethnocentrism, this orientation tends to lock identity within nationalist strictures.[284] Jennings suggests that this posture does not display a fundamental openness to the other as other but rather evaluates the non-Westerner according to the descriptive categories of whiteness. In this sense, nonwhite peoples tend to be reflected

278. Jennings variously describes this as Colenso's "depleted orthodoxy," "spent orthodox imagination," "the exhaustion of his orthodoxy" and "the poverty of his theology" (147–49).

279. Jennings, *Christian Imagination*, 139.

280. Ibid., 144.

281. Ibid., 145.

282. Walls, *The Missionary Movement*; and Sanneh, *Translating the Message*. Sanneh and Walls were at one time colleagues at the University of Aberdeen, Scotland.

283. Jennings, *Christian Imagination*, 155; Hauerwas, *State of the University*, 71.

284. Jennings, *Christian Imagination*, 167.

upon as concepts narrating the soteriological concerns of Western theology. As with Colenso's initial relationship with Ngidi, the nonwhite other becomes more prop than partner. This has many ecclesiological ramifications, several of which are considered in chapter 4.

As Jennings maintains, "What looks like a radical antiracist, anti-ethnocentric vision of Christian faith is in fact profoundly imperialist. Colenso's universalism undermines all forms of identity except that of the colonialist."[285] In this schema, a process which Jennings titles "rendering the African," the native becomes a set piece in a performance of "theological self-absorption."[286] Colenso's initial "didactic use of the native" discouraged the profound possibilities of the unlike "other" becoming a "theological conversation partner who would significantly affect the outcomes of modes of life."[287] The conversations had by Ngidi and Colenso pressed against Colenso's Christian imagination, leading the later Colenso to choose authentic relationship over the objectifying patterns of reflection characteristic of whiteness.

A Christology of Translation

In this section I will demonstrate that, because of the supersessionist imagination, framing the embodiment of Christian faith in terms of "mission" or "translation" may not be the most helpful ways of framing the particular-universal trajectory of the Gospel. Before interacting with Walls and Sanneh, I will describe a key heuristic device Jennings employs to demonstrate the deformities of Western Christian reflection upon transmission of the faith. Jennings maintains that Christian theology post-colonization tends to operate within heretical Christological "habits of mind."[288] He uses the poles of Docetism and adoptionism to demonstrate how Christians tend to reflect upon "divine entrance into the world."[289] Whereas the colonial Christian imagination tended to frame the Incarnation in spiritualized terms not unlike the historical contours of Docetism in which the Incarnation lost its "social and political character," modern missiology tends to imagine the Incarnation in material terms that Jennings refers to as the other side of "the same coin": "the theological heretical habit of mind" known as

285. Ibid., 145.
286. Ibid., 150.
287. Ibid., 150, 154.
288. Ibid., 166.
289. Ibid.

adoptionism.[290] Jennings maintains that "neither find[s] its way to a Christian theology that of necessity creates intimacy." Whereas the former tends to universalize Jesus in a way that underemphasizes particular embodiment reflective of the Incarnation, the latter tends to contextualize the Gospel in a way that posits the presence of God as "adopting" each particular people, thereby rendering unnecessary particular joining in the flesh of Jesus. Jennings is not anachronistically suggesting that the contours of the contemporary Christian imagination are equivalent to the historical problems of Gnostic Docetism or Ebionite adoptionism. He nevertheless finds it helpful to demonstrate the ways in which contemporary incarnational postures mime the imaginative habits of said Christological aberrancies. In both tendencies, the scandal of particularity is underemphasized, resulting in malformed conceptions of place and race.

Jennings traces the development of the "adoptionist" missiological imagination before interacting specifically with Sanneh and Walls. Jennings finds Colenso's vision to be a Protestant maturation of the "comparativist hermeneutic" modeled in the Renaissance Catholic Acosta.[291] However, whereas in Acosta the comparison functioned to denigrate the Peruvian natives, in Colenso, and by extension modern missiology, the comparison is intended to humble European arrogance.[292] Yet it characteristically does so by reflecting on, rather than with, those to whom the missionary is going. While Colenso evaluated Zulu religious practices positively, he read cultural difference within a racialized comparative schema that offered ethnicity as an index of cultural development. His commentary on Romans presented the movement of the Gospel from "European Christian" to "African heathen" as the movement out of Israel to the Gentile "pagan." In this hermeneutic framework, the Jews become, in the words of Jennings, "the foil to faith, the carrier pigeon of the gospel."[293] Gone are Israel's history and its story of liberation. The Gospel now functions fully within a European-centered soteriology:

> It is that [white] hubris that triggers what would become in the late nineteenth century and twentieth a formulaic way of articulating the relation between sin, damnation, and eternal punishment. What is concealed in that formulaic articulation is the

---

290. Ibid., 166–67.
291. Ibid., 133.
292. Ibid.
293. Ibid., 141.

centered white subject who discerns moral deficiency, salvific absence, and the eternal state after death.[294]

Jennings demonstrates that Sanneh and Walls, like Colenso, read modern missions into the biblical text as analogical of the relationship between Jew and Gentile, or what Walls calls the "carrier culture" and the "recipient culture."[295] This enacts an inherent theological relativism in which YHWH's history is of little consequence for faith.[296] For Sanneh and Walls, translation operates within the space between the eternal essence of the message and its particular embodiment.[297] Jennings contends that they fail to consider the simultaneous translation of indigenous peoples into the vernacular universe of European nations that valued the written word and individual literacy over against oral, more communal traditions.[298] Physical place and material realities are of little consequence to a spirituality so conceived. As with the colonial moment, flesh continues to serve as indicator of theological identity. Jennings maintains that, in primarily reflecting on the positive results of translation, Sanneh and Walls ignore the slow, steady historic development of translation within a colonialist and supersessionist Christian imagination.[299]

Since Jennings deals extensively with both Sanneh and Walls, I will not reiterate the entirety of the argument, but will rather briefly read both missiologists so as to demonstrate Jennings' divergence with them and to prepare the way for my consideration of Hauerwas in chapter 4. Sanneh, Professor of Missions, World Christianity, and History at Yale Divinity School, treats Christianity as a *religion* which exerts a "dual force in its historical development," on the one hand "relativiz[ing] its Judaic roots" and, on the other "destigmatiz[ing] Gentile culture" in order to "*adopt* that culture as a natural extension of the life of the new religion."[300] In his framework, Jewish identity is evacuated and every national identity adopted by the universal religious impulse of the Gospel.[301] With Israel superseded, Christianity proceeds as a translation movement in which its "vernacular character" results in various *ethnos* "all following a version of the faith expressive of

294. Ibid., 143.

295. Ibid., 155, and Walls, *The Missionary Movement*, xvii.

296. Jennings, *Christian Imagination*, 160.

297. Ibid., 156.

298. Ibid., 159, 207–20.

299. Ibid., 157.

300. Sanneh, *Translating the Message*, 1, italics mine.

301. See Greggs, *Theology Against Religion*, which offers an account of the ways in which faith in Jesus has been circumscribed by the modern category of religion.

their national character."[302] Sanneh's historiographic treatment of Christian faith reinscribes nationalist identity as reflective of divine providence. What initially sounds antiethnocentric strengthens racialized identity and resists the joining of difference in local space.

Sanneh's historiography operates according to a modern particular-universal dialectic: "Either believers accept the pluralist thrust of the gospel . . . as evidence of God's pilgrim purpose or they resist it with some arbitrary exclusivist cultural ideology."[303] For Sanneh, Christians must choose between a contextualizing theological relativism and a universalizing theological imperialism. As with Colenso, the scandal of particularity is overlooked. While European arrogance is criticized, left in place is the hidden assumption that the European body is constitutive of Christian faith. Sanneh is working against what he sees as the consensus within his discipline:

> Modern historiography has established a tradition that mission was the surrogate of Western colonialism, and that . . . together these two movements combined to destroy indigenous cultures . . . . I wish in this book to present another point of view, which . . . should help restore some objectivity to the subject.[304]

Sanneh believes that mission strengthened indigenous cultures. While Jennings maintains that the life of Christ was often imparted even through mangled colonial missionary translation,[305] he reads Sanneh's account as obscuring the sociopolitical nature of the Incarnation, which

> draws our imaginations not first to the translation of the gospel message but to the joining of peoples in the struggle to learn each other's languages in the process of lives joined, lives lived together in new spaces, and constituting a new history for a new people.[306]

Jennings' analysis suggests that translation has tended to function as a Kantian enterprise in which a universal moral ideal finds various contextual applications. The Scriptures maintain that the eternal Word *became* flesh;[307] translation does not entail *becoming* anything. The theological intuitions of

302. Sanneh, *Translating the Message*, 1–2.

303. Ibid., 6.

304. Ibid., 4.

305. See Jennings, *Christian Imagination*, 168: "In the end, William Ngidi and many others like him captured something in the missionary endeavor. Despite its multiple problems, a translation of the original had happened. And even if the original had been mutilated, tortured, and eventually killed in colonialist power, there was a resurrection."

306. Ibid., 160–61.

307. John 1:14.

Chalcedonian Christology point less to an unchanging ideal taking on a particular form than they do a conjoining of natures in a particular, unified person. While Jennings recognizes that the early Hellenization of orthodox Christology would lay groundwork exploited by later and more extreme supersessionism, his Christological heuristic affirms the same reality toward which Chalcedon was pointing: that two separate natures were joined in a single person without division or confusion.[308] It is this scandal which post-colonial Christology seems to be unable to adequately conceptualize. Jennings' Christology of joining proves to be more consistent with patristic sensibilities than is Sanneh's Christology of translation.

Additionally, translation itself is not as innocuous an enterprise as Sanneh suggests. While Jennings acknowledges that the vernacular translation movement achieved "tremendous missional, even redemptive, ends," he maintains that "literacy's redemptive possibilities were themselves drawn inside projects of nation building as well as burgeoning performances of class consciousness."[309] While he lauds "[t]he strength of salvation's witness in word," Jennings asserts that biblical literacy served as "a powerful catalyst for the transformation of [language and land] and for the formation of peoples as nations."[310] Within "the pedagogical conditions for Christian initiation," the world's peoples were nationalized and racialized. Within a paradigm of translation, there is "little room or energy for a vision that joins, mixes, or fuses peoples and their languages."[311]

Jennings' alternative linguistic vision is a Pentecostal one.[312] Rather than a universal ideal being translated into various tongues, thereby allowing people to remain separate, singing the praises of God within their

---

308. I suspect that Jennings' general evaluation of the early ecclesial development of Christology is similar to that of Justo Gonzalez, who states: "[I]n spite of a rather widespread opinion that the development of doctrines was an unwarranted Hellenization of Christianity—it was often the "heretics" that proposed the most radically Hellenized versions of Christianity, and that in condemning them the Church at large, while often using the tools of Hellenistic philosophy, in fact set a limit to the influence of that philosophy upon the understanding of the Christian faith . . . That Hellenization has to do not only with matters of form or vocabulary, but also with the very understanding of the nature of Christianity, and it therefore created problems that ideally could have been avoided by following other avenues of philosophical interpretation. But . . . the general development of Christian doctrine, while making use of a Hellenistic understanding of Christianity, instinctively excluded those extreme forms of Hellenization which would have denied the basic tenet of the Christian faith: that God was in Christ reconciling the world unto himself" (Gonzalez, *A History of Christian Thought*, 1:394–95).

309. Jennings, *Christian Imagination*, 218.

310. Ibid.

311. Ibid.

312. Ibid., 266–67.

national and ethnic identities, the coming of the Spirit entails a deep inter-penetration of various linguistic structures into a unified chorus of praise to the Father of Jesus Christ. Learning another's tongue entails entering into his spatially-constituted identity as intimate guest. The coming of the Spirit was the superfluity of the lips of Jewish disciples as an invitation to all peoples to together praise the God of Abraham, Isaac, and Jacob through Jesus the risen Christ.[313] Intellectual projects like Sanneh's allow for separatist eccle-siologies in which the "other" can be reflected upon and "respected" from a safe distance. Jennings' Christology of joining, on the other hand, suggests an ecclesiology requiring the sharing of space in the mutual enfolding of difference. I will take up this ecclesiology of joining in the Conclusion.

Walls, Professor of the History of Mission at Liverpool Hope Univer-sity and Professor Emeritus of the study of Christianity in the non-Western world at the University of Edinburgh, focuses on what he sees to be the shift of the center of global Christianity from West to East. However, he interprets that progression to be archetypical of the movement of salvation away from Israel to the Gentiles. Like Colenso and Sanneh, Walls reads European identity into Jewish identity. As he strives to relativize Eurocen-trism, he underemphasizes the significance of YHWH's history of salvation in the world.

Walls offers a dialectic between the "indigenizing principle" and the "pilgrim principle,"[314] which means that God takes people as they are, indig-enous culture and all, and transforms them into an itinerant people with no abiding home. Place is implicitly overcome in the movement from heathen "indigene" to Christian "pilgrim." For Walls, the indigenizing principle is indicative of the particular, whereas the pilgrim principle demonstrates a move to the universal through conversion. Walls finds this particular-uni-versal trajectory displayed at the Jerusalem Council in Acts 15, a passage he interprets as demonstrating a decisive rift between Christianity and Judaism as separate and distinct "religions." Walls contends that no society has ever existed, "in East or West, ancient time or modern, which could absorb the word of Christ painlessly into its system," including "Jesus within Jewish culture, Paul within Hellenistic culture."[315] For Walls, the "word of Christ" functions as universal, decontextualized content which finds expression through the adoption of local cultures. Jennings suggests that, for Walls, "the Son is always being translated."[316] In this adoptionist motif, the Incar-

---

313. Acts 2:1–41.
314. Walls, *Missionary Movement*, 7–8.
315. Ibid., 8.
316. Jennings, *Christian Imagination*, 158.

nation does not disrupt human patterns of living but reveals the divine approval intrinsic to them.[317]

Like Sanneh, Walls presents the Incarnation as a particular-universal dialectic: "The bewildering paradox at the heart of the Christian confession is not just the obvious one of the divine humanity; it is the twofold affirmation of the utter Jewishness of Jesus and of the boundless universality of the Divine Son."[318] Walls' formulation separates the universal divinity of the Divine Son from the particular humanity of the Jewish Jesus in a way that problematically mirrors the rough thought habits of early Dynamic Monarchianism and later Nestorianism. Walls' missiology tends to separate God's revelation in Jesus from time and space, rendering the Incarnation a "bewildering paradox" rather than a particular scandal. Jennings' thesis encourages the query: When would Walls identify as the point at which theological history ceased to be an account of YHWH's acts in particular time and place?

Jennings asserts that Walls reduces Christian community to "crosscultural communication," a process by which the Gospel is continually translated into new nationalities and linguistic structures, thereby dethroning the culture out of which it is translated.[319] For Walls, the historical problem is not so much that missiology functioned alongside colonization but that "representative Westerners" could not help but have transmitted their own cultural values.[320] Walls sees contemporary Christian mission as inaugurating a blessed "period of double identity" leading to a multiculturalism of "expression and application" in which the West will "come to terms with Christianity as a non-Western religion."[321] Walls posits that "Third World theology," shaped by "domestic tasks . . . so basic, so vital" and characterized by "*doing* things," will become "the representative Christian theology" while "Western theology," filled with "barren, sterile, time-wasting by-paths," will become a "specialist interest" to historians.[322] Walls' account tends to essentialize various peoples as either "thinking" beings or "doing" beings. Walls does not explore the possibility of an intermeshing of diverse understandings of rationality and variegated ways of being in the world.

For Walls, the missionary moment both confirms national identity and overcomes it:

317. Ibid., 166.

318. Walls, *Missionary Movement*, xvi.

319. Jennings, *Christian Imagination*, 159.

320. Walls, *Missionary Movement*, xviii, xix.

321. Ibid., xviii, xix.

322. Ibid., 9–12.

> That wise old owl, Henry Venn of the Church Missionary So-
> ciety, reflecting on the Great Commission in 1868, argued that
> the fullness of the Church would only come with the fullness
> of the national manifestations of different national churches:
> 'Inasmuch as all native churches grow up into the fullness of the
> stature of Christ, distinctions and defects will vanish . . . But it
> may be doubted whether, to the last, the Church of Christ will
> not exhibit marked national characteristics which, in the over-
> ruling grace of God, will tend to its perfection and glory.'[323]

For Walls and Venn, difference is locked within "national characteristics." It is divine grace that matures the "distinctions and defects" of native churches as they "grow up" into Christ. While disunity is imagined as overcome, static identity is reconfirmed. As Jennings suggests, a similar mental exercise was taking place in the thinking of another missionary theologian: "Colenso is reading salvation history inside settler-Zulu relations and attempting to render the particularities of identity inconsequential to Christian existence. In order to do this, Colenso must racialize those identities to then transcend them."[324]

Walls posits a cosmic unity between all Christians in all times and spaces in the *pleroma*: "It is as though Christ himself actually grows through the work of missions . . . The full-blown humanity of Christ requires all the Christian generations, just as it embodies all the cultural variety that six continents can bring."[325] While Jennings would not disagree with the heart of this contention, he suggests that an emphasis on such an invisible unity may serve to undercut visible joining in particular times and spaces. Walls misses the crucial distinction which Jennings discerns: The fullness of God was conjoined with the particular humanity of Jesus Christ so as to provide a concrete ground in which particular humanity is conjoined.

While Sanneh and Walls should perhaps be applauded for striving toward an antiethnocentric missiology, they are unable to satisfactorily theologically imagine reconciliation. Like Colenso, whose heart Jennings' commends, Sanneh and Walls demonstrate the dangers of doing missiology within a depleted Christological imagination. Their Christology of trans-lation is less radical than Jennings' Christology of joining, which suggests an ecclesiology of joining in which the racial gaze is resisted. As Jennings summarizes:

---

323. Ibid., 12.

324. Jennings, *Christian Imagination*, 139.

325. Walls, *Missionary Movement*, xvii.

Bishop Colenso marked a path that has been traveled by so many others before and since. One must in the end celebrate that path for showing a courageous Christian bishop who gave his life in missionary service and who in the mature years of his life acted for the good of an oppressed people. One must also grieve over that path for showing Christian theology in translation not only bound to colonialism, but still confining Christians to its options.[326]

A Christology of Joining

The stories of Acosta, Zurara, Equiano, and Colenso have been heard before. While their significance has been recognized in the tales told by historical studies, the theological academy has largely ignored the promise and limitation of their reflections. It is to another story that Christians must again listen if we are to recognize the deformities that we, like these four, have inherited:

> The story of Israel connected to Jesus can crack open a life so that others, strangers, even colonized strangers begin to seep inside and create cultural alienation for the translator, and even more, deep desire for those who speak native words. These implications are far greater than emancipatory possibilities for indigenes rooted in vernacular Christian agency of budding cultural nationalisms, but in joining—loving, caring, intimate joining. That joining is a sharing in the pain, plight, and life of one another . . . This, finally, is Christian translation. And such translation cost Bishop Colenso everything.[327]

In this chapter I have demonstrated Jennings' stance of interdisciplinary joining; in the next chapter I will suggest that his critique of a reclamation of Western virtue demonstrates that such a traditioned posture may be resistant to the vulnerability of joining, a vulnerability that costs everything.

326. Jennings, *Christian Imagination*, 168.
327. Ibid., 165–66.

Chapter 4: Jennings and Virtue Ethics

Alisdair MacIntyre: A Reasoned,
Traditioned Ethic of Virtue

I HAVE SUGGESTED THAT the work of Jennings, like that of Carter, can be understood best by positioning it between and beyond the disciplines of cultural studies and contemporary theological virtue ethics. In chapter 3, I read Jennings as joining with the discipline of cultural studies (as exemplified by Mignolo), while necessarily diverging from its naturalistic conclusions (as exemplified by Brion Davis). In this chapter, I will demonstrate that Jennings is content with neither the aesthetic and ethical hegemony of a MacIntyrian philosophy of virtue nor its theological deployment by Hauerwas. While I will contend that Hauerwas' theological invocation of virtue resists some of the more problematic aspects of MacIntyre's philosophical reclamation of virtue, and while I do not suggest that Hauerwas' theological program can be reduced to its more problematic MacIntyrian components, I will maintain that, to the extent that Hauerwas takes on board such an account of reality, his theological program tends to devalue non-Western (including Jewish) ways of conceiving the world. I will mirror my treatment of Carter and Milbank by first considering the manner in which MacIntyre understands ethics to function before examining how a tradition of Western virtue is extended through Hauerwas' vision of the University. I will contend that such an account of moral formation tends to produce Christian ministers and intellectuals who have a hard time not imagining themselves and their traditions from what Jennings calls "the commanding heights."[1]

Jennings explains how the Aristotelian-Thomist theological parent of MacIntyre's philosophical ethics functioned as a system of descriptive control:

> Theology will indeed become the trigger for the classificatory subjugation of all nonwhite, non-Western peoples. But that classificatory subjugation began simply as the reassertion of a

---

1. Jennings, *Christian Imagination*, 8.

doctrinal logic—that God created the world. Here, with Acosta, the theoretically sublime Christian doctrine will create space and then conceal in his own time and in the centuries to come the morally hideous.[2]

Jennings is interested in what I will call the "space between": the hidden presuppositions that provide a conceptual framework in which an embodied anti-Christianity can take root. It has too often been the paragons of formation in their respective traditions whose works most clearly encourage paternalism, thereby making room for objectifying relationality and even heinous practice. Jennings is primarily concerned with how Christian theology, a way of life predicated upon love for neighbor and focused on the central image of Christ's body, could have become a vehicle through which moral justification was provided for centuries of Western conquest, subjugation, racism, and ecclesial division. His work probes the ways in which similar theological currents to those undergirding colonization find expression through contemporary Christian intellectual and spiritual formation. As a confessing Christian, Jennings does not contend against the historic creedal affirmations of the Church but explores the manner in which such doctrinal confessions were used in service of grotesque ends. How could those who affirmed that God was in Christ engage in practices not consonant with the vulnerability of the Incarnation? In what ways is the Christian imagination beholden to these doctrinal sleights-of-hand and how do such distortions often remain hidden from substantive theological inquiry?

A Tradition of Virtue

In his influential *After Virtue*, MacIntyre laments the "interminable character" of "contemporary moral utterance."[3] He maintains that there is no modern rational standard by which ethical debates can be concluded nor is there a process of formation through which humans can order their passions, thereby becoming moral agents who choose the right. For MacIntyre, modernity signals the disintegration of a classical moral framework. He names the "distinctively modern standpoint . . . that which envisages moral debate in terms of a confrontation between incompatible and incommensurable moral premises and moral commitment as the expression of a criterionless choice between such premises, a type of choice for which no

---

2. Ibid., 87.
3. MacIntyre, *After Virtue*, 6.

rational justification can be given."[4] Much like Milbank, MacIntyre criticizes modernity's dialecticism and its lack of a shared, rational, moral foundation. He claims that Kant, Diderot, Hume, Kierkegaard, and Smith were all formed by a "highly specific shared historical background,"[5] which he terms "an independent rational justification of morality" characteristic of the late seventeenth and the eighteenth centuries.[6] Their "common philosophical project" suffers from an "internal incoherence."[7] Each thinker held in common a quest to locate ethics (as a discipline distinct from theology, law, or aesthetics) in something other than a communal tradition focused on inculcation of the virtues. According to MacIntyre, whether modern morality is a universal moral law (Kant) or a radical choice based in an absurd leap of faith (Kierkegaard), the criterion is located in the individual. Severed from a history, "the individual moral agent, freed from hierarchy and teleology," is "sovereign in his moral authority."[8] For MacIntyre, modern ethics are constructed in piecemeal fashion, producing people unformed to live virtuous lives. It is this Enlightenment project that is of necessity doomed to failure.[9]

MacIntyre's thesis is clear: A recovery of the virtue-based tradition as exemplified through an Aristotelian-Thomist framework is the remedy for the modern moral impasse. As he writes twenty-five years after the first edition of *After Virtue*, "I remain equally committed to the thesis that it is only from the standpoint of a very different tradition, one whose beliefs and presuppositions were articulated in their classical form by Aristotle, that we can understand both the genesis and the predicament of moral modernity."[10] As he expresses, "I became a Thomist after writing *After Virtue* in part because I became convinced that Aquinas was in some respects a better Aristotelian than Aristotle."[11] MacIntyre claims that his earlier views had lacked an appropriate *telos*, which was supplied later by Aquinas' Aristotelianism. Thomism provided MacIntyre a "metaphysical grounding" for his articulation of practices, traditions, and narratives as directed toward "the human

---

4. Ibid., 39.

5. Ibid., 51. I question MacIntyre's inclusion of Kierkegaard in his list of the philosophers of moral modernity. I interpret MacIntyre's inclusion as signaling that he interprets individualism as their common thread.

6. Ibid., 39.

7. Ibid., 51.

8. Ibid., 62.

9. Ibid., 51.

10. Ibid., x.

11. Ibid.

good" as well as a "biological grounding" for his anthropology of human beings as "rational animals."[12]

While Jennings grants that the culture of moral modernity is problematic in many ways, he finds the individualistic encyclopedic rationality of Enlightenment to be a descendant of theology done in the age of conquest. It is in the theological scholasticism of the colonial moment that imperialist patterns of reflection upon the non-European "other" took root. The philosophy of MacIntyre hearkens to a medieval tradition of virtue, the tradition that shaped Acosta. As we shall see, Acosta was not a fringe renegade at odds with his tradition. It was precisely from within his tradition that he was able to form a summative view of the New World which Spain would claim as its own. Jennings contends that philosophers such as MacIntyre and Jeffery Stout, and the theologians who follow their "thinking on tradition," "all have yet to face Jose de Acosta and what he means for Christian (and modern democratic) traditions embodied and articulated."[13] MacIntyre's critique is not of individuals but of a *culture*—the "culture of moral modernity," which he claims lacks "the resources to proceed further with its own moral inquiries."[14] Similarly, Jennings' genealogy does not single out Acosta alone as problematic; he is examining what it is about the *culture* and shared suppositions of Aristotelian Thomism that produced an Acosta and how it is that similarly denigrating forms of reflection are often channeled through contemporary philosophical and theological virtue ethics:

> This difficulty I shall face . . . is reckoning with the fact that this crisis of theological tradition was not discerned by Acosta, and for the most part has still not been discerned, as a crisis of Christian tradition. From the moment Acosta (and all those like him) placed his feet on the ground in Lima, the Christian tradition and its theologians conjured a form of practical rationality that locked theology in discourses of displacement from which it has never escaped.[15]

Acosta's Virtues

I will briefly relate Jennings' description of Acosta's intellectual and spiritual formation before directly reading Acosta's theological reflections in order

12. Ibid., xi.
13. Jennings, *Christian Imagination*, 71.
14. MacIntyre, *After Virtue*, x.
15. Jennings, *Christian Imagination*, 71.

to demonstrate the manner in which a classical virtue ethic tends to undertake reflection when faced with what MacIntyre calls an "epistemological crisis."[16] As Jennings relates, Acosta was a Jesuit theologian of first-rank order, schooled in the most prestigious academic institutions of his context and prepared to be a model of the integration of faith and praxis. He had a deep commitment both to theological orthodoxy and to spiritual formation. It was this "interpenetration of devotion and knowledge" that prepared him for a life of ministry and service to others.[17] His family was enmeshed with the Society of Jesus: Acosta's parents and siblings were deeply committed to spiritual zeal and religious orders. As a Thomist, Acosta had a "precise doctrinal understanding . . . joined to a conceptually clear vision of how the world is and ought to be ordered."[18] Not only did he embody a harmonization of the tradition, but he had a coherent account of societal relations and commutative justice by way of Aristotle's political ethics as refracted through Augustinianism.[19]

This same Acosta fashioned the theological vision for the ordering of the New World, speaking for the native peoples as he facilitated their incorporation into the "civilized" world.[20] In his *De Procuranda* and *Historia*, Acosta purposes to offer a comprehensive narrative of the origins of native peoples, their cultures and customs, and their land and traditions. Acosta intends to make the indigenes understandable to his home continent and to incorporate the natives into the story of salvation. Absent from these texts is sustained interaction with the indigenous people themselves.[21] With Acosta, nonwhite peoples become the soteriological counterweight to Christian Europe, an imaginary position that remains powerfully lodged in the consciousness of Western theology.[22] Jennings reads *De Procuranda* and *Historia* as presenting a salvation devoid of communion.

16. Ibid., 70.

17. Ibid., 67.

18. Ibid., 68. Jennings' observation is further evidenced by the very nature of St. Thomas Aquinas' theological method as one of a totalizing summation of the theological tradition for all aspects of existence. The name and structure of his primary work, the *Summa Theologica*, bears out this observation.

19. Jennings, *Christian Imagination*, 88–90.

20. Ibid., 91.

21. Ibid., 85–86.

22. Ibid., 31–38. This trajectory is described by Jennings through his utilization of the Jesuit Alessandro Valignano. By way of example, in contemporary parlance a common way to narrate soteriological concerns is to invoke the presence of "the native tribe who has never heard about Jesus" as the contrasting pole to the Westerner who most fully embodies salvific possibility. In such a comparative schema, the identity of both the white body and the nonwhite person are assumed to be known givens.

Acosta discerns a vast demonic and idolatrous network to be active in native beliefs and practices without engaging in relationships marked by the "generosity of spirit" which would accompany "simple Gentile remembrance."[23] In contradistinction to a biblical identification of idolatry as worship not directed toward YHWH and not connected to God's people, Acosta was "moving toward a more modern vision:" one in which "the hermeneutics of idolatry was modulating into something new—an ethnographic, anthropological vision of cultures arranged hierarchically," which is "not a movement away from a theological vision but a modulation within it."[24] Jennings does not discount the prophetic discernment granted to the seers of Israel in their condemnation of pagan practices, but maintains that Acosta claims this epistemological privilege for himself, failing to "position himself with the Indians within a history of Gentile . . . existence," thereby precluding "far more richly imagined possibilit[ies] of movement toward faith from within the cultural logics and spatial realities of Andean life."[25]

The power of Jennings' analysis is that it does not paint Acosta a diabolical character surreptitiously couching his colonizing intentions in theological jargon. If that were the case, Acosta would be easier to dismiss. On the contrary, as Mignolo maintains, "[t]he Jesuits were in general more open to learning from the cultures they sought to convert than the Dominicans and Franciscans were."[26] Acosta's doctrinal orthodoxy, theological prowess, and cogency in offering a precise summative account of creation were not in question. This is what makes Acosta so troubling. He is an example of a theologian, faithfully formed in a hallowed tradition, working beyond the limits of his knowledge.

The Spaniards of the sixteenth century believed that the "discovery" of the New World was the most momentous occurrence since the creation of the world.[27] Acosta was doing none other than narrating this new world through the lens of Christian Thomism. The very structure of his *Natural and Moral History of the Indies (Historia)* is formed in the pattern of a *summa*. Acosta addresses his new surroundings (including people, places, weather patterns, plants, animals, and "religious" practices) by renarrating them within the Christian story so as to procure the salvation of the natives. In this sense, his *De Procuranda Indorum Salute* was a form of "liberation

---

23. Ibid., 93, 98–99.

24. Ibid., 102.

25. Ibid., 98.

26. Acosta, *Natural and Moral History*, xviii.

27. Ibid., xx.

theology" characteristic of the era.[28] When reading Acosta's *Historia*, one gets the strong impression that he was attempting to paint the indigenous people in a more favorable light than some of his predecessors. As Acosta claims,

> I intend to write of their customs and polity and government, with two aims in mind. One is to refute the false opinion that is commonly held about them, that they are brutes and bestial folk and lacking in understanding or with so little that it scarcely merits the name. Many and very notable abuses have been committed upon them as a consequence of this false belief, treating them as little better than animals and considering them unworthy of any sort of respect.

On the contrary,

> [T]hey have a natural capacity to receive good instruction . . . [I]f . . . we enter by the sword and neither hear nor understand them, we do not believe that the Indians' affairs deserve repute but treat them like game hunted in the hills and brought to us for our service and whim . . . The most diligent and learned men who have penetrated and attained their secrets, their ancient style, and their government judge them in a very different way, amazed that there could have been so much order and reason among them . . . The other aim that can be achieved with knowledge of the laws and customs and polity of the Indians is to help them and rule them by those very laws, for in whatever does not contradict the law of Christ and his Holy Church, they ought to be governed according to their statutes.[29]

By undertaking the task of educating and ruling the natives, Acosta believes he is providing for them what they cannot provide for themselves. Pedagogy and governance become benevolent acts necessary to assist those with a "capacity" for achieving a more developed rationality. While the "most learned men" were surprised at the rationality of the natives, Acosta believes that this rationality can be formed, through proper education and rule, into something akin to his own tradition.

Acosta begins a process of extirpation of what he discerns as demonic deception in the beliefs of the "Indians," renarrating their history for them so as to provide them with the hope of attaining salvation. Since he finds that "it is easier to refute what is false about the Indians' origin than to

28. Ibid., xxi.
29. Ibid., 329–30.

discover the truth," he concludes that "[i]t is not very important to know what the Indians themselves are wont to tell of their beginnings and origin, for what they relate resembles dreams rather than history."[30] Although he marvels at their oral history, its mythical similarities to certain stories in the Genesis account, and the natives' ability to so accurately recall details, its lack of conformity to European patterns of reflection renders it unable to be considered actual *history*. Because of this *a priori* decision, Acosta finds it unnecessary to learn from the indigenous people's self-articulation of land, history, spirituality, and identity.

Acosta offers no criticism of the Spanish crown for the compulsory labor it forced upon the native people as they suffered and toiled in deathly conditions "in the bowels of the earth."[31] Rather, as Mignolo relates, "Acosta recalls a time in Spain's history when the Spaniards mined for the Romans, and he reasons that, in turn, the native Andeans now mine for the Spaniards in Potosí."[32] As Acosta discerns divine Providence at work in this hierarchical arrangement, he narrates the discovery of the *Indies Occidentales* as owing to God's wisdom in appealing to Spanish avarice for the purpose of the salvation of the "savages" of "the most remote and barbarous nations."[33] Acosta marries Christian mission with the beginnings of the modern market and a logic of land use that would develop into modern conceptions of private property. In his famous *hija fea* (ugly daughter) analogy, Acosta reflects:

> But it is a circumstance worthy of much consideration that the wisdom of our Eternal Lord has enriched the most remote parts of the world, inhabited by the most uncivilized people, and has placed there the greatest number of mines that ever existed, in order to invite men to seek out and possess those lands and coincidentally to communicate their religion and the worship of the true God to men who do not know it . . . Hence we see that the lands in the Indies that are richest in mines and wealth have been those most advanced in the Christian religion in our time; and thus the Lord takes advantage of our desires to serve his sovereign ends. In this regard a wise man once said that what a man does to marry off an ugly daughter is give her a large dowry; this is what God has done with that rugged land,

30. Ibid., 71–72.
31. Ibid., 179–82.
32. Ibid., 181.
33. Ibid., 163–64.

endowing it with great wealth in mines so that whoever wished could find it by this means.[34]

While Acosta does not justify the "excesses" committed "for the sake of gold and silver," he nonetheless finds God to be at work in utilizing the market to motivate "civilized" peoples to have contact with "uncivilized" peoples for the sake of the Gospel. The market becomes enfolded into soteriology, and vice versa. The native people become expendable in the quest for an eschatological *telos* of cultural and economic "development." In offering salvation to the "Indians," Acosta distances them from the Jews by denying the premise that the natives of the New World are descended from the Hebrews, thereby rendering them untainted and open to the Gospel.[35] Racialization, the market, and Christian mission begin to be articulated together within a supersessionist imagination.

Acosta inaugurated a systematic assimilation of the "other" to an Occidental frame of reference, a Western optic. According to Mignolo, Acosta's *Historia* became a sort of "encyclopedia of the exotic" for his European audience.[36] Acosta dedicated his work to "Her Most Serene Highness the Infanta Dona Isabel Clara Eugenia de Austria," whom he hoped would find his work "honourable and useful entertainment."[37] While he suspected that his works may not be of interest "owing to the fact that they deal with heathen peoples," he hoped that his cataloguing of the "remarkable and rare" might entice her because "speculation" was known to "cause natural pleasure and delight in persons of exquisite perception, and because news of strange customs and events also pleases by way of its novelty." While Acosta was most likely pandering for the sake of publication, Mignolo explains that the impact his work had upon the imagination of Europeans (especially white males) cannot be overestimated.[38]

In a world shaped by the Reformation and counter-reformations, embroiled in pre-modern tectonic cultural shifts, and involved in a Classical Renaissance of the Greek tradition, the newfound cross-cultural contact presented enormous epistemological complications. Acosta's response to the cultural shifts at home and the unfamiliar context in which he found himself abroad was to retreat into a Greek philosophical-theological tradition that could reinforce his identity as European and as Christian. While he found it necessary to question Aristotle's geographic theories with a

34. Ibid., 163–64.
35. Ibid., 69–71.
36. Ibid., 100.
37. Ibid., 5.
38. Ibid., xx.

laugh, he did not call into question their epistemic principles. As Mignolo notes, that which is "constantly absent and silenced in the narrative" is the Amerindians' own conceptualizations of the realities Acosta is renarrating, conceptualities that would be silenced by modernity and "progress."[39] Mignolo concludes that "Acosta's classical *Historia* should be read not only for what he says but, and perhaps mainly, for what he hides, certainly unintentionally, at the limits of his Christian beliefs."[40] Jennings suggests that such an unintentional silence (or what I have called the "space between") is characteristic of a retreat to Western virtue in the face of a newfound global cosmopolitanism and shifts in regnant Western philosophical assumptions.

Speaking for the Other

I now turn to demonstrating the manner in which MacIntyrian virtue ethics reenacts Acosta's pattern of reflection upon the "other." In *After Virtue*, MacIntyre tells a story of Captain Cook and his crewmen's famous third voyage and the Polynesian tribe they encountered on this journey.[41] MacIntyre uses this illustration as a parable to posit an analogous relationship between moral modernity and what he reads as pre-modern native ignorance. According to MacIntyre's read of Cook's journals, Cook's crew were surprised at the apparent juxtaposition of what they interpreted as lax sexual practices on the part of the natives and prohibitions against "men and women eating together."[42] When asked about these prohibitions, the Polynesians replied that such practices were *taboo*. Yet the seaman could come to little understanding about what the concept of *taboo* entailed. Rather than venturing the conclusion that there could have been a lack of ability to comprehend or interpret on the part of the crew, MacIntyre suggests that "the native informants themselves did not really understand the word they were using."[43]

This observation is refracted through three generations of Western interpretation (the crew, Cook's journals about their descriptions, and MacIntyre's analysis) in order to arrive at an apparently transparent understanding of the Polynesians. It is crucial that MacIntyre views *this* as the hermeneutical "problem" that generations of anthropologists since that fateful encounter have had to "struggle" with.[44] It is not the ability of the Westerner

39. Ibid., xxvii.

40. Ibid.

41. MacIntyre, *After Virtue*, 111ff.

42. Ibid., 111.

43. Ibid.

44. Ibid.

to discern the native that is in question; it is the lack of ability of the native to self-articulate. MacIntyre summarizes this conundrum by concluding that in cases such as these "the resources of a culture are too meagre to carry through the task of reinterpretation."[45] He postulates that if only the Polynesian culture had "enjoyed the benefits of analytical philosophy it is all too clear that the question of the meaning of taboo could have been resolved."[46]

While I recognize that it could be tempting to read MacIntyre's comment as ironic, it remains the case that whether or not MacIntyre intended it as irony does not change my point: that MacIntyre utilizes the native people as an intellectual exercise. I contend that MacIntyre would not talk about interactions between indigenous peoples and Europeans in this way if he were engaging in serious and sensitive dialogue about his thesis with people not from his own cultural tradition. It is unlikely that MacIntyre would reflect upon the nonwhite "other" in this manner if his account was in any way substantially informed by practices of reading together with unlike others. This is the hermeneutical center of my thesis: that joining opens doors for us to see, to read, to hear, and to "be" differently. My read of MacIntyre and Hauerwas is inescapable because I have lived in a world that has given me eyes to see that the white world has forgotten it lives in God's world.[47]

MacIntyre's interpretive method is placed in stark relief when compared with a direct read of Cook's own reflections on this encounter. While Cook's journals from his three sea voyages render examples of chauvinistic language and abhorrent practice, particularly in relation to the "use" of native women and the crew's recourse to violence when they sensed the threat of danger upon initial contact with the people of the land (who were presumably attempting to protect their homeland from the Europeans), Cook himself does not suggest that the indigenous people's invocation of *taboo* was in any way internally incoherent. He simply notes that in certain cases he was unable to understand what was happening. Cook does not venture, as does MacIntyre, that *taboo* had anything to do with rules governing mixed-gender dining; rather he praises the *taboo* ethic while acknowledging that he is not familiar with all its ramifications. After describing several quite gracious receptions from the tribal leaders of the island of Tonga, including two men named Poulaho and Mareewagee, and after relating that they had exchanged meaningful gifts and mutual invitations which resulted in the

45. Ibid., 112.

46. Ibid.

47. This manner of framing the matter has been influenced by Jennings' language as he blurbs Smith's *Weird John Brown*.

hope of being "joined in this friendship," Cook goes on to relate a story of returning the favor by hosting the leaders on his ship:

> Accordingly, the young prince, Mareewagee, old Toobou, three or four inferior chiefs, and two respectable old ladies of the first rank, accompanied me. Mareewagee was dressed in a new piece of cloth, on the skirts of which were fixed six pretty large patches of red feathers. This dress seemed to have been made on purpose for this visit; for, as soon as he got on board, he put it off, and presented it to me; having, I guess, heard that it would be acceptable on account of the feathers. Every one of my visitors received from me such presents as I had reason to believe they were highly satisfied with. When dinner came upon table, not one of them would sit down or eat a bit of anything that was served up. On expressing my surprize at this, they were all *taboo*, as they said; which word has a very comprehensive meaning; but, in general, signifies that a thing is forbidden. Why they were laid under such restraints at present was not explained. Dinner being over, and, having gratified their curiosity by showing to them every part of the ship, I then conducted them ashore.[48]

Unlike MacIntyre, who maintains that "Cook's seamen were unable to get any intelligible reply to their queries from their native informants,"[49] Cook himself neither presents the concept of *taboo* as internally inconsistent nor ventures a reason for its invocation on this occasion. Rather, he maintains that his own limited experience and the lack of an offered explanation prevented him from being able to interpret the "comprehensive meaning" of *taboo* in this particular case.

Cook does not suggest that the natives did not understand their own ethical system. He describes in detail the "decorum" observed by the Tongan people in deference to their leaders, who by use of the *taboo* ethic enact "wise regulation[s]" that guard against such disasters as improper cultivation of the land and famine.[50] In commenting on the extensiveness of the *taboo* ethic, Cook relates:

> It does not indeed appear that any of the most civilized nations, have ever exceeded this people in the great order observed on all occasions; in ready compliance with the commands of their chiefs; and in the harmony that subsists throughout all ranks, and unites them as if they were all one man, informed with and

48. Cook, *Three Voyages*, 347–48.
49. MacIntyre, *After Virtue*, 111.
50. Cook, *Three Voyages*, 459–62.

directed by the same principle . . . *Taboo*, as I have before observed, is a word of an extensive signification . . . Old Toobou, at this time, presided over the *taboo*; that is, if Omai comprehended the matter rightly.[51]

My purpose in presenting Cook's reflections on the *taboo* ethic is not to invoke the Tongan natives as "noble savages" nor is it to exculpate Cook from participation in processes that would have horrific consequences for indigenous people groups around the world. Rather, it is to tag the fact that Cook's own reflections are far more supple and nuanced than MacIntyre acknowledges. It is not until Cook's reflections are refracted through a Western tradition of virtue as extolled by MacIntyre that his observations take on such a pejorative tenor.

MacIntyre's purpose in invoking the Polynesian concept of *taboo* is to create what he calls an "imaginary debate" between modern philosophers that will demonstrate the superiority of the Greek philosophical tradition to Enlightenment modes of discourse.[52] He is not interested in the concept of *taboo* except as a means to narrate his own concerns. Interestingly, MacIntyre utilizes the ethical mandates of Judaism in this same regard as he equates Deuteronomic law with taboo rules deprived of their original context.[53] MacIntyre proclaims: "We from our standpoint *in the real world* know . . . that there is no way to understand the character of the taboo rules, except as a survival from some previous more elaborate cultural background."[54] MacIntyre laments the loss of a shared "original context" in which contemporary ethical rules as "fragmented survivals from an older past" could be understood.[55]

> What we need here is not only philosophical acuteness but also the kind of vision which anthropologists at their best bring to the observation of other cultures, enabling them to identify survivals and unintelligibilities unperceived by those who inhabit those cultures. One way to educate our own moral vision might be to enquire if the predicaments of our cultural and moral state

51. Ibid., 459–62.

52. MacIntyre, *After Virtue*, 112.

53. Ibid., 112: "So Mary Douglas has argued that the taboo rules of Deuteronomy presuppose a cosmology and a taxonomy of a certain kind. Deprive the taboo rules of their original context and they at once are apt to appear as a set of arbitrary prohibitions, as indeed they characteristically do appear when the initial context is lost, when those background beliefs in the light of which the taboo rules had originally been understood have not only been abandoned but forgotten."

54. Ibid., 112–13, italics mine.

55. Ibid., 111–12.

may not resemble those of social orders which we have hitherto
thought of as very different from ourselves.[56]

Stated differently, the purpose of reflecting upon Polynesians with the pierc-
ing gaze of anthropological clarity is to identify the ways in which Western
culture has digressed into more "savage" modes of ethical reflection.

In a stunning move, MacIntyre identifies his Enlightenment interlocutors with the Polynesian natives so as to discredit the modern philosophers.
He compares the modern moral quagmire with the supposed ethical confusion of aboriginal peoples. He uses the trope of native ignorance to demonstrate just how unintelligible are thinkers such as Moore, Ross, Prichard,
Stevenson, Hare, "and the rest."[57] In order to make Nietzsche the paragon
of incomprehension, he utilizes the name of the Hawaiian king who he
maintains removed the taboos several generations later with a "lack of social
consequence": "And why should we not think of Nietzsche as the Kame-
hameha II of the European tradition"?[58] In order for Nietzsche to be the
counterweight to MacIntyre's tradition, he is equated with a darker-skinned
counterweight to the European explorers. In the hands of MacIntyre, the
native becomes something he is accustomed to being: a prop used to narrate
the philosophical and theological concerns of the traditioned Westerner.

Not only are the Polynesians spoken *for*, but the caricature of their
voices fulfils the role of the counterbalance to the virtue-based tradition
being extolled. Tellingly, it matters not to MacIntyre that the Polynesians
encountered by Captain Cook, and the Hawaiian king whom he reads as
dismantling the ethical system of taboo, were not even located in the same
area of the Pacific. Native peoples in his schema are essentially movable,
understandable only by virtue of their shared classificatory status within
European ethical inquiry. At the close of the twenty-five years immediately
following the publication of *After Virtue*, MacIntyre confidently asserts that
"If there are good reasons to reject the central theses of *After Virtue*, by now
I should certainly have learned what they are."[59] Alongside the assumption
that a quarter-century of critique from patrons of his tradition is obviously
sufficient to render his position conclusive, it could be ventured that there
are voices which have not been included in the conversation.

The intellectual imperialism of MacIntyre's virtue ethics is evident
in the way he envisions interactions between various philosophical traditions. The Aristotelian-Thomist tradition is designated by MacIntyre as a

56. Ibid., 111.

57. Ibid., 113.

58. Ibid.

59. Ibid., ix.

"tradition of enquiry," bearing the dual characteristics of *truth* in its central theses and *soundness* in its rational argumentation.[60] MacIntyre does not explore the ways in which "rational" argumentation itself presumes certain cultural presuppositions nor does he allow that other modes of the appropriation of knowledge, such as divine revelation or some component of lived experience, may be equally "reasonable."

MacIntyre envisages engagement between traditions as antagonism between rivals who are trying to "defeat the claims" of the other.[61] MacIntyre does not consider the fact that a "rival tradition"[62] may not desire to engage with a tradition bound on its "defeat." I contend that, while there are certainly moments when contradictory elements between diverse philosophies become apparent (whether real or seemingly so), it is impossible to understand where these contradictions actually lie without knowing the other well enough to hear the other on the other's own terms. In a world that is animated by racial notions of peoplehood, I am convinced that appeals to "rational" criteria are often means to assert one's own sense of identity over against another.

Rather than being joined to the other, MacIntyre's claim is that one must "learn how to think as if one were a convinced adherent of that rival tradition," a process which "requires the exercise of a capacity for philosophical imagination that is often lacking."[63] The distinction here is easy to miss: MacIntyre is not speaking of a philosophical humility in which one is open to learning from (and with) the other; he is suggesting that one's own *imagination* be used to "think as if one were" the other. MacIntyre purposes to interact with the "rival tradition" to subdue it. Only secondarily does he suggest that a tradition "identify, from the standpoint of the adherents of that rival tradition, its crucially important unresolved issues and unsolved problems."[64]

MacIntyre recommends engaging with the other *for the purpose of discerning their "problems" and "issues."* MacIntyre's process of discernment involves refracting the other's philosophical frameworks through one's own system. It is not unimportant that language of *interrogation* rather than language of *listening* is used.[65] In a MacIntyrian framework, when a tradition

60. Ibid., xii.

61. Ibid., xiii.

62. Ibid.

63. Ibid.

64. Ibid.

65. Ibid., where MacIntyre insists that the goal of such acts of "imagination and questioning" is "to interrogate some particular rival tradition."

interacts with another, it utilizes its own internal logic to overcome the difficulties or impasses of the other. MacIntyre claims that while "defeat" can be accomplished, it may not be recognized by the rival tradition due to a lack of "neutral standards."[66] After it is established "which tradition is superior to which,"[67] the defeated tradition "will still take themselves to have excellent reasons for rejecting any invitation to adopt the standpoint of any other rival and incompatible tradition."[68] MacIntyre appears to not recognize the difficulty of maintaining any sense of real encounter with another if the outcome has been predetermined. He claims that his ethical stance "wins" by making "the rational case . . . for a tradition in which the Aristotelian moral and political texts are canonical."[69] In a racialized world, the call to "win" a clash of traditions can be heard in a racialized inflection. MacIntyre's vision of how a Western tradition of ethics interacts with another bears similarities to Acosta's vision of *extirpation*.

In much the same way as MacIntyre attempts to think *for* and *as* the other, Acosta narrated the other. A MacIntyrian "epistemological crisis" begins to sound like Acosta's laugh, which Jennings maintains demonstrates that one has "reached the epistemological limits of his theological vision."[70] In the pregnant pause in which Acosta laughed—a pause in which he admitted that he was facing that which he did not already know, a pause full of hope and potential for a new way forward—Acosta began a practice that is mirrored in white reflection upon nonwhite flesh throughout much of the Christian tradition in its wake: speaking *for* the other.[71] MacIntyre's virtue ethic continues this legacy.

Enthroning the West

While Jennings and MacIntyre agree that underemphasizing particularity in favor of universality is problematic, they disagree about which particularity should be normative for understanding the ethical life. In rejecting both the individualism and universality of modernity, MacIntyre appeals to the particularity of another tradition:

66. Ibid., xiv.

67. Ibid., xiii.

68. Ibid., xiv.

69. Ibid., 257.

70. Jennings, *Christian Imagination*, 91.

71. Ibid., 91.

The answer is that . . . all morality is always to some degree tied to the socially local and particular and that the aspirations of the morality of modernity to a universality freed from all particularity is an illusion; and secondly that there is no way to possess the virtues except as part of a tradition in which we inherit them and our understanding of them from a series of predecessors in which series heroic societies hold first place.[72]

For MacIntyre, where "Christianity or Judaism or Islam have prevailed," it is due to a pre-Christian "stock of stories" providing the "moral background" for "heroic society . . . classical society and . . . its successors."[73] MacIntyre asserts that "morality and social structure are in fact one and the same,"[74] asserting the importance of tradition and narrative for ethics. The narrative he offers is the Greek heroic tale, a structure which "assign[s] men their place in the social order and with it their identity," assuring that people be capable of "receiving recognition and response from others."[75] In order to reclaim the centrality of rational ethics, Western society must reconnect with its place in the story of Greek virtue. In contrast, Jennings relates that "Christians are, through Jesus the Christ, brought into the story of Israel, which is indeed God's story."[76] For Jennings, the narrative around which human history is oriented is YHWH's history through his people Israel, culminating in the person of Jesus Christ.

In this sense, MacIntyre's work supplants theological history with the "classical" history of the Occident. In the words of Jennings: "What is at stake is not simply particularity and certainly not the dialectic between the particular and the universal, but rather the scandal of particularity."[77] Jennings contends that the particularity of Israel does not function as that of whiteness. Whereas YHWH-centered particularity enfolds various traditions into each other as they are enfolded into the life of the Messiah, whiteness functions as universal hegemon, demanding assimilation by riding over various particularities on its way to universality. This is where the disciplinary frameworks of Jennings and MacIntyre collide: Jennings is a theologian; MacIntyre is a philosopher whose account of attainment of the virtues tends to function as a self-constitutive humanism. While MacIntyre is a Roman Catholic Christian, his account posits religious faith as little

72. MacIntyre, *After Virtue*, 126–27.

73. Ibid., 121.

74. Ibid., 123.

75. Ibid., 123–24.

76. Jennings, *Christian Imagination*, 160.

77. Ibid.

more than the fulfillment of a Western tradition of virtuous living.[78] I will contend that, while Hauerwas' account of ethics is more theologically astute than this, it tends to reenact the ethical voluntarism of a MacIntyrian account of ethics.

On the contrary, Jennings tends to think of ethics in a Barthian modality of receptivity to the divine command. It is not against virtue *per se* that Jennings contends. Rather, Jennings' invocation of joining suggests that virtue is received by being joined to the divine life through the divine Son, with whom people are connected as they are conjoined with the other in Jesus' body. In this sense, divine grace is mediated through the body of the other as "one new man" is made "in place of the two" in the flesh of Jesus, who "himself is our peace."[79] Jennings' account of ethics could be described in Andrew J. B. Cameron's phrase the "joined-up life."[80] Unlike MacIntyre, Jennings does not postulate the virtues as something to be possessed. Whereas MacIntyre appeals to heroic tales (which tend to function as morality plays for emulation), Jennings focuses on the story of divine condescension in covenantal history (thus the contention that Jennings thinks of virtue as received through joining with YHWH and his people).

MacIntyre recognizes that his reclamation of Greek virtue is not without difficulties, chief among them Aristotle's view of non-Greeks and slaves. However, he deems such difficulties peripheral to the general orientation of Western philosophical ethics. For instance, while MacIntyre rejects Aristotle's defense of slavery and its concordant anthropological implications, he does so on extremely problematic grounds. As MacIntyre relates, Aristotle held that only Greek males of high social status could possess the virtues. A virtuous life was impossible for a slave or a barbarian (which is a derogatory slur whose etymology, according to MacIntyre, derives from the sound, in Hellenistic ears, of non-Greek speech: "ba, ba, ba").[81] MacIntyre asserts that we are correct to be affronted by Aristotle's "writing off of non-Greeks,

---

78. See various points in *After Virtue*: MacIntyre sets up the New Testament as being syllogistically related to the Aristotelian tradition, 163; examines the relationship between the classical and Christian virtues, 165–80, where his conclusion that Catholic Thomism is constitutive of the virtuous life is contrasted with disparaging references to Luther, who he reads as mocking Aristotle, 165; contends that "the New Testament's account of the virtues" has "the same logical and conceptual structure as Aristotle's account" which allowed for Aquinas' synthesis of Aristotle and the New Testament, 184; invokes several saints as the clearest exemplars of the classical virtue-based tradition, 199, 263; and syntactically joins the terms "Aristotelian" and "Christian," 233, 236.

79. Eph 2:14–15

80. Cameron, *Joined-up Life.*

81. MacIntyre, *After Virtue*, 158.

barbarians, and slaves."[82] Yet he immediately tempers this assertion by identifying Aristotle's blindness as "part of the general, although not universal,
blindness of his culture." Yet this classical culture is the very culture that MacIntyre exhorts us to reclaim in order to live a life of virtue. How can classical culture be the paragon of virtuous formation and simultaneously be
exculpated from the derogatory frameworks perpetuated by those formed
according to its commitments? MacIntyre insists that

> It remains true that these limitations in Aristotle's account of the
> virtues do not necessarily injure his general scheme for under-
> standing the place of the virtues in human life, let alone deform
> his multitude of more particular insights.[83]

The only grounds MacIntyre has for rejecting Aristotle's defense of a
stratified society is that Aristotle was unable to envision how "men might
pass from being slaves or barbarians to being citizens of a *polis*" because of
his conviction of the intransience of the polis and the primitive nature of
those outside it.[84] The most rousing critique MacIntyre can muster is that
it was unavailable to Aristotle to envision how non-Greeks or marginalized
socioeconomic groups could assimilate into Greek society. Surely such an
Aristotelian posture toward the "other" has contributed to the formation of
this tradition's proponents, including Acosta and MacIntyre.

Aquinas, Acosta, and Locke

A primary aspect of the Aristotelian-Thomist tradition of virtue that has
allowed for the racial imagination to flourish is its theological anthropology.
As a student of St. Thomas Aquinas, Acosta understood theology to be a
summary catalogue of the accumulated body of human knowledge. Within
this framework, Acosta had inherited an understanding of the *imago Dei* as
an *analogia entis*. The *imago Dei* was understood to reside in the rationality
of human beings, qualifying them to enact dominion over the rest of creation. The doctrine of creation and the dominion of "man" over it propelled
Acosta forward in his descriptive project. As Aquinas writes in his *Summa
Theologica*, "This natural dominion of man over other creatures, which is
competent to man in respect of his reason wherein God's image resides, is
shown forth in man's creation."[85]

82. Ibid., 159.
83. Ibid., 160.
84. Ibid., 158–159.
85. Aquinas, *Summa Theologica*, II–II, Q. 66, Art. 1.

As heir to a tradition that viewed itself as the paragon of human rationality, Acosta assumed that it was necessary to educate and govern the peoples of the Americas. The West has by and large imagined itself to be the most complete picture of the flourishing of human life as God intended it. Occidental self-conception has often tended to be that of "image-bearers." MacIntyre's vision of the unity of the transcendentals—aesthetics, ethics, and ontology—communicates that being itself is bound to certain aesthetic performances. MacIntyre's anthropological designation of "rational animals"[86] is the same phrase that Mignolo identifies as the Renaissance expression utilized to distinguish humanity from the rest of the "animal kingdom."[87] It is this anthropology which encouraged Acosta to imagine cultural modes of being along a hierarchical spectrum from God-like to animal-like and which can be read as influencing MacIntyre's confidence in the superiority of Western ethical systems. The image of God understood in terms of rationality has profoundly influenced a myriad of identity assessments, including racialization, gender essentialisms, and conceptions of people with disabilities.

A further conception of Aquinas that has fueled this hierarchical impulse is the dictum that "the imperfect is directed to the perfect"[88] or alternately stated as "the imperfect is always for the sake of the perfect."[89] Humanity's dominion over the rest of creation is to be understood according to a teleological framework within which those things of lesser capacity and rationality are meant to be used for the service of that which is higher-functioning or more perfect. Aquinas applies this logic to not only inanimate objects and various forms of life, but to people.[90] He maintains that "dumb animals and plants,"[91] "external things,"[92] and "individual person[s]"[93] can all be located within this framework of subservience to the higher good. Acosta's and MacIntyre's virtue ethics assume the Greek tradition to be indicative of a more perfect form of rationality than other modes of inquiry. MacIntyre follows a Thomist logic as he relates: "According to Aristotle then excellence of character and intelligence cannot be separated

86. MacIntyre, *After Virtue*, xi.
87. Acosta, *Natural and Moral History*, xxiv.
88. Aquinas, *Summa Theologica*, II–II, Q. 64, Art. 1.
89. Ibid., II–II, Q. 66, Art. 1.
90. Ibid., II–II, Q. 64, Art. 2.
91. Ibid., II–II, Q. 64, Art. 1., ad. 2.
92. Ibid., II–II, Q. 66, Art. 1.
93. Ibid., II–II, Q. 64, Art. 2.

. . . for Aristotle stupidity of a certain kind precludes goodness."[94] If Acosta's tradition encouraged him to connect his conceptions of rationality with ethics and ontology, it is unsurprising that he was unprepared to join with people unfamiliar to him.

The subjugation of native peoples was in large part enabled by a late medieval theological appeal to creation and natural law. As I have claimed, a belief in God as Creator does not necessitate this conceptual jump. Rather, I am interested in identifying the sort of middle work that Jennings is expos-ing throughout his analysis. Aquinas reflects that "by sinning man departs from the order of reason, and consequently falls away from the dignity of his manhood, in so far as he is naturally free, and exists for himself, and he falls into the slavish state of the beasts, by being disposed of according as he is useful to others."[95] Aquinas quotes Aristotle, whom he calls "the Philosopher," as stating that "a bad man is worse than a beast, and is more harmful."[96] Therefore, "it may be good to kill a man who has sinned, even as it is to kill a beast."[97] Within such a framework, it is a small step from identifying sin and distortion in others to justifying colonial dominance. It is compelling to read Acosta's identification of idolatry in the indigenous peoples of the New World in this light. Confronted with the unknown, Acosta turns to Thomist metaphysics and anthropology to find some orien-tation, thereby using his own tradition as the plumb-line against which to narrate non-Western peoples, who are identified as in need of being freed from the demonic.

Jennings' analysis suggests that modernity should not be understood as the triumph of liberty and autonomy over heteronomy as much as it is the maturation of the colonial moment, which carried forward the theological anthropology of late medieval scholasticism. This reading is buttressed by the fact that Lockean political anthropology carries forward the tradition of Thomist theological anthropology. This reading is perhaps counterintuitive given the propensity of virtue ethicists to distance themselves from modern moral autonomy. However, John Locke utilized the anthropological formu-lations of the scholastic natural law tradition to get his political theories up and running. In his *Two Treatises of Government*, Locke finds the image of God in humanity to be located in reason, which is "the voice of God in him."[98] Like Aquinas, Locke maintains that when people are held to have

94. MacIntyre, *After Virtue*, 154–55.
95. Aquinas, *Summa Theologica*, II–II, Q. 64, Art. 2, ad. 3.
96. Ibid.
97. Ibid.
98. Locke, *Two Treatises of Government*, 205.

fallen away from reason, they have become "things noxious" and "may be destroyed as a Lyon or Tyger."[99]

While I am not claiming that Lockean political theory is to be interpreted as a direct descendant of Thomism, it remains the case that European Manifest Destiny was built in large part on Lockean assumptions borrowed from the Anglo-Catholic natural law tradition. According to Locke, a person who could be categorized as childlike or as lacking an acceptable "degree of reason" was "never capable of being a Free Man," needed to be "continued under the Tuition and Government of others," and was subject to the dictum: "he that understands for him must will for him too."[100] Locke proclaimed Native lands to be the "uncultivated waste of America" providing "the needy and wretched inhabitants" only a small fraction of the possible "conveniencies of life" because "ninety-nine hundredths" of the value of land was to be found in "labour" and not creation.[101] Because the Indians failed to utilize land to its fullest potential, the land could be "appropriate[d]" by another for the good of "the common stock of mankind." Locke specifically appeals to a translation he owned of "Josephus Acosta's" *The Naturall and Morall Historie of the Indies* in its descriptions of "the People of *America*," whom he invokes to display his theories about free consent in "the State of Nature" and "Politick Societies."[102] Acosta's theological narration of indigenous peoples, MacIntyre's invocation of native ignorance, and Locke's myth of the noble savage are each related in important ways to the Aristotelian-Thomist tradition, a tradition reclaimed by ethics of virtue.

Pierre Bourdieu and a Forgetting of Being

As a link between my analyses of MacIntyre's virtue ethic and its theological deployment by Hauerwas, I will relate Jennings' critique of the manner in which the academy tends to imagine identity: what sociologist Pierre Bourdieu calls the "scholastic disposition."[103] As academician and pastor, Jennings relates that he has witnessed firsthand the embodied effects of "the Christian theological imagination [being] woven into processes of colonial dominance."[104] This distorted imaginary has produced what is

99. Ibid., 272, 274.

100. Ibid., 305–8.

101. Ibid., 294–96.

102. Ibid., 335, 337.

103. Bourdieu, *Pascalian Meditations*, 16.

104. Jennings, *Christian Imagination*, 7–8.

"fundamentally the resistance of theologians to think *theologically* about their identities."[105]

> One crucial site where I have watched the display of this in-
> terrupted social imagination is in the theological academy. As
> student, professor, and academic dean, I have watched with a
> sense of melancholy the formation process of Christian intel-
> lectuals. I watched what at first I took to be a cultural and social
> clumsiness that seems bound to what the sociologist Pierre
> Bourdieu calls "the scholastic disposition." Later I realized that
> what I was witnessing was not a social clumsiness at all but a
> highly refined process of socialization. I watched a complex
> process of disassociation and dislocation that was connected to
> the prescribed habits of mind for those who would do scholarly
> theological work.[106]

In *Pascalian Meditations*, Bourdieu describes the social conditions that have given rise to the scholastic disposition,[107] calling this complicated pattern of disassociation "the forgetting of Being."[108] Bourdieu claimed a somewhat complex relationship with the academy, disliking "the intellec- tual in [him]self," recognizing the "*negative philosophy*" in which he was engaged, and feeling "the ricochet of [his] own words."[109] He maintained that the academic environment fosters in scholars, including himself, the ability to "forget" the privileged social conditions "resulting from a long process of autonomization" that "make possible a view of the world and of cultural products that is characterized by self-evidence and naturalness."[110] The "scholastic point of view" thereby assumes an "ontological difference" between the "thinker" and the "common man" connected to the menial cycles of everyday life, including labor and production. Bourdieu suggests that this posture is "rooted in the sense" of "natural election through gift" and paradoxically strives to "repress the differences of condition" that have been produced by "academic procedures of training and selection." The academy functions around a "theodicy of . . . privilege."[111] Bourdieu's work shares important thematic connections with Jennings' concerns about the

---

105. Ibid., 7.
106. Ibid.
107. Bourdieu, *Pascalian Meditations*, 16.
108. Ibid., 25.
109. Ibid., 7.
110. Ibid., 25.
111. Ibid.

contributions of the university, the natural law tradition, and distorted views of election to the racial imagination.

Bourdieu finds these tendencies to be rooted in an "epistemic posture" made possible by "being able to withdraw from the world so as to think it."[112] By "universalizing" this "vision of the world," the realms of aesthetics, ethics, and knowledge constitute "three forms of fallacy" able to be engaged in precisely because they have broken away from "the urgencies of practice."[113] According to Bourdieu, the problem is that many scholars have "forgotten" and "repressed" the "social conditions of possibility" that have allowed for this presumed objectivity. This forgetting entails a lack of remembrance of one's own identity. Jennings finds these "social conditions" to be connected to the habits of mind he calls *whiteness*.

Bourdieu's analysis suggests that there is a vested interest in being unable to remember the conditions which gave rise to the academic's descriptive posture. This "forgetting" fosters a resistance to the giving up of power or the adjustment in posture that would allow for the possibility of being changed by the other. Jennings finds the "scholastic disposition" resistant to the vulnerability of joining. He maintains that this resistance to the life of the Incarnation is not to be explained by many of the well-trod paths of debate surrounding all manner of problems associated with modernity, including

> the theory/practice split in conceptual work, or the split between the classical and practical disciplines, or the separation of the church from the academy, or a split between orthodox and orthopraxis; neither can it be characterized through the arguments regnant in the tired debates about the nature, purposes, and values of abstract thinking versus situated thinking and all the permutations of that conflict.[114]

Rather, the difficulty is that

> theology lacks the ability to see the profound connections between an embrace by very different people in the chapel and theological meditations articulated in the classroom, between connecting to the earth, to strangers, and to the possibilities of identities formed and reformed precisely in and through such actions.[115]

---

112. Ibid., 49.

113. Ibid., 50.

114. Jennings, *Christian Imagination*, 7.

115. Ibid., 7.

It is this connection with people and with land—which should guide our understanding of race and place—that is lacking in the formulation of many theological identity reflections. Jennings suggests that relationships of intimate knowledge with those from whom we differ will carry with them resistance to the problematic stance of whiteness as manifested in the scholastic disposition.

Stanley Hauerwas and the University

Hauerwas and a Contemporary Virtue Ethic

As Jennings reflects on the failure of the church and the academy to recognize the "epistemological crisis" embodied in Acosta, he maintains that "one could fault MacIntyre but more importantly those theologians who have followed his thinking on tradition for not seeing the effects on the Christian tradition triggered by the modernist elements at the beginning of the age of Iberian conquest."[116] Christian theology's "pedagogical performances reflect and fuel the problem, further crippling the communities it serves."[117] This "deep pedagogical sensory deprivation" reflects the tendency of Western Christian intellectuals to "imagine the world from the commanding heights."[118]

The theologian who most clearly appropriates MacIntyre's thinking on tradition, carrying it forward into Christian intellectual formation in the university, is Hauerwas, a key figure in the contemporary rise of Western virtue ethics. Like MacIntyre, Hauerwas has been tenured at both Notre Dame and Duke. He now holds a chair in theological ethics at the University of Aberdeen. He is a renowned ethicist and public intellectual, having been named "America's Best Theologian" by Time Magazine in 2001[119] and having delivered the prestigious Gifford Lectures at the University of St. Andrews in the same year. Hauerwas has been a champion of a pre-Constantinian Christian orthodoxy over against the shrill debates between modern liberals and conservatives, who in his view are both bound into the project of the nation-state and the Enlightenment. Hauerwas has been a controversial peace advocate and an outspoken defender of active non-violent resistance. He has challenged the academy to consider for whom it exists and how its identity is tied into modern capitalism, Mammon, and

116. Ibid., 71.
117. Ibid., 7.
118. Ibid., 8.
119. Elshtain, "Theologian."

the legitimization of state power.[120] Hauerwas, like Yoder, has been helpful in initiating Christians into recognizing the problematic alignment of the Church with the "principalities and powers."

Hauerwas maintains that the structures of modernity have problematically formed "a certain kind of social imaginary" indicative of the ideal of the disembodied moral agent, the production of the "distinction between the public and the private," and the correlative social forms of "the market economy, the public sphere, and self-governing people."[121] While there is common ground between Hauerwas' concerns and the issues that trouble Jennings, Jennings reads Hauerwas' assessments as truncated diagnoses that underestimate the racialized character of the problems he is observing.[122] The title of Jennings' work, *The Christian Imagination*, can be read, at least in part, as a response to Hauerwas' diagnosis of the "social imaginary" of modernity, as Jennings instead focuses on what he calls the "diseased social imagination" forged in the intersection of theology and colonization.[123]

There are important distinctions to be drawn between the works of Hauerwas and MacIntyre. Much in the same way as I read Raboteau's historical account as more theologically satisfactory than modern historiography in general, I read Hauerwas as offering a more satisfactory theological account of virtue than MacIntyre's philosophical account. It is not insignificant that Jennings explicitly criticizes MacIntyre but leaves his critique of Hauerwas largely implicit. While this might stem from a desire to not overtly overemphasive his disagreement with Hauerwas, it could also suggest that Hauerwas' theological manner of framing virtue is to be preferred to MacIntyre's philosophical methodology. Be that as it may, given Jennings' diagnosis of the theological roots of the racial imagination, while he finds the core of the problem in the philosophy of MacIntyre, he is in actuality *more concerned* with its theological deployment in the moral formation of Christians. Jennings' basic contention is that Hauerwas' MacIntyrian trajectory produces Christian ministers and scholars who tend to see themselves and their traditions as constituting the center of God's saving activity in the world, thereby devaluing the identity of the nonwhite other.

Hauerwas' relationship to an ethic of virtue can best be demonstrated through his work *Christians Among the Virtues*.[124] In a chapter entitled *The*

---

120. Hauerwas, *State of the University*, 76ff.

121. Ibid., 37.

122. See Jennings, *Christian Imagination*, 7, where he claims that these types of diagnoses "touch on" the issue but are ultimately "tired debates."

123. Ibid., 9.

124. Hauerwas, *Christians Among the Virtues*.

Renewal of Virtue and the Peace of Christ, Hauerwas interacts with both Milbank's and MacIntyre's accounts of virtue. Hauerwas focuses on virtue in order to avoid an ethics of obligation, where "acts are determined and stated to be objectively right or wrong," an ethic he sees as "invariably ignor[ing] the importance of the subject."[125] Hauerwas is attempting to avoid both Kantian and utilitarian modes of ethical reflection by reclaiming a more holistic conception of ethics in which the moral formation and character of the subject (and not only that subject's actions) matter. Hauerwas prefers Milbank's account of virtue to MacIntyre's, which he reads as not sufficiently distinguishing between Greek and Christian accounts of virtue: "Milbank holds that we can never recommend virtue in general, but rather only Christian virtue in particular."[126] In Hauerwas' read of Milbank, the difference between Greek and Christian accounts of virtue is that the former is founded on violence and exclusivity, while the latter is founded on peace. Therefore, for Hauerwas, Christian accounts of peace "radically challenge . . . Greek notions of virtue."[127] However, in chapter 2, I argued that Milbank's "peace" is an imperialistically-tinged assimilation to Western aesthetic and pedagogical norms. Preferring Milbank's theological account to MacIntyre's philosophical account does not solve the problem.

For Hauerwas, it is not so much the hegemony of a Greek view of the world (or the manner in which it has been used to supersede a Judaic view of the world) that is the problem. According to Hauerwas, the crucial distinction should be that the Christian community is a counter-culture of peace opposed to the *polis* of war.[128] For this reason, Hauerwas maintains that MacIntyre does not sufficiently distinguish the Christian body politic from the State *polis*: "Crucial to his project is the possibility that the Christian account of the virtues can be successfully grafted onto the Greek heritage."[129] This is why Hauerwas prefers Milbank: he finds Aquinas' theological account of virtue preferable to Aristotle's philosophical account. Hauerwas maintains that "Christianity is not a continuation of the Greek understanding of the virtues, but rather the inauguration of a new tradition that sets the virtues within an entirely different telos in community."[130]

This is where Hauerwas and Jennings most clearly differ. Hauerwas calls Christianity a "new tradition" (as opposed to a continuation of

125. Ibid., 58.
126. Ibid., 61–63.
127. Ibid., 63.
128. Ibid., 65.
129. Ibid., 62.
130. Ibid., 63.

YHWH's work in the world). Jennings contends that it is this tendency for
Christians to see themselves as replacing the divine work through YHWH's
people Israel that animates the racial imagination. As was demonstrated by
Givens, Yoder helps us see that early Christianity largely saw itself (and was
largely seen) as Jewish. Even though the boundaries would quickly begin to
be navigated in a variety of ways (leading up to what Yoder sees as the definitive break: Constantinianism), early Christianity should not be understood
as a "new" tradition in a thick sense of that term. The tendency to view
Christian tradition as in some sense discontinuous with Hebrew tradition
can be identified in Hauerwas' account. He favorably summarizes Milbank's
position: "At best, Greek views are redeemable from a Christian perspective
only typologically. Speaking analogically, they can help constitute the true
city only as the Old Testament allegories foreshadowed Christ."[131] Hauerwas suggests that the Greek tradition is to be understood as analogically
equivalent to the Hebrew Bible in foreshadowing Christianity. While analogy should not be pressed too far, my point is that Hauerwas' account of the
virtues does not sufficiently view the Hebrew faith as a constituting reality
for Christian life but simply as an allegorical *foreshadow*.[132] Such a formulation can easily slip into conceptions of the Greek philosophical tradition as
a "replacement" of sorts for God's historical work in space and time through
the Judaic covenants. That Hauerwas uses language of "grafting" demonstrates that he understands the gravity of the theological issues at work in
his account of virtue. However, while he resists "grafting" the Christian life
onto a Greek tradition of the virtues, he still finds a return to a Greek way of
conceiving the ethical life to be the best option.

Hauerwas maintains that contemporary Western society is in a similar
moment to the world in which the ancient Greek philosophers found themselves. He concludes that:

> This tension in MacIntyre's position should not be taken as a
> weakness in his larger position, particularly his assessment of
> our present moral crisis . . . A reappropriation of the ancient
> Greek accounts of virtue is a fitting strategy for moral reform,
> at least for non-Christians, for despite obvious differences there
> *is* a strong resemblance between our own world and that of the
> Greeks.[133]

131. Ibid., 62.

132. It can be contended that early allegorical interpretation (such as was common
in Alexandrian hermeneutics) contributed to the increasing Hellenization of the faith
and its decreasing ability to see itself as part of another people's history.

133. Hauerwas, *Christians Among the Virtues*, 62–63.

Hauerwas does not expound upon the differences between contemporary Western society and ancient Greek society. He sees both societies as locked in a strain between virtue and liberalism.

He insists that, because of the similarities, "MacIntyre's return to the sages of the ancient Greek world is entirely fitting."[134] The distinction between Hauerwas and MacIntyre is one of nuance rather than one of contrasting theological trajectories.

To be fair, Hauerwas does acknowledge that the contemporary "strong disquiet" about returns to virtue, while it may signal "battles for turf as the hegemony of liberalism is challenged," "is not a false alarm."[135] He claims that it is "quite right to ask what sort of politics matches or is entailed by the so-called return to the virtues" and that "the liberal suspicion of the return to virtue is not to be dismissed."[136] However, when asking if Christians must "join liberals in repudiating the return to virtue," Hauerwas concludes that Christians need not "deny the link between Greek virtue and Christian virtue, between Aristotle and Aquinas" as long as they "carefully distinguish the true God from the gods of this world, including the Greek gods of virtue."[137]

What this means in concrete terms for Hauerwas is that Christians must decry the false gods of violence and the nation-state in order to follow the God whose church is a community of peace. While this is a point well-taken, Jennings' account suggests that Hauerwas underestimates the manner in which violence in the nation-state is justified and made possible primarily because of racialization, that violence is the means of policing the boundaries of peoplehood. In other words, the problem with a return to Greek virtue is not so much the temptation to return to a politics of war as it is the manner in which such a return is a rearticulation of the racialized politics that are intrinsic to this manner of viewing the world. In this sense, the Aristotelian *polis* and its attendant proto-racial classifications can be seen as foreshadowing the modern democratic polity that is undergirded by the sort of racialized violence that was built into the founding of America and is regularly seen on her streets. Jennings' account also suggests that, due to supersessionism, it is not sufficient to give theology a sort of "free pass" by distinguishing it from philosophy without also carefully distinguishing the God of Christian theology from the gods of Greek philosophy by clearly recognizing that the Christian God is first another people's God.

134. Ibid., 67.
135. Ibid., 66.
136. Ibid., 66–67.
137. Ibid., 67–68.

Given the manner in which Hauerwas frames the competition be-tween virtue and liberalism, it could be tempting to interpret Jennings as raising a classically liberal critique of virtue and tradition. However, as I have demonstrated in the last chapter, while Jennings is sensitive to the con-cerns that liberalism has with Western expansionism and racial violence, he finds the liberal trajectory to be ultimately unsuccessful in dislodging the racial imagination. On the contrary, Jennings presents Christianity itself as a form of cultural joining that is able to challenge racialized notions of peoplehood. At the same time, he demonstrates that appeals to traditioned moral inquiry bring with them the racialized optic of whiteness—the racial imagination. This means that liberalism alone should not be faulted with creating a racialized anthropology any more than it should be contended that violence is peculiar to liberalism. Jennings demonstrates that the racial imagination had its roots in early-modern theological moves that, while they may have paved the way for the later frameworks of modernity, were prior to it. Therefore, Jennings' critique of the virtues cannot be read as a classically liberal criticism of the sort against which Hauerwas contends.

I maintain that Hauerwas' account of ethics is helpful in demonstrat-ing how virtue is formed in the life of Christians: "Christian virtue is not so much initiated action but response to a love relation with God in Christ."[138] Christian virtue is not acquired suddenly but through a process of being transformed by the Spirit of God, often through training in particular prac-tices. However, Hauerwas does not recognize that racial formation also fol-lows a path of discipleship, a pattern to which we have grown so accustomed that we are no longer able to see it. Jennings names this path "whiteness." A MacIntyrian ethic of virtue leads its proponents down a path of racial formation in the ways already demonstrated. Hauerwas appears to have a blind spot in regard to how his thinking on tradition is tied in to the con-struction of race. Jennings is critical of the tendency to follow MacIntyre's thinking on tradition because it tends to close theologians off to resources from the broader Christian tradition (and contemporary scholarly and neighborly relationships) from which a racialized view of personhood may be combatted.

Hauerwas recommends particular practices as constitutive of moral formation in the body of Christ. Among these are Eucharist and feeding the hungry.[139] In the pages that follow, I will demonstrate how the Eucharist of a reclamation of virtue and its practices of caring for the poor tend to disciple Christian ministers and scholars into racialized habits of mind and

138. Ibid., 68.
139. Ibid., 69.

paternalistic conceptions of the "other." In the Conclusion, I will suggest a different path forward for Christian practices that can resist such distortions. This path involves joining together, in a community marked by difference, with each other and with another people's God in Jesus Christ.

My interaction with Hauerwas is intended neither to reduce his theological legacy to a tradition of virtue nor to reflect on his complete oeuvre. I will be limiting my treatment to the manner in which Hauerwas imagines the formation process of Christian intellectuals as traditioned inculcation in the virtues. I contend that inasmuch as Hauerwas' work reenacts a MacIntyrian virtue ethic it is subject to the limitations Jennings identifies in that tradition. I will take as the key text Hauerwas' *The State of the University*, which I read as paradigmatic of the tradition of theological formation from which Jennings distinguishes his work in *The Christian Imagination*. I suggest that while Jennings may commend Hauerwas' heart as he did Colenso's, he asserts that, in following MacIntyre's "thinking on tradition," Hauerwas fails to recognize how "traditioned Christian existence" animated Iberian conquest so as to create "traditioned imperialist modernity."[140]

Because Hauerwas is a better doctrinal and ethical theologian than either Milbank or MacIntyre (both of whose accounts are arguably primarily philosophical, even if Milbank's account should be categorized as philosophical theology), the problematic implications of his work for a theology of race may be harder to see. Hauerwas does not utilize what I read as the overtly racialized rhetoric of Milbank. I will focus less on his overt claims than on the manner in which his tradition of virtue tends to affect his views on education, aesthetics, the "poor," race, and mission. As with Milbank, my read of Hauerwas is intimately connected to relationships with real people who are affected by being categorized as "poor," as "other," and as "recipients" of Christian education, mission, and charity. In this manner, my criticism of Hauerwas is a criticism of myself and the manner in which I tended (and sometimes still do) to view Christian mission at the beginning of my journey toward joining.

The University

In *The State of the University: Academic Knowledges and the Knowledge of God*, a collection of Hauerwas' essays, he writes that

> The problem, of course, is not the university or the subjects that constitute the university. The problem is with those like myself

140. Jennings, *Christian Imagination*, 71.

who identify ourselves as Christians. Namely the challenge is whether any of us live lives as Christians that are sufficient to force us to think differently about what is and is not done in the university.[141]

While Jennings would not be so confident that the structure of the university itself is immune from criticism, heir as it is to the "universal" cataloguing of late medieval scholasticism, he agrees that there are problems associated with the identities formed within the university. However, he disagrees with Hauerwas as to how those problematic aspects are to be understood. Jennings' analysis of the "scholastic disposition" contends that Christian training and formation often suffers from a "forgetting of Being." He contends that this "forgetting of Being" is tied in to the production of the racial imagination. Jennings is not singling out Duke Divinity School or Hauerwas for criticism. Rather, he is attempting to demonstrate how "the best" of contemporary theology is not immune from an imagination affected by "colonial dominance."[142]

Hauerwas identifies the primary challenge faced by Christian theology as "Constantinianism"[143] and offers an ecclesiological "disavowal of Constantine" as the solution.[144] Hauerwas is concerned that the church and the nation-state have operated in such deep collusion for so long that the church has lost its identity as an alternate polis. He refers to this illicit union with the term "Christendom."[145] Hauerwas is working primarily in the realm of ecclesiology, or more precisely, the connection between ecclesiology and political theology. While Jennings would not disagree with Hauerwas' basic contention that the church-state order is problematic, Jennings implies that the medieval and modern church-state alliance is simply a nexus that increased the reach and violence of theological distortions already developing within the tradition. He does not name the problem "Constantinianism" as much as the supersessionist Christologies and rationalized theological anthropologies which allowed for early-modern theology to categorize, control, and manipulate certain bodies. Whereas Hauerwas is working in ecclesiology, Jennings finds Christology to be the site at which to locate the distortions of modernity, distortions partially recognized by Hauerwas and many other theologians.

141. Hauerwas, *State of the University*, 32.

142. Jennings, *Christian Imagination*, 8.

143. Hauerwas, *State of the University*, 34, 38, 187–88.

144. Ibid., 74.

145. Ibid., 31.

Hauerwas' primary concern with the church-state order is the violence which attends the State and is blessed by the Church. Jennings contends that this violence is inherently racialized and has been made possible by traditioned theological patterns of reflection upon the "other." Without reimagining its Christological habits of mind and the patterns of embodiment that accompany them, a reclamation of the church as an alternative *polis* will not remedy the modern distortions of peoplehood partially recognized by scholars such as Hauerwas and Givens. Because reclamation projects often carry the racialized imagination with them, Jennings clarifies that his own method is not best understood as "an exercise in retrieval."[146]

Hauerwas and Jennings both contend against the modern liberal genealogy of the nation-state, but in different ways. Hauerwas claims that the modern liberal story in which the privatization of religion saved the world from the violence of religious faith is simply "not true."[147] Hauerwas' alternative read is that wars between religious parties should not be seen as religiously motivated but are better understood as State attempts to gain political power in the wake of the decentralization of the Church after the Reformation. By utilizing Cavanaugh (one of Hauerwas' students), Hauerwas contends that the State, in its rise to power, is that which relegated religion to the private sphere.[148] In his schema, religion needs to be centralized in public discourse again primarily through the historic institution of the university.

While Jennings also does not find the modern liberal story compelling, he views Hauerwas' solution as equally problematic. Jennings contends that Anglo-Catholic theology in the age of colonization (represented by Acosta) provided the State with the intellectual architecture upon which to build its Christian Empire. Jennings' thesis suggests that Hauerwas lets Christian theology off the hook a bit too easily, missing the opportunity for critical self-engagement with the tradition. Jennings reads the modern category of "religion" not so much as a "secular" invention but as a comparative construct made possible in the maturation of traditioned theological reflection upon native peoples in the age of New World contact. Scholastically trained theologians attempting to live as faithful Christians often provided the missional framework for the cultural "development" of the nonwhite body through European pedagogy. He suggests that Hauerwas' vision of pedagogical formation in the virtues reenacts this discursive stance.

146. Jennings, *Christian Imagination*, 10.
147. Hauerwas, *State of the University*, 62–63.
148. Ibid., 63.

The Teaching of Universal Knowledge

In decrying the disconnection of academic disciplines within the fragmentation of modernity, Hauerwas paints a compelling holistic picture of "education as moral formation."[149] A key part of his vision for the university is a reclamation of what John Henry Newman called the "teaching of universal knowledge."[150] Hauerwas echoes MacIntyre on this point, who bemoans that education has lost the belief in "the order of things of which there could be a unified, if complex, understanding."[151]

In interacting with Stanley Fish's critique of the modern university, Hauerwas contends that the world in which we live "is a world in which there no longer exists any common judgments about the true, the good, and the beautiful."[152] The phrase "no longer" implies that there was a time past in which a universal body of knowledge was satisfactorily maintained and disseminated. For Hauerwas, the institution entrusted with the communication of this body of knowledge is the university (whose name implies the "universal" scope of its knowledge). While Hauerwas does not commend the idea of a "Christian" university, he contends that Christian thinking about what is done in the university includes a return to "the unity of the transcendentals, that is, the inseparability of beauty, truth, and the good."[153] We have already seen how a similar invocation of "the transcendentals" enabled MacIntyre to distinguish between the rationality of the human, the non-rationality of the animal, and the underdeveloped rationality of Polynesian natives. While Hauerwas does not intend to build his anthropology upon rationality, he nonetheless states that

> MacIntyre argues, for example, that 'it is from *within* the practice of painting in each case that shared standards are discovered, standards which enable *transcultural judgments of sameness and difference to be made*, both about works of art and about the standards governing artistic practice and aesthetic evaluation.'[154]

While Hauerwas' point is that one must be engaged in particular practices in order to be able to render aesthetic judgments (as opposed to modern rationalistic disengagement), he maintains that there are universal criteria by which transcultural aesthetic judgments can be made. This places

149. Ibid., 51.
150. Ibid., 30.
151. Ibid., 48.
152. Ibid., 77.
153. Ibid., 203.
154. Ibid., 112, italics mine.

the university student in the posture of learning how to adjudicate the relative merits of cultural difference. While Hauerwas does not reference race at this point, his invocation of the intrinsic connection between the moral, the ontological, and the aesthetic does implicitly offer the ability to determine the merits of particular cultural modes of being. My point is not so much to contend against the study of ethics, aesthetics, or philosophy (or even to suggest that connections cannot be made between them), but rather to tag the fact that neatly presenting them as a holism functions to make whiteness the standard by which beauty, goodness, and peoplehood are judged. Jennings maintains that this process "points to the slow, steady surrender to the theological power of whiteness and how it became determinative of the true (intelligence), the good (morality), and the beautiful (aesthetics)."[155] Jennings' analysis of Acosta and MacIntyre demonstrated that an appeal to a unified "natural order" has often catalyzed discourses of subjugation. Late medieval intellectual formation encouraged its adherents to "civilize" the world's peoples through assimilation to similar aesthetic, ethical, and ontological standards. Jennings maintains that such a universalization initiates the non-Westerner into the role of "perpetual student" in a Sisyphean exercise of "pedagogical imperialism."[156]

I contend that Jennings is working in a Barthian actualist ontology in which the veracity of the study of eternal essences is called into question. An emphasis on essence (as opposed to action) assumes an epistemological privilege which Jennings connects with the hubris of whiteness. In Paul Nimmo's treatment of Barth's theological ethics, *Being in Action*, he contends that, for Barth, participation in the divine is not an ontological continuity but an actualistic, or historical, correspondence.[157] As such, Barth's ontology resists essentialism. God is not known by humans in his eternal essence (nor as a "substance") but rather is known by his acts in history, culminating in the saving actions of Jesus Christ. God's self-revelation is personal; it is not to be found in ideas *about* God. As Brian Brock maintains, "Religious practice and utterance are . . . understood to be true only as uttered performatively, as a way of life."[158] For Barth, the object of theology is an event: the Incarnation. This is why, for Jennings, the church is not so much an invisible mystical union with God as it is visible, particular identification with others in the body of the Jewish Jesus. This is why "joining" is Jennings' core term rather than something akin to either deification (Carter's

155. Jennings, *Christian Imagination*, 277.
156. Ibid., 112.
157. Nimmo, *Being in Action*.
158. Brock, *Singing the Ethos of God*, 250.

tendency) or ethical correspondence (which tends to be Hauerwas' view of the church). Nimmo criticizes Hauerwas' critique of Barth's ecclesiology (in which Hauerwas maintains that Barth underemphasizes the moral witness of the church):

> Barth has certainly radically relativized the importance of the community, with a view to prioritizing not only the transcendence of God but also the living relationship of God with the Church as a whole and with the ethical agent in particular. Precisely in its continual dependence on the grace of God, the Church cannot arrogate to itself the role of moral teacher or former of moral character without also insisting that it is such only in a relative and indirect manner. The consequent lack of concretion that Hauerwas finds so problematic is, for Barth, ultimately unavoidable.[159]

This is in part why Jennings tends to speak of supersessionism in terms related to the "imagination" of Christians (as opposed to doctrinal terms) and tends to speak of joining in terms that do not dictate what that joining will look like in particular places (although he does give examples, like the life of Colenso). Jennings does not want to predetermine the shape of the joined community by engaging in talk about essences or ethics that is ultimately disconnected from real life shared by real people in real place. For Hauerwas to follow MacIntyre in asserting the need to reclaim the centrality of aesthetics, ontology, and ethics (in a world held to have no rational standard of adjudication) is to fall into an abstraction that tends to reconfirm white ways of being.

Whereas MacIntyre and Hauerwas lament the lack of agreed-upon aesthetic and ethical criteria, Jennings' genealogy suggests that this lack of a universalizable standard is recognizable largely because the newfound cross-cultural contact made possible in modern globalization calls into question the veracity of making claims about transcendental essences. In other words, what Hauerwas calls a lack of "common judgments" may signify that, as people have come to appreciate differing expressions of beauty, they have realized that their own assumptions about aesthetics may not be as objective as once thought. In this way, the postmodern distrust of universalizable rational norms can be read, at least in part, as undergirded by a heretofore unexperienced modern global cosmopolitanism. Jennings contends that judgments about beauty cannot be made apart from relationships marked by difference, relationships out of which flow unexpected experiences of beauty, truth, and goodness. In this sense, Jesus Christ, the one who

---

159. Nimmo, *Being in Action*, 84.

is beauty, truth, and goodness, is known primarily in *action* through his communal body, and not in reflection upon his *essence* (the latter of which tends to slip into the default settings of white rationality).

Jennings contrasts his aesthetic of joining with Hauerwas' aesthetic of virtue. An aesthetic of joining points to shared expressions of beauty in the body politic of Jesus Christ. In communion with the "other" in shared space, the One who is Beauty and Truth is encountered. Jennings' aesthetic of joining may be described as mutually performative, whereas Hauerwas' aesthetic of virtue tends to discern the "good" performance from within the resources of its own tradition. This posture often produces paternalistic patterns of relationality. Paternalism names a quest to teach or to guide rather than to walk along beside, to be a father rather than a brother. Paternalism as a strained form of relationality is found when one person or group of people offers anything in unilateral agency toward another as recipient without a reciprocal action from the other party constituting mutuality, interdependence, and intimate knowledge of one another. In the following sections, I will suggest examples of paternalism in Hauerwas' theological deployment of a MacIntyrian tradition of virtue. As with Acosta, such an orientation "outlines the presentation of salvation without the desire for communion. The analogy witnesses a strained ecclesiology and a troubled church in the New World."[160] Hauerwas' reflections may subtly reenact such a problematic ecclesiology.

The Other as Prop

In this section, I will demonstrate the manner in which a reclamation of Western virtue tends to encourage paternalist and assimilationist relational patterns. As with my analysis of Milbank, the "will" or "intentions" of Hauerwas are not the focus. I will specifically point to Hauerwas' "us-them" language as evidence that he tends to think of identity as static. Additionally, I claim that Hauerwas' invocation of the "poor" refers less to real people in real space than it does an imaginary social field upon which the virtues of the university student may be exercised. I suggest that invoking poverty in generalized terms tends to play into racialized notions of peoplehood and reconfirms the static social images repeated *ad nauseam* in Western society.

One of the themes Hauerwas returns to several times is the need for universities to "produce" people who can "love the poor."[161] In his analysis, "the poor" are identified solely by their status as "poor." They have no

160. Jennings, *Christian Imagination*, 93.
161. Hauerwas, *State of the University*, 10, 189–201.

voice in the narrative. There is no indication that "the poor" are people with agency. Who are "the poor"? Is the reference to be understood as a State designation of those who fall "below the poverty line" in federal descriptive processes? Is it referring to people in materially "impoverished" nations who are living on the equivalent of a few dollars a day? Is the designation a material or a spiritual classification (i.e. the "poor in spirit")? Does invoking "the poor" leave space for recognizing the ways in which the virtuous Christian subject may also be impoverished?

I contend that, much like MacIntyre's invocation of the "natives," Hauerwas' reflections on poverty are most easily understood if "the poor" are read as props used to further his reflections about moral formation. They exist as recipients of the goodwill of the virtuous student. While I am not psychologizing Hauerwas' invocation of "the poor" as demonstrating some sort of hidden racism, nor am I suggesting that Hauerwas is speaking in racial "code," I am suggesting that his use of this language demonstrates that he imagines people in static categories, the sort of identity structures in which a racial logic flourishes. Generalized reflections upon "the poor" too easily create phantoms invoked for intellectual exercise. As with Jennings' account of Bishop Colenso, who used the trope of native personhood to further his own theological considerations, turning "native questions into occasions for theological self-absorption,"[162] so Hauerwas utilizes the trope of poverty to narrate his own concerns about the moral formation of the university student:

> But I do want to put Gregory's reflections on poverty, and in particular lepers, to show why Christians have a stake in sustaining the work of the university.[163]

> You may well wonder what lepers have to do with universities, but I take it that Fred Norris's life work has been to make unlikely connections . . . I lack Norris's erudition, but like him I want to be a free-church Catholic who refuses to leave behind the institutions of Christendom, institutions like the university, simply because they too often are in service to Caesar rather than the poor.[164]

> So it is not impossible for there to be a connection between the university and the poor, a connection that I hope . . . also can

162. Jennings, *Christian Imagination*, 150.
163. Hauerwas, *State of the University*, 188.
164. Ibid., 188.

help us to rethink as Christians what we ought to be about as people committed to love learning and the poor.[165]

Christianity is the faith of the poor.[166]

In these accounts, "the poor" and "lepers" are invoked in service of many causes, including the financial sustenance of the university, praise for a fellow religious thinker, self-deprecation of skills in erudition, concerns with Christian identity and tradition, and proclamation of an anti-Empire stance. Hauerwas' linguistic structure objectifies "the poor" alongside another *concept* to be loved, that of "learning." Ultimately, the conceptualized prop of poverty is granted unilateral ownership of the Faith as a gauge for discerning the virtues of Christians formed in the university. It remains unclear, however, how anyone privileged enough to engage in vocational theological reflection can properly be considered Christian if Christianity belongs to "the poor" from whom the university student is syntactically distinguished. Neither the manner in which Hauerwas' Christians are impoverished, nor the ways in which his "poor" may have something to teach the university, is explored.

Hauerwas' hope is that universities will be able to "produce people" who will be able "to see and describe the poor as beautiful."[167] Not only does the article "the" function as a term of classification distinguishing "them" from "us," but the vocation Hauerwas envisions for the university student suggests a posture of descriptive analysis and social control. His grammar is characteristic of the encyclopedic enterprise and relationships constituted around capital: *categorization* (i.e. "the poor"), *description* (i.e. "see and describe"), and *production* (i.e. "produce people"). While it is certainly preferable to view people as "beautiful" rather than as "ugly," it remains that such a posture is still a descriptive project through which the educated and moneyed populace engages in evaluating the aesthetic value of the "other." A more "satisfactory" classificatory schema does not necessarily encourage the binding of one's life with another. It is through joining that beauty is mutually experienced, not "seen" or "described." Hauerwas' conjuration of the "other" renders difficult a real identification in real space with real people, precluded by the economic boundaries of the university.

Much like the assumed ontological difference between the scholar and the common man as identified by Bourdieu, Hauerwas' appeal to poverty as identifier assumes an ontological juxtaposition between "Christians" and

165. Ibid., 189.
166. Ibid., 10.
167. Ibid., 198.

the "poor." The "poor" exist on the periphery of Christian identity as recipients of charity and salvation. Hauerwas' invocation of poverty is substantively different from that which we saw in Maximus the Confessor, who proclaimed the poor man to *be* God in a process of mutual *theosis*, as all participants were together divinized through their relationships across socioeconomic boundaries. This distinction is all the more important in the wake of coloniality-modernity, which aligned racial designations with impoverished conceptions of being. While I would not suggest that Hauerwas intends a skin color for his "poor," his conjuring of poverty does not challenge the racial order but rather gives consent to it. The Christian imagination has comfortably joined "darkness" with impoverishment of being, and has communicated this conflation over and again through images, sociological analyses, and soteriological debates. In other words, it is unwise to use such classificatory language in a world shaped by racial classifications.

While it is true that the Scriptures regularly reference "the poor," the later intertwining of poverty with modern race was nowhere in sight of the biblical authors. Biblically, invocations of poverty tend to serve the purpose of proclaiming God's identification with those who are marginalized. In the *kenosis*, the Word took on poverty in order to make humanity "rich."[168] This latter orientation places Jesus of Nazareth's exhortations about poverty within his own identification with impoverished humanity. Hauerwas' invocation of Christianity *as* the faith of the poor who need to be loved *by* Christians implies an ontological dichotomy foreign to the theological anthropology of the Scriptures.

Historical Remembrance and the Forgetting of Being

While neither MacIntyre nor Hauerwas speak about race often, they are not silent on the subject. Both speak about the evils of slavery and its continued socioeconomic ramifications. While this is a welcome corrective to many theologically conservative accounts, which often shy away from substantively engaging race or do so in a hurtful manner, MacIntyre's and Hauerwas' reflections tend to use the subject of race primarily to advance broader debates about ethical methodology. This suggests the self-reflexive nature of ethical reclamations of virtue. In this section, I will explore two of their rare reflections on race. In *After Virtue*, MacIntyre invokes slavery to pit historical remembrance against modern individualism:

168. Phil 2:5–11; 2 Cor 8:9.

From the standpoint of individualism I am what I myself choose
to be . . . I may legally be a citizen of a certain country; but
I cannot be held responsible for what my country does or has
done unless I choose implicitly or explicitly to assume such responsibility. Such individualism is expressed by those modern
Americans who deny any responsibility for the effects of slavery
upon black Americans, saying 'I never owned any slaves'. It is
more subtly the standpoint of those other modern Americans
who accept a nicely calculated responsibility for such effects
measured precisely by the benefits they themselves as individuals have indirectly received from slavery. In both cases 'being an
American' is not in itself taken to be part of the moral identity
of the individual.[169]

Similarly, in an essay entitled *Duke University: The Good of this Place*, Hauerwas writes

That Duke is marked by its being a place of the South means
that Duke can never forget slavery flourished here and racism
remains a present reality. This is a memory and reality that cannot and should not want to be lost in the "mists of history." In
particular, we should never forget that Christians owned slaves.
In other words, Duke cannot be Duke unless we are dedicated
to the truthful telling and retelling of the story of slavery and
racism.[170]

In both of these accounts, racism is referenced not in order to consider its theological ramifications, nor is it presented in a light that demonstrates sustained and substantive relational interactions with the implied
"objects" of the account: African Americans. While this may seem like an
inconsequential observation, the point is that the "subject" in both accounts
remains the white body who is thinking about virtue by thinking about the
black body. The plight of blackness is used to demonstrate, respectively,
that individualism is bad and that the university is good. This suggests that
while both accounts entail historical remembrance, they betray a forgetting of Being. They function so as to hide the identity of the subject from
himself. In such cases, historical remembrance can be a mask for theological
forgetfulness.

First, racism is presented as American slavery, from which the authors
are safely separated by a century and a half. This way of framing the subject
reduces it to discourses about explicit historical *racism* while missing the

169. MacIntyre, *After Virtue*, 220.
170. Hauerwas, *State of the University*, 204.

unconscious *racial imaginary* that is sustained through Christian theology. Second, the guilt for slavery is upon those who owned slaves in the past or those who have benefitted in the present from their ancestors having owned slaves. This suggests that responsibility for the racial quagmire of the West is limited to slaveholders and those who have profited from it (which begs the questions: 'Who hasn't?' and 'How should such profit be "calculated"?'). Such a formulation may function to exculpate the scholar from participation in the racial project to the extent that he is learned enough to have an historical memory (i.e. "the scholastic disposition").[171] Third, neither account offers a constructive ethic of how to live today in a racialized society (e.g. Was the last instance of the racial imagination in 1863?). For instance, traditioned ethical reflection is not of necessity at odds with conceptions of justice that allow for judgments like the verdict of the Zimmerman trial or the exoneration of dozens of police officers who were just "doing their jobs." I am not suggesting that ethics of virtue contribute to violence but rather that their manner of imagining right and wrong does not have the internal mechanisms to criticize racism on grounds other than "bad character."

Fourth, these reflections on race tend to buttress a view that the university is inherently virtuous. For Hauerwas, "Duke cannot be Duke unless . . . " talk about slavery happens within its walls. Such a formulation buttresses the moral identity of the academy by engaging in conversations about the subjugation of African Americans. The limitations of his particular institution stem from its being "a place of the South" and have little to do with the university-as-place. Commenting on the traditioned moral formation of the individual, MacIntyre astutely recognizes that "being an American" is "part of the moral identity of the individual."[172] Virtue ethics' recognition that morality is shaped by community (and not just "choice," as in liberalism) is a welcome conclusion. However, this recognition should encourage ethicists of virtue to consider what being committed to the retrieval of Western philosophical ethics may mean for the "moral identity" of the scholar.

This is not to suggest that historical remembrance should be forsaken. Rather, it is to acknowledge that such traditioned historicism may serve to distract from what Jennings calls "a compelling new invitation to life together,"[173] an identity forged in "the embrace by very different people in the chapel."[174] This embrace will necessarily initiate both persons into a pro-

---

171. Cf. Matt 23:30: "[You say], 'If we had lived in the days of our fathers, we would not have taken part with them in shedding the blood of the prophets.' Thus you witness against yourselves that you are the sons of those who murdered the prophets."

172. MacIntyre, *After Virtue*, 220.

173. Jennings, *Christian Imagination*, 294.

174. Ibid., 7.

cess of learning the historical realities that predicated the embrace and the ways in which one's theological suppositions extend the racial imaginary contending against such an embrace. It is this embrace that encourages the type of historical confession that is needed in the sustenance of a reconciling body politic. This embrace is not a punctiliar event, but an invitation to a continued life together that becomes ever more authentic.

A Truncated Christological Imagination

While Jennings does not imply that a tradition of virtue fails to affirm a high Christology, he suggests that missiological reflections in this trajectory tend to reproduce the adoptionist habits of mind characteristic of Sanneh. In the last chapter, I suggested that Jennings utilizes Sanneh in order to contrast his work with that of Hauerwas. In this section, I will suggest that Hauerwas' distinction between "church" and "world" is not the correct theological distinction when discussing mission and soteriology. Jennings' account of the biblical distinction between "Jew" and "Gentile" is more compelling and theologically satisfactory. I suggest that Hauerwas tends to imagine the distinction between church and world in a supersessionist motif characteristic of modern missiology. I maintain that this tendency is related to Hauerwas' Yoderian ethical voluntarism as the basis for his ecclesiology.

While Hauerwas works primarily in ecclesiology, his Christology is stronger and more satisfactory than Milbank's Christology. In Hauerwas' stress on particularity, he avoids what Jennings describes as a docetic Christological imagination. He recognizes the importance of embodiment and understands that the Incarnation has a political nature. However, there are signposts that suggest that Hauerwas tends to slip into adoptionist modes of imagining the Incarnation. I maintain that this is because he desires to more favorably evaluate the identity of non-Christians than do many conservative accounts of missiology. However, because of his strong distinction between church and world (of which his own tradition would belong to the former) rather than between Jew and Gentile (of which his own tradition would belong to the latter), his desire to envision non-Christians in a respectful light forces him to imagine the Gospel as in effect "adopting" all people without satisfactorily retaining the particularity of its Jewish center. This universalization is foreign to his otherwise particularist account, suggesting that there are supersessionist tendencies at work in his missiology. I will build on these contentions by briefly sketching the contours of Hauerwas' use of Sanneh and Yoder. This analysis suggests that before we can ask who we are in relation to each other, we must attend to the question posed to us: "Who do you say that I am?"[175]

Hauerwas favorably appropriates Sanneh's rejection of "religious privatization" and his acclamation of "public ethics."[176] Hauerwas advocates a return to some form of "natural theology," offering a defense of Thomist thought as an adequate framework in which to envision proclamation of the Gospel.[177] Hauerwas reads Sanneh as offering a compelling account of the church having a "public role in the world," a role exemplified in Catholicism's "resistance to colonialism" among Native Americans.[178] While he recognizes that "the word 'mission' has become a negative word for many because of its colonial history,"[179] Hauerwas does not explore the manner in which colonization was energized within a theological atmosphere similar to the one to which he is advocating return. For all his positive rhetoric about the "other," he has trouble imagining interaction with other traditions as substantively more than a MacIntyrian "confrontation," albeit a non-violent one. By way of Yoder, Hauerwas maintains that, "when confronted by the religious 'other,'" a witness that is "nonviolent," "non-coercive," and "non-Constantinian" is the appropriate response to "alien claims."[180] Not unlike Acosta, he assumes that "the prophetic denunciation of paganization" is a primary role of the "local" and "visible" ecclesial community.[181] Unfortunately, he does not explore the difference between the prophetic role of Israel and the mission of the Church.

These difficulties presumably stem from Hauerwas' attempt to reimagine "mission" in a favorable light while holding on to the theological architecture that rendered mission so problematic. As he rejects a docetic (i.e. neo-Gnostic) posture, Hauerwas is left with an adoptionist (i.e. contextualist) posture concordant with his read of Yoder and Sanneh:

> The existence of other significant traditions is not a "problem" for Christians, but rather a gift. That is why Christian missionaries who went and continue to go to make Christ present to those they assumed did not know Christ so often return confessing

175. Mark 8:29

176. Hauerwas, *State of the University*, 71.

177. Ibid., 68.

178. Ibid., 71. Hauerwas recommends Damien Costello's study, *Black Elk: Colonialism and Lakota Catholicism*, but does not examine the ways in which colonialism was animated by scholastic Catholic theology.

179. Hauerwas, *State of the University*, 67.

180. Ibid., 66–68.

181. Ibid., 69.

they discovered Christ in those they went to serve. The great missionary effort of the nineteenth century was no doubt sometimes sponsored by a western arrogance, but it may well turn out to be one of the ways God used to humble that same arrogance.[182]

Hauerwas strives for an antiethnocentric missiology that resists Western hubris. Yet he has trouble pinpointing the center of God's saving activity in the world. While he intuitively recognizes that to privilege the Western church is arrogance, he has no remaining imaginative framework other than envisaging the other as effectually unilaterally "adopted" by Christ. This begs the question: If it is the case that all peoples are "adopted" independently of each other, then why the "going" of missions? Hauerwas recognizes that to "go" into "mission" in a way that privileges the West is problematic (a docetic posture) but strives to remedy it by viewing the "going" of "mission" as a means by which the Western subject might recognize that God was already with the "other" (an adoptionist posture). Jennings' invocation of the "going" of mission as a movement from Israel to the world more satisfactorily retains the scandal of particularity and the particular center of theological history. This movement from near to distant neighbors presents the need to "go" as born out of a desire for the other, a joining through which diverse peoples are together drawn into the Jewish flesh of Jesus Christ. While Hauerwas, by way of Yoder, understands that Israel is important in some way, he does not emphasize joining to Israel's story in a substantive manner. Jennings suggests that while there are certainly elements of truth in recognizing the divine in all places, such a conceptuality renders joining in physical place unnecessary.

Jennings claims that emptying the Incarnation of its scandalous particularity and postulating the presence of Christ as in some sense "adopting" all peoples is a "tragedy":

> At one level, [this] assumption appears to be an ecumenical breakthrough, a ray of theological sunshine announcing not only religious tolerance for indigenous peoples but possibly even celebration of and respect for their religious sensibilities. Indeed, this has become a way of articulating divine presence serviceable for multiple intellectual projects. Yet at another level, what is apparent in [these] conclusions is the formation of a cultural nationalism that fully captures Christian theology. It is theology of and for the nation, for a people, any people, and every people. And in this conceptualization, Israel is historicized

182. Ibid., 71.

as an exhausted theological moment because God is now with everyone else . . . God has always been with everyone, they just didn't know it. Once this is expressed, theology must come to exist wholly as a nationalist intellectual exercise.[183]

Hauerwas is one of the contemporary theologians who has most clearly resisted nationalism from a traditioned and orthodox Christian perspective. Yet his adoptionist reflex suggests that his imagination is captive to nationalist conceptions of peoplehood (which are, finally, racialized views of identity). When the divine becomes the property of each particular national people, Jesus' particular Jewish identity is of little consequence, opening the door to racialized conceptions of peoplehood grounded in whiteness. While not completely capitulating to this schema, Hauerwas' "church versus world" dialectic leads him into problematic places.[184] Jennings eschews this dichotomy as he maintains that the presence of God was revealed in and through Israel and inasmuch as peoples are joined with her Messiah Jesus Christ and with other peoples being so joined, those peoples can echo the words "God with us."[185] He explains:

> The point here is easy to miss. The tragedy is not contextual reflection; the tragedy is the way divine entrance is imagined among peoples. God's history is missing—no Israel, no Jesus, no apostles, no material struggle, no divine walking through time and indeed space, real space. Such a walking, such an entrance would be messy, carrying forward Israel's election and carrying forward many peoples, places, voices, ways of life bound to the Jewish Jesus, always announcing that God is with us . . . Divine entrance, therefore, requires no relationships with anyone. Just as God is with Christians in Jesus, God is present among all people. But is God present among all peoples, all cultures?

---

183. Jennings, *Christian Imagination*, 166–67.

184. Hauerwas, *State of the University*, 66–67. It is worth noting that the dichotomy of "church" and "world" was most clearly articulated in late medievalism, the era Jennings pictures as the staging ground for colonization. The Christian Latin term *saecularis* (as a means by which to distinguish the world from Christendom) had its genesis in this era. While I do not suggest that Hauerwas imagines "secular" in a medieval fashion, it is worth noting that "secular" may not best be understood as a construct of modernity, which is the way Milbank and Hauerwas both present it. Seen in this light, that which animated the ecclesial logic of sacred and secular was an embryonic racial logic. Read this way, the "teaching of universal knowledge" is historically predicated upon the preeminence of the sociopolitical order of whiteness over against "darker" and "heathen" peoples. Surely a revitalization of the university along the lines of a scholastic virtue ethic will not resist this distortion of identity.

185. Jennings, *Christian Imagination*, 167; Isa, 7–8 and Matt 1:22–23.

Only on this side of the colonialist moment and its antecedent supersessionism does one see this as a legitimate question. It is not. Divine presence revealed in the Jewish Jesus is a disciplining presence, guiding not only what Christians say about God in the world but how they see God at work in the world. That seeing . . . draw[s] [Christian bodies] toward other peoples, calling them to become one and to love concretely.[186]

While Hauerwas invokes the Jewishness of Jesus, it is in the context of attempting to maintain the primacy of the church in interfaith dialogue. Hauerwas emphasizes what he terms Yoder's "Christological maximalism," that Jesus is the end and goal of history in a way that is consistent with the uniqueness of the God of the Jews.[187] Yet he parses this to mean that when confronting "alien" communities, the Church can have "confidence" in what Yoder calls the "final primacy" of Jesus Christ. Hauerwas uses Jewish centrality to buttress Western church-centrality in interfaith dialogue; he misses the fact that the Gentiles are the "aliens" throughout biblical history. He appears to miss the further implication that the Gentile Church itself is decentered through proclamation of the Lordship of the Jewish Son of God, into whose flesh those "far from God" are invited as into a particularity not their own. While emphasizing the Jewishness of Jesus, Hauerwas appears to underestimate the significance of his tradition's Gentilic identity.

Jewish existence in Hauerwas' reflections functions in a similar manner to his invocation of "the poor." It is there, but usually functions to support the prominence of a Western tradition of moral enquiry. Perhaps this theological imprecision in his account of Jewish identity is what prompted one of his students to describe Hauerwas' thought as being "haunted by the Jews."[188] It may be worth noting that Yoder's own account is more thorough than Hauerwas' in exploring the ways in which "Radical Protestantism" has been animated by "its concern for the particular, historical, and therefore Jewish quality and substance of New Testament faith in Jesus."[189] Yoder fills out this claim through several specific ways in which the Jewishness of Jesus should influence the Christology of those who advance counter-cultural ecclesiologies. Rather than exploring these concrete suggestions, Hauerwas utilizes the particularity of Jesus as a defense for particularity in general. He has his finger on the pulse of Jennings' critique as he writes, "Christians are often tempted to jettison the particular, the local, the specific biblical content

---

186. Jennings, *Christian Imagination*, 167.
187. Hauerwas, *State of the University*, 67.
188. Bader-Saye, "Haunted by the Jews," 191–209.
189. Yoder, "The Disavowal of Constantine," 246–47.

in an attempt to correct the Christian imperialism associated with Christian Europe."[190] However, he ends by acclaiming "specificity" without examining how this specificity might render peripheral his tradition of virtue.

Hauerwas laudably seeks to eschew missional coercion in favor of "the concrete encounter with the neighbor who is different from me."[191] Yet it is unclear what Hauerwas means by "encounter" and how we are to understand "encounter" as anything other than a MacIntyrian wrestling match between traditions. He maintains that "vulnerability" means that "the herald cannot be in a position to make anyone who refuses to believe be destroyed or persecuted."[192] If "vulnerability" is primarily an eschewal of violent punishment rather than a fundamental posture of openness to the other, then Hauerwasian "encounter" must be distinguished from Jenningsian "joining." As Jennings summarizes:

> The theological imagination that deploys divine presence without concomitant real presence and real relationship may be enacting a form of Gentile hubris that believes we have the right to claim the very reality that was only announced over us by a gracious act of the Holy Spirit in the presence of Jewish believers (Acts 10, 11) . . . [T]his adoptionist habit of mind turns peoples toward an isolating theological creativity, imagining the divine among one's own people. Such imagining is not wholly wrong, but it is impoverishing. And Christian theology in modern times has been set in place by this very poverty. So the gospel transmitted means in many imaginations the ways in which different peoples have culturally adopted and adapted Christian faith, ideas, doctrine, and language. And thanks to a supersessionist mistake and a colonialist sensibility, few Christians would discern the tragic history and the ongoing tragedy inside that statement about transmission.[193]

Hauerwas remains one of the contemporary theologians who has most compelling reminded the church that faithfulness to her Lord means resisting violence and Empire. However, his MacIntyrian tradition of virtue has limited his recognition that, since the colonial moment and its attendant supersessionist imagination, violence and Empire are fundamentally racialized realities. It has also limited his recognition that these racialized realities are strengthened by theological accounts of Western virtue. While Hauerwas'

190. Hauerwas, *State of the University*, 67.

191. Ibid., 70.

192. Ibid., 68.

193. Jennings, *Christian Imagination*, 167.

account is to be preferred to Milbank's and MacIntyre's, traditions of Western virtue extend the tragic legacy of reflection on the "other" characteristic of theological currents at the "dawn" of Western expansionism.

Barth and Bonhoeffer

The Image of God

Jennings often speaks in terminology drawn from Barth and Bonhoeffer and shares several key methodological tendencies with their general theological sensibilities.[194] While resisting designations such as "Barthian" as examples of "the obsessive labeling and positioning of theological trends" characteristic of "continuing encasement in racial logics and agency,"[195] he tends to frame his theological anthropology in a modified divine command modality.[196] Two key differences between Jennings' divine command ethic and an ethic of virtue are the way in which they conceive of the *imago Dei* and the manner in which they understand ethnic diversity. As I did with Carter, I will now close my treatment of Jennings by summarizing his constructive vision. In this section, I will briefly contrast the *anologia relationis* of Bonhoeffer and Barth with the Thomist *analogia entis*, which I briefly referenced in my previous analysis of MacIntyre.

Contrary to the proclivity of both the Anglo-Catholic tradition and modern liberalism to present anthropologies constructed around *rationality*, Bonhoeffer offers a theological exegesis of Genesis 1:26–27 in which he claims that the only characteristic common to God and humanity is *relationality*. Created male and female by a God whose being is referenced in the plural, humanity bears the *imago Dei* in an *analogia relationis*.[197] It is in freedom for the other that what is created displays the glory of and sings the praises of the Creator:

194. Ibid., 60–61, 260–61. Also, 286, where he utilizes Barth's phrase "near and distant neighbors" to describe his own vision of the joining of peoples with the land and with each other.

195. Ibid., 8.

196. I use the term "modified" because of the manner in which Barth sometimes slips into abstraction (what Givens calls his overly formal Christology). While Barth's divine command ethic is Christocentric, Jennings' divine command ethic more clearly expresses a Christology of Jesus as a Jew. For Jennings, the divine command is always received in particular time and place and is realized in joining between particular people. In this sense, I read Jennings' ecclesiology as having similarities to Luther's account of the estates, particularly in how it resists abstraction by focusing on the particular spaces and communities in which we receive the Word of God.

197. Bonhoeffer, *Creation and Fall*, 60–65.

Freedom is not a quality that can be uncovered; it is not a possession, something to hand, an object; nor is it a form of something to hand; instead it is a relation and nothing else. To be
more precise, freedom is a relation between two persons. Being
free means 'being-free-for-the-other,' because I am bound to the
other. Only by being in relation with the other am I free.[198]

Bonhoeffer is clearly thinking out of Luther when, against conceptions
of the *imago Dei* which find it to reside in attributes inherent to humanity, he emphasizes the *justitia passiva*, the righteousness of God imputed to
humanity by His grace contra the works of the flesh.[199] Because the Gospel
is gift and grace, God's free choice alone is what separates humanity from
other created beings over which they are granted dominion. By contrast, an
analogia entis tends to assume the existence of qualities intrinsic to humanity, such as rationality, by which they share in the divine nature. This is one
key area where Hauerwas breaks with the Thomist (and MacIntyrian) tradition. Influenced by his interest in medical ethics and disability theology,
Hauerwas proclaims it "morally indefensible" to construct an anthropology
by "privileging rationality."[200] While I have argued that his invocation of the
unity and objectivity of aesthetics, ethics, and ontology may render similar
judgments about rationality, Hauerwas clearly finds MacIntyre's anthropology of "rational animals" to be problematic.

Barth's and Bonhoeffer's anthropologies were influenced by their experiences of the racial imaginary at work in early twentieth-century Germany as the myth of the Nordic or Aryan people as pure "master race" rose
to prominence through Nazi ideology. The Jews became what Givens calls
the "foil" for nationalist peoplehood,[201] similar to the manner in which they
had been classified as the contagion threatening those with "pure blood"
in fifteenth-century Iberian taxonomy. While Bonhoeffer's resistance to the
Third Reich is well known, Barth's refusal to pledge allegiance to the Führer
led to his dismissal from his theology post at the University of Bonn and his
return to his native Switzerland. Barth had long recognized the problematic
nature of liberal German theologians' use of an *analogia entis* in laying anthropological groundwork that would later be exploited by National Socialism. In reference to what he considered their pseudo-exegesis of the Genesis
account, Barth noted:

198. Ibid., 63.
199. Ibid., 65.
200. Hauerwas, "Abortion," 615.
201. Givens, *We the People*, 139.

It is obvious that their authors merely found the concept in the text and then proceeded to pure invention in accordance with the requirements of contemporary anthropology, so that it is only by the standard of our own anthropology, and not according to the measure of its own anthropology and on exegetical grounds, that we can decide for or against them.[202]

Barth accuses such expositors of being "too tied to an anthropology" that expected a "full description" of the inherent qualities of mankind that they "found it impossible to think that it could consist only in this differentiation and relationship."[203] While I am not insinuating that the theological problems against which Barth and Bonhoeffer were contending are directly connected to contemporary accounts of virtue, I am simply tagging the manner in which a "traditional" Anglo-Catholic account of the *imago Dei* was utilized by modern German Protestantism to support a supersessionist racialized logic as means to demonic ends. This is presumably why Barth made his famous early assertion: "I regard the *analogia entis* as the invention of Antichrist."[204]

Barth finds that the New Testament writers located the fullness of the *imago Dei* in the One who is the visible image of the invisible God (Colossians 1:15). He maintains that it is not the individual or his attributes that reflect the glory of the image of God (2 Corinthians 3:18). Rather, the image of the invisible God, displayed in the person of Jesus Christ, is reflected in the body of which he is Head and Lord:

> It is with them that Jesus Christ is God's image. It is from among them, representing the basis of their own existence, that Paul makes this equation. He has no abstract Christological interest in this equation. Or rather, this Christological equation has at the root an inclusive character, so that it is also an ecclesiological and therefore even an anthropological equation.[205]

Barth suggests the connections between Christology, ecclesiology, and anthropology upon which Jennings expounds in his theology of race. While Barth's account of the church remains somewhat abstract and does not sufficiently distinguish the church from Israel (as Givens contends), Jennings fills out this abstraction with a Christology of Jewish particularity. We shall see in the next section that Barth mostly avoids the problem of

202. Barth, *Church Dogmatics III.1*, 193.
203. Ibid., 195.
204. Barth, *Church Dogmatics I.1*, xiii.
205. Barth, *Church Dogmatics III.1*, 205.

supersessionism in his ecclesiology by recognizing Israel as the locus of divine salvation for "near and distant neighbors."

Near and Distant Neighbors

A second distinction between the tradition within which Jennings is working and that of Hauerwas becomes apparent in their respective conceptions of the multiplicity of peoples. Hauerwas conceives of the existence of diverse *ethnos* in light of his read of Yoder's interpretation of the account of the tower of Babel in Genesis 11. Hauerwas claims that the differentiation of languages and the scattering of the peoples is "too often . . . interpreted as punishment."[206] Rather than divine judgment, he relates that Babel should be understood as a gracious act of God demonstrating God's desire for ethnic diversity. The "confusion of tongues" is, in Yoder's words, "the gift of new beginnings."[207] The sin of Babel, then, was that the human community was trying to "absolutize itself" in resistance to divinely-ordained diversification. God's "gracious intervention" at Babel means that "we are forced to learn to respect the other and learn humility."[208]

Again, while Hauerwas admirably strives against ethnocentrism, his ecclesiology falls prey to several of the limitations of the theological anthropology of an Anglo-Catholic tradition of virtue. Seen in a Barthian light, what sounds in Hauerwas like radical anti-ethnocentricity subtly inscribes race within a divine *ordo* of creation. Ascribing ethnic difference to divine decree can serve to reify race. It is this type of anthropological essentialization which Barth recognized in the pseudotheological moves of his early twentieth-century German interlocutors.[209] According to Barth, in creation God specifically ordained the distinction between male and female and between parents and children. All humanity is either male or female, either parent or child.[210] Barth suggests that since all humanity is of common

---

206. Hauerwas, *State of the University*, 70.

207. Ibid., 70–71.

208. Ibid., 71.

209. Barth, *Church Dogmatics* III.4, 307–9.

210. While I recognize that critical queer theory and transgender studies would question this claim, these criticisms were not on Barth's radar. Additionally, while I am sympathetic with critical queer studies' post-structuralist critique of gender essentialism, I am unconvinced that gender can be done away with as an appropriate anthropological and theological description. Likewise, my theological suppositions make me sympathetic to the claim that gender dysphoria is in some sense related to a postlapsarian existence.

ancestry, the term "race" is not a proper theological category.[211] Barth prefers to speak of one's own people in close proximity as "near neighbours," while referencing wider humanity as "distant neighbours," maintaining that the command of God directs humanity toward both. It is in this relationality that the image of God lies; there is no quality inherent to mankind that makes humans like God. In Bonhoeffer's account, to be like God (*sicut Deus*) is the temptation that, since the garden, has been the attempt of mankind to absolutize itself.[212]

According to Barth, the sin of Babel was not humanity's attempt at unity. He reflects that if God created all peoples from one man, how then could it be sin to join together as one?[213] For Barth, the sin of Babel was that mankind was attempting to reach God on its own terms, through its own capacities. This self-actualizing trajectory is what Barth found expressed in the *analogia entis*. It was not sin to build a tower, construct a city, or "to want to have a name and not to be scattered."[214] Rather, the problem was that the people were not satisfied with being called by the name of YHWH:

> It is wrong not to be satisfied with this name and this unity, to try to make another city and tower and name, to try to assure and assert by human resolve and enterprise the unity already given and not really threatened from any quarter. What is wrong is the anxiety underlying this construction, the forgetting of the name and unity already enjoyed, and the resultant arrogance of thinking that man himself can and must take himself as he takes brick and mortar, and make himself the lord of his history, constituting the work of providence his own work. This building is wrong to the extent that it is obviously a departure from grace. [215]

Barth maintains that an abstract unity centered on anything or anyone or any people other than the God of Israel in the person of the Jewish Jesus is idolatrous. Jennings suggests that whiteness names an attempt to construct a universal "city" other than the house of YHWH.

Jennings explicitly utilizes Barthian language as he constructs his vision of the joining of peoples: "The space of communion is always ready to appear where the people of God reach down to join the land and reach out

---

211. Barth, *Church Dogmatics III.4*, 286.
212. Bonhoeffer, *Creation and Fall*, 111.
213. Barth, *Church Dogmatics III.4*, 314.
214. Ibid.
215. Ibid.

to join those around them, their near and distant neighbors."[216] Jennings stresses *place* more thoroughly than does Barth, although such a focus is not foreign to the latter. For Barth, a people are to be understood by means of language, location (or place), and history.[217] Barthian theological anthropology resists racial essentialization by stressing these three aspects as constitutive of a people. For Barth, the Word of God is a particular Word that comes to humanity in the "natural and historical place" in which he finds himself. The command of God does not "float in empty space"[218] and seek contextualization, as is suggested by contemporary missiology's focus on "disentangling" the Gospel from its cultural "baggage." The command of God always comes to humanity as particular people in particular place, demonstrating that "he is this individual and not another."[219] God's Word is spoken in the relationship between near and distant neighbors. For Barth and Bonhoeffer, the command of God is received in the material and mundane spheres of life (cf. Luther's "estates": *oikos*, *ecclesia*, and *politia*).[220] Jennings joins Barth and Bonhoeffer in maintaining that the particularities of humanity are constituted through the particularities of place and land, not in divinely ordained ethnological differentiation.

As Barth exposits theological history around the heuristic of near and distant neighbors, he notes that while the nations as such are given only supporting roles in the biblical accounts, Israel remains the focal point of the entire narrative. The *goyim* take their entrances and exits as they relate to the story of YHWH's salvation. The *ethnos* take their place in the narrative of salvation as those brought from distance to nearness, those whom Jennings refers to as "near belonging."[221] As Jennings interprets Paul's letter to the Ephesians, the *ethnos* are those who were once far off but have now been brought near through the blood of Jesus Christ.[222] The nations approach Israel's table as dogs who eat the crumbs that fall from the table of the children of the Kingdom.[223] The place of the *ethnos* in YHWH's story is a very real place, a very near place, but it is the proper place. It is this place that is held open in invitation by Peter on the day of Pentecost when the Holy Spirit enabled women and men of Israel to speak in a multiplicity of

---

216. Jennings, *Christian Imagination*, 286.

217. Barth, *Church Dogmatics III.4*, 288–98.

218. Ibid., 288.

219. Ibid.

220. Bonhoeffer, *Ethics*, 380.

221. Jennings, *Christian Imagination*, 250.

222. Ibid., 271–72.

223. Ibid., 262.

tongues so that residents of the entire known world could hear the message of salvation in their own languages and be drawn near and added to their number. Theology entails a movement from the near to the distant, from the particular to the universal, but it does not begin in Europe, Africa, or the Americas. It began in Jerusalem, extended to Judea and Samaria, and only by way of that particularity does it encompass the whole earth. Jennings' account demonstrates that Hauerwas does not sufficiently distinguish the church from Israel in his ecclesiological formulations regarding the "people of God."

For Barth, the movement from near to distant neighbors is the means by which to properly conceive reconciliation: "Christian ethics cannot espouse an abstract internationalism and cosmopolitanism. On the other hand, it cannot espouse an abstract nationalism and particularism."[224] Whether stressing the universal (the liberal move of cultural studies) or the particular (the conservative tendency of virtue ethics), whiteness names an abstraction of being foreign to a theology of race and place grounded in the trajectory of YHWH's salvation. Jennings contends that until the church and the academy reckon with the supersessionist Christian imagination, they will reenact the "conceptual confusions and political struggles" surrounding contemporary "multicultural discourse."[225] Jennings hopes that he might "intervene helpfully in this conversation" by "seek[ing] a deeper soil" than the cosmopolitanism of "an imagined democratic spirit." While this "deeper rich soil is not easily unearthed,"

> Christianity marks the spot where, if noble dream joins hands with God-inspired hope and presses with great impatience against the insularities of life, for example, national, cultural, ethnic, economic, sexual, and racial, seeking the deeper ground upon which to seed a new way of belonging and living together, then we will find together not simply a new ground, not simply a new seed, but a life already prepared and offered to us.[226]

Until reconciliation is reimagined along these lines and embodied accordingly, the Christianity offered to the world will be "necessary . . . and living but not very appealing."[227] Jennings' Christology of joining suggests an equally radical ecclesiology of joining:

---

224. Barth, *Church Dogmatics III.4*, 312–13.

225. Jennings, *Christian Imagination*, 11.

226. Ibid.

227. Ibid., 202.

My hope is for a joining of peoples not only to each other but to the God who calls them to touch his body. For some, this deeply erotic image is disturbing. But it should be far less disturbing to us than bodies that never embrace, that never walk together on a moonlit night awaiting the dawn of a new day.[228]

228. Ibid., 288.

Conclusion: An Ecclesiology of Joining

A Theology of Race and Place

I INTRODUCED THIS TEXT with an autobiographical narrative describing the limits of the theological imagination bequeathed to me in penetrating the problem of race in the modern world. This limitation became especially apparent through pastoring a local ecclesial community marked by difference and striving for reconciliation. The schemas of the theological architecture of whiteness strained to the point of breaking when faced with the task of articulating the work of joining. I intuited that my theological imagination was insufficient to the task of conceptualizing the life and ministry in which I was engaged. I was aware that the theological accounts of reconciliation available to me tended to encourage white persons to reflect upon, rather than commune with and learn from, nonwhite persons. The works of Jennings and Carter, on the other hand, have helped me to discern where the problem lies in most of these constructs. Through their language of supersessionism, they are able to pinpoint the manner in which the Christian-qua-Westerner imagines other peoples on a continuum of salvific potential. It is as if, in the post-colonial Christian imagination, non-European peoples play the roles of spokes radiating outward from a hub occupied by the Occidental Jesus-as-cultural-reflex. This hierarchical presumption inaugurated the modern concept of race and remains the field upon which race continues to function.

Since Christian self-identity in the modern world tends to function within the trope of race, skin color is the assumed index of the distance one has had to travel to be grafted into the narrative of salvation. The darker the body, the more miraculous is its salvation within common Christian missiology. While many Christians, schooled as they have been in an ethic of "colorblindness," would be loath to admit that the soteriological framework of the Western church tilts on a racial axis, the common parlance and imagery of both missions and social justice work betrays this reality. A more honest appraisal of the visceral reactions of our collective Christian imagination would reveal this racial calculus. Jennings utilizes the offense of the story of the Syrophonecian woman to illustrate just how tortured are such theological assumptions. The scandal of this story is not that a "Christian" Jesus discourages the "heathen" body from coming to table but that Gentiles can be invited to a table not their own only by taking the name of the Messiah of Israel upon their lips. In the gospels, Jesus is amazed when the faith of a non-Jew is displayed through that person's submission to a story not her own.[1] For the white subject to be brought into communion with YHWH, he or she must approach the divine as "Other": as another people's God. The white subject is grafted into the story of Jesus as an alien and stranger whose identity becomes conjoined with the identity of others who are likewise making the journey out of static self-actualization into ecstatic identity-as-gift.

I have demonstrated the ways in which Carter and Jennings discern the limitations of common ways of theologically imagining Christian identity in a globalized world. I have suggested that both Milbank's Radical Orthodoxy and Hauerwas' MacIntyrian virtue ethic, while helpful in introducing the church to distortions common to liberal modernity and the nation-state, reproduce problematic racialized conceptions of moral formation characteristic of a retreat into Anglo-Catholic ways of imagining the world. As highly influential theological trajectories, offering compelling ways to imagine Christian identity, their contours are replicated through many popular Incarnational and missional frameworks. At the same time, neither Carter nor Jennings trusts modern liberal religious or cultural studies to offer a less paternalistic assessment of the world's peoples. If Western Christian reclamation projects are assimilationist, the relativizing sensibilities of studies related to "religion" or "ethnography" tend to be segregationist. My account has suggested that joining is possible only inasmuch as diverse peoples share local space in the field of a new body politic. Carter and Jennings have proposed that this sociopolitical order is the person of Jesus Christ. While such a claim may initially sound imperialist, a denial of the particularity of the central revelation of God proves to be profoundly imperialist, as it denies the revelatory nature of particularity. Particularity itself can be maintained only inasmuch as its existence is a scandal. Frameworks that jump straight to the universal trample the particularities of all peoples underfoot or require that those particularities exist at a safe distance from one another.

If, as Jennings and Carter have claimed, the way forward out of racialization is a radical joining not unlike miscegenation, an ecclesiology of joining is required. Since both Radical Orthodoxy and Hauerwasian virtue

---

1. See, for example, Matt 8:8–10.

ethics are framed primarily in ecclesiological terms, I propose to illustrate the practical entailments of a contrasting ecclesiology shaped around the Christology of joining offered by Jennings and Carter. I offer these concluding reflections in order to draw together the shared emphases of Jennings and Carter, and to develop this trajectory in light of my own discoveries as a pastor being remade through joining. I begin with a theological exegesis of two biblical passages, one from the Lucan Jesus and one Pauline, which I interpret against the grain of Occidental hegemony.

As I briefly reengage an oft-quoted Lucan pericope, I hope to arrive at an unfamiliar alternative narrative reading. This approach echoes that of Jennings, whose theological exegesis of the second chapter of Ephesians, teamed with the story of Jesus and the Syrophoenician woman, displays the aesthetic power of joining. Through his autobiographical introduction, his narrative of four seemingly unrelated historical characters, and his invitation to share hermeneutical space, Jennings displays a posture of joining which I would like to inhabit. Likewise, Carter indicates that racialization is challenged by "a particular way of reading Scripture—reading against rather than within the grain of the social order."[2] I will present an interpretation of the Scriptures influenced by having my ears attuned to the interests of Jennings and Carter and the perspectives of my neighbors.

I will then briefly investigate the Christological politics of Bantum, a theologian whose work is intellectually indebted to Jennings and Carter, and whose work I read as stopping short of articulating the scandalous ecclesiology toward which his own Christology points. Following this brief excursion, I will develop Bantum's incipient ecclesiology by discussing practices which I propose are consonant with the ecclesial embodiment delineated by Carter and Jennings. I will organize these reflections around the practice of eating together as paradigmatic for additional components that invite further study. Like Carter, I will look to a helpful moment in Eastern Orthodox practice as I offer my constructive ecclesiology of joining. As I begin to sketch an outline of what such an ecclesiology may entail, I will be guided by aspects of my own experiences in conversation with the scandalous Christology of the theological race theory of Jennings and Carter. My aim, in the end, is to offer a theological account directing the reader to the dynamics involved in Christian joining in particular places. It is my hope that, in discovering a nonsupersessionist and miscegenistic conceptualization of Christian identity, the church will find a way of life in which objectification of the "other" is inconceivable.

2. Carter, *Race*, 344.

Theological Exegesis

The "Good" Samaritan

Perhaps no biblical text is referenced more often in modern popular par-lance than the parable of Jesus in Luke 10 about a man beaten and left for dead, who was shown mercy by a traveler who cared for his wounds and provided him patronage at a hostel. The title "The Good Samaritan" has become a proverbial image of a person who demonstrates unusual compas-sion and courage by giving of herself to care for the needs of another. This New Testament story is one of the few into which white rationality unam-biguously reads itself as the non-Jewish persona in the tableau of characters. The white subject is apparently uncomfortable identifying with the Jewish characters in this parable, one of whom is lying on the side of the road in need of assistance, and the others of whom pass by unwilling to come to his aid. Whiteness is accustomed to assuming the power position of "Savior" status. It is instinctual for expositors of this text to encourage the hearer to identify with the Samaritan by committing deeds of benevolence on behalf of those "unable" to help themselves.

The familiar title given this passage comes not from the biblical text it-self but from Western hermeneutical traditions.[3] As with many designations formed in the wake of the racial imagination, the irony of this title appears to be lost on modern commentators. The application of an adjective in order to clarify that a specific person is "this" one and not "another" clearly carries with it the implication that "this" one is qualitatively different than all the "others" like him. For a specific Samaritan to be called "good" betrays the assumption that the collective character of those designated as "Samaritan" must be flawed. The foregoing analysis indicates why such a generalization is the reflex of a racialized calculus. Were a title of this sort to be newly applied to any ethnic group or other identity designation, this characteristic would become obvious. "The good Jew"; "the good European"; "the good African";

---

3. While it is not known when the phrase itself was first used, the figurative use of "Samaritan" as one to be emulated by Europeans in caring for the poor may be traced to a book published in London by Peter Chamberlen in 1649 entitled *The Poore Mans Advocate, or, Englands Samaritan*. The book was subtitled: "*Powring oyle and wyne into the wounds of the nation. By making present provision for the soldier and the poor, by reconciling all parties. By paying all arreares to the Parliament army. All publique debts, and all the late kings, queenes, and princes debts due before this session.*" Imagining the Samaritan as a Christian engaged with the "world" is carried forward through many popular accounts of Christian identity, including that of Francis Schaeffer in *The Mark of the Christian*, 18: "Christians are not to love their believing brothers to the exclusion of their non-believing fellowmen. That is ugly. We are to have the example of the Good Samaritan consciously in mind at all times."

"the good woman"; "the good white man"; these would all clearly display assumptions about virtue and identity. Perhaps Jesus' story undermines such static ethical and ontological categories. If this is the case, this profound irony has largely escaped notice. I maintain that while whiteness has identified itself with the Samaritan, it has classified this particular Samaritan as "good" in order to distance itself from ethnic hybridity in general. The supersessionist imagination can be seen in these interpretive moves.

Following Jennings, I suggest that ethnic identities and cultural self-identifications (particularly regarding the relationship of Jew and Gentile) should not be read as incidental in stories told by Jesus. If the scandal of particularity is expressed through sharing the space of the body of Jesus of Nazareth, then Jesus' incorporation of ethnicity and cultural identity into his parables can be taken as instructive for a contemporary ecclesiology of race and place. The Lucan pericope in question opens as a Jewish legal expert, a *nomikos*—a teacher and arbitrator in the Mosaic law—addresses Jesus. He is offered in turn a story in which a person of mixed ethnic ancestry is presented as an exemplar of neighborly care.

> 25 And behold, a lawyer stood up to put him to the test, saying, "Teacher, what shall I do to inherit eternal life?" 26 He said to him, "What is written in the Law? How do you read it?" 27 And he answered, "You shall love the Lord your God with all your heart and with all your soul and with all your strength and with all your mind, and your neighbor as yourself." 28 And he said to him, "You have answered correctly; do this, and you will live." 29 But he, desiring to justify himself, said to Jesus, "And who is my neighbor?"[4]

The text maintains that the intention of the legal expert was to "put [Jesus] to the test;" his motivation was a desire "to justify himself." Jesus affirmed that the lawyer's textual interpretation was accurate; he had read the Scriptures correctly. He understood that election emanated from Israel, yet he interpreted the Law in a way that tightly drew the borders of neighborly kinship relations around himself. Could it be that Jesus' intention in this passage is to undermine a self-reflexive posture? There are good reasons in the text to read some form of attraction to a myth of racial purity in the behavior depicted of the Jewish lawyer. It is as if Jesus recognized in the legal expert's question regarding the identity of his neighbor the assumption of an insular mode of being. Jesus' narratival answer undermined a static ontology by clarifying how Jewish identity is to be understood. This suggests

4. Luke 10:25–29.

that the lawyer understood Jewish identity as "hermetically sealed"[5] rather than as reception of divine gift for the blessing of all peoples.[6] If this parable was Jesus' critique of one who was correct in claiming election for himself but incorrect in doing so in a way that ran contra to the particular-universal trajectory of the covenant, then how much more devastating would be the critique of Christ toward a Gentile people claiming for themselves ownership of a table at which they were guests and doing so in an even more totalizing and universalizing fashion? The latter, of course, is a quite accurate rendering of the sort of hubris evidenced by colonization and the modern pedagogical mandate adopted in its wake. While I recognize that my comments thus far could be interpreted as subtly reading whiteness into Jewish identity as "pure" racial identity and concomitantly reading "mixed" or bastardized ethnic identity (as categorized by whiteness) into the Samaritan figure, I am intentionally trying to carry my reflections in a different direction altogether in order to push against these static ontological categories.

The *nomikos* had been educated into an orthodox tradition; his pedagogical vision as an expert in the Mosaic Law was not in question. "You have answered correctly," Jesus replied in affirmation of the legal expert's assertion that loving YHWH and loving the neighbor is the path to inheritance of eternal life. The problem was not with the man's virtue or the orthodoxy of his tradition. The problem was the "middle work": the theological sleight-of-hand that privileged the speaker as the one defining the parameters of neighborly kinship relations. Jesus' answer came in the form of a narrative that unseated static ontological designations. He picked as the protagonist of his narrative a Samaritan: a man of mixed ethnic ancestry whose lineage in the prophetic imagination represented the unfaithfulness of the northern kingdom in forsaking YHWH and intermarrying with the *ethnos*.[7] The one whom the religious imagination of the day saw as a symbol of impure hybridity Jesus privileged as faithfully embodying the trajectory of joining.

As Jennings has articulated, the reason that stories such as that in which Jesus apparently rebuffs the Syrophoenician woman are so scandalously offensive to our modern ears is because we have misinterpreted the theological scandal of particularity.[8] It is precisely because the modern Western interpreter places himself in the position of Jesus "looking down" on the Gentile woman that our contemporary liberal hermeneutic dictates

5. Carter, *Race*, 366.

6. See the Abrahamic covenant in Gen 12:1–3.

7. See the historical account of 1 Kgs 16:24–34 and the prophetic reflection of Ezek 16:44–55, in which Samaria is used as a counterweight to Israel in order to magnify the magnitude of the sins of Israel.

8. Jennings, *Christian Imagination*, 160, 262.

that it is of necessity offensive. Because the modern interpreter reads Jewish identity within the strictures of modern racialized identity and because whiteness has privileged itself as "chosen" (and has designated blackness or hybridity as "taint"), Jesus' response to the Canaanite woman is of necessity racist. However, if it is the case that the universal offer of salvation and provision extends from the particular table of Israel-Jesus, then Jesus' response should be interpreted in exactly the opposite direction. Jesus' offer of crumbs to the non-Israelite becomes an extreme offer of grace in that such inclusion is undeserved and does not rely upon the ability of the creature to self-actualize.

As is the case with Jesus' parables, the hearer is expected to find himself in this Lucan story. Herein lies the scandal of the parable, a scandal that whiteness seems to have failed to recognize. It is clearly implied that the legal expert would identify with the Jewish man in the ditch:

> 30 Jesus replied, "A man was going down from Jerusalem to Jericho, and he fell among robbers, who stripped him and beat him and departed, leaving him half dead. 31 Now by chance a priest was going down that road, and when he saw him he passed by on the other side. 32 So likewise a Levite, when he came to the place and saw him, passed by on the other side.[9]

Because of ceremonial purity laws, the Jewish legal expert would likely sympathize with the priest's and the Levite's avoidance of a bleeding body near death.[10] Similarly, the *nomikos* would not desire to be identified with the Samaritan, especially a man who touched an "unclean" body lying in a ditch. It would not be the logical option for the lawyer to read himself into the position of the ones avoiding the beaten man or the one doing the "helping." It would naturally be the case that he would place himself in the position of the man whose identity proceeded from Jerusalem, the one who was "going down" from there, the man whom Jesus scandalously pictures as lying naked and half dead alongside the road, the man in the position of being helped. It is this man who has no speech; it is this man who is not self-articulating; it is this man who is forced to receive his very life back from the unlike other. It is this man who was refused help by his own people, with whom his own people refused to be identified, "pass[ing] by on the other side" presumably so as to follow the tenets of the Levitical law of which the lawyer was an expert. Like the man who had been beaten, the lawyer was the one who needed to receive his identity from another.

9. Luke 10:30–32.

10. See Lev 21 and Num 19, where to touch a human corpse is to incur the state of uncleanness.

33 But a Samaritan, as he journeyed, came to where he was, and when he saw him, he had compassion. 34 He went to him and bound up his wounds, pouring on oil and wine. Then he set him on his own animal and brought him to an inn and took care of him. 35 And the next day he took out two denarii and gave them to the innkeeper, saying, 'Take care of him, and whatever more you spend, I will repay you when I come back.' 36 Which of these three, do you think, proved to be a neighbor to the man who fell among the robbers?" 37 He said, "The one who showed him mercy." And Jesus said to him, "You go, and do likewise."[11]

The only person to speak in the parable is the one who challenged the assumption of self-constitution. The Samaritan, the one who millennia later could be identified as "mulatto" in the Iberian *limpieza de sangre* laws, is the one who is given a voice by the Lord. He is the one who is moved by compassion; he is the one who unguardedly sets the wounded man "on his own animal;" he is the one who "took care of him;" he is the one who provided out of his own resources for the continued care of the man. Jesus asked the legal expert: "Which of these three, do you think, proved to be a neighbor to the man who fell among the robbers?"

The syntax of Jesus' question is telling: He is asking the expert in the Law which of the characters "proved to be a neighbor *to the* man," not which person *to whom* the wounded man was a neighbor. This is a critical distinction. Jesus was not putting the lawyer in the driver's seat of being able to choose his own neighbors or in the powerful position of being the one to help another, thereby becoming a good neighbor. The question Jesus asked was in response to the previous query from the lawyer: "And who is *my* neighbor?" The Jewish lawyer had (not incorrectly) positioned himself in the center and asked who the neighbor was in relation to himself.[12] Perhaps he had been developing an intimation that the invitation to YHWH's table extended further than he had originally expected. Jesus assumed the lawyer's stance in order to expand it by positioning the broken, beaten man in the center and asking who the neighbor was *in relation to* the Jewish

11. Luke 10:33–37.

12. Again, the *nomikos* was certainly right to identify Jewish identity as central to divine redemption. The problem seems to be that he failed to remember how this identity was to function: as a center of blessing for all peoples. My point is not to present the lawyer in a "bad light," but to demonstrate that inasmuch as whiteness does something similar in its identity reflections it is even more problematic. Additionally, it should be remembered that I have interpreted Jennings' terminology of supersessionism as primarily a problematic mode of imagination and secondarily as a systematic doctrinal misstep. Therefore, my interpretation of this parable is an attempt to identify Jesus' response to similarly problematic modes of imagination.

man. Jesus did not decentralize Jewish identity but rather challenged the narrow stance of relationality posed by the legal expert. In assuming that the *nomikos* would not identify himself with a Samaritan, Jesus intended that the lawyer be encouraged to identify the neighbor as the unlike other from whom he could receive his very life.

The question posed by Jesus, in reply to the lawyer's original question, required a difficult answer: "Which of these three . . . proved to be a neighbor?" This question necessitated a response that identified in the affirmative the "other" of mixed ethnic ancestry who, in this story, occupied the position of power through service. The legal expert was constrained to identify himself as broken and in need of help in the form of mutuality. He hesitated to name the "helper" in his feeble reply: "*The one* who showed him mercy." The lawyer did not allow the title "Samaritan" to pass his lips. The "Samaritan" of Jesus' story became "the one" within the legal expert's classificatory response. Much in the same way as traditions of virtue tend to designate people as "poor" or as "other," tacitly assigning them space somewhere along a racialized continuum, the legal expert of generations past categorized "the one" who pressed on his own borders of kinship and called his static identity formulations into question.

This Lucan pericope, from the Gentile Evangelist who focused his narrative upon the marginalized, ends with Jesus' simple command: "You go, and do likewise." Generations of Christians have taken this command as a mandate for service out of a position of power, a sort of exhortation for helping the poor and broken out of their own self-sufficient means.[13] Yet a simple reading of the story does not encourage such a potentially paternalistic interpretation. The character in Jesus' story pictured as "going" was the "man" who "was going down from Jerusalem": the one with whom the lawyer had cast his lot. It was the "going" one who would be incapacitated,

---

13. Martin Luther King Jr. can be said to have followed a similar interpretive tendency when, in his last sermon, in Memphis, "I've Been to the Mountaintop," he asked what would happen to people wounded along the road if he did not help them. However, there are several important distinctions between King's speech and traditional "white" interpretation. First, King recognized that issues of race were at play in this parable. Second, he was explicitly resisting the distinction between the "I" and the "thou," thereby contending against static views of race. Third, his audience and the sanitation workers he was encouraging them to join with were both largely African American (which demonstrates that he was not assuming the paternalist tendency of many white Americans to read themselves as the "Samaritan" helping the poor "other"). Fourth, King was clear in this speech (as in many others) that his work would help heal those whom he called his "sick white brothers." Therefore, while King was employing the Samaritan as a means to "help" rather than "be helped," he was doing it from the underside of power and not from its pinnacle (the latter of which is the common interpretive posture of whiteness).

laid out on the side of the road, and unable to sustain himself through his self-appropriated resources. It was the *nomikos* who was told by Jesus to "go" and "do." Would this not have encouraged the legal expert to recognize that the mandate to "go" required that in his "going," he would "do" that which the "man" had done: allow himself to be helped by the unlike other so as to receive his own being back from that one? The posture of whiteness discourages such an interpretation. While whiteness has consistently read itself into Judaic election in the Scriptures, in this case it has most often firmly ensconced itself in Gentile identity so as to miss Jesus' point about the destruction of a static ontology through a process of joining with Israel.[14]

A similar claim can be made about the interpretive tendency of whiteness as it relates to Pauline language about the body of Christ. Unable or unwilling to recognize the theological scandal of particularity as the hermeneutical horizon within which to read somatic language of joining, whiteness interprets language of reconciliation (*katallage*, or exchange) as an invitation to *koinonia* extended from its own resources. Contrary to this assumption of hermeneutical privilege, Jennings draws from his exegesis of Ephesians 2:11–22 the Pauline conclusion that Gentile existence is that which had been without hope and "without God in the world."[15] While Paul is the apostle to the Gentiles, and while he characteristically waxes eloquent that "[t]here is neither Jew nor Greek, there is neither slave nor free, there is neither male nor female, for you are all one in Christ Jesus," he recognizes that to become "Christ's" is to become "Abraham's offspring."[16] For Paul, election is not distended into a conception of divine predestination of the individual either to approbation or reprobation.[17] Pauline reconciliation is that which takes place within the divine election of a particular people as an invitation to all peoples to be joined to her.[18]

14. Even if it is a valid interpretive move to recognize in Jesus' parable the need to help others, white interpretation should at least recognize that the call in this case would be to join with the Jewish brother in his moment of need (rather than a blanket appeal to helping "the poor" out of its own self-sufficiency).

15. Jennings, *Christian Imagination*, 271–75.

16. Gal 3:28–29.

17. This view is characteristically held by the American Reformed tradition as narrowly refracted through the Synod of Dort. This is the theological legacy embodied in Puritanism and within which the election of the "settlers" of the New World was affirmed.

18. See the progression of Romans chapters 9–11, which, read in totality and in context, does not have the election of individuals on its thematic "radar," so to speak. Even where an individual is referenced, as in the case of Pharaoh, that individual stands in as representative for a people. See especially Rom 11:25–36, in which Paul invokes the complete salvation of Israel and maintains that her election is for the purpose of

The Body of Christ

It is within this latter framework that we approach Paul's great invocation of the body in 1 Corinthians 12. This passage presents the body of Christ as existent precisely in the shared space in which diverse peoples are joined one to another. It is this image which will provide the backdrop for my constructive ecclesiology of joining.

According to a Pauline somatic ecclesiology, the church is present inasmuch as there is a diversity of ethnic and socioeconomic groups functioning together in whole and healthy bodily unity as they are joined to their head, the Jewish Lord. This image is predicated by the Eucharistic language of 1 Corinthians 11, in which the existence of ecclesial divisions along socioeconomic lines is "not the Lord's supper" but is rather an "unworthy" feast that "profane[es] the body and blood of the Lord."[19] My constructive ecclesiology will suggest a path forward for joining in which table fellowship does not replicate this mistake.[20] In the context of eating, Paul turns his attention to the existence of the body *as* the diversity of *ethnos* being joined together in local space. For Paul, the scandal of the body of Christ is that people who have no business being together are intentionally intermeshing their lives in shared space so as to constitute a new creature (a new "people"), an inseparable whole in which difference is maintained while being conjoined.

> 12 For just as the body is one and has many members, and all the members of the body, though many, are one body, so it is with Christ. 13 For in one Spirit we were all baptized into one body—Jews or Greeks, slaves or free—and all were made to drink of one Spirit. 14 For the body does not consist of one member but of many. 15 If the foot should say, "Because I am not a hand, I do not belong to the body," that would not make it

---

mercy being offered to all. After this affirmation of mercy for all *ethnos* through the election of Israel, Paul breaks into ebullient doxology at the wisdom and knowledge of the God whose judgments are inscrutable.

19. See 1 Cor 11:17–34, especially verses 20 and 27.

20. While I use language of Eucharist, I do so not to replicate Anglo-Catholic views of Eucharist but to subvert their tendencies toward aesthetic elitism. I suggest that the Lord's Supper is not so much a liturgical act with definable contours as it is a local process of entering into a characteristically Jewish practice with connections to the land: dining together from the fruit of creation as entrance into relationship with YHWH. This feast will be enacted differently in different locations: its form must not be "imported" but intimately connected with the local place in which it is practiced. The Lord's Supper is the practice of joining with a Jewish feast (Passover) with all the historical significance and particularity that it entails.

any less a part of the body. 16 And if the ear should say, "Because I am not an eye, I do not belong to the body," that would not make it any less a part of the body. 17 If the whole body were an eye, where would be the sense of hearing? If the whole body were an ear, where would be the sense of smell? 18 But as it is, God arranged the members in the body, each one of them, as he chose. 19 If all were a single member, where would the body be? 20 As it is, there are many parts, yet one body. 21 The eye cannot say to the hand, "I have no need of you," nor again the head to the feet, "I have no need of you."[21]

The Eucharistic imagery of 1 Corinthians 11 extends into this passage as Paul invokes "Jews" and "Greeks," "slave" and "free" together being made "to drink of one Spirit." Contrary to the proclivity of modern interpretation, this passage does not first and foremost invoke the ideal of a multiplicity of spiritual gifts functioning together in pragmatic fashion,[22] but rather paints a picture of different peoples together battling static identity formulations through a process of intermingling those identities with each other within the identity of the Jewish Messiah. Lest the church be tempted to interpret "body" language as being solely a coexistence of a multiplicity of charismata, or as an ethereal "spiritual" affiliation of all Christians of all ages in imaginary agreement, Paul clearly intends a much more radical interpretation. He rhetorically anticipates the conclusion that if various body parts—representative of socioeconomic and ethnic designations—are not physically joined together in particular local space, there is no body: "Where would the body be?"

That which Jennings and Carter describe as "joining," "mutual articulation," "miscegenation," and "speaking in tongues," afforded by an "*ekstasis*" of being, is that which Paul pictures as a shared somatic constitution. It should go without saying that a body is not present where only similar body parts are grouped or where certain body parts are attempting to manipulate

---

21. 1 Cor 12:12–21.

22. A popular example of this view, which demonstrates that prominent Evangelical Christians think of diversity in the body as primarily related to self-realization is the following text produced and marketed by Willow Creek Community Church: Bugbee, Bruce. *What You Do Best in the Body of Christ: Discover Your Spiritual Gifts, Personal Style, and God-Given Passion*. Grand Rapids: Zondervan, 2005. While I do not discount the importance of discerning spiritual gifts, that Paul's body language is interpreted in popular parlance as foremost a path toward self-fulfillment demonstrates the depth of the deformities of whiteness. The ecclesiological scandal toward which Paul is pointing is missing. Such accounts tend to reinforce the self-reflexive character of whiteness and to draw Christians away from recognizing the central importance of joining.

other body parts to assimilate to their form or function. A collection of like body parts or a positive evaluatory stance toward the unlike other cannot be regarded as a body. Utilizing Pauline language, it should be clear that a group of "feet," a collection of "hands," an assembly of "ears," or a gathering of "eyes" does not constitute a body. These grotesqueries instead constitute a dismembered corpse. A living and healthy body must share space and must include variegated body parts; it is of necessity a scandal to all the pseudo-theological evaluations of whiteness, including the oppositional logic of the identity politics that whiteness instigated. Neither assimilation nor separatism, even if that separatism is posed within a framework of imaginary unity or equality, amounts to a proper ecclesiology. Both movements initiated by whiteness, that toward assimilation to particular cultural ideals (through a retrieval of Occidental philosophical and didactic resources), and that toward a Jim Crow logic of mutual respect (through modern missiology and religious or cultural studies), are ecclesiologically aberrant.

The posture of whiteness must be exited in order for its particularities to be included in the body. This is not to say that white people should try to not be "white." While the spatially-constituted identity of European particularity is not in itself heretical, we have seen that this is not the manner in which such particularity has functioned. Practically speaking, white folks must realize that they have to submit to other parts of the body or they are living as if they are limbs "cut off" from the body. Additionally, they must remember that *they do not constitute the body*—that the Head of the body[23] is Jewish: not Western, not European, and not white. This is why Cone and Carter can allow for the possibility of "white" universality being subdued through joining to "black" particularity. In a world re-created by colonialism-modernity, the scandal of reconciliation must be expressed in terms of impurity. Miscegenation and joining as erotic imagery appear to be the only options available to approach the significance of the scandal toward which Jesus and Paul are pointing.

Bantum and the Christological politics of "Mulatto"

In his book *Redeeming Mulatto*, Bantum explores a Christology of miscegenation as reflective of the logic of Chalcedon.[24] I read Bantum as being quite helpful in dismantling the false gospel of racial purity by focusing his reflections upon the existence of the scandalous body of the mixed-race child as transgressive of idolatrous notions of essentialized identity. His work is

23. Col 1:18.
24. Bantum, *Redeeming Mulatto*.

important in breaking the black-white dichotomy in which identity politics such as those displayed in the work of Cone are entrenched. His Christology of miscegenation does this in a manner that retains the importance of the particularity of ethnicity without rendering it ontologically static. Early in his text, Bantum describes race as a reality that must be either lived into or resisted.[25] In this sense, the colonial-modern construction of race is a habitus into which one is discipled. As such, Christian discipleship into the life of the mulatto Christ, and the ecclesial community that bears his name, is a profoundly counter-cultural practice.[26] Bantum fills out these claims through an invocation of the definition of Chalcedon, which he reads as an apophatic formulation that resists static identity structures.[27] By articulating the person of Jesus in terms which Bantum characterizes as a "neither/nor—but" arrangement, orthodox Christology bears striking similarities to the body of the person of mixed-racial ancestry, whose identity is classified within modernity as "neither" white "nor" black. The disruptive presence and personhood of the "mulatto" body is the "but" which is a type of Christ in its scandalous conjoining of "natures." In this sense, Bantum's Christological reflections bear similarities to Carter, who speaks of the Body as miscegenated, and Jennings, who finds in the vulnerability of the Incarnation the formation of "habits of mind" able to resist the distortions of racialization. It is when Bantum is constructing this framework, and deconstructing racialized modernity, that his work is most penetrating and compelling.

As Bantum turns his attention to the "politics of identification," the "politics of presence," and the attendant "practices" which initiate and disciple the convert into the mulattic community, his theological schema begins to insufficiently distinguish itself from the Occidental retrieval impulse and the shape of its attendant practices. While Bantum's descriptions of the efficacy of practices such as baptism, the Eucharist, and prayer are theologically thick, he does not demonstrate how the specific shape of the practices he extols differs from the shape of the praxis enacted within the Anglo-Catholic tradition. To be sure, Bantum is quite careful to emphasize continually the myriad ways in which the practices of the church should be indicative of a "mulattic" Christology and an ecclesiology of "impure" mixing. However, his work tends to present discipleship into the life of the mulatto Christ, and out of the life of the hierarchical arrangements of racialization, as automatic given the presence of said practices properly performed. One is left

25. Ibid., 17.

26. This manner of formulating the issue reveals a Hauerwasian tendency in Bantum that I will analyze in some detail later in this section.

27. Bantum, *Redeeming Mulatto*, 90–91.

with the strong impression that when such practices "hit the ground," the didactic process of formation initiated by them will not of necessity differ from that which inculcates people into the virtues of whiteness. Bantum does not clarify *how* the Lord's Supper resists racialization or what it would look like to share in a feast of this nature. Bantum's strong and scandalous Christology gives way to an ecclesiology that is considerably less surprising.

I intend to utilize Bantum's radical Christological insights in order to draw out the more incipiently radical aspects of his ecclesiology. My basic contention is that Bantum draws on a Hauerwasian ecclesiology that, for all its emphasis on the counter-cultural nature of the practices of the Church, does not clearly challenge the assumptions and practices of racialization. If, as Bantum so compellingly concludes, whiteness has initiated a habitus into which all bodies must be discipled, how then should Christian disciple-ship function so as to resist the disciplines of whiteness? Surely the material practices of baptism, the Eucharist, and prayer do not in and of themselves produce an ecclesia potent to resist the assimilationist motif of coloniality-modernity. For instance, the Eucharistic practices of Christopher Columbus and Acosta were not aberrant from the standpoint of orthopraxy. Likewise, the contemporary weekly reception of the body and blood in homogenous local worshipping communities throughout the West is not performed in a manner that is contrary to the received tradition of the Church. In fact, it is precisely in such a tradition that a racialized hierarchy was constructed and continues to flourish. In a post-colonial world, the assumption that, through performance of the sacraments, novitiates will be formed into a maturity potent to subvert the principalities of racialization begins to look rather naïve. Bantum's claim, in relation to the spiritual disciplines, that the person of Jesus Christ "is" reconciliation (i.e. "faith, hope, and love") tends to assume a direct correlative relationship between practices such as the Eucharist and the interrelationship of particular lives.[28]

It is my contention that these limitations in the work of Bantum exist because of the complexities of his dual relationship at Duke to Hauerwas' school of virtue-ethics and Jennings' and Carter's school of theological race theory.[29] It is telling that in his *Acknowledgements*, Bantum thanks Hauer-was, his doctoral supervisor, that he "*allowed* [him] the freedom to pur-sue this research,"[30] but names Carter an "endless reservoir of ideas" and

28. Ibid., 135.

29. See ibid., 3, where Bantum situates his theology according to Carter's poles of Milbank and Cone, which he calls "*the* theological trajectories before the contemporary church."

30. Ibid., ix, italics mine.

Jennings the one who "taught [him] to be a theologian."[31] The suggestion seems to be that the tradition of virtue is a transitional system that "allows" for inquiry related to race, while the Jenningsian/Carterian school is that which properly locates that inquiry theologically.

Associate professor of religion at Baylor University and former student of Hauerwas,' Tran, has written an essay for one of Hauerwas' festschrifts, *Unsettling Arguments*, entitled "Time for Hauerwas' Racism."[32] Tran reads the silence of Hauerwas in regard to race as a blessed silence of repentance intentionally inhabited by Hauerwas due to a recognition of his own "provinciality" as a child of Southern "Klan culture."[33] Tran references Bantum in order to demonstrate that Hauerwas, by recognizing the limitations of his own particularity, is able to give consent to projects he would not himself author.[34] While providing a positive evaluation of the morality of Hauerwas' personal praxis, Tran does not explore the myriad ways the aesthetic elitism of a tradition of virtue may discourage its proponents from satisfactorily conceptualizing the theological problem of race. Tran, like Bantum, does not entertain the possibility that a MacIntyrian virtue ethic is itself encouraging of the sort of "sophisticated" racism which Tran finds to exist among academic "elites."[35] Is it not the case that Tran is gracious with Hauerwas and Hauerwas gracious with Bantum precisely because of the deep bonds of friendship formed between them? Recognition of the beauty of mutuality should not preclude recognition of the ways in which a particular tradition might produce a lacuna in the theological views of its proponents in regard to race. Instead, Tran maintains that Hauerwas' theologically unsatisfactory comments on race are "downright un-Hauerwasian!"[36] Whereas I read Tran as working primarily in a tradition of virtue, I read Bantum as more thoroughly influenced by the theological race theory of Jennings and Carter. I suggest that Bantum's ecclesiology does not as sufficiently inhabit this trajectory as does his Christology.

Tran tends to presuppose a sort of determinism about the ability of people of various ethnicities to employ or understand appropriate speech about race.[37] His reflections imply that a white author is limited in his ability

31. Ibid., x.

32. Tran, "Time for Hauerwas' Racism," 246–64.

33. Ibid., 254.

34. Ibid., 251.

35. Ibid., 254.

36. Ibid., 255.

37. See Ibid., 255–56, where Tran recounts the way a "white audience" might respond to an unsophisticated assertion about race, as compared to "befuddled colored folks" like himself. This move may have the net effect of further encasing whites in an

to articulate the distorting effects of the rationality of whiteness without collapsing into "nervous verbosity."[38] This formulation implicitly calls whites to greater internal scrutiny in the face of what he frames as the paradoxical nature of a white person commenting on race, in which case he finds silence to be the generally better option.[39] This trajectory may further enclose whites in a self-centered intellectual spiral and may tend to reaffirm the binary logic of identity politics against which Jennings' thesis contends. Silence does not encourage the sort of mutuality and interdependence that allows for confession, correction, and redirection.

It remains that Bantum better discerns the problematic self-reflexive nature of whiteness than does Tran. He articulates the impossible place in which white people, through the hubris of "the European colonial project," have attempted to stand.[40] As he articulates the question posed to African Americans by Du Bois over one hundred years ago, "How does it feel to be a problem?," Bantum recognizes that the "fundamental assumption" of colonialism is lodged in the question, "How does it feel to be the answer?" As I move into the constructive portion of my treatment, I join with Bantum by suggesting a possible answer to his question: It is dizzying to assume the ultimately self-referential mode of existence that is whiteness. There is a deep anxiety attendant to this attempted way of living beyond the limits of creaturely bounds. One can only wonder if a large part of the compulsion, objectification, and therapeutic obsession characteristic of Western society is fundamentally the maturation of the posture of whiteness. Surely anthropological assumptions that position the human body in the place of the Creator carry with them deeply unhealthy patterns of creaturely life. While the subjugation wrought upon non-white peoples is comparably the greater tragedy by far, it is at least worth noting that the inculcation of young white intellectuals, ministers, and scholars into the deeply self-reflexive patterns of reflection characteristic of whiteness is a tragedy of lesser magnitude. I am firmly convinced that *the only path to redemption* is in intimacy with the unlike other from whom one can receive his own identity. I now turn to suggesting a path toward this mutuality in shared space. I will orient my ecclesiology of joining around the practice of eating together, which intimates the practices of sharing place, participating in one another, and engaging in a mutually-articulated proclamation.

---

obsessively introspective racial logic while granting nonwhites a sort of "free pass" in speaking about race.

38. Ibid., 251.
39. Ibid., 257–61.
40. Bantum, *Redeeming Mulatto*, 7.

An Ecclesiology of Joining: Practices

Eating Together

Within the local community I pastor, we somewhat unintentionally stumbled upon the Lord's Supper as a genuine outgrowth of the community. As a congregation comprised largely of residents of our economically disadvantaged neighborhoods, we desired that each Sunday be an opportunity to be fed both spiritually and physically. Without initially having the resources to spread a feast each week, and having witnessed the objectification and kinship fragmentation characteristic of soup kitchens, food pantries, and the like, we began a carry-in meal for which people could bring a dish to share, rather than a hand-out in which power disparities were maintained. As the congregation grew in size, we found it necessary to develop a rotation whereby a diverse variety of people prepared the main dish for the day, the ingredients being paid for from the church budget and selected by that week's "chef." While people are still encouraged to bring a side dish, there is neither an effort to coordinate a culinary theme nor to identify those who may have been unable or unwilling to bring a dish to share on a given day. If we are lucky, someone will have picked fresh vegetables from our community garden in which neighborhood residents can "work together—eat together." I have often been humbled and amazed that those who are most generous are often those who have the least economically to share with others. Food stamps being used to make large pots of chili and aluminum cans being redeemed for money to buy drinks for children upset assumptions about identity. While in our congregation economic disparity and ethnic identity are by no means aligned, there is little that is more beautiful than witnessing a normally self-reliant person receiving the bread of life from the hand of one who may otherwise have been objectified as "poor" or as a recipient of "charity." Like the man in the ditch, those who normally have the resources to go where they would like begin to recognize their need to be helped and healed by another (and, in so doing, be given eyes to see and ears to hear what they would not otherwise have seen or heard).

An unforeseen aspect of this shared meal is that preconceived assumptions about identity as static are beautifully upset as people who should not be eating together receive their daily bread from the hand of the unlike other. There is not much that requires more vulnerability than white folks trying to figure out how to eat collard greens with ham hocks and hot sauce and black folks wondering what in the world a soupy green bean casserole is all about. It is especially poignant when a relocator to our neighborhood or a visiting person interested in "mission" or "social justice" (usually a curious

Caucasian) is unable to classify "who is who" in such a meal.[41] It is a regular reminder that if various socioeconomic distinctions and ethnic identities are not being enfolded into one another, "Where would the body be?" The lines between *oikos* and *ecclesia* are blurred as foods which are commonly served only in homogenous familial settings are now extended throughout the family of God. Both static socioeconomic status and racialized identity are called into question as a person experiences being provided for by a person she did not expect. While as a church we still regularly partake in the Pauline-Christocentric words of institution around a shared cup and loaf, hosted by an intentionally diverse and ever-changing rotation of community members, the post-service meal remains one of the most important practices for discipling people out of racialized (and "economized") identity and into Gentilic identity as mutual participants in the miscegenated body of the Jewish Jesus.

I want to stress that the shape of this meal was not a pre-planned practice for the purpose of producing joining. Rather, it was an outgrowth of the joined, albeit imperfect, community. People had already been invited, by someone of another ethnicity or socioeconomic group, to be guests at tables not their own in homes not their own. Many uncomfortable social interactions and humbling experiences had preceded the mutual recognition of the beauty of intermingling identities in ways that questioned preferences, positions, and power. Eating together did not "automatically" produce joining; the vulnerability of mutuality produced a table that repeatedly catechizes the community in an ecclesiology of joining. Jennings' historical analysis suggests that the aesthetic shape of Christ's table is not to be "exported," as is often the case with Western Eucharistic practice or orchestrated events aimed at "reconciliation." The litmus test of joining is not how much Communion you have had together or how many services of "Christian unity" you have participated in but who comes to your children's birthday parties and who you call on when burdened and alone.

---

41. Who is who? Who is being served? Who is serving? Conceptions of mission and social justice forged in whiteness usually operate around being able to clearly distinguish such matters. Notice the propensity of those in "helping professions" to guard against what is considered "role confusion." In fields such as pastoral ministry, social work, and psychology, reciprocity between parties is often seen as an impediment to the process. Distance is purposely maintained. The relationship is often predicated upon an imbalance of power which must be sustained in order for the relationship to continue. This suggests that there is often a vested interest for those in service professions that the one being "helped" remain reliant upon the one doing the "helping." My thoughts on this matter (and some of my language) have been influenced in part by Nouwen, *In the Name of Jesus* and several of the aforementioned works by Lupton.

The table suggested by this analysis is a shared place where the diverse body joined in Jesus is hosted by the Nazarene as mediated through the community. In this case, a lived ecclesiology of joining drives the "liturgical" practices, not the other way around. What may be a doctrinally "thick" liturgy may in fact be ecclesiologically and Christologically "weak" if it does not encourage the lived unseating of static identity structures in the community formed by its observance. These are some of the signposts that point to the radical ecclesiology suggested by Jennings and Carter and that distinguish an ecclesiology of joining from reclamations of "tradition."

Before exploring several contemporary theological accounts of eating together, I want to briefly indicate the three additional practices that I will suggest for further study at the end of this Conclusion. Our eating together has been shaped by the practices of place-sharing, participation in the life of the unlike other, and mutual proclamation in previously unfamiliar linguistic cadences. By practicing what Jennings has called "living where we should not," by participating in each other's lives through submission as guests, and by learning to hear and speak the promises of God in cultural expressions not our own, our eating together more fully reflects the life of the joining community. This eating together is not something to be had nor does it reflect something that has been achieved. Rather, it is a stepping stone in a messy and beautiful journey of together walking in faith into the unknown. As a practice, it is as imperfect as the community that it images. As will be seen, it is something different than what is commonly described in contemporary theological literature regarding the Eucharist. It is an eating consonant with the ecclesiology suggested by Jennings and Carter. I now turn to analyzing four contemporary theological accounts of sharing table in order to demonstrate the peculiar contours of an ecclesiology of joining.

Bantum

As I have suggested, Bantum discerns the formative nature of practices such as sharing table yet does not clearly demonstrate how he imagines their deployment to differ from their enactment within a tradition that produced the claims to racial purity that he is resisting. His constructive work tends to assume a causal relationship between practices performed and particular lives joined:

> This life of discipleship can be rendered only through the mulattic shape of its birth and life . . . This life of discipleship birthed in the baptismal moment bound us to the very bread of life, the Lord's Supper or Eucharist. Discipleship is the daily existence

arising out of and stretching toward. This yearning, this con-
forming . . . constantly displays a mulattic re-creation and disruption conceived in the desire of the Father for us. It is birthed
through the womb of Christ and enfolded within the enduring
presence of the Spirit in our very bodies.[42]

Bantum utilizes patristics and the wisdom of the tradition in regard
to the spiritual disciplines to suggest that a life marked by the practices of
the church *is* a life that is resistant to a racialized hierarchy. While I do not
disagree that this *can* be the case, I purpose to fill out his claim by offering
a theological account of eating together that bears within it the seeds of
an ecclesiology that combats racialization. Surely more or better-performed
Eucharist, baptism, and prayer do not in and of themselves pose a direct
challenge to the distortions inherent in the colonial-modern Christian
imagination. On the contrary, as Paul contends, liturgical eating can be
either a "participation"[43] in the body and blood of the Lord or something
that is "not the Lord's supper."[44] Rather than the practice constituting the
community, Paul finds that the feast "discern[s] the body."[45] Pauline Communion is a heuristic to explore the lived ecclesiology at work in local
communities of faith. If it is eaten in a manner that reinforces factions, socioeconomic distinctions, or static ethnic identity, the Eucharist becomes a
feast of judgment.[46]

Many theological accounts of Eucharist do not acknowledge that the
feast has the potential to *not* be the body and blood of the Lord if performed
by an ecclesial community that reinforces divisions. Paul utilizes a similar
argument two chapters later in 1 Corinthians 13 as he contends that any
practice has the potential to be nothing more than noise and disruption,
working *against* the constitution of the body of Christ.[47] For Paul, the validity of Christian communion comes not from aesthetic practices properly
performed but from the vulnerability of love displayed in Christian communities marked by difference.[48] Jennings' and Carter's work suggests that
if the enactment of table-fellowship does not proceed from the scandalous
shared life of a diverse people joined in a particular place, it may work
against the Body.

42. Bantum, *Redeeming Mulatto*, 169.

43. 1 Cor 10:16–17.

44. 1 Cor 11:20.

45. 1 Cor 11:29.

46. 1 Cor 11:29–30.

47. 1 Cor 13:1.

48. 1 Cor 13:5, 12.

Bretherton

In *Hospitality as Holiness*, Luke Bretherton presents an account of Christian ethics as hospitality.[49] Bretherton interacts extensively with MacIntyre, whose account of Christian ethics as rational moral debate grounded in a Thomist account of the virtues he finds to be compelling, while taking issue with several points.[50] Chief among these criticisms is that Bretherton does not find ethical discourse to be imagined best as "rivalry between competing traditions."[51] He contends that such an account lacks an emphasis on the eschatological dimension of relations between Christians and non-Christians. He softens Hauerwas' emphasis on the distinction between the Church and the world and suggests that the life of the Church is intrinsically interwoven with the life of her neighbors.[52]

Yet Bretherton's emphasis does not amount to a critique of the Western tradition of virtue as the best path to reconciliation with one's neighbor. He explains that his motif of hospitality is "in line with the model for tradition-situated reflection and deliberation" he draws from MacIntyre and Oliver O'Donovan.[53] Bretherton is attempting to chart a course that is less objectifying than many accounts of virtue ethics and does not maintain such a sharp distinction between Church and world. He emphasizes a "fluid" line between "Christians and non-Christians"[54] and stresses the need for both continuity and discontinuity with Christian and worldly "moral and social practices."[55] At several points, he explains that the Church is both host and guest to its neighbors[56] and mentions that the Church is host in a way that does not leave her "unaffected" by the "encounter" with the "stranger."[57]

Despite this effort to envision a more "open commensality"[58] in his assessment of how the Church should relate to its neighbors, I do not read Bretherton's conception of the relationship between Christ and world to be as satisfactory an account of reconciliation as that offered by Jennings' and Carter's theological race theory. This can be demonstrated through Breth-

49. Bretherton, *Hospitality as Holiness*.

50. Ibid., 30.

51. Ibid., 115.

52. Ibid.

53. Ibid., 128.

54. Ibid., 115.

55. Ibid., 121.

56. Ibid., 128, 146.

57. Ibid., 140.

58. Ibid., 129.

erton's examination of the Scriptural witness to hospitality. I contend that Bretherton's exegesis does not escape the problem of supersessionist ways of imagining the "other." On the contrary, he consistently describes the relationship between Christians and their neighbors as analogous to the relationship between Jew and Gentile. His central text is the parable of the Great Banquet in Luke 14:15–24, in which those invited by the banquet's host refuse to come, prompting the host to compel those in the "highways and hedges" to fill the banquet house.[59] Bretherton recognizes that the scholarly evidence connects this story of Jesus to the messianic feast of Isaiah 25, in which all Gentile nations are invited to the table of the Jewish Messiah.[60] However, he immediately reads the Church into the place of Israel as host at the table. He makes the same interpretive move as he mentions the story of Jesus' interaction with the Syrophoenician woman and the story of the Roman Centurion whose servant Jesus healed.[61] He parses each of these examples as demonstrating the necessity for the Church "elite" to "subvert . . . the existing patterns of social stratification" by welcoming the poor, outcasts, crippled, blind, and lame.[62]

Likewise, Bretherton views "Peter's meeting with Cornelius" and "the mission to the Gentiles" as "a picture of how Christians should relate to their neighbours."[63] While this hermeneutic trajectory is not entirely unhelpful, it does not encourage the author or his readers to find themselves in the position of Gentile "outsider" and thus be decentered. It does not allow the Gentile Christian to see himself as in need of hospitality at the table of another. While Bretherton labors extensively to relativize and soften what it means to be the "elite,"[64] his ecclesiology retains the centrality of the Western church as host to the "other." Unsurprisingly, the sole biblical text in which Bretherton reads the Western Church into Gentilic identity (apparently unintentionally) is the "Good Samaritan," which Bretherton reads as a mandate for Christians to mirror the hospitality of the Samaritan in hosting the "vulnerable."[65] In this one example, Bretherton departs from his usual identification with Israel so as to retain the Church's position as giver and host.

59. Ibid., 131–35.
60. Ibid., 131.
61. Ibid., 134–35.
62. Ibid., 132–33.
63. Ibid., 136–37.
64. Ibid., 132.
65. Ibid., 131 (cf. 139).

While Bretherton's account is not focused primarily upon race, he does give several indications that, while he reads the Western Church as Israel, he imagines those of non-European ancestry to be functionally synonymous with the "unclean" and the "pagan" in the biblical texts he exegetes. His account of eating positions the Church as welcoming "pagans, the unclean, and sinners . . . the impure . . . and the Gentiles,"[66] whom he quotes N.T. Wright as calling "all the wrong people."[67] Bretherton maintains that the "Christocentric performance of hospitality is the call to welcome the stranger," which he interprets as "the imperative to enter into relationship with, and accommodate, those who are different."[68] Bretherton uses two examples to illustrate what he means by "difference." First, he desires that hospitality extend to "the refugee." Second, he shows that he thinks of nonwhite people as the outsiders needing to be included at the table of Christ. One example will serve to demonstrate this contention.

Bretherton rightfully criticizes British statesman and linguist Enoch Powell's "Rivers of Blood" speech to a conservative political body in 1968.[69] In this speech, Powell whipped up a frenzy of fear against immigration, citing the opinion of one of his constituents, "a decent, ordinary fellow Englishman," that if the tide of immigration in Great Britain did not abate, within a generation "the black man will have the whip hand over the white man."[70] Bretherton criticizes Powell, claiming that the churches had the better response in their call for "integration."[71] However, while Bretherton criticizes racism (albeit a fairly extreme fifty-year-old example[72]), he still uses this example of black immigrants in England in order to picture the Western church as "host" to the nonwhite "other" as "guest" in need of "hospitality." Bretherton's account of reconciliation operates according to a European-as-Israel versus nonwhite-as-Gentile dialectic: "As the story of the encounter between Peter and Cornelius illustrates, and Paul constantly emphasizes, Christ breaks down the barriers between different races and nations. The Church has no stake in preserving the kind of unity Powell

---

66. Ibid., 130,

67. Ibid., 129.

68. Ibid., 148.

69. Ibid.

70. "Enoch Powell's," para. 7.

71. Bretherton, *Hospitality as Holiness*, 148.

72. I wrote these words before Donald Trump began to whip up fears about immigrants in 2015 in the American Republican presidential primary debates. I never dreamed that the type of rhetoric used by Powell in 1968 would ever again become acceptable in a major political party.

advocated, one based on language or race."[73] It is in this way that Bretherton claims that Christians are not identified by "race" or "culture" but by "union with Christ."[74] While Bretherton goes to great lengths to overturn elitism, separatism, and a view of the sacraments that stresses the isolated purity of the Church, his picture of Christ and world is not as theologically satisfactory as that of Jennings and Carter because he has not as carefully explored the relationship between Jew and Gentile.

My preceding analysis of Jennings indicates why Bretherton's Christological imagination reveals distortions of supersessionism that could have been avoided by a simple remembrance of what it means to be a Gentile. Bretherton claims that "hospitality can only be understood within a particular tradition, and different traditions will have different forms of hospitality."[75] Yet he does not entertain the possibility that different traditions could be joined in such a way as to be re-traditioned. He maintains his adherence to tradition-situated enquiry as the path to "living with those who are different" and frames those relations within the motif of hospitality. For Bretherton, "the church . . . is to host the world."[76] The Western church is the benefactor to whose table the world is invited.

The practice Bretherton pictures as the embodiment of Christian hospitality is the Eucharist. However, the manner in which he presents this feast as liturgical enactment reveals the aesthetic elitism at work in his sacramental imagination. While he provides abundant examples of patristic calls for a literal hosting and feasting with one's neighbors, he reinterprets them in his contemporary theological framework as "the sacramental enactment of feasting and fasting" characteristic of the liturgical church calendar.[77] It is an aesthetic practice properly performed that becomes for Bretherton the "means by which to assess whether or not particular forms of Christian life together constitute a faithful witness to Jesus Christ."[78] Western conceptions of aesthetics and ethics are again presented as an inseparable whole.

For Bretherton, the makeup of the local ecclesial community takes a back seat to proper liturgical performance. It is the sustained performance of a practice that determines the particular shapes of communal life rather than an ecclesiology of joining that drives the particular shapes of Christian practices. Bretherton's purpose in offering the enactment of sacramental

73. Bretherton, *Hospitality as Holiness*, 148.
74. Ibid., 121.
75. Ibid., 127.
76. Ibid., 138.
77. Ibid., 145–46.
78. Ibid., 146.

eating as hospitality is that the "church [which] host[s] the life of its neigh-bours" not be "assimilated to, or colonized by . . . the world."[79] Bretherton's aesthetic elitism does not allow him to explore the significance of the world's peoples having been colonized within the sort of liturgical framework he extols.

McBride

A text that comes closer to exemplifying the sort of Christological imagina-tion offered by Jennings and Carter is Jennifer M. McBride's *The Church for the World.*[80] McBride reads with and beyond Bonhoeffer to explicate the church's relationship with the world as one of public repentance. With Bon-hoeffer, McBride argues that "the work of the sinless Christ may be under-stood as repentance." She provocatively argues that in the Incarnation "God repents in Christ in accordance with the fallen human nature Jesus bears, what Paul calls in Romans 8:3, 'the likeness of sinful flesh.'"[81] Beyond Bon-hoeffer, McBride maintains that the witness of the church is neither a full apprehension of truth nor a championing of morality but a confession of its own guilt and the sin of the world.[82] This Christocentric posture is rooted in a "theology of the cross" rather than a "theology of glory."[83] McBride sug-gests that the distorted public witness of the American Evangelical church "arises from lack of sustained reflection on the simultaneous inclusive and exclusive nature of Christ's person and work."[84] She offers

> Bonhoeffer's penetrating critique, written after his second visit to the United States in 1939, that (white) North American the-ology is essentially ethics uprooted from its christological and ecclesiological grounding and thus disconnected from christo-logical ways of thinking about the identity and mission of the church.[85]

---

79. Ibid., 146.

80. McBride, *Church for the World.*

81. Ibid., 18. Although race is a part of McBride's analysis, she does not investigate the connections between racialization and historical conceptions of "sinful flesh," con-nections Carter unveils in his treatments of Douglass and Lee.

82. Ibid., 17–19.

83. Ibid., 5.

84. Ibid., 18.

85. Ibid., 18.

She suggests an alternative Christological grounding for ecclesiological witness:

> The church witnesses to Christ in a nontriumphal manner and demonstrates Christ's being for the world when it takes the form of the humiliated, crucified God by accepting guilt or confessing sin unto repentance.[86]

While it may be beyond the scope of McBride's argument to consider the posture in which nonwhite persons have already been called to stand as they have often been forced to bear the reproach of and suffer the sin of Western society, her critique of ecclesiologies characteristic of whiteness bears similarities to that found in Jennings and Carter.

McBride suggests that if, as Bonhoeffer has maintained, Christ being "truly lord of the world," means that the Church is not "religiously . . . privileged" but instead "belong[s] wholly to the world," then a thick Christology offers "the foundation for an ecclesial witness that is free to belong wholly to a world already reconciled to God and to enact concrete redemption from that place."[87] McBride recognizes that a lived ecclesiology is demonstrative of the Christological presuppositions of the ecclesial community. While McBride does not explore the connection between a supersessionist imagination and a truncated Christology, she has her finger on the pulse of Jennings' diagnosis that the distortions of white ecclesiology stem from mental habits that mime early Christological heresies. McBride's Bonhoefferian Christology points to an ecclesiology that "maintain[s] both the concreteness of the . . . local church-community with all its failings *and* the theological claim that the church is Christ's contemporary bodily presence in the world."[88] She argues that because Christ's body is comprised of sinful human beings, its redemptive witness is embodied as it takes the form of Christ in "accept[ing] guilt" and taking "responsibility for sin."[89]

McBride's contention that a "closed theological system" may be "guard[ed] against" by "welcoming lessons learned from an enfleshed

---

86. Ibid., 19.

87. Ibid., 17, 19.

88. Ibid., 19.

89. Ibid. Again, it is problematic to make a Christology of repentance a blanket description of the posture the Church needs to assume. For instance, black flesh on New World soil has experienced enough of "accepting the guilt" and taking "responsibility for the sin" of the white world. Bonhoeffer's call to repentance is a posture more fitting for white theology. It is to be remembered that Bonhoeffer's theology was influenced by the necessity for him as a white aristocratic male to bear the reproach poured upon his Jewish sisters and brothers by a white power structure.

church"[90] is a reminder of Jennings' contention that theological convictions demand a life consistent with those confessions.[91] She recognizes that Bonhoeffer's theology was forged in actual church communities engaged in social resistance in New York and Germany and that "philosophical theologians and practitioner-activists need one another to engage more fully the task of cultivating just and redemptive communities."[92] While McBride's account, like Bretherton's, strives to resist paternalistic ways in which the church often relates to the world, and while her account is arguably more effective in doing so, she does not discern the supersessionist problem in her framing of the church-world dichotomy. Therefore, she does not adequately decenter the Gentile church in relation to its "neighbors." I contend that, by limiting her Christology to a Bonhoefferian modality of repentance, McBride does not utilize a thorough enough range of theological resources to effectively resist racialization.

The constructive portion of McBride's text ends with a case study of an urban ministry in Washington, D. C. called *The Southeast White House*. McBride provides a theological analysis of the manner in which this community shares meals. McBride presents the SEWH's ministry as "an ongoing activity of repentance" that "fosters relationships and draws other people into its communal life together, connecting people normally divided by race, religion, politics, economics, social standing, geography, and culture."[93] She suggests that the SEWH's presence in their community is grounded in "an initial act of repentance as the cofounders turned toward the forgotten quadrant and moved into the neighborhood in order to encounter the neighbor."[94]

While I am experientially aware that an initial act of relocation is often prompted by repentance (which may be an appropriate and necessary framework in which to view this initial step toward resisting a world reshaped by whiteness), it would be problematic for an ecclesial community to maintain, as its raison d'être, that sort of a theology of the Incarnation. Doing so would reinforce the "othering" frameworks and "us-them" rhetoric characteristic of supersessionist ecclesiologies. If the theological basis

90. Ibid., 20.

91. Jennings, *Christian Imagination*, 164.

92. McBride, *Church for the World*, 21.

93. Ibid., 21. It is unclear why McBride includes "geographical" diversity in this list while simultaneously extolling an urban ecclesial community grounded in a particular place and living in proximity to one another. This suggests that her account of place is not as thick as that of Jennings.

94. Ibid., 21. It would also be interesting to understand what McBride means by the "forgotten" quadrant. Forgotten by whom? Surely not those who live there . . .

for relocation remains a long-term emphasis on repentance, the community shaped by it may begin to take on Savior or martyr complexes and paternalistic ways of relating to others. In other words, Barth's emphasis on the qualitative distinction between God and humanity may be collapsed. Worse yet, such a community may implicitly call the neighbors it views as "marginalized" to join with them in a state of contrition rather than themselves entering in to the celebration of the joined and resurrected local community. Those marginalized by racialization and "otherness" should not bear the burden of repenting for it. A more satisfactory theological framework than relocation-as-repentance is Jennings' account of transgressing the boundaries of commodified space because of desire for the other.

To be sure, McBride neither presents SEWH as a community embodying paternalism and objectification nor as a group free from recognizing the messiness attendant to the pursuit of joining. On the contrary, neighborhood residents, staff, volunteers, and founders of this diverse community candidly relate the inherent power disparities and economic imbalances encountered when resisting static identity formulations through relationship.[95] It is important to note that members of SEWH's community do not themselves speak of their mission as an act of repentance, a fact which McBride acknowledges "challenged the terms of [her] constructive theology."[96] I fear that in narrowing reconciliation to repentance,[97] McBride's Christological schema could be interpreted as centering the white body as the active agent in redemption and as calling nonwhite peoples to bear an undue burden of conviction for the distorted relationality inaugurated by whiteness. To call relocation to space not one's own an act of repentance acknowledges (I believe rightly so) that the commodification of space and the reification of identity attendant to segregation is a revolt against creation. If, as Jennings and Carter maintain, and as McBride appears to assume, this distortion of place is enacted according to the rationality of whiteness, then the trespassing of place is to be understood as repentance from white rationality and its reach through the market. Yet McBride does not make this clear. While her Bonhoefferian Christology is to be preferred to the implicitly Occidental Jesus of a tradition of virtue, her ecclesiology of repentance is unable to decenter whiteness as effectively as Jennings' and Carter's emphasis on the Gentile identity of the *ethnos*.

This can be seen in the way in which McBride describes the "Reconciliation Luncheons" hosted by the SEWH. Her theological descriptions

95. Ibid., 180–86.
96. Ibid., 21–22.
97. Ibid., 190.

have trouble unseating the host/guest dialectic the SEWH so clearly strives to undermine. Similarly to Bretherton, McBride compares the SEWH inviting their marginalized neighbors to their meals as Israel opening its doors to the outcasts in the Great Banquet of Luke 14.[98] These weekly meals, hosted by the SEWH, are described as foreshadowing "the wedding festival in the eschaton where individuals, regardless of merit or status, feast at the eternal wedding supper of the Lamb."[99] McBride's eschatalogical paradigm subtly reads the "staff"[100] and "mentors"[101] into Christocentric "host" status and does not explore the manner in which the hosts of the meal may also possess a poverty of merit. While she emphasizes that all, including the "neighbor," are given the opportunity to serve and thereby become "host,"[102] her Eucharistic theology is unable to picture various Gentile peoples as together being guests at someone else's table.

McBride's important insights into the strides made by the SEWH toward equality, mutuality, and interdependence are made at the expense of the systematic integrity of her Christology of repentance. For instance, in order to fit the celebratory experience of the community into her ecclesiology of repentance, McBride has to clarify that the "festive character" of the meal which "fosters right relationships between people normally estranged from one another . . . exemplifies that repentance includes joy."[103] Repentance as a category must be expanded to include the variegated experiences of the community. McBride's quotes from community residents reveal that they understand themselves to be the "guests" of staff and volunteers, who confess a quest to "throw . . . elitist attitude[s] out the window" and "see people as God sees them—as always equal."[104] While this candor and vulnerability may be beautiful, it reveals a poverty of Gentile remembrance in the Christological imagination of American Christians, a poverty that groups such as the SEWH strive to resist. The theology of Jennings and Carter opens a more satisfactory path toward escaping this identity gridlock.

98. Ibid.
99. Ibid., 193.
100. Ibid., 191.
101. Ibid., 193.
102. Ibid., 192.
103. Ibid., 193.
104. Ibid., 191.

Du Boulay

The theological account of sharing table which perhaps comes closest to that which I am attempting to present in my ecclesiology of joining comes from what may be an unlikely source. In order to orient my reflections on eating together, I would like to use the central sacrament of the church as practiced in the Greek mountain village of Ambeli in Juliet Du Boulay's *Cosmos, Life, and Liturgy in a Greek Orthodox Village.*[105] While this is arguably an unusual place to turn, given the monochromatic nature of Ambeli, I find it quite compelling for several reasons. A homogenous mountain community in Greece populated by Greek people is a much different reality than contemporary communities of segregated homogeneity generated by Western expansion and divided according to the market logic of whiteness. Likewise, I am persuaded by Carter that there are resources within an Eastern Orthodox imagination that can be used to challenge the racial logic of the church. As a practicing member of the Orthodox Church, and having resided in Ambeli for several years, Du Boulay is attempting an ethnography of which she is a part, *"observ[ing] life by participating in it."*[106] My methodology shares important aspects with Du Boulay's lived ethnography. What I find to be instructive in Du Boulay's study is the deep interconnectedness of land, people, work, food, life, and worship.

In her chapter *Work and Bread*, Du Boulay describes a world in which house, economy, and liturgy function in continuity as people reach out to one another and to the land.[107] Rather than sharp lines of demarcation between *oikonomia* and *ecclesia*, Du Boulay finds in Ambeli that the "seasonal cycles" of the agrarian society and the "liturgical ordering" of the church enter "into daily life by being continually replicated in a multitude of diverse forms down to the minutest area of man's activity."[108] The Eucharist in Ambeli is birthed out of a community "living almost entirely off their own land."[109] It is not proper liturgical enactment but the day in and day out life of the community that provides the hermeneutical lens through which

105. Du Boulay, *Cosmos.*

106. Ibid., 10.

107. While I recognize that presenting the three estates in language of "holism" risks sounding like the MacIntyrian "unity of the transcendentals," it will be seen that I am utilizing this language to demonstrate that the continuity which DuBoulay is experiencing comes from lives lived together connected to land. In this sense, I am not invoking an ideal sort of convergence between various disciplines or a holism in the studies of essences. Rather, I am attempting a more realist account influenced by an actualist ontology.

108. Du Boulay, *Cosmos*, 134–36.

109. Ibid., 7.

to understand the local ecclesial practices: "Neither eating nor not eating, therefore, carry in themselves moral connotations; the connotations are given to them by the nature of the time to which they are related."[110] For Du Boulay, time is to be understood as constituted by place. The church calendar in Ambeli arises from the created order and the particular land upon which the people live; it is not an artificial construct imported to structure the activities of a worshipping community.

In Ambeli, a village connected by the land to the time cycles of planting and harvest, feast and fast, celebration and lamentation, the medium of wheat is of utmost importance in the constitution of the community.

> Wheat is thus a food which pre-eminently unites the physical and spiritual worlds, material and immaterial brought together in a single substance, and it is because of this that bread, above all other food and in all sorts of different forms, is used to define and to express the meaning of the great variety of ceremonial occasions.[111]

Bread becomes an icon of the divine inasmuch as it is furnished from the place in which the feast is experienced and inasmuch as it is fashioned by the people connected to that land. The body politic, therefore, is an image of Christ inasmuch as it is a genuine expression of the particularities of the people/s shaped by specific place. It is not wheat loaves (above any other medium) that are the means of grace. Rice or maize or corn bread or chapatti would carry the same significance. The Eucharist, therefore, cannot be aesthetically exported or imported. Rather, the Lord's Supper is the bringing together of the sustenance of the particularities of the community into a blessed intermingling of various expressions of what it means to be human.

It is in this way that the bread of Ambeli, provided by God in creation, harvested from the field, and fashioned into loaves in the bakery, is brought to the priest to be distributed in turn as sacrament in the *ecclesia*. Traditionally Western gender roles are subverted in this process as the man reaps the grain in the field; the woman shapes it, carves the sign of the cross upon it, and fires it in the mud oven; and the priest then receives it from the female body as the body of the Lord.

> In their periodic offering of the liturgical loaves the individual households are therefore related directly to the Holy Gifts in the action of the liturgy, and when these loaves are offered as *andidhoro* [blessed bread] at the end of the liturgy, these households

110. Ibid., 146.
111. Ibid., 148.

stand alongside Christ himself as the hosts of a symbolic meal eaten by the community as a whole.[112]

The intermediary between God and man, rather than the priest, is the communal body of the crucified and risen Lord. Inasmuch as all are joined together, all are hosts and all are guests. The table of the Jewish Messiah is that to which the community has been invited. As with any gathering, "quarrels and disagreements" are not absent. Yet "for however brief a moment, the reintegration of a world fragmented by sin" is experienced and "a kind of reconciliation is achieved not only between people and their neighbours but also between the villagers and the natural world in which the celebration is set."[113] In other words, reconciliation is an imperfect prolepsis of the eschaton in which land, bodies, and food are joined together as one.

The End of "Hosting"

Of these four contemporary theological accounts of eating together, the first two do not sufficiently distinguish themselves from the accounts of tradition that they are criticizing. While Bantum's account is not focused primarily on eating, and while he demonstrates how orthodox Christology is resistant to claims of racial purity, his account of practices does not palpably differ from a tradition of virtue. I contend that Bretherton's treatment of eating as hospitality is the most problematic of the four because it assumes a hierarchy of aesthetic performance foreign to the eating texts in Scripture. While I am not suggesting that the Christian tradition has nothing of value to teach in regard to practices (and while my account is very "traditional" in many ways), I join Barth and Jennings in suggesting that tradition is not a watertight motif in which to consider the Christian life. As I have already suggested, I read both Jennings and Carter as being sensitive to the tradition while utilizing liberating undercurrents found within it (and within contemporary discourses) to subversive effect. This is why Jennings and Carter read Barth in a generally favorable light. He both affirms a high Christology and recognizes the ways such a commitment calls into question the self-assured cataphatic formulations of the "tradition," formulations that are characteristic of what Jennings and Carter call "whiteness."[114]

112. Ibid., 153.

113. Ibid., 159.

114. It may be helpful for Jennings and Carter to, in future works, more explicitly clarify their relationship to the "tradition." While I am sympathetic with their recognition of the problematic nature of appeals to "tradition," and while I am resistant to the racialized implications of reclamations of Western traditions of virtue, it remains

Appeals to "the tradition," while safeguarding important aspects of how earlier followers of Christ have understood God's revelation in Jesus, also carry forward the mistakes inherent to those understandings. As Barth reminds us, because we are creatures we cannot rely on our own apprehension of knowledge (nor can we apprehend the divine in its "essence") but must receive the revelation of the Creator (which comes to us in the saving "acts" of God in history, most notably through the people Israel and her Messiah, Jesus). As the "tradition" became increasingly estranged from its Judaic center and was subsequently married to colonization (through late medieval Catholicism and refracted through early-modern Protestantism), it became increasingly difficult to imagine the Christian faith as connected to Israel in any thick sense. The modern missological mandate increased the reach of these distortions as it spread the Gospel throughout the world. Many opportunities for rich experiences of relationship and vulnerability were precluded.

Even so today, the manner in which many Christian scholars and leaders see themselves as "traditioned" mitigates against relationships of humility and postures of openness to learning from those not part of their tradition. "Tradition," then, can overdetermine the shape local ecclesial communities must take to the exclusion of the work of the Spirit in joining people to Christ and to each other. A thick Christological account of ethics will find instructive the way communities in other places and times have sought to embody the life of Christ but will not privilege the way in which the Word of God encountered other contexts to the detriment of the particular shape of Christ's continued work in joining particular people in space and time. Additionally, accounts that assert the prominence of the "tradition" often tend to underemphasize the more central "tradition" of YHWH's work through his particular people Israel. Contemporary Christian ethics must reckon with the racial imagination inherent in "traditioned" moral enquiry. While mitigating against MacIntyre's tendency to view interaction between

---

that Jennings and Carter reference the tradition in important ways (as well as broaden conceptions of the "tradition"). While I have suggested that this utilization is often subversive in positive ways, I cannot help but wonder if Jennings and Carter have at times underemphasized their convergence with orthodox Christian thought. I read their affinity for early patristic and Eastern Christology (Irenaeus, Chalcedon, Gregory of Nyssa, Maximus) to sharpen their critique of the liberal religious studies methodology of scholars like Cone as well as provide a contrast with late medieval scholastic missteps. While they do not carry forward patristic capitulations to Hellenistic philosophical thought (which can be read as proto-supersessionist), they nonetheless welcome reading alongside ancient mothers and fathers of the Faith. My point is that we cannot help but read as part of a community. In this sense, Jennings' and Carter's works have provided a means by which to question what communities we are reading with.

"traditions" as "rivalry," Bretherton reenacts the limitations of traditioned virtue ethics.

Of the four contemporary theological accounts of eating together, I find the last two to hold more promise for resisting the objectifying patterns of relationality characteristic of whiteness. Yet I contend that neither treatment expresses the relationship between Christ, his people, and the world as satisfactorily as the Christological accounts of Jennings and Carter. McBride's picture of Christ and world explicitly denounces the triumphalism often attendant to traditioned theological reflection and its ethical and aesthetic hegemony. Her practical picture of ecclesiological embodiment offers a serious challenge to the kinship fragmentation and objectification often implicit in theological accounts of interacting with the "other." However, much like Colenso, McBride's theological system begins to break down when actually reflecting *with* the other. Her narrow view of reconciliation as repentance is challenged by the evidence she cites from the local urban ecclesial community in Washington, D.C. Yet McBride's Christological posture is much to be preferred to postures of the church triumphant which have often been embraced in the Empires of the West.

In the fourth account I have utilized, Du Boulay is headed in a promising direction as she describes how the love feast functions in a particular, local community marked by the joining of lives to land. As all guests together bring the fruits of creation to the celebration of worship, the body of Jesus Christ is present in a way that transcends both proper aesthetic performances and hierarchical ontological arrangements. Because of its contextual constraints, Du Boulay's work does not explore how the particular flesh of the Jewish Jesus Christ could be constitutive of a community marked by difference. I am attempting to demonstrate how similar connections between people and place may be experienced in a community transgressing the boundaries of modern commodified space and race.

I contend that the Israel-centric and particularist Christology offered by Jennings and Carter more sufficiently describes the relationship between Christ and world than the other literature I have analyzed, thereby positioning the church with a more supple ecclesiology. As I have presented it in this text, Jennings' and Carter's theological race theory posits that colonization and the modern observatory stance have together produced a supersessionist Christological imagination that centralizes white flesh and marginalizes the nonwhite other. I am claiming that envisioning the Gentile Church as host to the world carries forward this trajectory in ways harmful to a communal life marked by difference. Contrary to this orientation, the biblical narrative knows nothing of the West spreading a table for other nations to share. The Scriptures present YHWH's hosting of a particular people through which he elects to host all *ethnos*. The biblical salvation narrative positions Israel as host to the world; supersessionism names the Church replacing Israel as host.

For these reasons, I argue that "hosting" and "hospitality" are not the best motifs in which to imagine the relationship between Church and world. As Carter argued in his study of Cone, Christ does not relate to the world as an abstract universal but as a concrete universal, a particular One for the many. The theological imagination of whiteness, including its Eucharistic reflections, relates to the world as an abstract universal, an imperialist hegemony. This relationality is sustained through aesthetic performances and practices such as a Eucharist of hospitality. On the contrary, the Lord's Supper in the biblical text was and is an invitation to a Jewish feast, the Passover. The scandal of this practice is that Gentiles are welcomed to partake of matzah and Seder wine.

This does not mean that contemporary local ecclesial communities need to mime the particular practices of historic Jewish community life, which would be to assume the sort of ethical voluntarist continuity with Israel posited by Yoder (as opposed to the more satisfactory conception of "election" as understood by Barth and presented by Givens). Doing so might also cause local ecclesial communities to be legalistic about observing practices not connected to their local places, or to engage in practices stripped of their particular significance, thereby running the risk of using Israel's community life as a cipher on the way to their own self-realization. On the contrary, every time an ecclesial community eats together, it should reconfirm its participants in their identity as guests at another people's table and recipients of the grace of another people's God. Through Gentile remembrance, multiple *ethnos* are joined together in particular shared feasts because of the particularity of the Host. A universal invitation to a particular center requires convergence. Universality in abstraction (which is the stance of whiteness) allows for separatism and spells a distortion of mutuality.

Forsaking "hospitality" as an appropriate motif for reconciliation means forsaking the idea that the Church has anything of its own to offer.[115] In concrete terms, it means that both worship and social justice work should no longer take place as unidirectional action through which the Church claims to "feed" the world. On the contrary, we must recognize that both Christians and our neighbors, in the communities in which we reside, are mutual participants in receiving God's good and generous gifts of

---

115. "What do you have that you did not receive? If then you received it, why do you boast as if you did not receive it?" (1 Cor 4:7). Luther: "We are beggars; that is the truth."

provision.[116] It means recognizing that the "whole earth is YHWH's"[117] and therefore no people has the right to claim "stewardship" over its bounty to the exclusion of others; its fruits have been given to all.[118] To restrict access to the shared fruits of the earth (or to present those fruits as "belonging to" or "stewarded by" the church) is to revolt against creation.[119]

How different would be a world in which George Zimmerman saw himself as a guest in the same space in which Trayvon Martin walked. How different would be a city in which Officer Daniel Pantaleo recognized that he was an invited guest to the same table as Eric Garner. How different would be a nation in which nonwhite people were not forcibly "hosted" in prisons and ghettos, nonwhite immigrants were not forcibly "uninvited" from the shared table through deportation, and place was not distorted through the drawing of districting lines and neighborhood boundaries for the purpose of diluting the power of the nonwhite body. Only those who see themselves as "hosts" claim the means by which to exclude and enact violence; mutual guests have no place from which to uninvite or perpetrate violence against others. As long as ecclesiological identity and national conceptions of peoplehood are presented in motifs of "hosting," invitation and exclusion will take place at the whims of whiteness. Positioning the church or the state as host rather than seeing YHWH as Host and Lord makes possible both segregation and assimilation.

Rather than a local church "hosting" her neighbors, the community should join in "guesting" each other, pointing toward a Host who is "Other," yet in whose body particular bodies may be conjoined. By recalling the "impure" grace that invites us as Gentiles to a table not our own, the local community can participate in an ecclesiology of joining each time it gathers. An ecclesiology of joining means exploring a richer imagination of how diverse peoples could together receive the bounty of God's harvest from the land. It means that our joined feasts may be unfamiliar to all and include moments of discomfort on the way to new mutual aesthetic appreciation.

116. See Luther, "Exposition of Psalm 127," 327, in which he explains that all human work is nothing but the finding and collecting of God's good gifts. He reminds us that we cannot cause grain to grow or ore to accumulate.

117. Ps 24:1

118. "And God said, "Behold, I have given you every plant yielding seed that is on the face of all the earth, and every tree with seed in its fruit. You shall have them for food" (Gen 1:29). As noted by Aquinas, the "you" is plural.

119. See Matt 5:45, where Jesus reminds his followers that the Father sends rain and sun on both the just and the unjust. See also Matt 13:24–30, where Jesus proclaims that it is not up to his followers to discern between the wheat and the weeds. Augustine appealed to this passage in arguing against the Donatist desire to judge between "saints" and "sinners."

It means that laughter, confession, forgiveness, and grace must abound as we try to together figure out what it means to be joined to one another as we are joined to Jesus. It means acknowledging that the ways our Christian imagination has taught us to see the world are so deeply deformed that the path to resisting static identity is quite a rocky one. Yet it also means that we do not walk this road alone; we walk it together, led by the One who in his "impure" flesh has already walked its way.

I will now suggest three additional components of an ecclesiology of joining that shape the contours of the eating experienced by the joined community. While it is beyond the scope of this analysis to investigate these components with the same detail with which I have explored the theological significance of eating, I propose that similar extensions to the theological race theory of Jennings and Carter along these lines would be fruitful.

Place

Jennings suggests that one of the most important practices for living beyond the patterns of racialization enacted by whiteness is the transgression of space.

> We who live in the new space of joining may need to transgress the boundaries of real estate, by buying where we should not and living where we must not, by living together where we supposedly cannot, and being identified with those whom we should not . . . For us in the racial world, the remade world, a crucial point of discipleship is precisely global real estate. Where we live determines in great measure how we live. Where we agree to the spatial configurations of the land inevitably means a tacit agreement to the racial formation of the world. We must enter the struggle of land acquisition, space and place design, targeted housing development, buying, and selling which constantly re-establishes and strengthens segregationist mentalities and racial identities . . . Our imaginations must be drawn to new possibilities of living arrangements that capture our freedom in Christ and turn them toward desiring a journey of joining enabled and guided by the Spirit of God.[120]

Jennings maintains that living according to the dictates of commodified space and market "preference" gives "tacit consent" to racialization. His historical-theological analysis of place suggests that a refusal to transgress the boundaries of modern space betrays an assumption of segregation as an

---

120. Jennings, *Christian Imagination*, 287.

act of divine providence: as if the world as we have it has not been reordered according to white rationality and "use-value." As Prather has maintained through his use of Jennings, adherence to the spatial mandates of the modern world indicates obedience to Mammon rather than to Christ.[121] Jennings neither suggests a chimerical attempted return to a "pre-race" world nor advocates a colonial move in which a "missionary" enters space for the purpose of changing it. Rather, he recommends entering a place as guest, making it one's own home, being claimed by the people of that place, and claiming the other as one's own. His work suggests that the problem with colonization was not the traversing of waters. Historical research demonstrates that many peoples traversed the waters before Europeans reshaped the New World. The problem was that the West entered space not their own *as if it was their own*, or more precisely, *as if it had been given them by God.*

As Carter's analysis proposes, a community marked by the miscegenistic mixing of blood will be a community marked by the scandalous sharing of local space. There are no easy answers; the theological dynamics at play require further research to more fully articulate. I can confirm that if my family had not moved into a place where we "should not" have moved, I would not have been prepared to recognize what Jennings and Carter are getting at in their works.

Prompted by McBride's analysis of relocation as repentance and Prather's analysis of the maintenance of modern space as subservience to Mammon and racialized conceptions of peoplehood, I will briefly indicate what is at stake in our theological descriptions of place. Because contemporary pursuits of reconciliation take place in a world remade by colonial displacements and the relentless aesthetic comparisons of slavery's auction block, transgression of space entails an encounter with all sorts of economic inequalities and power disparities. Without rendering relative socioeconomic status static or aligning it with ethnic identity, we must acknowledge that the pursuit of joining requires us to recognize the socioeconomic marginalization that has been disproportionately visited upon those marginalized by racialization. Jennings' tale of Equiano indicates that the lived problem of racial reconciliation necessarily involves reflecting on the sociological and relational implications of the market as racialized system of social control.

For instance, it is not insignificant that in 2011, the median income for black households was roughly 60 percent that of white households.[122] Such

121. Prather, *Christ, Power, and Mammon*, 232–33.

122. The median income for white families in 2011 was $55,412. The comparative figure for black families was $32,229 ("Income, Poverty, and Health Insurance Coverage in the United States: 2011." https://www.census.gov/hhes/www/hlthins/data/incpovhlth/2011/index.html).

a comparative figure aligns exactly with the anthropological designation enacted by the constitutional three-fifths compromise of 1787, which valued black being at 60 percent that of white being. The practices of redlining in lending, historically segregationist urban planning, targeted law enforcement, the "War on Drugs," police profiling, creation of the suburbs and interstates, and rapid changes in the job market have conspired to create an intransient "underclass" from which those on the underside of the racialized hierarchy theologically described in this analysis must often fight to escape. As Carter maintains: "[M]odernity's biopolitical organization operates according to a logic that separates wealth and poverty, aligning the former with certain groups and the latter with others, according to discourses of race that hide themselves precisely as racial discourses."[123] It may be the case that an informed transgression of space will entail a complex interplay of both economic "downward" and "upward" mobility. For instance, I have noticed this complicated interchange in the disconnect between "prosperity" and "poverty" theology. It is often the privilege of white Christians on "mission" to claim purchase on being "poor," which is usually radically disingenuous. As McBride quotes Dr. David Hilfiker, who writes about living and working in a medical shelter for homeless men in the same city as SEWH:

> The poverty of inner-city Washington is not to be sought. The spiritual discipline of "voluntary poverty" has nothing in common with the oppression and despair of the ghetto. There is nothing beautiful or romantic . . . in lives crushed by the weight of indifferent history and cultural negligence. The poverty of the inner city is evil, and we betray those caught in its web by romanticizing it or imagining that we—by divesting ourselves of some bits of our privilege—can choose to enter into it.[124]

This is why McBride suggests the formative practice of sharing table in shared space. Although simple "renunciation" of white privilege may not be possible, she notes that the proper theological *telos* is an "existence with and for others through a reconciliation that resists dualisms that destroy community."[125] An unlikely community sharing space is a concrete practice that resists racialization.

123. Carter, *Race*, 227.
124. McBride, *Church for the World*, 186.
125. Ibid., 186.

Participation

Jennings maintains that the community shaped by shared land will conflict with "class and economic stratification":

> The space of communion is always ready to appear where the people of God reach down to join the land and reach out to join those around them, their near and distant neighbors . . . This joining . . . involves entering into the lives of peoples to build actual life together, lives enfolded and kinship networks established through the worship of and service to the God of Israel in Jesus Christ. Such kinship networks would, of necessity, come into contention with the permeation of class and economic stratification inherent in the transformation of land into private property. The space of communion draws into itself the social divisions enacted by and facilitated through that stratification in order to overcome them.[126]

Rather than being ignored, caste-like stratifications are drawn into the spatially-constituted joined community and resisted through mutuality and interdependence. Carter's claim that, by means of participation in the body politic marked by the relationality of the Triune God, "being" itself is experienced as *transcendent* suggests a communal hypostasis in which differences are neither static nor separated, but are ecstatic and conjoined. As I maintained in my critique of a Christology of translation, the significance of the Incarnation is that together we are afforded the opportunity to *become* something new: a "new creation" in Christ.[127]

Much as Jennings has contended that Christology is best understood as joining rather than translation, I have claimed that ecclesiology is best understood as joining: a participation with one another rather than a "hospitality" in which some are "hosts" and others are "guests." In this sense, the church is not a counter-culture that hosts the world but a body politic made up of those far from God who together are being drawn to the center: the Father of Jesus. Describing Christian witness as hospitality tends to underemphasize the manner in which those assuming the position of "host" find themselves discipled by submission to the "neighbor."

I maintain that this process of mutual participation is suggested by the Biblical concept of mutual submission (despite its problematic historical deployment).[128] Many of the experiences of people who have been hosted

---

126. Jennings, *Christian Imagination*, 286–87.

127. 2 Cor 5:17

128. I hesitate to use language of submission because of its misappropriation in

in communities not their own (by submitting to the people of that place) call for further theological examination. Examples of these experiences include seeking out local leadership and mentorship, intentional partnership as "yokefellows" between people different from one another, participation in the joys and pains of the community, and submission to local people in any attempts toward constructive change in that space. There is no way to prevent this being messy. I am aware that what I am describing opens a door to all sorts of misunderstandings and misrepresentations. This risk is part and parcel of resisting the segregated power-alliances that have been created through the navigation of race in the modern world.

A guest allows a host to welcome him with all the attendant cultural practices that such hospitality entails. While these practices may at first be unfamiliar or perhaps seem contrived, over time he will grow to appreciate the aesthetic he is experiencing. A guest will begin to long for and attempt to reciprocate, however fumblingly, the practices that bid him welcome. A guest will not rush into action, assuming knowledge of a people and a place which has hitherto been foreign to him. Questions suggested by this encounter are: Can "mission" any longer be an appropriate rubric under which to consider cross-cultural interaction? In a post-colonial world, do calls to live "incarnationally" mean anything? If Christ is the New Human who inaugurates a new way of being in the world for all peoples (a new theological anthropology) how can the Incarnation be embodied in anything other than a joined life? As a subversion of the motif of hospitality, the theological significance of participation as guest begs to be considered further.

Proclamation

Carter maintains that "what is common" to both the "pseudotheological aesthetic of whiteness" and an "aesthetic of the black religious consciousness" is that neither "speaks in tongues," that is to say, "neither knows how to

---

gender and race relations. However, much like my use of language connected to Lordship and reconciliation, I do not believe language of submission to be irredeemable. For instance, I have intentionally submitted to mentors from the place in which I live and my marriage is a relationship in which I submit to my wife as we are joined to one another. I am attempting to reclaim what I consider to be a biblical usage of these terms. For instance, in regard to the much maligned *haustafeln*, Paul attempts to subvert the social order by beginning his treatment in Ephesians 5 with "submit to one another out of reverence for Christ" (v. 21). While I recognize that the white male body has often been the reference point for identity-constitution, I am reading mutual submission as resistance to self-constitution. A political arrangement constituted only by competing hegemonies will further conceptions of self-constitution and will not ultimately dislodge the white male body as aesthetic standard.

inhabit languages not its own."[129] Jennings finds the monolinguistic speech of both blackness and whiteness to be rooted in the tragic legacy of slavery, in which literacy meant "reading alone and apart."[130] In this manner, the history of black-white relations on New World soil should not be considered "multicultural" as much as a single culture of division locked in a sort of mutually-defining death dance. The polyglot associations of the religious academy remain locked in this macabre embrace. Carter and Jennings find the path of escape to be what I have termed *poly-glossolalia*.

At the same time, both scholars have presented examples of African American church experience as offering openings through which a fuller ecclesiology than that of whiteness may be explored. While not finding adherence to a particular "tradition" to be the most satisfactory ecclesiological posture, both theologians offer pictures of the manner in which the lacunae in the pseudotheology of whiteness may be filled by joining with nonwhite particularities. While not presenting a monolithic view of the "black" church, Jennings and Carter are suggesting that elements of her proclamation of the *kerygma* may better represent an ecclesiology of joining than those enacted by whiteness. Jennings, Carter, and Cone each pull on this thread in important ways as they assert the importance of black particularity for the process of exiting the universal sway of whiteness.

It is beyond the scope of this analysis to theologically consider the particular shape of black-white mutual rearticulation. Perhaps a musical metaphor will suffice to intimate the manner in which this matter could be explored. As with a participatory jazz modality, many historically Afro-Christian churches create space for a multidirectional proclamation and reception of the Word. Rather than a "classical" aesthetic in which the intentions of the composer must be replicated before ornamentation can be added, proclamation in black linguistic space tends to be shaped by all participants adding elements of improvisation to the theme that is being played. Among other practices, a "call and response" aesthetic and a "shared" platform in which various ministers participate in directing the shape of the proclamation bear striking similarities to the manner in which proclamation arises out of the *ecclesia* in the Psalms. The Psalmist proclaims God's praise "in the congregation,"[131] and recognizes the responsorial nature of proclamation in the interrelationship of hearing and speaking.[132] It is in a similar sense that Paul proclaims: "When you come together, each one has

129. Carter, *Race*, 227.

130. Jennings, *Christian Imagination*, 240.

131. See Pss 22:22, 25; 35:18; 107:32; and 111:1.

132. See Ps 62:11–12.

314   A Theology of Race and Place

a hymn, a lesson, a revelation, a tongue, or an interpretation. Let all things be done for building up."[133] An ecclesiology of joining will value a circular shared hermeneutic not unlike that offered by Jennings and Carter.

By sharing space and table, and by submitting to the proclamation of one from whom we differ, our Biblical hermeneutics and cadences of proclamation begin to be reshaped: the Spirit enables us to speak in tongues not our own. As I related in the Introduction, I have experienced the grace of the ecstasy of worship being extended to me as I have been invited into worship traditions not my own and have experienced the Spirit of God overflowing through me with tongues heretofore unlearned. Ludwig Wittgenstein maintains that "to imagine a language means to imagine a form of life,"[134] or as John J. Ross calls it, a "way of life."[135] Experiences of linguistic interdependence point to a shared way of life in the body of the One who is the Way and the Life.[136] Jennings' and Carter's works maintain that the Word who became flesh is not a universal ideal but the Incarnation of the God who is relationality. Proclamation of this God is marked by linguistic interpenetration, a Trinitarian term that indicates a hypostatic reality ecclesiologically embodied. As languages heretofore locked in hegemonic competition and binary opposition redirect their relationship toward a mutual embrace, new tongues will be spoken and understood. This process warrants a fuller theological and practical examination along the lines of what I have pursued with sharing table.

Conclusion

As the joined community marked by difference shares table together in shared space, it becomes clear that there is no host other than the Risen Lord glorified in the communal flesh of the body politic that bears his name. The gathered community recognizes the grace that invites them to a table not their own; the participants reflect on the unlikelihood of walking the way of life with each other. It is this uniquely joining function of sharing a common loaf, prepared by many different hands, about which the community of the *Didache* rejoices:

> We thank Thee, our Father, for the life and knowledge which
> You madest known to us through Jesus Thy Servant; to Thee be

133. 1 Cor 14:26.
134. Wittgenstein, *Philosophical Investigations*, §19, pg. 11.
135. Ross, *Reading Wittgenstein's*, 18.
136. John 14:6.

the glory forever. Even as this broken bread was scattered over the hills, and was gathered together and became one, so let Thy Church be gathered together from the ends of the earth into Thy kingdom; for Thine is the glory and the power through Jesus Christ forever.[137]

It is the life of the community scattered by racialization but pressed together within the particular body of the Jewish Jesus of Nazareth that is the sacrifice of praise and thanksgiving to the Father of life. It is this community that brings both its poverty and its abundance together in practices that proceed from the particularities of its place. It is this community that violates commodification by scandalously sharing space. It is this community that participates in each other's lives so as to participate in the life of the Incarnate One. It is this community that experiences aesthetic conversion and renewal by hearing and speaking the proclamation of the Gospel in tongues not their own. The components of an ecclesiology of joining name the ways in which we look for the resurrection of the body politic within the flesh of the risen Lord. The theological race theory of Jennings and Carter points toward an ecclesiology that is able to live beyond the pseudotheological legacy of whiteness.

---

137. "The Didache," *Early Christian Writings*, chap. 9.

Bibliography

Acosta, Jose de. *Natural and Moral History of the Indies*. Edited by Jane E. Magnan. Durham: Duke University Press, 2002.

Alexander, Michelle. *The New Jim Crow: Mass Incarceration in the Age of Colorblindness*. New York: The New Press, 2012.

Andrews, William L. *To Tell a Free Story: The First Century of Afro-American Autobiography, 1760-1865*. Urbana: University of Illinois Press, 1986.

Aquinas, Thomas. *Summa Theologica*. London: Burns Oates & Washbourne, 1920-1922.

Athanasius. *The Orations of St Athanasius Against the Arians: According to the Benedictine Text*. Edited by William Bright. Cambridge: Cambridge University Press, 2014.

Bader-Saye, Scott. "Haunted by the Jews: Hauerwas, Milbank, and the Decentered Diaspora Church." In *Unsettling Arguments: A Festschrift on the Occasion of Stanley Hauerwas's 70th Birthday*, edited by Charles R. Pinches, Kelly S. Johnson, and Charles M. Collier, 191-209. Eugene, OR: Wipf & Stock, 2010.

Balmer, Randall. "The Real Origins of the Religious Right." *Politico Magazine* (May 27, 2014). http://www.politico.com/magazine/story/2014/05/religious-right-real-origins-107133.

Bantum, Brian. "Bloodlines: Race, Cross, and the Christian—A Review." *The Other Journal* (February 2012). http://theotherjournal.com/2012/02/06/bloodlines-race-cross-and-the-christian-a-review/.

—————. *Redeeming Mulatto: A Theology of Race and Christian Hybridity*. Waco: Baylor University Press, 2010.

Barth, Karl. *Church Dogmatics I.1: The Doctrine of the Word of God*. Edited by G. W. Bromiley and T. F. Torrance. Translated by A. T. Mackay and T. H. L. Parker. Peabody, MA: Hendrickson, 2010.

—————. *Church Dogmatics III.1: The Doctrine of Creation*. Edited by G. W. Bromiley and T. F. Torrance. Translated by A. T. Mackay and T. H. L. Parker. Peabody, MA: Hendrickson, 2010.

—————. *Church Dogmatics III.4: The Doctrine of Creation*. Edited by G. W. Bromiley and T. F. Torrance. Translated by A. T. Mackay and T. H. L. Parker. Peabody, MA: Hendrickson, 2010.

—————. *The Epistle to the Romans*. Translated by Edwyn C. Hoskins. 6th ed. London: Oxford University Press, 1968.

Blair, Leonardo. "Pastor Calls Trayvon Martin 'Pot-Smoking, Paranoid 17-Year-Old Boy,' Rails at Church for Being 'Black' on Verdict." http://www.christianpost.com/news/pastor-calls-trayvon-martin-pot-smoking-paranoid-17-year-old-boy-rails-at-church-for-being-black-on-verdict-100472/.

Blackburn, Robin. *The Making of New World Slavery: From the Baroque to the Modern, 1492–1800*. London: Verso, 1997.

Bonhoeffer, Dietrich. *Dietrich Bonhoeffer Works*. Vol. 3, *Creation and Fall*. Edited by John W. de Gruchy. Translated by Douglas Steven Bax. Minneapolis: Augsburg Fortress, 1997.

———. *Dietrich Bonhoeffer Works*. Vol. 4, *Discipleship*. Edited by Geffrey B. Kelly and John D. Godsey. Translated by Barbara Green and Reinhard Krauss. Minneapolis: Augsburg Fortress, 2001.

———. *Dietrich Bonhoeffer Works*. Vol. 6, *Ethics*. Edited by Clifford J. Green. Translated by Reinhard Krauss, Charles C. West, and Douglas W. Stott. Minneapolis: Fortress, 2005.

Bourdieu, Pierre. *Pascalian Meditations*. Stanford: Stanford University Press, 2000.

Bretherton, Luke. *Hospitality as Holiness: Christian Witness Amid Moral Diversity*. Surrey, UK: Ashgate, 2006.

Brock, Brian. *Captive to Christ, Open to the World: On Doing Christian Ethics in Public*. Eugene, OR: Cascade, 2014.

———. *Singing the Ethos of God: On the Place of Christian Ethics in Scripture*. Grand Rapids: Eerdmans, 2007.

Brueggemann, Walter. *The Land: Place as Gift, Promise, and Challenge in Biblical Faith*. Minneapolis: Augsburg Fortress, 2002.

Buber, Martin. *I and Thou*. Translated by Walter Kauffman. New York: Touchstone, 1970.

Cameron, Andrew J. B. *Joined-up Life: A Christian Account of How Ethics Works*. Nottingham: InterVarsity, 2011.

Capeheart, Jonathan. "George Zimmerman Should 'Regret' His Hannity Interview." *The Washington Post* (July 19, 2012). https://www.washingtonpost.com/blogs/post-partisan/post/zimmerman-should-regret-hannity-interivew/2012/07/19/gJQAwTNovW_blog.html.

Carretta, Vincent. *Equiano, the African: Biography of a Self-Made Man*. New York: Penguin, 2005.

Carson, Clayborne, ed. *The Autobiography of Martin Luther King, Jr*. New York: Warner, 1998.

Carter, J. Kameron. "Race: A Theological Account." PhD diss., University of Virginia, 2001.

———. *Race: A Theological Account*. Oxford: Oxford University Press, 2008.

Chamberlen, Peter. *The Poore Mans Advocate, or, Englands Samaritan*. London: Giles Calvert, 1649.

Coakley, Sarah. *God, Sexuality and the Self: An Essay "On the Trinity."* Cambridge: Cambridge University Press, 2013.

Cone, James H. *Black Theology and Black Power*. Maryknoll, NY: Orbis, 1997.

———. *A Black Theology of Liberation*. 40th anniversary ed. Maryknoll, NY: Orbis, 2010.

———. *The Cross and the Lynching Tree*. Maryknoll, NY: Orbis, 2011.

———. *God of the Oppressed*. Maryknoll, NY: Orbis, 1997.

———. *Martin and Malcolm and America: A Dream or a Nightmare*. Maryknoll, NY: Orbis, 1991.

Cook, James, and James King. *The Three Voyages of Captain James Cook Round the World*. Vol. 5, *Being the First of the Third Voyage*. London: Longman, Hurst, Rees, Orme, and Brown, 1821.

Costello, Damian. *Black Elk: Colonialism and Lakota Catholicism*. Maryknoll, NY: Orbis, 2005.

Dahmer, David. "The Harsh Truth about Progressive Cities." *Madison365* (September 3, 2015). http://madison365.com/index.php/2015/09/03/what-no-one-wants-to-talk-about-race-and-progressive-cities/.

Davis, David Brion. *Inhuman Bondage: The Rise and Fall of Slavery in the New World*. New York: Oxford University Press, 2006.

———. *The Problem of Slavery in the Age of Revolution: 1770-1823*. Oxford: Oxford University Press, 1999.

Dawkins, Richard. *The God Delusion*. New York: Houghton Mifflin, 2006.

D'Costa, Gavin. *Theology in the Public Square: Church, Academy, and Nation*. Oxford: Blackwell, 2005.

Deloria, Vine, Jr. *Custer Died for Your Sins: An Indian Manifesto*. New York: Macmillan, 1988.

———. *God Is Red: A Native View of Religion*. Golden, CO: Fulcrum, 2003.

"The Didache: The Teaching of the Twelve Apostles." In *Early Christian Writings*, translated by Alexander Roberts and James Donaldson. http://www.earlychristianwritings.com/text/didache-roberts.html.

DuBois, W. E. B. *The Souls of Black Folk*. Oxford: Oxford University Press, 2007.

Du Boulay, Juliet. *Cosmos, Life, and Liturgy in a Greek Orthodox Village*. Limni, Greece: Denise Harvey, 2009.

Dussel, Enrique. *The Underside of Modernity: Apel, Ricoeur, Rorty, Taylor, and the Philosophy of Liberation*. Translated by Eduardo Mendieta. Atlantic Highlands, NJ: Humanities, 1996.

Elshtain, Jean Bethke. "Theologian: Christian Contrarian." *Time* (September 17, 2011). http://content.time.com/time/magazine/article/0,9171,1000859,00.html.

"Enoch Powell's 'Rivers of Blood' Speech." *The Telegraph* (November 10, 2007). www.telegraph.co.uk/comment/3643823/Enoch-Powells-Rivers-of-Blood-speech.html.

Foucault, Michel. *Discipline and Punish: The Birth of the Prison*. New York: Random House, 1995.

———. *The Order of Things*. New York: Random House, 1970.

Fuder, John E., and Noel Castellanos. *A Heart for the Community: New Models for Urban and Suburban Ministry*. Chicago: Moody, 2009.

Gates, Henry Louis, Jr. *The Signifying Monkey: A Theory of African-American Literary Criticism*. Oxford: Oxford University Press, 1988.

Gates, Henry Louis, Jr., and Cornel West. *The Future of the Race*. New York: Knopf, 1994.

Givens, Tommy. *We the People: Israel and the Catholicity of Jesus*. Minneapolis: Fortress, 2014.

Gonzalez, Justo L. *A History of Christian Thought*. 2 vols. Nashville: Abingdon, 1970.

Gordon, Wayne. *Real Hope in Chicago: The Incredible Story of How the Gospel Is Transforming a Chicago Neighborhood*. Grand Rapids: Zondervan, 1995.

Gordon, Wayne, and John M. Perkins. *Making Neighborhoods Whole: A Handbook for Christian Community Development*. Downers Grove, IL: InterVarsity, 2013.

Greenblatt, Stephen, and Catherine Gallagher. *Practicing New Historicism*. Chicago: Chicago University Press, 2000.

Greggs, Tom. *Theology Against Religion: Constructive Dialogues with Bonhoeffer and Barth*. London: T. & T. Clark, 2007.

Gutierrez, Gustavo. *A Theology of Liberation: History, Politics, and Salvation*. Edited by Caridad Inda. Translated by John Eagleson. 15th anniversary ed. Maryknoll, NY: Orbis, 1988.

Guy, Jeff. *The Destruction of the Zulu Kingdom*. London: Longman, 1979.

Haley, Alex, and Malcolm X. *The Autobiography of Malcolm X*. New York: Ballantine, 1964.

Harris, Sam. *The End of Faith: Religion, Terror, and the Future of Reason*. New York: Norton, 2004.

Hauerwas, Stanley. "Abortion, Theologically Understood." In *The Hauerwas Reader*, edited by John Berkman and Michael G. Cartwright, 603–22. Durham: Duke University Press, 2001.

———. *Hannah's Child: A Theologian's Memoir*. Grand Rapids: Eerdmans, 2010.

———. *The Peaceable Kingdom: A Primer in Christian Ethics*. Notre Dame: Notre Dame University Press, 1991.

———. *The State of the University: Academic Knowledges and the Knowledge of God*. Oxford: Blackwell, 2007.

Hauerwas, Stanley, and Charles Pinches. *Christians Among the Virtues: Theological Conversations with Ancient and Modern Ethics*. Notre Dame: Notre Dame University Press, 1997.

Hauerwas, Stanley, and William H. Willimon. *Resident Aliens: Life in the Christian Colony*. Nashville: Abingdon, 1989.

Hinchliff, Peter. *John William Colenso: Bishop of Natal*. London: Thomas Nelson, 1964.

Hitchens, Christopher. *God is Not Great: How Religion Poisons Everything*. New York: Hachette, 2007.

Hopkins, Dwight N. *Down, Up, and Over: Slave Religion and Black Theology*. Minneapolis: Augsburg Fortress, 2000.

———. *Shoes that Fit Our Feet: Sources for a Constructive Black Theology*. Maryknoll, NY: Orbis, 1993.

Hopkins, Dwight N., and George C. L. Cummings, eds. *Cut Loose Your Stammering Tongue: Black Theology in the Slave Narratives*. Louisville: Westminster John Knox, 2003.

Jennings, Willie James. *The Christian Imagination: Theology and the Origins of Race*. New Haven: Yale University Press, 2010.

Johnson, Clifton H., ed. *God Struck Me Dead: Voices of Ex-Slaves*. Cleveland: Pilgrim, 1969.

Jones, William R. *Is God a White Racist? A Preamble to Black Theology*. Boston: Beacon, 1998.

Kant, Immanuel. *Religion within the Boundaries of Mere Reason, and Other Writings*. Edited by Allen Wood and George di Giovanni. Cambridge Texts in the History of Philosophy. Cambridge: Cambridge University Press, 1998.

Katongole, Emmanuel, and Chris Rice. *Reconciling All Things: A Christian Vision for Justice, Peace, and Healing*. Downers Grove, IL: InterVarsity, 2008.

Kierkegaard, Soren. *Fear and Trembling*. Cambridge: Cambridge University Press, 2006.

King, Martin Luther, Jr. "'I Have a Dream . . . ' Speech by the Rev. Martin Luther King At the 'March on Washington.'" 1963. http://www.archives.gov/press/exhibits/dream-speech.pdf.

Locke, John. *Two Treatises of Government*. Edited by Peter Laslett. Cambridge Texts in the History of Political Thought. Cambridge: Cambridge University Press, 1988.

Long, Charles H. *Significations: Signs, Symbols, and Images in the Interpretation of Religion*. Philadelphia: Fortress, 1986.

Loughlin, Gerard, ed. *Queer Theology: Rethinking the Western Body*. Oxford: Blackwell, 2007.

Louth, Andrew, ed. *Maximus the Confessor*. Early Church Fathers. New York: Routledge, 1996.

Lupton, Bob. *Compassion, Justice, and the Christian Life: Rethinking Ministry to the Poor*. Ventura, CA: Regal, 2007.

———. *Theirs Is the Kingdom: Celebrating the Gospel in Urban America*. New York: HarperCollins, 1989.

Luther, Martin. "Exposition of Psalm 127: for the Christians at Riga in Livonia." In *The Christian in Society*, edited by Walther I. Brandt and Helmut T. Lehmann, 2:317–37. Philadelphia: Muhlenberg, 1962.

MacCormack, Sabine. *Religion in the Andes: Vision and Imagination in Early Colonial Peru*. Princeton: Princeton University Press, 1991.

MacIntyre, Alisdair. *After Virtue*. Notre Dame: Notre Dame University Press, 2007.

———. *Three Rival Versions of Moral Inquiry: Encyclopedia, Genealogy, and Tradition*. Notre Dame: Notre Dame University Press, 1991.

Marable, Manning. *Malcolm X: A Life of Reinvention*. New York: Viking, 2011.

McBride, Jennifer M. *The Church for the World: A Theology of Public Witness*. Oxford: Oxford University Press, 2012.

Mignolo, Walter D. *The Darker Side of the Renaissance*. Ann Arbor: University of Michigan Press, 1995.

Milbank, John. *The Future of Love: Essays in Political Theology*. Eugene, OR: Wipf & Stock, 2009.

———. *Theology and Social Theory: Beyond Secular Reason*. Oxford: Blackwell, 2006.

Milbank, John, Catherine Pickstock, and Graham Ward, eds. *Radical Orthodoxy: A New Theology*. London: Routledge, 1999.

Miller, Joseph Calder. *Way of Death: Merchant Capitalism and the Angolan Slave Trade: 1730–1830*. Madison: University of Wisconsin Press, 1996.

Moltmann, Jürgen. *The Crucified God*. Minneapolis: Fortress, 2015.

Niebuhr, H. Richard. *Christ and Culture*. New York: HarperCollins, 1951.

Nietzsche, Friedrich. *The Gay Science: With a Prelude in Rhymes and an Appendix of Songs*. Translated by Walter Kaufmann. New York: Random House, 1974.

Nimmo, Paul T. *Being in Action: The Theological Shape of Barth's Ethical Vision*. London: T. & T. Clark, 2007.

Noel, James. "African American Art and Biblical Interpretation." In *True to Our Native Land: An African American New Testament Commentary*, edited by Brian Blount, 73–84. Minneapolis: Augsburg Fortress, 2006.

———. "African American Religions (An Overview)." In *Encyclopedia of Religion*. Detroit: Cengage Gale, 2005.

———. *Black Religion and the Imagination of Matter in the Atlantic World*. New York: Palgrave, 2009.

Nouwen, Henri J. M. *In the Name of Jesus: Reflections on Christian Leadership*. Chestnut Ridge, NY: Crossroad, 1989.

Patte, Daniel. *Ethics of Biblical Interpretation*. Louisville: Westminster John Knox, 1995.

Perkins, John M. *Beyond Charity: The Call to Christian Community Development.* Grand Rapids: Baker, 1993.

———. *Let Justice Roll Down.* Ventura, CA: Regal, 1976.

———, ed. *Restoring At-Risk Communities: Doing It Together and Doing It Right.* Grand Rapids: Baker, 1995.

Piper, John. *Bloodlines: Race, Cross, and the Christian.* Wheaton, IL: Crossway, 2011.

Prather, Scott. *Christ, Power, and Mammon: Karl Barth and John Howard Yoder in Dialogue.* London: T. & T. Clark, 2014.

Raboteau, Albert J. *A Fire in the Bones: Reflections on African-American Religious History.* Boston: Beacon, 1995.

———. *Slave Religion: The "Invisible Institution" in the Antebellum South.* New York: Oxford University Press, 1978.

Rediker, Marcus. *The Slave Ship: A Human History.* New York: Viking, 2007.

Roberts, J. Deotis. *Liberation and Reconciliation: A Black Theology.* Louisville: Westminster John Knox, 2005.

Robles, Francis, and Scott Hiaason. "FBI Records: Agents Found No Evidence that Zimmerman Was Racist." *Miami Herald*, July 12, 2012.

Root, Andrew. *Revisiting Relational Youth Ministry: From a Strategy of Influence to a Theology of Incarnation.* Downers Grove, IL: InterVarsity, 2007.

Rogers, Eugene F., Jr. *Sexuality and the Christian Body: Their Way Into the Triune God.* Oxford: Blackwell, 1999.

Ross, John J. *Reading Wittgenstein's Philosophical Investigations.* Lanham, MD: Lexington, 2009.

Ruether, Rosemary Radford. *Gaia and God: An Ecofeminist Theology of Earth Healing.* New York: Harper-Collins, 1992.

———. *Sexism and God-Talk: Toward a Feminist Theology.* Boston: Beacon, 1993.

Russell-Brown, Katheryn. *The Color of Crime: Racial Hoaxes, White Fear, Black Protectionism, Police Harassment, and Other Macroaggressions.* New York: New York University Press, 1998.

Sanneh, Lamin. *Translating the Message: The Missionary Impact on Culture.* Maryknoll, NY: Orbis, 1989.

Schaeffer, Francis. *The Mark of the Christian.* Downers Grove, IL: InterVarsity, 2006.

Schussler Fiorenza, Elisabeth. *But She Said: Feminist Practices of Biblical Interpretation.* Boston: Beacon, 1992.

———. *In Memory of Her: A Feminist Theological Reconstruction of Christian Origins.* New York: Crossroad, 1994.

Sims, Angela D. *Ethical Complications of Lynching: Ida B. Wells's Interrogation of American Terror.* New York: Palgrave Macmillan, 2010.

Smith, Ted A. *Weird John Brown: Divine Violence and the Limits of Ethics.* Stanford: Stanford University Press, 2015.

Sullivan, Nikki. *A Critical Introduction to Queer Theory.* New York: NYU Press, 2003.

Thomas, Hugh. *The Slave Trade: The Story of the Atlantic Slave Trade: 1440–1870.* New York: Touchstone, 1997.

Thurman, Howard. *Jesus and the Disinherited.* Boston: Beacon, 1976.

Tillich, Paul. *The Courage to Be.* New Haven: Yale University Press, 2000.

Todorov, Tzvetan. *The Conquest of America: The Question of the Other.* New York: Harper & Row, 1984.

Tran, Jonathan. "The New Black Theology." *The Christian Century* 129/3 (February 2012). https://www.christiancentury.org/article/2012-01/new-black-theology.

———. "Time for Hauerwas's Racism." In *Unsettling Arguments: A Festschrift on the Occasion of Stanley Hauerwas's 70th Birthday*, edited by Charles R. Pinches, Kelly S. Johnson, and Charles M. Collier, 246–64. Eugene, OR: Wipf & Stock, 2010.

Walls, Andrew F. *The Missionary Movement in Christian History: Studies in the Transmission of Faith*. Maryknoll, NY: Orbis, 1996.

West, Cornel. *Race Matters*. New York: Vintage, 1994.

Williams, Gregory Howard. *Life on the Color Line: The True Story of a White Boy Who Discovered He Was Black*. New York: Plume, 1995.

Williams, Reggie L. *Bonhoeffer's Black Jesus: Harlem Renaissance Theology and an Ethic of Resistance*. Waco, TX: Baylor University Press, 2014.

Wilson-Hartgrove, Jonathan. *Free to Be Bound: Church Beyond the Color Line*. Colorado Springs: NavPress, 2008.

Wink, Walter. *The Powers that Be: Theology for a New Millennium*. New York: Doubleday, 1998.

Wittgenstein, Ludwig. *Philosophical Investigations*. Rev. 4th ed. West Sussex: Blackwell, 2009.

Yoder, John Howard. "The Disavowal of Constantine." In *The Royal Priesthood: Essays Ecclesiological and Ecumenical*, edited by Michael Cartwright, 242–61. Grand Rapids: Eerdmans, 1994.

———. *The Politics of Jesus*. Grand Rapids: Eerdmans, 1994.

Zimmerman, George. "Full Transcript Zimmerman." http://www.documentcloud.org/documents/326700-full-transcript-zimmerman.html.

Name Index

Abraham, 140, 170–73, 181, 184, 195, 211, 276, 280
Acosta, Jose de, 18–19, 27–28, 149–67, 185, 201, 207, 214, 216–24, 230, 233–36, 239, 247, 249, 251, 258, 285
Alexander, Marissa, 10n11
Alexander, Michelle, 10, 111
Allen, Richard, 44
Anderson, Oswald, 174
Anderson, Victor, 51
Andrews, William L., 47, 193–95
Aquinas, Saint Thomas, 38, 123, 157–58, 217–19, 232–35, 241, 243, 307
Aristotle, 118, 150, 157–58, 161, 186–87, 190, 217, 219, 223, 232–35
Athanasius, Saint, 135n159

Bader-Saye, Scott, 261n188
Balmer, Randall, 44n53
Bantum, Brian, 16–18, 35, 273, 283–87, 290–91, 303
Barth, Karl, 17, 22n41, 23, 28, 32, 49–50, 54, 74, 120, 134n154, 153, 156, 165–67, 169, 179–80, 184n176, 193n211, 232, 249–50, 263–69, 299, 303–4, 306
Blackburn, Robin, 185, 187–8, 190n195, 192
Bonhoeffer, Dietrich, 28, 66, 69, 169, 174–76, 263–69, 297–99
Bourdieu, Pierre, 236–68, 253
Bretherton, Luke, 292–96, 298, 300, 303, 305
Brock, Brian, ix, 97, 164, 249
Brown, John, 173–76, 202, 225n47
Brown, Michael, 1
Brueggemann, Walter, 170, 172–73
Buber, Martin, 62

Bush, George W., 172n121

Cameron, Andrew J. B., 232
Carmichael, Stokely, 12
Carretta, Vincent, 193, 197–8
Carter, J. Kameron, vii, x, 6–7, 10–28, 29–92, 93–144, 145, 149n16, 155, 215, 249, 263, 271–73, 282–86, 290–92, 295–97, 299–301, 303–6, 308–15
Cavanagh, William T., 127n119
Chamberlen, Peter, 274n3
Charlemagne, Emperor, 109
Cicero, 161
Clayton, John, 97
Coakley, Sarah, 13n17
Colenso, John William, 27, 151, 185, 201–14, 245, 250, 252, 305
Coleridge, Samuel Taylor, 108–9, 202
Columbus, Christopher, 285
Cone, James H., 12–14, 16, 19, 25, 31–34, 39, 49–71, 73–75, 83–86, 89, 91–2, 93, 114–16, 119–22, 128, 132, 143, 283–85, 304n114, 306, 313
Cook, Captain James, 224–28
Costello, Damien, 258n178

Davis, David Brion, 85, 185–86, 190–92, 215
Dawkins, Richard, 22
D'Costa, Gavin, 78
Derrida, Jacques, 90
Descartes, Rene, 31, 35, 43, 94, 123, 169
Deloria Jr., Vine, 12–13, 83–85, 167
Douglas, Mary, 226n53
Douglass, Frederick, 32, 34, 63, 74, 113, 134, 174, 296n81
DuBois, W. E. B., 3, 174

Subject Index

liberation, 8, 44, 53–60, 65–67, 87, 112,
117, 135, 142–43, 186, 207
liberation theology. *See* theology,
liberation
limpieza de sangre. See blood purity
liturgy, place of, 28, 126–27, 139, 144,
152, 183, 281n20, 290–91,
295–96, 301–2
Lord's Supper, the. *See* Eucharist
love, conceptions of, 48, 67–69, 96ff,
110, 114, 131–32, 136–38,
141–42, 147–48, 154, 205, 216,
244, 251–54, 261, 274n3, 275,
285, 291
lynching, 13, 52–53, 60–71

Mammon, 23, 198, 201, 239, 309
Manifest Destiny, 23, 45–46, 112, 114,
172, 236
metaphysics, 109, 217, 235
methodologies, distinctions between
differing, 6n7, 21, 26–27, 32–33,
37–38, 41, 44, 46–47, 50–52, 73,
75, 77, 82–86, 94, 100, 111–19,
122–23, 133–36, 155–57,
163–68, 203, 240, 254, 263, 301,
304n114
Middle Passage, the, 41, 132, 193
miscegenation, 20, 24, 38, 44, 54, 57,
61, 67–69, 77, 102, 127, 272,
282–84, 289
missiology, 14, 24, 27, 147, 156, 205–8,
212–13, 257, 259, 268, 271, 283
missionary work, 42–43, 146–50, 155,
157–59, 163, 194, 198, 222–23,
245, 247, 271–72, 288–90, 293
mission, definitions of, 206–14, 257–62
modernity, development of, 6, 9n10,
19–21, 29–34, 94–106, 133–36,
160, 164, 216–18, 235, 238,
240–46, 260n184, 283–85
morals / morality, 5, 9, 18, 19–22, 43,
45, 55, 68, 96, 99, 102–6, 109,
126, 128, 147, 154, 156, 161,
164, 173–74, 187, 189, 200, 205,
208–9, 215–18, 220, 224, 227–
28, 230–32, 235, 240–42, 244,

248–50, 252, 255–56, 261, 264,
272, 286, 292, 296, 302, 304
mulatto, 11, 16, 24, 61, 188, 278, 283–91
multiculturalism, 21, 26, 121, 152, 212,
269, 313
musical theory, 126, 129, 154, 313
mutual articulation, 64n136, 89, 129,
140, 143, 282, 313
mutuality, 8, 10n10, 15–16, 24, 28, 38–
40, 53, 62, 78, 118, 127–29, 132,
138, 144, 149, 151, 154, 205,
251, 279, 286–89, 300, 306, 311

nation-state, the, 110, 164–65, 172, 179–
180, 239, 243, 246–47, 272
Native American theology, 12–13,
83–85, 167, 258
native peoples. *See* indigenous peoples
nations, the. *See ethnos*, the
natural law / theology, 104–5, 121–22,
131, 134n154, 142, 167, 185,
187, 221, 233–38, 249, 258
near and distant neighbors, 153, 169,
259, 263n194, 266–69, 311
neighbors / neighborhood, 1, 7, 14–15,
23, 64, 93, 128, 144, 146–47,
151, 174–75, 200, 216, 244, 262,
273, 275–76, 278–79, 288, 292–
96, 298–300, 303, 306–7, 311
New Atheism, 22
Noble Savage, myth of the, 85, 227, 236

oikos / oikonomia, 33, 268, 289, 301
ontologies of peace / love, 114, 124, 127,
130–39
ontologizing identity, 29, 32, 49–51,
53–71, 91
ontology, actualist, 249, 301
ontology, 7, 20, 24–25, 82–83, 86–87,
95, 100, 116, 118, 128, 234–35,
237, 249–50, 253–54, 264, 275–
76, 284, 305
ontology, static, 12, 34, 57, 60, 90, 177,
275, 280
ontology of violence, 129
opacity of being, 12, 82–91
oppressed, the, 4, 12, 48–67, 72, 83, 86,
88–89, 115–17, 132, 186, 214

www.ingramcontent.com/pod-product-compliance
Lightning Source LLC
Chambersburg PA
CBHW070902080426

R18103500001B/R181035PG41932CBX00013B/5